D0850783

THE CASE OF IRELAND'S BEING BOUND BY ACTS
OF PARLIAMENT IN ENGLAND, STATED

William Molyneux

The Case of Ireland's Being Bound by Acts of Parliament in England, Stated
Dublin, 1698

EDITED, TOGETHER WITH AN INTRODUCTION, CRITICAL
APPARATUS, APPENDICES AND NOTES

by

PATRICK HYDE KELLY

FOUR COURTS PRESS
in association with
THE IRISH LEGAL HISTORY SOCIETY

Typeset in 10.5pt on 12.5pt EhrhardtMt by
Carrigboy Typesetting Services for
FOUR COURTS PRESS LTD
7 Malpas Street, Dublin 8, Ireland
www.fourcourtspress.ie
and in North America for
FOUR COURTS PRESS
c/o IPG, 814 N Franklin St, Chicago, IL 60622

References to this publication should cite the publisher as Four Courts Press
in association with the Irish Legal History Society.

A catalogue record for this title is available
from the British Library.

ISBN 978-1-84682-741-9

Printed in England
by CPI Group (UK) Ltd, Croydon CR0 4YY

Contents

Acknowledgments

OVER THE THREE DECADES WHICH this work has been in gestation, I have benefited enormously from the help and kindness of fellow scholars, librarians and institutions, whether in direction to relevant material, discussion of problems, the opportunity to publish interim findings, or encouragement to persevere in what at times seemed an unending task. These debts have been many and the period over which they have been incurred has been long, so I must ask those whom I have failed to mention not to think that I have been unappreciative of their help.

First, I must thank the Board of Trinity College for permission to edit the text of *The Case* using Molyneux's holograph and the printer's copy manuscript preserved in the college library, without which the aspiration to produce a critical edition of the work could never have been achieved.

Next I should like to pay tribute to three mentors no longer with us for their help and encouragement, namely Mary (Paul) Pollard, William O'Sullivan and Gerald Simms, the last of whom first introduced me to Molyneux and his work.

James McGuire and David Hayton generously read the entire work in manuscript, and have made valuable suggestions for its improvement.

Peter Crooks and Caoimhe Whelan have patiently acquainted me with recent scholarship in the medieval background, with particular reference to the Modus Tenendi Parliamentum and Magna Carta in the one case, and Giraldus Cambrensis and the Expugnatio Hibernica in the other. Paul Brand kindly gave permission to cite his forthcoming paper 'Magna Carta in Ireland'.

I should also like to express thanks to the following for their assistance over the years: Robert Armstrong, Sir John Baker, Toby Barnard, Terry Barry, the late Charles Benson, David Berman, Mark Box, Ciaran Brady, Andrew Carpenter, Aidan Clarke, David Dickson, Martin Flaherty, Loraine Frazer, Raymond Gillespie, Jack P. Grene, Jackie Hill, James Kelly, the late James Lydon, Charles Ludington, Ian McBride, Richard McMahon, Jane Maxwell, Bernard Meehan, Jane Ohlmeyer, Felicity O'Mahony, Nial Osborough, Micheál Ó Siochrú, John Pocock, Jim Smyth, Bill Vaughan, Isolde Victory, James Wood and Neil Langley York. Particular thanks are due to my former secretary, Olive Murtagh, whose transcription of the text of *The Case* enabled the project to start, and to Fiona Fitzsimons of Eneclann, who undertook the checking of the manuscript variants against the originals. I should also like to thank the staffs of the Manuscript and Early Printed Book departments of Trinity College Library for their unstinting help and support over the decades, together with the staffs of the other Dublin libraries where I have regularly worked, namely the Gilbert Library, Dublin City Library and Archive, Pearse Street; the National Library of Ireland; Marsh's Library; and the Royal Irish Academy Library.

I also wish to express my gratitude to the Irish Legal History Society for undertaking to sponsor the publication of this extensive critical edition of William Molyneux's *The case of Ireland's being bound by acts of parliament in England, stated*, and to thank the members of the publication committee, Robert Marshall and James McGuire, who have helped bring the project to completion. Sam Tranum of Four Courts Press has brought efficiency, patience and courtesy to seeing the edition throught the press, and the typesetter, Josette Prichard, has proved remarkably creative with its complex demands.

Finally, I should like to thank my wife Margaret for her support and assistance in the writing of this book, as well as for putting up with two decades of Molyneux after the earlier decades dominated by Locke.

All remaining errors and omissions are of course my own responsibility.

PATRICK H. KELLY,
Dublin, June 2018.

Abbreviations

app. crit.	the apparatus criticus of this edition
Atwood, *History*	Atwood, *The history, and reasons, of the dependency of Ireland upon the imperial crown of the kingdom of England* (1698)
Autobiography	Molyneux, *Anecdotes of the life of ... William Molyneux* (1803)
BL	British Library
Bolton, 'Declaration'	Sir Richard Bolton, 'A declaration setting forth how, and by what means, the laws and statutes of England, from time to time, came to be of force in Ireland' [1644]
British chronology	Powicke & Fryde (eds), *Handbook of British chronology* (1961)
brs.	broadsheet
C.	combined with the appropriate numeral to denote century in notes
Cal. S.P., dom.	*Calendar of State Papers, domestic series*
Cary, *Vindication*	Cary, *A vindication of the parliament of England, in answer to a book, written by William Molyneux* (1698)
The Case	Molyneux, *The case of Ireland's being bound by acts of parliament in England, stated* (1698)
Clement, *Answer*	[Clement], *An answer to Mr Molyneux* (1698)
Coke, *Inst.*	Sir Edward Coke, *Institutes of the Law of England*
Coke, *Reports*	Sir Edward Coke, *Reports*
Commons Jnl [Eng.]	*Journal of the house of commons* [of England]
Commons Jnl [Ire.]	*Journal of the house of commons of the kingdom of Ireland*
Commons, 1690–1715	Cruickshanks et al., *The house of commons, 1690–1715* (2002)
Complete peerage	Cokayne, *The complete peerage of England ...* (1910–59)
corr.	corrected
dedic.	dedication
del.	deleted
Derry MSS	Moody & Simms (eds), *The bishopric of Derry and the Irish Society of London, 1602–1705* (1968 and 1983)
DIB	*Dictionary of Irish biography* (2009)
Domville, 'Disquisition'	Sir William Domville, 'A disquisition touching that great question, whether an act of parliament made in England shall bind the kingdom and people of Ireland' (2007)

DPS	Dublin Philosophical Society
ECI	*Eighteenth-Century Ireland: Iris an dá chultúr*
edn	edition
ESI	Berry & Morrissey (eds), *Statutes and ordinances ... of the parliament of Ireland* (1907–39)
ESTC	*Eighteenth-century short title catalogue*
Gilbert Library, Dublin	Gilbert Library, Dublin City Library and Archive, 138–44 Pearse Street, Dublin 2
HMC	Historical Manuscripts Commission
IHS	*Irish Historical Studies*
IMC	Irish Manuscripts Commission
intro.	introduction
Johnson, *Dictionary*	Samuel Johnson (ed.), *A dictionary of the English language* (1770)
King, William	Letters from William King, bishop of Derry, 1691–1702, and archbishop of Dublin, 1702–1729, from the King Letterbooks, TCD MSS 750/1–6 (unless indicated otherwise), identified solely by date
'Legislative power in Ireland'	'That the legislative power in Ireland doth belong to the king by the advice of his parliament of Ireland ...' (MS TCD 888, ff 127–30)
Locke Corr.	Locke, John, *The correspondence of John Locke*, ed. E.S. de Beer (1976–); letters are cited by de Beer's list number
Lords Jnl [Eng.]	*Journal of the house of lords [of England]*
Lords Jnl [Ire.]	*Journal of the house of lords [of Ireland]*
Lords MSS	*Manuscripts of the house of lords*
manu	in the handwriting of
Methuen Letters	Letters to and from the Irish Lord Chancellor John Methuen, in BL Add. MS 61653, cited by date
Molyneux library catalogue	Molyneux, *A catalogue of the library of the Honble Samuel Molyneux, deceas'd ...* (1730)
NLI	National Library of Ireland
ODNB	*Oxford dictionary of national biography* (2004)
OED	*Oxford English dictionary* (1989)
para.	paragraph
ser.	series
TCD	Trinity College, Dublin
transl.	translated/translation
Treatises	Locke, *Two treatises of government*, ed. Peter Laslett (Cambridge, 1960)
Vernon letters	James Vernon, *Letters illustrative of the reign of William III, from 1696 to 1708* (1841)

Illustrations

General introduction

I. INTRODUCTORY

The case of Ireland's being bound by acts of parliament in England, stated by 'William Molyneux of Dublin, Esq;' is widely regarded as the most celebrated political pamphlet published in Ireland before the union with Britain in 1801, and with good reason. Aptly described in 1779 as 'the Manual of Irish Liberty', it was admiringly cited by a line of patriots from Swift to Wolfe Tone, and has continued to be held in high regard to the present day.[1] Other than offended officialdom, very few in Ireland have been critical of Molyneux's stance. Yet at first sight *The Case* would seem to have scant potential for popular appeal. Presented in the form of a legal case as submitted to a court, the work is in danger of coming across to present day readers not so much as a vindication of Ireland's legislative independence of the English parliament as a sourcebook from which such a right might be constructed.[2]

Explaining the attraction which *The Case* exercised for Molyneux's countrymen in the century following its publication in 1698 poses, therefore, a major challenge for the editor of his text. One set of answers, and the one which supplies the major rationale for this introduction, would seem to lie in a careful consideration of the various contexts which illuminate why and how the work came to be written. These include the immediate political background, and the recent history of the conflict between the English and Irish parliaments over the right to make laws for Ireland; the colonists' experience of the Jacobite War and its aftermath; Molyneux's intellectual and personal history, and the myth that the English house of commons had condemned the pamphlet to be burnt by the common hangman. At the centre lies the internal history of the text, substantiated not only by Molyneux's autograph version but also, uniquely for Ireland in the age of the hand press, the manuscript actually used by the printer to set the text. Two letters from Molyneux to his revered friend, the philosopher John Locke, throw further light on the circumstances of the work's composition, while considerable material illuminates the immediate fate of *The Case* at the hands of the English house of commons, culminating in its condemnation as 'of dangerous Consequence to the Crown and People of *England*, by denying the Authority of the King and Parliament of

N.B. References to the text of *The Case* are to the 1698 pagination (printed at the top of the page).
1 *The alarm, or the Irish spy* (Dublin, 1779), p. 53.
2 For the format adopted for the work, see further pp 28–9 below.

England, to bind the Kingdom and People of *Ireland*'.[3] Five published replies to
the book, and the comments of a range of other figures including Isaac Newton as
well as a small number of Irish readers – mostly unenthusiastic ones, shed further
light on the immediate reaction to the work. Collation of the two manuscript
versions and the printed text of the first edition of 1698 have made it possible to
establish a critical text of *The Case*, while consideration of the three major sources
on which Molyneux based his composition further illuminates what he was seeking
to do. However, uncertainty remains: without the discovery of further material, one
cannot know, for example, whether Molyneux's reference to legislative union with
England as 'an Happiness we can hardly hope for' (*Case*, pp 97–8) was a serious
call for union or merely a rhetorical challenge to the English parliament, or what
his reaction was to the three answers to *The Case* published before his death in
October 1698.[4]

What follows considers the historical context in which *The Case* appeared,
starting with a brief account of the author, proceeds to the broader historical
background, the circumstances of publication, and the response first in the English
parliament and then in the published replies to the work, as well as other
contemporary reactions. The second section focuses on Molyneux's ideas and the
format in which he chose to present them; his use of history and legal precedent
and his reliance on natural law thinking, particularly Locke; followed by an
aftermath looking at the later reprintings of the book, particularly in the eighteenth
century. Finally, the textual introduction gives an account of the chief manuscript
sources on which Molyneux drew and an overview of the printed sources, followed
by a description of the manuscripts of *The Case*, and consideration of the variants
found in the first edition of 1698.

II. THE HISTORICAL CONTEXT

'William Molyneux of Dublin, esquire'

By birth and education William Molyneux belonged to the Protestant elite that had
dominated the city of Dublin since the Reformation. His paternal great-
grandfathers included the late Elizabethan lord chancellor and archbishop of
Dublin, Adam Loftus; Sir William Ussher, Elizabeth's last secretary of state in
Ireland, and Loftus' protégé Thomas Molyneux, the first of the name to settle in
Ireland, who eventually became chancellor of the Irish exchequer. Though
sometimes thought of as French Huguenots, the Molyneux family were in fact
former inhabitants of the English enclave of Calais.[5] William's grandfather, Daniel

---

3 *Commons Jnl [Eng.]*, xi, p. 331.
4 For the call for legislative union and the answers to *The Case*, see intro. pp 36–7 and 20–3,
   respectively. Reference to the survival of family papers as recently as Fraser, 'The Molyneux
   family', *Dublin Historical Record*, 16 (1960), p. 11, suggests they might still come to light.
5 Biographical information is derived mainly from Simms, *William Molyneux* (Dublin, 1982), and
   Molyneux entries in *DIB* and *ODNB* .

Molyneux, had been a less successful figure, who ended his career as Ulster king of arms, though it was he who secured the marriage connection with the prestigious Ussher dynasty. Daniel's son, Samuel Molyneux, the elder, did much to re-establish the family's position, acquiring from land dealings during the Cromwellian period and Restoration the substantial landed properties that would justify his elder son, William, designating himself 'esquire'.[6] Though he had trained as a lawyer, the wars that followed the 1641 rebellion transformed Samuel Molyneux into a professional soldier. In his capacity as master gunner of Ireland and through his personal intellectual concerns, Samuel was responsible for the start of the family's connection with the New Science of Copernicus, Kepler and Galileo. Besides William, Ireland's first major home-educated scientific figure, and the moving spirit behind the Dublin Philosophical Society (founded 1684), his younger brother Thomas, was a physician educated at Leiden who became an FRS, while William's son Samuel, junior, was a distinguished astronomer and writer on optics.

William Molyneux received his schooling at the grammar school linked to St Patrick's cathedral, and entered Trinity College, Dublin in 1671 when barely 15, graduating BA in February 1674. His university education was traditionally Aristotelian, though abbreviated to three years rather than four because of his status of fellow commoner.[7] His college contemporaries included the future political writer Robert (later 1st Viscount) Molesworth, and St George Ashe, who as provost of Trinity in the early 1690s would introduce Locke's philosophy into the curriculum, at Molyneux's recommendation. His college tutor was William Palliser, later archbishop of Cashel, a notable bibliophile who bequeathed much of his collection to Trinity College library. What remains unclear about Molyneux's upbringing is the role of religion in the Molyneux household. Consonant with Archbishop Loftus' patronage, which had brought them to Ireland, the family had strong Anglican connections, and there is no indication of puritan sympathies in the 1640s and 50s. Little in the correspondence of William or Thomas Molyneux suggests, however, that religion was a deep concern for either of the brothers, while religious matters played almost no role in Molyneux's celebrated correspondence with Locke.[8] And all except one of the references to the importance of religion for Irish Protestants in *The case of Ireland* are shown by the manuscripts to have been afterthoughts.[9]

Molyneux's formal career was to be the law, and though his 1694 autobiography claimed that he found his legal studies unfulfilling, this, as the legal learning and

---

6 See p. 6, n. 21 below for details of Molyneux's property.

7 Fellow commoners were a category of students who, in return for higher fees, received various privileges including the shortening of their BA courses: Simms, *William Molyneux* (Dublin, 1982), p. 18.

8 There are some conventional references in the *Autobiography* to divine mercy having reconciled William to his wife's blindness and other family calamities. He later claimed to have broken with the astronomer Flamsteed because of his 'ill nature and irreligion': *Autobiography*, pp 7, 13, 35, 44–5.

9 Namely, that in the dedication to King William, *The Case*, A4v.

culture of *The Case* demonstrate, was by no means the whole story.[10] Like all intending members of the Irish bar, he was obliged to study at one of the London inns of court, duly passing the years from 1675 to 1678 at the Middle Temple, an inn then much favoured by Irishmen.[11] What and how Molyneux studied is by no means clear, particularly as his attendance coincided with the final transition from the old method of teaching provided by the Inns, in the form of biannual 'readings' (lectures delivered by a senior member of the Inns) and more informal exercises such as moots, to entirely private study. He must therefore have relied largely on private reading in such works as *Littleton on tenures*, *Coke on Littleton*, Coke's *Institutes*, and FitzHerbert's *New natura brevium*, perhaps with guidance from some senior lawyer engaged by his family.[12] He later claimed to have been an active compiler of legal commonplace books and to own a number of rare legal texts, and his manuscript 'Abridgement of the law' was sold to an unidentified purchaser in 1730.[13] Of Molyneux's other experiences during these years in London we know nothing: his return to Dublin took place in June 1678, just before the outbreak of the Popish Plot.

In September 1678, as he embarked on his legal career, Molyneux married Lucy Domville, the youngest daughter of the Irish attorney general, Sir William Domville. Tragically, her sight rapidly deteriorated, and the search for a cure for Lucy's blindness awoke her husband's interest in scientific theories of vision. Thanks to the 'Molyneux problem' that William subsequently propounded to John Locke, and to his *Dioptrica nova*, 1692, a pioneering work on lenses and refraction in English, it was to be a branch of science with which his name would long remain associated.[14] In 1683–4 he assumed a leading role in setting up an Irish scientific association that was to be the local equivalent of London's Royal Society. An informal society was started in 1683; a more formal body with fourteen members, established in 1684 and known as the Dublin Philosophical Society, flourished until the uncertainties of Tyrconnell's administration early in 1687. Scholarly Dublin in the 1680s also showed an interest in topographical studies and Irish antiquities. Descriptions (intended as contributions to Moses Pitt's abortive atlas of the British Isles) survive for a number of parts of Ireland among Molyneux's papers, such as the account of Connaught by the Gaelic antiquary Roderick O'Flaherty. After the Jacobite War, Molyneux's brother-in-law, Anthony Dopping, bishop of Meath,

---

10　*Autobiography*, pp 3–4.

11　Lemmings, *Gentlemen and barristers* (Oxford, 1990), pp 26–9.

12　Lemmings, *Gentlemen and barristers* (Oxford, 1990), ch. 4, esp. pp 78–92. *Molyneux library catalogue*, pp 75–6, lists a group of introductory legal texts with imprints from the 1660s and 1670s, perhaps acquired to launch his studies.

13　*Autobiography*, pp 9, 42–3. His 'Abridgement of the Law' was sold for 10s. 6d. (*Molyneux library catalogue*, p. 77, item 877); it is not known whether it still survives. See further P. Kelly, 'The one that got away' in Vaughan (ed.), *The Old Library* (Dublin, 2013), pp 95–8.

14　Namely, whether a man born blind would, on acquiring sight, be able to distinguish correctly by sight alone between the cube and sphere that he had previously differentiated by touch. On the problem and subsequent efforts to solve it, see Degenaar, *Molyneux's problem* (Dordrecht, 1996).

published the Irish *Modus tenendi parliamenta et consilia in Hibernia* (1692).[15] Dopping's collection of historical and antiquarian material was begun in the 1670s, while another brother-in-law, John Madden, was also a distinguished collector, as was William King, the future bishop of Derry. In 1683 Molyneux became involved in history of a more recent sort, through acting as an intermediary for Bishop Borlase of Chester with Dublin critics of his father's account of the Irish Rebellion.[16]

In 1684 Molyneux became joint surveyor of the king's buildings in Ireland, through the purchase of a half-share in the patent held by William Robinson, architect of the Royal Hospital at Kilmainham. This office was acquired through the favour of the viceroy, the duke of Ormonde, under whom Molyneux's father had served at the Battle of Ross in 1643. In view of this family link, it is strange that the *Autobiography* stressed that Molyneux owed his introduction to Ormonde not to his father but to Ormonde's protégé, the Franciscan priest Peter Walsh, promoter of the Catholic oath of loyalty to the Stuart monarchy, known as the Irish Remonstrance.[17] Among the responsibilities of the surveyor was supervision of Ireland's fortifications, and Molyneux received official backing for a journey of several months in the Low Countries, parts of Germany and northern France in the summer of 1685 to familiarize himself with developments in the field. The tour provided the opportunity to travel with his brother, Thomas, who was studying medicine at Leiden, and to meet distinguished scientists such as Christiaan Huygens, the microscopist Leeuwenhoek and G.B. Cassini, first director of the new observatory in Paris. Returning through London Molyneux met the astronomer John Flamsteed, with whom he had corresponded since 1681, and once back in Dublin was elected a fellow of the Royal Society.

By now, however, James II had been six months on the throne, and the balance of power in Ireland was beginning to tilt against Protestants such as the Molyneux family and their kinsfolk. Molyneux established good relations with James' first viceroy, and brother-in-law, the High Tory Lord Clarendon, to whom he dedicated *Sciothericum telescopicum* (1686). With Clarendon's replacement in early 1687 by the Catholic Tyrconnell, the position of Protestants deteriorated further. Money became scarce as debts and rents went unpaid; Thomas Molyneux had to be summoned home from further studies in London, while William and his partner were forced to surrender the Surveyorship. However, given the general scarcity of government funds, the substantial payment that Molyneux received in late 1688 for building work at Dublin Castle suggests he was rather more *persona grata* with the Jacobite regime than might be expected.[18] According to the *Autobiography*, this

---

15 Copies are also found with a cancelled titlepage, reading '*Modus Tenendi Parliamenta in Hibernia*'. There are no apparent changes to either Dopping's intro. or the text of the Modus.
16 Borlase, *A history of the execrable Irish rebellion* (London, 1680). See further BL, MS Sloane 1008, ff 233, 251, 301, 333.
17 *Autobiography*, pp 15–18. For Walsh, see further *DIB*, s.v.
18 Loeber, 'The rebuilding of Dublin Castle, 1661–90', *Studies*, 69 (1980), pp 48, 66–8.

money was sufficient to support the brothers together with William's wife and child when they fled to Chester in February 1689. Thomas practised in the local area, while William worked on his *Dioptrica nova*, which did not finally appear until the family had been back in Dublin for over twelve months.

After the surrender of Dublin in July 1690 William briefly visited Ireland, though the family did not ultimately return home until December. While opportunities emerged for self-advancement following the collapse of the Jacobite regime, William does not seem to have been tempted; although he and Robinson regained the Surveyorship, the latter was now the sole active partner. Molyneux served briefly as a commissioner for army accounts, and was then appointed a commissioner for forfeitures (administering estates confiscated from the Jacobites). The unsavoury reputation of the other commissioners led him to decline to act, a piece of altruism which the *Autobiography* claimed enhanced his reputation.[19] However, he did get elected to the post-war parliament of 1692 as member for Dublin University, along with Ormonde's former secretary, Sir Cyril Wyche, secretary to the new lord lieutenant, Henry Sydney. This choice was an indication of official favour, as the university's restricted constituency was virtually at the disposal of the viceroy. The parliament, however, lasted barely a month, being dismissed for insistence on the right to initiate financial legislation (the so-called 'sole-right' issue that would bedevil parliamentary relations with the executive for the remainder of the decade).[20] Molyneux also resumed his legal practice, while the death of his father in 1693 brought him a substantial landed estate in counties Armagh, Kildare and Limerick, though rents were slow to recover after the war.[21]

In June 1692 Molyneux made the most important intellectual contact of his career as a result of presenting a copy of his recently published *Dioptrica nova* to the philosopher John Locke, for whose *Essay concerning human understanding* the preface expressed warm admiration. From this developed first a correspondence between the two men and then a friendship. As a result of its publication in *Some familiar letters between Mr Locke and several of his friends* (1708), this correspondence constituted Molyneux's major claim to philosophic consideration in the eighteenth century. More than sixty letters between the two men survive. Their most important areas of common interest were philosophy, in which Molyneux substantially influenced the second and third editions of the *Essay*, and education, leading the now-widowed Molyneux to adopt Locke's system for the education of

19 *Autobiography*, 35–8, 40–1.
20 Sydney's recommendation of Molyneux to Secretary Nottingham, 19 Dec. 1692 as one of 'the best that are to be had here': *Cal. S.P., dom., 1695* (addenda 1689–95), pp 96–7, makes it highly unlikely he was a sole-right man. Cf. Molyneux's claim to have pleased 'both the Government and the University by my Temper and Moderation' in the 1692 parliament: *Autobiography*, p. 40.
21 Samuel had received 1,000 acres in Limerick as arrears of army pay in 1661; his main estate at Castle Dillon, near Armagh, was acquired in 1664 for £3,444, and he subsequently purchased lands in Kildare and elsewhere. In 1665 he bought land near Gormond (or Ormond) Gate in Dublin for the erection of a town house, where William subsequently lived. For details, see Robinson Library, Armagh, Poo1937770.
22 See further P. Kelly, 'Locke and Molyneux', *Hermathena*, 126 (1979), pp 41–2.

his son Samuel.[22] From 1696 their correspondence became increasingly dominated by public affairs, particularly following Locke's appointment to the board of trade and the board's being directed to investigate competition from Irish woollen exports to the Continent. In September 1696 Molyneux responded with an account of recent attempts to establish a linen manufactury in Ireland, asserting that 'no Country in the World is better adapted for it'.[23]

Molyneux's friendship with Wyche gave him an entrée to the administration that in 1693 replaced Sydney in the persons of three lords justices: the Whig politician Henry Capel; the Tory banker William Duncombe and Wyche himself. This influence survived Capel's superseding his colleagues as sole governor in May 1695, when Molyneux was again elected for Dublin University in the parliament summoned later that year. The Commons Journal reveals Molyneux as a regular participant, whose standing was demonstrated by his membership of several important committees. His interest in parliamentary procedure is attested by his compendium of precedents compiled in 1693 from the (seventeenth-century) Commons Journal, together with an extensive analytic index.[24] For his services in the 1695 session Molyneux was rewarded with one of the prestigious masterships in chancery, carefully drawing up a list of his new duties.[25] He was again active on committees in the 1697 session, and provided Locke with accounts of the difficulties in the commons that led to the loss of the bills to restrict woollen exports and encourage the linen manufactury (which had partly originated with the board of trade).[26] Early in 1698 Molyneux received further signs of official confidence with a temporary appointment as a chancery judge during Lord Chancellor Methuen's absence in London, and another as one of three guardians of the Irish estate of Lord Woodstock, heir to William III's Dutch favourite, Lord Portland.[27]

The background to the publication of *The Case*

As Molyneux's introductory remarks made clear, the immediate background to *The case of Ireland* involved the controversy over competition from Irish woollen exports; the Irish Society of London's appeal to the English house of lords against the Irish lords' verdict in favour of the bishop of Derry; the disposal of forfeited Jacobite estates and a number of other issues that reflected the tensions that had developed between the kingdoms of England and Ireland since the end of the Jacobite War in 1691. Other than the replacement of James by William and Mary, no major constitutional change was effected in Ireland by the Glorious Revolution (such as occurred in England with the Bill of Rights or in Scotland with the Claim of Right). However, several important developments, constitutional and otherwise, did take place between 1691 and 1697. Some, such as the surge in woollen exports,

23 Molyneux to Locke, 26 Sept. 1696: *Locke Corr.*, 2131.
24 TCD MS 622.
25 TCD MS 889, ff 65–6.
26 Molyneux to Locke, 4 and 16 Oct. 1698: *Locke Corr.*, 2324, 2331.
27 *Cal. S.P., dom., 1698*, p. 34 (17 Jan. 1697/8); Simms, *William Molyneux* (Dublin, 1982), p. 96.

originated within Ireland itself; others were the result of developments in England brought about by the Nine Years War against France; and yet others occurred as a result of the impact on Ireland of post-revolution political and constitutional changes in England. Perhaps most notable was the growing importance of the Irish parliament, despite its precipitate prorogation in November 1692 as a result of controversy over the so-called 'sole-right' issue, and dissolution in July 1693. Interestingly, the question of whether English statutes required re-enactment in Ireland had arisen in the preparations for this parliament. The London and Dublin administrations had concurred in not re-enacting the 1691 English act abrogating the oaths of supremacy and allegiance in Ireland in case doing so conveyed the (to them) unacceptable message that English legislation did indeed require re-enactment before becoming applicable here.[28] Once assembled, the parliament had showed other signs of self-confidence in its concern to re-establish its rights, precedents and ceremonial, as well as a desire for constructive legislation. A committee (which included Molyneux) was set up to consider what English laws needed to be re-enacted in Ireland, and a list of fifteen English statutes was identified before the prorogation on 3 November.[29] A similar committee was established early in each subsequent session to 1698–9, and re-enacted English statutes amounted to more than 30 per cent of all statutes passed in Ireland in these years.[30] The majority of Irish politicians must therefore have regarded the re-enactment of some English statutes as a normal and desirable practice. Immediate practical concerns rather than theoretical commitment to legislative independence would seem to have been the motive for these re-enactments, even as the practical necessity of adapting English legislation to Irish conditions must (given the requirements of Poynings' Law) have disposed the English administration to accept the practice under normal circumstances. In 1695, however, the former lord justices, Wyche and Duncombe, claimed that the Irish parliament's demand for statutory abrogation of the acts of the Jacobite parliament despite the English act 1 W. & M., ses. 2, c. 9, was motivated by the desire for legislative independence, while Lord Chancellor Porter was struck by the degree of support for the principle among 'Leading Men in the Lawe' in Dublin.[31]

28 McGuire, 'The Irish parliament of 1692' in Bartlett & Hayton (eds), *Penal era and golden age* (Belfast, 1979), pp 8–9.
29 *Commons Jnl [Ire.]*, ii, pp 15–19; *Lords Jnl [Ire.]*, ii, pp 470–5; the lords established a similar committee, ibid., p. 454. See also Dopping, *Modus tenendi parliamenta et consilia in Hibernia* (Dublin, 1692) (which included a reprint of the 1657 *Orders of the English house of commons*), pref. The commons also adopted the recent English practice of printing a brief, near-instantaneous record of their proceedings in *The votes of the [Irish] house of commons*: Englefield, *The printed records of the parliament of Ireland* (London, 1978), pp 4–5.
30 The figures are complicated by instances of re-enactment of an English statute in some clauses of an Irish act, with the remaining clauses being new legislation (e.g. 7 Will. 3, c. 25 'An act for the prevention of vexations and oppressions by arrests, and delays in suits of law'). The highest proportion of re-enactments occurred in 1695, reflecting the backlog of nearly four decades without a successful legislative session.
31 Cf. Bergin & Lyall (eds), *The acts of James II's Irish parliament* (Dublin, 2016), p. lvii; Porter to Sir William Trumbull, 9 July 1695, cited in Rose, *England in the 1690s* (Oxford, 1999), p. 250.

A constitutional *modus vivendi*, rather than a formal settlement, was achieved in the 1695 session through a successful compromise on the 'sole-right' issue, which would provide a basis for the operation of the Irish constitution for much of the eighteenth century.[32] The commons achieved the right to determine finance, subject to first passing a money bill originating with the administration. More frequent meetings of parliament were ensured by limiting revenue grants to two years. At the same time a measure of legislative initiative was achieved through the consolidation of the heads-of-bills procedure that facilitated a limited circumvention of the English administration's monopoly under Poynings' Law of initiating legislation in the Irish parliament (cf. *Case*, p. 167).[33] The 1695 session also saw the beginnings of what would become known as the 'undertaker system', as the administration entered into an understanding with a specific group of local politicians to manage the business of the house.[34] In addition, the Irish political world began to adopt the English party divisions of Whig and Tory, though what these terms stood for in Ireland was not always the same as in England. What also resulted in Ireland from the revolution was the working out of the implications of the transfer of sovereignty in England from the crown alone to the crown in parliament. Its effect was to render obsolete the 'dual-monarchy' model interpretation of relations between the kingdoms of England and Ireland favoured by many Irish politicians and thinkers, though this change took time to work itself through. Perhaps most remarkable, however, of all of the changes during the Nine Years War against France (1689–97) was the speed with which the English parliament, which had once (along with the king) appeared the saviour of the Anglo-Irish, came to be perceived as a threat to their liberties.[35] Anglo-Irish politicians realized that the practical application of revolution principles was restricted to the English context, and that the English parliament did not regard the parliament in Dublin as its equal in rights, nor once the counters were down distinguish very clearly between different categories of Irishmen, seeing when it suited them little difference between former Jacobites and former Williamites.

As indicated, the major contention (in English eyes) between England and Ireland by the mid-1690s arose from commercial jealousy over the remarkable expansion in the export of Irish woollen cloth to Europe following the end of the Jacobite war, at a time when the English woollen industry was severely hampered by depressed demand on the Continent, currency crisis at home and rising food costs from the mid-1690s. The woollen industry in its various branches was not only England's major export industry but the very backbone of its economy,

---

32 McGrath, *The making of the eighteenth-century constitution* (Dublin, 2002), pp 116–17.
33 This somewhat cumbersome procedure provided for draft proposals for legislation ('heads of bills'), raised in the Irish parliament and approved by the Irish privy council, to be forwarded to the English privy council. If agreed to, they were returned as bills to the Irish parliament (in accordance with Poynings' Law), and either rejected or accepted without amendment: J. Kelly, *Poynings' Law* (Dublin, 2007), p. 116.
34 Hayton, *Ruling Ireland* (Woodbridge, 2004), pp 106–9.
35 Cf. lords' address at beginning of 1692 parliament, 24 Oct. 1692: *Lords Jnl [Ire.]*, ii, p. 460.

England's 'Darling Mistris', as Molyneux described it to Locke in 1696.[36] The perceived threat led to a call for the prohibition of Irish woollen exports, first voiced in print in the autumn of 1695 by the Bristol philanthropist and economic writer John Cary.[37] The parts of England most seriously affected in the mid-1690s were the West Country and East Anglia, which produced mainly bays and serges, collectively known as the 'new draperies', the field in which Irish competition was most strongly felt. With the soaring cost of war on the Continent, 1696 was a year of major economic crisis in England, as the reform of the currency began to be implemented in the Great Recoinage of 1696–8, liquidity collapsed and the terms of trade turned significantly against English exports to the Continent. The problem was further exacerbated by rising food costs resulting from a run of bad harvests from 1693 to 1698, particularly in the West Country. Not so seriously affected by this prolonged harvest disruption as other parts of Western Europe, Ireland enjoyed a wage-cost advantage over England (estimated by contemporaries at between 30 and 50 per cent), which stimulated her exports of woollen cloth to the Continent. In late 1696, as we have seen, the newly established board of trade was instructed to investigate competition from Irish woollens, and legislation was brought forward (unsuccessfully) in 1697 to prohibit their export from Ireland. The king and ministry, aware of the problems that this would cause in Ireland, did their best to moderate English demands. The Board preferred a gradual approach through fiscal incentives to diversify from woollen manufacture to linen in place of straightforward prohibition, and it had been to help understand the background to the issue that Locke had sought Molyneux's advice. The king and English ministers believed that in order to placate English opinion the Irish parliament would need to give a lead in effecting the change over, but the necessary response was not forthcoming.[38] Instead the 1697 session sought to intensify the legislation against Catholics, repudiate some important concessions in the Treaty of Limerick and maintain the initiative in financial matters against the English administration in Ireland, leading the new lord chancellor, John Methuen, to describe Irish MPs as 'very uneasy under the strict dependence on England'.[39]

Following the end of the war against France in September 1697, the last session of William's third English parliament opened in December 1697, with the inevitability of an election within twelve months, under the terms of the 1694 Triennial Act. Almost immediately, Robert Harley and Paul Foley, leaders of the 'new Country Party', opened a campaign for the restriction of the size of the military forces in England and Ireland, initiating the Standing Army Crisis, which

36 *Locke Corr.*, 2131, 26 Sept. 1696.

37 Cf. Cary, *An essay on the state of England* (Bristol, 1695).

38 Thanks largely to opposition claims that the bounties proposed in the linen bill violated the 'sole-right' agreement of 1695: P. Kelly, 'The Irish Woollen Export Prohibition Act of 1699', *Irish Economic and Social History*, 7 (1980), pp 31–3.

39 Methuen to Shrewsbury, 8 Oct. 1697: *Buccleuch MSS* (London, 1903), ii, p. 563. Methuen's appointment was intended to provide effective management of the 1697 session, an experience he found extremely frustrating.

would prove the major issue of contention during this session and the first session of the following parliament. Simultaneously, the prominent Tory leader Sir Edward Seymour moved to revive a modified version of the 1697 bill against the export of Irish woollens. Shortly afterwards there appeared a brief but virulent attack on Ireland in the form of *A letter from a gentleman in the country, to a member of the house of commons; in reference to the votes of the 14th instant*.[40] This inflammatory tract almost single-handedly transformed the nature of the Anglo-Irish conflict from largely commercial rivalry to an overtly political and constitutional issue. An unidentified correspondent of Bishop William King named John Toland as author of the piece, an ascription the bishop found convincing in the light of the Irish parliament's condemnation and subsequent burning of Toland's pamphlet, *Christianity not mysterious*, the previous autumn.[41] *A letter from a gentleman* sparked off an extensive pamphlet controversy, in which Toland's claims were angrily refuted by defenders of Irish exports, and counter-claims advanced in support of English woollen interests. The spate of pamphlets continued into the early summer of 1698, with many of the works being rapidly reprinted in Dublin.[42]

Posing as a regular trader to Ireland and occasional visitor there, the author of *A letter from a gentleman* argued that Ireland represented the most insidious threat to English trade, being well placed by nature to exploit resources in fishing, woods and cattle products such as hides and tallow, while enjoying cheap provisions with which war-impoverished England could not hope to compete. But more serious was the political threat afforded by Ireland, which from the 1630s had served as a nursery for arbitrary government in England, particularly through its pliant judiciary. Forgetting that theirs was a conquered country at the victor's disposal, the post-revolution Irish parliament had sought to challenge English dominion by disposing of the lands forfeited by the Jacobite rebels. This monstrous ingratitude for 'the vast expenditure of [English] blood and treasure' could best be checked by abolishing the Irish parliament and treating Ireland on a par with England's other colonies, as Cary had called for.[43] The impact of these proposals was enhanced by the virulence with which they were expressed, and the barely veiled implication that there was little to choose in terms of disloyalty between the current Anglo-Irish and the supporters of James II. Such violent language suggests the *Letter* was intended to provoke an equally outspoken response from Ireland that could be used

40 Namely, for introducing the Irish woollens bill and for setting up a committee on Anglo-Irish trade: *Commons Jnl [Eng.]*, xii, p. 7. For Harley and Seymour, see *ODNB*, s. vv.
41 King to Sir Robert Southwell, 6 Jan. 1697/8, which included a detailed response to the *Letter*, that King may have intended for publication; see further P. Kelly, 'A pamphlet attributed to John Toland', *Topoi*, 4 (1985), which reprints both texts.
42 Some seventeen titles preceded the publication of *The Case* in mid-April, see further pp 15–16 below, and appendix C.
43 The emotive and widely echoed phrase, 'vast expense of blood and treasure' occurred in both Sidney's opening speech to parliament, 5 Oct. 1692 (*Commons Jnl [Ire.]*, ii, p. 9), and the Irish Act of Recognition, 4 W. & M., c. 1. A slightly different version (with 'treasure' preceding 'blood') was found in the Irish commons' remonstrance of 7 Nov. 1640: ibid., i, p. 162.

to justify severe measures against the colonists, such as Molyneux's *Case* would unfortunately supply.

The second major conflict in Anglo-Irish relations in late 1697 was over the appeal brought in the English house of lords by the Irish Society of London against a decision by the Irish lords in favour of the bishop of Derry. At issue was the refusal of the Irish lord chancellor, John Methuen, to make a determination in relation to a lease granted by the Irish Society to the corporation of Londonderry in 1694 for 1,500 acres, known as Termonderry or the Quarter Lands, which the corporation had previously rented from the bishop. This dispute was the current manifestation of a wider, long-standing conflict between the company set up to manage the Londonderry Plantation on behalf of the London Livery Companies, who were the original undertakers of the plantation, and the bishops of Derry, which involved both lands and valuable fisheries.[44] Bishop King's decision to appeal to the Irish house of lords in August 1697 was prompted by the belief that in issuing a further interlocutory order after the court of chancery had ruled in his favour on possession in June, Methuen was dragging out proceedings for political reasons.[45] The lords quashed this order and gave King possession, leaving the question of title to be tried at common law.[46] King initially saw his case as involving not only the interests of the see of Derry but those of the Irish episcopate and church in general, if a lease based on ancient title and undisputed for five decades could be collusively overset in this fashion. But, when the society in turn appealed to the English house, he came to fear that victory for the society would mean that all Irish land titles would ultimately be subject to determination outside the country, thereby reducing Ireland to a state of slavery.[47] In English eyes the Irish Society's appeal to the English lords raised the broader issue of whether the Irish house of lords had the right to hear appeals from the court of chancery. Beyond that again lay the fundamental constitutional question of where the ultimate right of appeal for Irish cases lay – the so-called *dernier resort*. Finally, this issue once more raised the question of England's right to legislate for Ireland, since the society had concluded its state of the case with specific reference to this power.[48]

That the Irish lords' right to hear appeals from the Irish court of chancery was far from clear in the later seventeenth century was by no means surprising. Even in England the current role of the house of lords in hearing appeals only went back

---

44 See *Derry MSS*, i, intro., and ii, pp 126–235 passim. The case that King appealed did not directly involve fishery issues, though other disputes between the bishop and the society over fisheries were currently before the courts.

45 *Derry MSS*, ii, p. 187; King to Robert Southwell, [?] Aug. 1697. While the June ruling had been made by Methuen and the two chief justices, the interlocutory order was issued by Methuen alone.

46 *Lords Jnl [Ire.]*, i, p. 636. King's preparations for the appeal included a search of the Rolls Office with Molyneux and St George Ashe (Marsh's Library, Dublin, MS Z.3.2.5, ff 301–6).

47 King to James Sloane, 4 Nov. 1697; 18 Jan. 1697/8.

48 *Derry MSS*, ii, p. 198. Authorities such as Coke had earlier argued that judicial subordination necessarily implied legislative subordination: Coke, *1st Inst.*, ff 253r, 260r. See further *The Case*, p. 131 nn.

to the 1620s, and had twice been significantly challenged by the commons in Charles II's reign.[49] Failure to hold a parliament in Ireland after 1666 had seen the English house become by default the sole resort for Irish appeals.[50] Moreover, as King conceded in a letter to Bishop Burnet, the Irish lords' willingness to hear his appeal rested more on analogy with English practice rather than specific precedents for their exercising such jurisdiction in the past.[51] Their decision to hear King thus had strong parallels to the way in which the house had assumed a right to hear impeachment proceedings against Strafford's associates and Lord Chancellor Bolton in 1641, a not altogether encouraging precedent, as the Irish lords had been forced to expunge the records of these proceedings from their Journal at the Restoration.[52] Appeal to medieval precedent was also resorted to, particularly by King, who asserted that the Irish Modus Tenendi Parliamenta established that all weighty and important cases were to be determined in Ireland itself, and that in the Prior of Llanthony's case the English house of lords had abstained in 1429 from interfering with a decision of the Irish parliament.[53]

The third major issue to which Molyneux alluded in the preface was the question of the estates forfeited by the Irish Jacobites. The failed efforts to deal with these forfeitures by both Irish and English parliaments in 1692–3 had allowed William to continue to dispose of these lands to successful commanders in the Irish war, English politicians and personal favourites including Portland, Albemarle and the king's sometime mistress Lady Orkney. With the ending of the Nine Years War the fate of former Jacobite estates in Ireland was once more reopened, though the forfeitures question was by now complicated by bona fide interests acquired by purchase from the original grantees, particularly by Irish office holders. In English politics the Irish forfeitures question melded with the controversy over William's extensive grants to favourites in England and Wales, from which his Dutch associates were held to have unduly profited. And, given the enormous increase in the public debt since 1689, arising from the continental war, the question of making Ireland pay for its liberation once more became pressing. However, though the issue would burgeon into a further exercise of English legislative authority over Ireland in the Resumption Act of 1700, following a major inquiry driven by the English parliament, the forfeitures question remained as yet merely a substantial cloud on the horizon when Molyneux came to write *The case of Ireland*.

49 See Hart, *Justice upon petition* (London, 1991), esp. ch. 6. Though Hart argues that the 1670s conflicts arose from perceived threats to commons privileges rather than the desire to strip the lords of their judicial role, King was informed that the commons greatly resented the lords' jurisdictional powers: King to Robert Southwell, 4 Dec. 1697; same to Annesley, 19 May 1698.

50 As can be seen from the precedents put forward in the Derry appeal: *Lords MSS, 1697–9*, pp 26–33; King to Annesley, 16 Apr. 1698.

51 King to Bishop Burnet, 29 Jan. 1697/8.

52 For the 1641 impeachment proceedings, see Perceval-Maxwell, *Outbreak of the Irish rebellion of 1641* (Dublin, 1994), pp 166–72. King, however, included some records excised in 1661 among his 1698 precedents: *Lords MSS, 1697–9*, pp 44–7.

53 See list of King's precedents in *Derry MSS*, ii, pp 234–6, which differed from those submitted by the Irish administration.

The publication of *The Case* and the reaction in the English parliament

'[T]he worst enemy of Ireland could by no way have done us so much mischief'
—Lord Chancellor Methuen on English parliamentary reaction to *The Case*, 7
June 1698[54]

The original date of 26 March 1698 in Molyneux's preface to the reader indicates
that *The Case* was completed for the printer by late March.[55] Its fourteen quires
would have needed some two weeks to print and bind, a time span that accords
with the earliest reference to the work's appearance, in a letter from Bishop King
to Francis Annesley, dated 16 April 1698.[56] As the bishop reported extensive
disagreement with the contents, while claiming he had known nothing of the book
before publication, he had presumably therefore received his presentation copy a
day or two earlier.[57] On 19 April, Molyneux informed Locke that his pamphlet had
now been published, adding that copies were on their way to London for him and
his friends.[58] He reported that friends in Dublin had persuaded him to dedicate the
work to the King (rather than publish it as a remonstrance to the English
parliament, which the manuscripts show was his original plan).[59] He also expressed
dissatisfaction with the book, explaining that it had been hastily written to
influence the English parliament's decisions over Ireland, adding tantalisingly
'were it again under my Hands I could considerably amend, and add to it'. Both
letters referred to Molyneux's intention of having the work formally presented to
King William, with the timing of the presentation decided by unnamed friends in
London.[60] While Bishop King feared the impact of the book in England,
particularly on his appeal before the English lords, Molyneux was more sanguine
– though sufficiently aware of danger from what he called 'Captious Men' to tell
Locke that he could not visit England till parliament had 'Risen'. The only other
thing known of the immediate fortunes of *The Case* in Ireland is that by early May

54 Methuen to Galway, 7 June 1698: BL Add. MS 61653, f. 65. All further letters between them from
this manuscript are identified by date alone.
55 Subsequently altered to 8 Feb. 1697/8 (cf. *The Case*, A8r app. crit.), a change probably made to
avoid compromising the Derry appeal, in relation to which the English lords had made an official
request for precedents to the Irish privy council on 8 Jan.: *Lords MSS, 1697–9*, pp 24–5.
56 For Annesley, see *DIB*, and *Commons, 1690–1715*, s.v. Annesley acted as King's managing counsel
for the Derry appeal, together with James Sloane.
57 This copy is now in NLI, shelf mark LO 2589/Bd. King's substantive objections are considered
on p. 23 below.
58 Although Molyneux had invited Locke to consider 'How justly [the English parliament] can bind
us without our *Consent* and *Representatives*' on 15 Mar. 1698, the latter had not realized that he
intended to publish on the topic: Locke to Molyneux, 6 Apr. 1698: *Locke Corr.*, 2407, 2414, 2422.
59 Cf. *The Case*, p. 1 app. crit.
60 King's letter of 16 Apr. also passed on a request from Molyneux asking Annesley to help George
Tollet find someone suitable to present the pamphlet to King William. A former member of the
DPS, Tollet had become secretary to the English commons' public accounts committee: *DIB*, s.v.

Molyneux had presented the work to the lords justices (the Huguenot earl of Galway and the marquess of Winchester).[61]

The reaction in England, particularly in parliament, was very different; Molyneux's hope that reason and 'strict Justice' might be expected from his appeal to 'that Illustrious Body of Senators' proved vain (*Case*, pp 1–2). When the session had opened in early December 1697, there was (as we have seen) already potential for conflict over several issues relating to Ireland, and the Irish Lord Chancellor John Methuen had been recalled from Dublin to manage Irish interests in parliament and elsewhere.[62] What soon became apparent was how closely the various Irish issues were now linked together, particularly the woollen exports, the appeal against the bishop of Derry and the size of the military forces in Ireland – all of which provided opportunities to drive a wedge between the interests of the Junto Whig ministry and the king.[63] As Seymour's woollens bill proceeded through the commons to the lords, anti-Irish feeling was intensified by a spate of pamphlets prompted by Toland's anonymous *Letter from a gentleman*.[64] Most prolific in defence of Irish woollen exports was the Irish MP and writer on trade, Sir Francis Brewster, currently in London, who produced *An answer to a letter from a gentleman* over his own initials, which was soon reprinted in Dublin along with the original *Letter*.[65] Brewster followed this with the anonymous *Discourse concerning Ireland ... in answer to the Exon and Barnstaple petitions* (1697/8), and yet another piece over the initials 'F.B.', entitled *A letter to a member of the house of commons, on a proposal for regulating and advancing the woollen industry* (1698).[66] Preliminary proceedings in the Derry appeal also opened in January, with the lords seeking evidence from the Irish administration relating to the Irish peers' right to hear chancery appeals, while Bishop King simultaneously gathered his own precedents.[67]

Seymour's bill cleared the commons in late February but did not surface in the lords till the end of March, when counsel were heard for and against it, together with various experts, including Brewster. The lords' proceedings gave rise to the

---

61 Their public acceptance of the book led to adverse reactions in England: Methuen to Galway, 7 June 1698.

62 Ironically, not only was Methuen's English constituency of Devizes an important woollen-manufacturing town, but his own family was prominent in the trade: *Commons, 1690–1715*, s.v. John Methuen.

63 The Irish lobby in London was already co-ordinating responses on the Derry appeal and on the woollen bill in Jan. 1698 (Methuen to Galway, 25 Jan. 1697/8), while a group of Irish merchants and gentlemen was collectively represented by Sir Thomas Powys at the lords' hearing on the woollen bill at the end of March (*Lords MSS, 1697–9*, p. 107).

64 For Toland's piece, see above pp 11–12. For details of these publications, see appendix C.

65 Brewster further sought to discredit the anonymous author by depicting him as a Catholic: Brewster, *An answer to a letter* (Dublin, 1698), p. 6. For Brewster, see further *ODNB*, s.v.

66 Cf. McBride, *Eighteenth-century Ireland* (Dublin, 2010), p. 167. Exeter proved a major source of attacks on Irish woollens both in the spring and in the parliamentary elections in the following autumn, which chose the leading Tories Sir Edward Seymour and Sir Bartholomew Shower to represent the city.

67 *Lords MSS, 1697–9*, pp. 16–33; King to Annesley, 27 Feb. 1697/8.

most influential publication in Ireland's favour, *Some thoughts on the bill depending before ... the house of lords for prohibiting the exportation of the woolen manufactures of Ireland into foreign parts*, attributed to Sir Richard Cox by Walter Harris in 1746, but more probably written by Francis Annesley.[68] *Some thoughts* soon produced two anonymous replies, Simon Clement's *The interest of England as it stands in relation to the trade of Ireland*, and *The substance of the arguments for and against the export of woollen manufacture from Ireland ...*, attributed in the British Library copy to '_____ Gardiner'.[69] Both Brewster and the author of *Some thoughts* highlighted the harm the prohibition would do to the English Protestant interest in Ireland, while leaving the Scottish Presbyterians in Ulster (whose numbers had been greatly swollen by recent immigration) and the bulk of Irish Catholics relatively unaffected.[70] Undermining the only group consistently loyal to England would necessitate increasing military forces in Ireland, and so threaten England's own prosperity and security. By early April the controversy had become increasingly ill-tempered, and the demand for punitive measures widespread. Tragically, both for Molyneux and for Ireland, the appearance of *The Case* proved the final straw. The deal that Methuen had brokered with the moderate group in the lords that the bill against Irish woollen exports be allowed to lapse, in return for a promise of legislation in Ireland, was imperilled.[71]

The extent to which feeling had been polarized became clear when the Derry appeal was finally heard before the lords on 20 May. The society's counsel, Sir Bartholomew Shower, asserted that the fundamental issue was whether the parliament of England was superior to that of Ireland. In response to Serjeant Wright's contention for the bishop that the issue depended on the nature of the kingdom of Ireland, the lords (with Lord Chancellor Somers in the chair) refused to hear arguments challenging their jurisdiction in Ireland.[72] All that remained to be decided was therefore whether the Irish lords had the right to hear appeals from chancery. The extensive precedents assembled by both the Irish privy council and Bishop King were dismissed as inadequate, along with the statement in the Irish Modus (the full text of which King had produced in evidence) that 'all weighty matters were to be determined in Ireland *in pleno parliamento et non alibi* [in full

---

68 P. Kelly, 'The Irish Woollen Export Prohibition Act of 1699', *Irish Economic and Social History*, 7 (1980), pp 34–5. Cf. King to Annesley, 30 Apr. 1698, commenting on the Dublin reprint of *Some thoughts*.

69 Perhaps the Mr Gardiner who spoke at the lords' hearing on the bill on 30 Mar.: *Lords MSS, 1697–99*, p. 108.

70 Alderman Hovell's anonymous *Discourse of the woollen manufactury of Ireland* (1698) made much of the financial benefits that England derived from Irish woollens.

71 Just before *The Case* appeared, Methuen had informed Galway (14 Apr. 1698) of his success with the moderate group: 'if the indiscreet Zeal and Diligence of the Gentlemen of Ireland do not hinder who are every day publishing books and papers not suiting with this climate'.

72 *Lords MSS, 1697–9*, pp 17–19. Shower reported on the Derry appeal in Shower, *Cases in parliament* (London, 1698), pp 78–82, a breach of privilege that earned him the censure of the house.

parliament and not elsewhere]'.[73] Rather than submit to the denigration of their parliament, Irish peers with English titles withdrew from the house, led by the duke of Ormonde (who incidentally was also high steward of Exeter, the centre of opposition to the Irish woollen trade).[74] The following day the house declared King's appeal to the Irish lords *coram non judice* (i.e. that the court did not have jurisdiction to hear the appeal), and an unidentified correspondent informed him that the outspoken views in *The Case* had tipped the balance against him.[75]

The onus of defending *The Case* fell to Methuen, helped by the Irish MP and privy councillor Robert Molesworth, who was also member for Camelford in Cornwall. The latter's sympathy for his college friend, Molyneux, was probably heightened by his own experience in 1694, when the Danes had called on the king to suppress Molesworth's *Account of Denmark* and punish its author.[76] Methuen's earlier failure to support the Junto in the standing army debate left him uncertain, however, of ministerial backing, despite William's strong support; his greatest difficulties were with Somers, whom at times he believed well-intentioned towards Ireland, and at others inexplicably opposed – particularly on the constitutional front.[77] Initial success came with Molesworth's persuading Molyneux's friends not to present the work to the king, thereby forestalling the English publication of the book.[78] The king and Methuen then sought to pre-empt further trouble by laying the *The Case* before the commons on 21 May, and inviting them to pursue the author and those who had supported him. Members' anger was not so easily assuaged.[79] The committee examining the book extended its inquiry to broader questions of Anglo-Irish relations, even expressing doubt that Molyneux was sole author of the work. Deliberations on *The Case* dragged out over six weeks; and though in early June Methuen still hoped the book would escape condemnation, the committee's outrage on discovering the extent to which the heads-of-bills procedure had – as they saw it – subverted Poynings' Law sealed the pamphlet's fate.[80]

The lead in attacking the book in the committee came from what to Molyneux must have been a most unexpected source, namely Locke's closest friend and

---

73 This version of the Modus differs in minor matters from Dopping, *Modus tenendi parliamenta et consilia in Hibernia* (Dublin, 1692), see further appendix A.

74 *Lords MSS, 1697–9*, p. 19; *Ormonde MSS*, n.s., viii, p. 35.

75 Probably Annesley or James Sloane: *Derry MSS*, ii, pp 201–4. Methuen to Galway, 21 May 1698, also blamed *The Case* for King's defeat. Cf. verdict, 20 May, and resulting order, 24 May: *Lords Jnl [Eng.]*, xvi, pp 292, 294.

76 See *ODNB*, s.v. Robert Molesworth.

77 Methuen to Galway, 2 Apr., 31 May, 2 June 1698, but Somers told Galway, 18 Aug. 1698, that Methuen had misrepresented his position.

78 Cf. King to Annesley, 14 May 1698. Methuen informed Galway of the seizure of 100 copies by the London customs, 24 May 1698.

79 Methuen to Galway, 21 May 1698; *Vernon letters*, ii, pp 83, 21 May 1698; anonymous newsletter, 21 May, *Cal. S.P., dom., 1698*, pp 261–2.

80 Thanks to Undersecretary Yard's providing a set of the printed *Votes of the Irish house of commons*: Courthorpe, 'Minutebook', *Camden Miscellany*, 20:3 (1953), pp 48–50. See further *Vernon letters*, 7 June 1698.

political associate, Edward Clarke, who acted as Somers' spokesman in the commons.[81] Determined to prevent Locke's name being drawn into the controversy, Clarke turned to establishing what in Ireland had given Molyneux confidence that such an attack on the English parliament would be acceptable to his countrymen. Methuen's belief that Clarke was merely voicing Somers' opinions was only partially true; as member for Taunton, Clarke also had a personal interest in championing West Country woollen interests, particularly with the forthcoming election under the Triennial Act.[82] The main issues raised were the Irish parliament's failure to discourage competition with the English woollen industry and its efforts to evade the restrictions imposed by Poynings' Law. Considered particularly offensive was the re-enactment of various English post-revolution statutes specifically directed at Ireland, above all the unsuccessful attempt to amend the English 1696 Act for the Better Security of the King's Person and Government in the 1697 session. In accordance with their terms of reference,[83] the committee identified thirty-two specific passages from *The Case* to the commons on 22 June as 'tend[ing] to the disowning and denying the Authority of the Parliament of *England* over *Ireland*'. These ranged from the definition of conquest as 'an *Acquisition of a Kingdom by Force of Arms*' (*Case*, pp 12–13), through the assertion that no English act expressly claimed the right to bind Ireland (*Case*, pp 67–8), to the claim that Ireland had as good a right to be considered an independent kingdom as Scotland (*Case*, p. 84).[84]

The much-cited finding (drawn from the committee's report) that *The Case* 'is of dangerous Consequence to the Crown and People of *England*', was unanimously adopted in a commons resolution of 27 June 1698. Two days later a draft address characterized the doings in Ireland that had given rise to the pamphlet as 'an open and explicit Act of Disobedience to the Legislative Authority ... of *England*'. Although in calling on the king to prevent 'any thing of the like Nature for the future', the draft spoke of 'punishing and discountenancing those that have been guilty thereof', Molyneux was not mentioned by name. The house as a whole, however, took a softer line, dropping the reference to 'Disobedience', as well as the demand for regular scrutiny of the Irish parliamentary journals.[85] When the address was presented to William on 2 July (along with a second address, calling for the suppression of Irish woollen exports), the king's desire to avoid further

81 Vernon to Shrewsbury, 21 May 1698.
82 Methuen to Galway, 31 May 1698, though Somers may have prevented a lords' inquiry into *The Case*: same to same, 21 May.
83 '[A]nd report such Passages, as they find, denying the Authority of the Parliament of *England*': *Commons Jnl [Eng.]*, xii, p. 281.
84 All such passages are identified in the explanatory notes to the text. For Clarke's involvement in their selection, see Somerset RO, DD/SF/13/2909, a reference for which I am indebted to David Hayton.
85 Cf. newsletter to Ambassador Joseph Williamson, 30 June 1698: *Cal. S.P. dom., 1698*, p. 332. As Donaldson, 'The application in Ireland' (PhD, QUB, 1952), pp 331–2, pointed out, this address was, ironically, the first occasion on which the English parliament formally asserted the right to legislate for Ireland.

conflict between the two kingdoms led to a brief and low-key response: 'Gentlemen I will take Care that what is complained of may be prevented, and redressed, as you desire'.[86] Instructions were sent to the Irish lords justices (7 July) to prepare legislation to restrict woollen exports and encourage linen manufacture. A second letter, dealing with 'Independency' and the circumvention of Poynings' Law, echoed the commons' complaints and instructed the lords justices not merely to discountenance this tendency but to punish those responsible – though no such action was apparently taken. *The Case* itself was denounced as likely to raise 'Passions [which] will be so fatall to this our Kingdom and even Ireland itself', but again no specific mention was made of Molyneux.[87]

Following presentation of the address, the session ended on 5 July, and Molyneux finally considered it safe to travel to England for his long-awaited meeting with Locke. What transpired between the friends in relation to *The Case* can only be surmised. Given Locke's angry reaction to previous revelations about the *Two treatises*, Molyneux's overt deployment of arguments from that work and barely stopping short of identifying of Locke as its author, can scarcely have been welcome.[88] In response to a no-longer-extant letter from Clarke undertaking to keep Locke's name out of the parliamentary inquiry, Locke had confided at the end of May that 'as there is no fence against other people's folly, so I think nobody is to answer for other people's follies but they themselves'.[89] On the other hand, before realizing Molyneux intended to publish on the subject, Locke had professed himself eager to discuss in person the question of 'How justly [the English parliament] can bind us without our *Consent* and *Representatives*'.[90] The extent to which Molyneux was aware of Locke's reservations remains unknown. The two friends spent several weeks together, first in London (where Locke had come to attend the board of trade) and later at Oates, near Bishop Stortford in Essex, where he had lived with the Masham family since 1691. While the subject of *The Case* and its treatment by parliament could scarcely have failed to come up, it certainly did not mar the occasion. In his letter of thanks, Molyneux referred to the visit as one of the happiest experiences of his life, a view cordially reciprocated by his host. Any possibility of future conflict was dispelled by Molyneux's unexpected death from a kidney stone a bare four weeks after returning to Dublin, a loss that Locke assured Thomas Molyneux affected him very deeply.[91]

Though it has long been asserted that the action taken against Molyneux's book by the English house of commons culminated in an order condemning *The Case* to be burnt by the common hangman, there is no contemporary evidence to

---

86 *Commons Jnl [Eng.]*, xii, pp 321–39 passim.
87 *Cal. S.P., dom., 1698*, p. 332. Cf. drafts in BL Add. MS 28942, ff 228–30.
88 Woolhouse, *Locke* (Cambridge, 2007), pp 281–2.
89 *Locke Corr.*, 2447, 30 May 1698; it was not unusual for Locke to destroy potentially compromising correspondence.
90 See further p. 14, n. 58 above.
91 Molyneux to Locke, 20 Sept. 1698; Locke to Molyneux, 29 Sept. 1698; Locke to Thomas Molyneux, 27 Oct. 1698: *Locke Corr.*, 2490, 2492, 2500.

support this. While such treatment of offending works was still meted out, in Ireland as well as England, there is no mention of such action in the *Commons Journal* nor any other contemporary reference to *The Case* having suffered this fate. Given the enormous interest the investigation into the pamphlet provoked, it is hard to believe that such an event would have gone unremarked at the time. Moreover, the earliest mention of the burning of *The Case* is not found till 1719, and there is no specific reference to it in print till Lucas' *Tenth address to the free citizens ... of the city of Dublin* in early 1749.[92] What did occur in the 1698–9 parliamentary session, however, was the final passing of an act (10 & 11 Will. 3, c. 10) prohibiting the export of Irish woollen cloths to the Continent, despite all the efforts of both the English and Irish administrations to prevent it, as well as an act appointing commissioners of inquiry into the Irish forfeitures (10 & 11 Will. 3, c. 9). By that stage William had had to submit to the dismissal of his cherished Blue Dutch Guards, and the sustained assault on the Junto ministry had borne fruit in the resignations of Shrewsbury and Montagu, leaving the ministry no longer able to, nor much interested in, resisting the pressure from the English woollens lobby. This triumph over Irish interests by the English parliament would be taken further in the following session, with the 1700 Act of Resumption (11 & 12 Will. 3, c. 2) revoking William's land grants in Ireland and thereby compounding the defeat of the cause Molyneux had sought to defend.

Contemporary responses to *The Case*

Answers in print were not long in appearing. The earliest, *A vindication of the parliament of England, in answer to ... The case of Ireland's ... stated*, came from the pen of John Cary (1650–1720), who identified himself in his dedication to Lord Chancellor Somers as the literary instigator of the campaign to ban the export of Irish woollens.[93] A merchant living in Bristol, where he dated his answer from on 16 June 1698, Cary's interests extended to the currency crisis and poor relief, as well as commercial relations with Ireland and Scotland.[94] His major work, *An essay on the state of England in relation to its trade, its poor & its taxes ...* , 1695 (which Locke praised as the best book he had read on the subject), had called for Ireland's reduction to the status of a colony like those in North America and the extirpation of its woollen industry.[95] In the autumn of 1698 Cary would stand unsuccessfully as an anti-Irish-woollens candidate at Bristol, his defeat perhaps attributable to a

92 William Nicolson, bishop of Derry, to Archbishop Wake, 1 Sept. 1719 (BL Add. MS 6112, item 115). The earliest indirect reference in print was an anonymous, allegorical reply to Swift and Sheridan's *Intelligencer*, no. 16, in the *Daily Journal* (London, 8 Feb. 1728/9), signed 'Philo-Britannicus', reprinted in Swift & Sheridan, *The Intelligencer* (Oxford, 1992), pp 259–60. The claim achieved widespread circulation with Charles Lucas' *A tenth address* (Dublin, 1749), see further p. 47 below.

93 Cary, *To the free holders* (Bristol, 1698), dedic.

94 For his career, see *ODNB*, s.v.

95 Locke to Cary, 2 May 1696: *Locke Corr.*, 2079.

perceived connection with Somers.[96] Despite his commercial background, Cary's critique of Molyneux focused chiefly on matters of law and precedent. His main contention in 1698, as in 1695–6, was that the Irish needed to acknowledge their colonial status, and accept the inevitability of commercial subordination to England. Cary's subsequent career involved him further with Ireland. In 1700 he was appointed an Irish forfeitures trustee, and it was presumably in connection with this that he brought out the second edition of *A Vindication* in 1700, in which a brief dedication to the two (English) houses of parliament preceded his original one to Somers.[97] By 1718, however, Cary had somewhat softened his position, accepting in the preface to his pamphlet *The rights of the commons in parliament assembled* ..., that acts of parliament made in England since 10 Hen. 7 did not automatically bind Ireland.

The second answer, William Atwood's *History and reasons for the dependency of Ireland ... Rectifying Mr. Molyneux's state of the case of Ireland's being bound* ... was listed in the *Term catalogue* for Trinity 1698, and subsequently advertised (without mention of its author) in the *Post Man* for 2–5 July 1698.[98] Atwood (1652–1712) was a radical Whig lawyer, who had been a collaborator of William Petyt in the 1680s, and subsequently justified the 1688 revolution in *The fundamental constitution of the English government* (1690), one of the earliest works to mention Locke's *Two treatises of government*.[99] Despite his professed admiration for the then anonymous *Treatises*, Atwood held no brief for what he called Molyneux's 'wheadling Notions of the *inherent*, and unalienable Rights of Mankind'.[100] His approach to *The Case* was primarily antiquarian, and (though not immediately relevant) his ideological obsessions with the elective nature of the English monarchy, and tracing the origins of the commons in parliament back to Saxon times, both featured prominently. Atwood's support for the Junto Whigs finally paid off with an appointment as chief justice of New York in 1700, where his autocratic behaviour, however, brought about his dismissal by the Tory governor Lord Cornbury in 1702. Atwood's final publication in 1704, attacking Scottish pretensions to independence, was burned by order of the Scottish parliament.[101]

---

96 Cf. Cary, *To the free holders* (Bristol, 1698); Sachse, *Lord Somers* (Manchester, 1975), p. 140.

97 The new dedication voiced concern that Cary's earlier defence of parliament had been understood to advocate 'arbitrary power'.

98 Atwood's dedication to the house of commons cited their resolution on *The Case* of 27 June 1698. Two forms of imprint are found; the first for 'Dan. Brown' and 'Ri. Smith', and the second for 'Dan Brown' and 'Tho. Leigh'. The first was advertised in the *Post Man*, 2–5 July, and the second, July 7–9. Apart from the titlepages, the two texts are identical.

99 Atwood, *Fundamental constitution* (London, 1690), pp 4, 97. See further, Ludington, 'From ancient constitution to British empire' in Ohlmeyer (ed.), *Political thought* (Cambridge, 2000), pp 244–52.

100 Atwood, *History*, p. 211, which suggested that his admiration for *Two treatises* owed more to mutual hostility to Filmer than appreciation of Locke's natural-law arguments. See further Atwood, *Fundamental constitution* (London, 1690), app. 9, p. 19.

101 Namely, *The superiority and direct domination of the imperial crown of England over the crown and kingdom of Scotland* (London, 1704): *ODNB*, s.v.

The third work, *An answer to Mr. Molyneux his case of Ireland* ... whose author speaks of not having read Atwood's book till he had finished his own, probably appeared sometime in July 1698.[102] Unlike its predecessors, the *Answer* was anonymous: only in recent years has its attribution to Simon Clement been definitively confirmed by the discovery of a signed presentation copy in Locke's library.[103] Clement too had already had a distinguished career as an economic pamphleteer, contributing two pamphlets to the 1695–6 recoinage controversy, and one on the general commercial and credit crisis of the mid-1690s. According to Charles Davenant, he was also the author of *The interest of England in relation to the trade of Ireland*, the most economically sophisticated of the attacks on the Irish woollen trade in the spring of 1698.[104] Despite his assurance that he was not a lawyer, Clement's comments on Prince John's revolt in 1194 demonstrated a clearer understanding of feudalism than the professed antiquary Atwood.[105] He also came across as the best informed of the three Whig critics about conditions in Ireland, displaying a sympathy for the Old English, which went beyond the merely rhetorical.[106] He appealed to the Protestant people of Ireland to repudiate Molyneux's specious claims and demonstrate their gratitude to England by banning woollen exports and repaying the cost of their liberation from James and the French. He too was a beneficiary of Junto Whig patronage; early in 1698 he had been named secretary to Locke's friend, Lord Bellomont, on the latter's appointment as governor of New York, though he eventually failed to take up the post.[107] Clement's was by far the most intemperate of the three replies, referring to *The Case* as 'little better than *Sheba*'s Trumpet of Rebellion', and accusing Molyneux of speaking like an Irishman rather than the English colonist that his name showed him to be.[108]

The Case subsequently attracted the attention of two Tory critics. The earlier was the non-juring clergyman Charles Leslie, whose brief and anonymous *Considerations of importance to Ireland* was dated 26 Dec. 1698; the second was the economist and pioneer statistician, Charles Davenant, whose critique of Molyneux had until recently gone largely unnoticed in his lengthy 1699 *Essay upon the probable methods of making a people possible gainers in the ballance of trade.*[109] Listed

---

102 The mention of 'answers' to *The Case*, in King's letter to Annesley, 16 July 1698, points to its availability by mid-July. Clement's references to Atwood (epist. ded., p. b2v, and pp 169–70) may hint at a concerted approach; both works appeared over the imprint of 'Dan. Brown' and 'Ri. Smith'.

103 Harrison & Laslett, *The library of John Locke* (Oxford, 1971), p. 110 (item 745). The *Answer* was previously generally attributed to Cary.

104 Davenant, *An essay* (London, 1699), p. 123.

105 Clement, *Answer*, p. 125. Cf. their different reactions to Molyneux's claim that John's title to the crown of Ireland was by 'two discents': *The Case*, p. 54, nn. See further Atwood, *History*, pp 90–1.

106 Clement, *Answer*, p. 125.

107 *Cal. S.P., col. 1693–6*, p. 461 (12 Dec. 1696); ibid., *1697–8*, p. 541 (12 Nov. 1698).

108 Clement, *Answer*, epist. ded., and p. 11.

109 A lacuna made good by István Hont's analysis of Davenant's critique in Hont, *Jealousy of trade* (Cambridge, MA, 2005).

in the *Term catalogue* for Hilary 1699, the Essay probably appeared in January or February 1699. Molyneux's Tory critics published therefore in support of the third (and finally successful) bill to prohibit Irish woollen exports of December 1698, rather than in the immediate aftermath of the pamphlet's appearance. A sixth contemporary critique of Molyneux's *Case* was provided by Isaac Newton, though it has remained unpublished among his mint papers. It was probably written in the late summer of 1698 when Newton, as warden of the mint, was instructed, along with the master, Thomas Neale, to investigate the establishment of a mint in Ireland.[110] His reflections on *The Case* consisted of factual notes from the book, interspersed with personal conclusions often directly at variance with Molyneux's. Most striking was the claim that Henry II's army had terrified the Irish into submission, so enabling the king to impose English laws and customs, and thus subsequently entitling the English parliament to legislate for Ireland.[111] Though Molyneux would presumably have been flattered to have his work examined by a man whose scientific eminence he so much revered, it may be doubted that he would have taken much comfort from Newton's conclusion, still less from that of his joint report with Thomas Neale to the Treasury, 18 August 1698: 'We are unwilling that any opinion of ours should be made use of … to make [the Irish] of equal dignity and dominion with [the English] and perhaps at length desirous to separate from this Crown …'[112]

No response to *The Case* was published in Ireland, whether by way of attack or defence. Nor, interestingly in view of the spate of Irish reprints of the woollens controversy pamphlets of early 1698, were any of the English answers to Molyneux reprinted in Dublin. The most extensive assessment of *The Case* in Ireland came in King's letter of 16 April 1698, already cited as the first mention of the work's being in print.[113] King's main objections were in relation to Molyneux's apparent acceptance of English Restoration legislation forbidding things like growing tobacco in Ireland, and his conceding that Ireland was subject to the Navigation Acts. Since King's observation that Ireland was no more subject to the latter than France or Spain was a point that Molyneux himself had made, his initial perusal of *The Case* was perhaps fairly perfunctory.[114] Despite these reservations, King subsequently expostulated at the English parliament's fixing on the opinions of 'a private gentleman' as justification for denigrating a whole kingdom.[115] By 1720,

110 It is printed in appendix D below.
111 This reading was perhaps influenced by Grotius' assertion that surrender in the face of overwhelming force amounted to a conquest rather than voluntary submission: Grotius, *De jure belli ac pacis* (London, 1715), iii, p. 142, a work available in Newton's library: Harrison, *The library of Isaac Newton* (Cambridge, 1974), p. 155 (item 719).
112 *Calendar of Treasury Books*, 14 (1698–9), p. 107. For Molyneux's admiration for Newton, see Hoppen, *The common scientist* (London, 1970), pp 124–5.
113 Page 14 above. Cf. King to Annesley, 24 Mar. 1697/8, 19 May 1698; same to Bishop Hartstonge of Ossory, 3, 13 May 1697.
114 Cf. *The Case*, pp 102–4.
115 King to bishop of St Asaph, 7 June 1698.

however, he had come to admire the book so much as to recommend its republication, albeit with an appendix pointing out where Molyneux had gone wrong.[116] King's private letters relating to the Irish Society's appeal to the English lords were far more outspoken than anything Molyneux published, referring to the Irish being reduced to a state of absolute slavery by England's assertion of judicial and legislative supremacy.[117] Of the various other comments found in correspondence etc., only the non-juror and former Trinity College fellow Henry Dodwell (by then living in England) seems to have voiced a measure of approval in an indirect reference to *The Case* in a letter from England to Molyneux's brother-in-law John Madden of 7 December 1700. Replying to a letter from Madden that he had subsequently mislaid, Dodwell inquired whether he was correct in remembering that this had informed him that Molyneux's 'defence of our Irish libertyes' drew on a paper inspired by 'the opinions of Hussey and my Lord Cook', which he believed Madden had credited to Sir Richard Bolton.[118] Equally interestingly, Archbishop Marsh recorded, in a doggerel note on the copy presented to him by Molyneux, that *The Case* was a reissue of Domville's 'Disquisition': 'Unhappy he,/ Who could not see/ What mischief would betide him,/ If he did write/ With so much spite/ And Domville's name not hide him.' Taken literally, this comment suggests Marsh had received his information at second-hand rather than drawn on personal knowledge of Domville's paper.[119]

The other contemporary Irish reference to Molyneux and *The Case* was also unfortunately indirect. In October 1699 Sir Richard Cox assured a correspondent, who was probably Edward Harley, that 'upon first view of Mr Molyneux's book, I gave you my thoughts that the doctrine was false, and unseasonably published, and would have ill consequences'.[120] Cox's remarks have an added interest in the light of his assertion in 1714 that he planned a detailed refutation of Molyneux's arguments for private circulation, though nothing seems to have come of this.[121] Finally, given Leibniz's complimentary remarks on *Dioptrica nova* and subsequent contribution to the debate over the Molyneux problem, it is interesting to note that he received a brief summary of *The Case* from Thomas Burnett of Kemney in February 1699, though he does not seem to have commented on Molyneux's views.[122]

116 King to Samuel Molyneux Jnr, 2 Jan. 1719/20. He had previously mentioned the need for an appendix in a letter to Bishop Lindsay of Killaloe, June 1698.

117 King to James Sloane, 18 Jan. 1697/8; same to Annesley, 16 Apr., 19 May 1698.

118 TCD MS 1995–2008/741; printed in full in *HMC 2nd Report* (1874), app. ii, p. 241. The earliest mention of the debt to Bolton in print was Morres, *The history of the Irish parliament* (London, 1792), i, p. 360. I have not been able to trace St George Ashe's letter of 10 Feb. 1699/1700 praising Molyneux for publishing *The Case*, referred to in Hoppen, *The common scientist* (London, 1970), p. 185.

119 J. Wood, 'William Molyneux and the politics of friendship', *ECI*, 30 (2015), pp 30–2.

120 Cox to [? Edward Harley], 28 Oct. 1669: *Portland MSS*, iii, p. 609.

121 Cox to Edward Southwell, 16 Oct. 1714: BL Add. MS 38157, f. 136, a reference for which I am indebted to David Hayton.

122 Simms, *William Molyneux* (Dublin, 1982), pp 71, 125–7; O'Gara, 'Leibnitz and "la liberté Anglois"', 2000: *The European Journal*, 3:1 (2002), pp 1–3.

III. THE SUBSTANCE OF *THE CASE*

> '*That* Ireland *should be Bound by Acts of Parliament made in* England, *is against Reason, and the Common Rights of all Mankind.' —The Case*, p. 150

The context of Ireland's claim to legislative independence[123]

The claim that English acts of parliament were not binding in Ireland until they had been re-enacted by the Irish parliament had surfaced intermittently during the seventeenth century. Opinion differed strongly within both countries. At times the Irish claim was apparently accepted at the highest levels of the English administration, as when the chief justices and chief baron had advised James I during the preparations for the Irish parliament of 1613 that English legislation did not automatically apply in Ireland.[124] In 1643 Charles I and his privy council had taken a similar view in the light of forthcoming negotiations with the Irish Confederates.[125] At other times, however, as notably in the Adventurers' Acts of 1642, the pretensions of the Irish parliament were simply disregarded.[126] Although as might be expected, Irish opinion tended to favour legislative independence, some prominent Anglo-Irish figures, from the future archbishop Ussher in 1611 to Richard Cox in 1689, accepted and approved England's claimed right to legislate for their country.[127] Earlier in the century two notable treatises justifying the right to legislative independence had been written by prominent Irish lawyers; Lord Chancellor Richard Bolton in 1644, and the newly appointed attorney general, Sir William Domville, in 1660 (both of which Molyneux would employ as major sources for *The Case*).[128] The issue resurfaced during the Irish parliament of 1661–6, particularly in relation to legislation for the land settlement in the acts of settlement and explanation. Occasional reflections on the matter can be found between 1666 and the Glorious Revolution, though the absence of parliaments in Ireland during these years meant that the issue was of little immediate practical concern.[129]

---

123 The term 'legislative independence' (which did not become current until C.18) is used as a shorthand for the principle that English statutes needed to be re-enacted by the Irish parliament before becoming of force in Ireland.

124 Coke, *12th Rep.*, pp 110–11; *4th Inst.*, pp 349, 351; and comment in Domville, 'Disquisition', p. 56.

125 Carte, *James, first duke of Ormonde* (Oxford, 1851), ii, pp 442–3. See further P. Kelly, 'Sir Richard Bolton and the authorship of "A declaration"', *IHS*, 35 (2006), pp 6–7.

126 Cf. 17 Car. 1, c. 33, which also overrode the Irish legal process by declaring people rebels without trial and confiscating their property.

127 Ussher, 'Of the first establishment of English laws' in Gutch, *Collectanea curiosa* (Oxford, 1781), i, p. 24; Cox, *Hibernia Anglicana* (London, 1689), epist. dedic.

128 Bolton, 'Declaration'; Domville, 'Disquisition'. It should be pointed out that Molyneux would not seem to have known Sir Samuel Mayart's lengthy 1644 'Answer to the declaration' (published along with Bolton's 'A declaration' in Harris' *Hibernica*). See further pp 54–9 below.

129 E.g. the relatively favourable opinion of Attorney General Finch in Feb. 1671 (cf. *The Case*, p. 100 nn.), and the more hostile comments of Lord Chancellor Guilford in 1685: Clarendon, *The correspondence of Henry Hyde* (London, 1828), i, pp 183–7.

A major caesura in the debate was created by the actions of the parliament summoned by James II in Dublin in 1689 after his abandonment of the English throne. Prominent among its statutes was 'An act declaring that the Parliament of *England* cannot bind *Ireland* ...', which also prohibited appeals to England in both common law and chancery cases, and only James' determined resistance prevented the revocation of Poynings' Law.[130] Traumatised by their treatment by the Jacobite regime, Irish Protestants, particularly those who sought refuge in England, abandoned for the short term their aspirations to the status of an independent kingdom in the triple monarchy. Instead, they boasted of the fact that Ireland was a conquered country, seeing in Henry's conquest of 1171–2 a compelling imperative for William to reconquer Ireland from the Jacobites and the French.[131] The process of recovering their confidence and reasserting Ireland's status as an independent kingdom of the English crown after 1691 was hastened by what they saw as unjustified concessions to the defeated in the settlement at Limerick. This dissatisfaction was increased by the subsequent behaviour of English officials in Ireland, above all the new lord chancellor, Sir Charles Porter, who appeared overly sympathetic to Catholics and Jacobites, and by English jealousy of Ireland's surprisingly rapid recovery from the devastation of war, notably the burgeoning export of woollen cloth to the Continent. In English eyes, Irish constitutional aspirations (especially for legislative independence) had been compromised by their enthusiastic espousal by the Jacobite parliament, and the various efforts to assert Irish Protestant interests in the parliamentary sessions of 1695 and 1697 were seen as early manifestations of what by the early eighteenth century would be stigmatized as 'Independency'.[132]

Legislating for Ireland in medieval times

As A.G. Donaldson showed more than half a century ago, understanding the claim that English legislation did not become operative in Ireland without re-enactment in the Irish parliament requires consideration of the process of legislating for the colony in Ireland from its beginnings in medieval times.[133] Among the various methods resorted to had been direct legislation for Ireland (both general and

---

130 5 Jac. 2, c. 10; text in Bergin & Lyall (eds), *The acts of James II's Irish parliament* (Dublin, 2016), pp 54–7. The lords' address on the lord lieutenant's speech in 1692 described the act as most detrimental to 'the King of England and to this Kingdom': *Lords Jnl [Ire.]*, ii, p. 460.

131 E.g. Cox, *Hibernia Anglicana* (London, 1689), epist. dedic.; [Wetenhall], *The case of Irish Protestants* (London, 1691), p. 6.

132 For the use of the term in relation to Molyneux and *The Case*, see J. Ellis to Ambassador Williamson, Oct. 1698 (*Cal. S.P., dom., 1698*, p. 409); Shower, *Cases in parliament* (London, 1698), p. 81, employed it to describe the Irish lords' claim to be the final court of appeal for chancery cases. During the Drapier's letters controversy in 1724, Marmaduke Coghill specifically linked the term 'independency' with 'Mr Molyneux's Book'. See further p. 47, n. 222 below. For other early C.18 use, see Hayton, 'The Stanhope/Sunderland ministry', *English Historical Review*, 113 (1998), p. 619.

133 See Donaldson, 'The application in Ireland' (PhD, QUB, 1952), intro.

specific) in England; extending English legislation to Ireland by writ; and confirmation (i.e. re-enactment) by the Irish parliament. Occasional examples were found of more unusual procedures, such as the general grant of English laws when King John visited Dublin in 1210; legislation enacted when Irish representatives were present at Westminster; and issuing certificates as to what the law was in doubtful matters, as in the case of coparceners (cf. *Case*, pp 86–7, 133–4).[134] By the early fourteenth century, Ireland was commonly included together with England and Wales in statutes dealing with commercial matters, while by the end of the century petition from Ireland had become an important means of initiating legislation for the country. The last example of extending English legislation to Ireland by writ is found in 13 Hen. 4, about the time of the first of the reputed Irish statutes confirming legislative independence in 10 Hen. 4 (1409). Later in the century, various re-enactments took place of all English statutes dealing with particular matters, such as purveyors, customs regulations, provisors and rape (cf. *Case*, pp 68–70), while at its end, Poynings' parliament of 1494 re-enacted 'all English Statutes late ... made in *England*, concerning the Common and Publique Weal'.[135] Following this, only two methods remained of legislating for Ireland: namely, direct legislation in the English parliament and legislation in the Irish parliament, including re-enactment of English acts for Ireland (henceforth subject to the restrictions on Irish legislative initiative imposed by Poynings' Law). As is shown in *The Case* (esp. pp 72–6), a substantial body of English legislation was re-enacted in Ireland in the century and a half to the outbreak of the 1641 rebellion.

Until the early 1640s, the case for legislative independence was held to rest on two fifteenth-century Irish statutes, namely 10 Hen. 4 and 29 Hen. 6, though no text had survived of either. The earliest mention of them is found in the officially sanctioned *Statutes of Ireland*, published in 1621 by Richard Bolton, who was then solicitor general and would later become lord chancellor. In a gloss on the Irish statute 10 Hen. 7, c. 22 (which had extended the operation of all English public acts to Ireland in 1494), Bolton claimed to have personally seen copies of both 10 Hen. 4 and 29 Hen. 6, 'exemplified under the great seale, and the exemplification remayneth in the Treasory of the citie of Waterford'.[136] These 'missing acts' were not, however, the only medieval Irish parliamentary declarations of legislative independence, nor indeed the most forceful. The act 38 Hen. 6, c. 6, issued by parliament in Dublin in 1460 during the viceroyalty of Richard, duke of York, is generally regarded as the high point of Irish medieval claims to legislative autonomy. It spoke of Ireland being a kingdom in itself with its own special law and customs, and:

134 Nine such certificates were sent to Ireland, 1223–38: Brand, 'Ireland and the literature' in *The making of the common law* (London, 1992), pp 445–60.
135 10 Hen. 7, cc 4, 5, 22.
136 Cf. Bolton, *Statutes of Ireland* (Dublin, 1621), p. 67 n., which also stated that the second statute was merely a re-enactment of the first (see further appendix B below). There had been parliamentary sessions in 1408–9, in which 10 Hen. 4 could have been enacted: Richardson & Sayles, *Irish parliament* (Philadelphia, 1952), pp 348–9.

freed of the burthen of any special law of the realm of England, save only of
such laws as by the lords spiritual and temporal and the commons of the said
land [Ireland] had in Great Council or Parliament there held, admitted,
accepted, affirmed and proclaimed, according to sundry ancient statutes
thereof ... [137]

Given such an unequivocal enunciation of the principle, commentators have
wondered why Molyneux failed to refer to this 1460 act, conjecturing that since it
did not figure in Bolton's 1621 *Statutes* he was perhaps unaware of its existence.[138]
However, the papers relating to Bishop King's search for precedents in the Rolls
Office in 1697 include a copy of the declaration in the hand of Molyneux's long-
term amanuensis, with minor corrections by Molyneux himself.[139] Thus, whatever
else led him to neglect the 1460 declaration in *The Case*, it was not ignorance of its
existence.

When the issue of legislative independence came once more to the fore in the
conflict of the mid-seventeenth century, the two 'missing' fifteenth-century acts of
10 Hen. 6 and 29 Hen. 6 that had satisfied Bolton in 1621 no longer appeared
sufficient to establish Ireland's independence from the resurgent English
parliament. As first Bolton and, building on his work, William Domville, realised,
what was necessary was to go back to the very foundation of the English polity in
Ireland and demonstrate Ireland's right to legislate independently of the English
parliament by establishing that from the very beginning the latter had not
possessed legislative competence here. By showing that '*ab initio non fuit sic* [from
the beginning it was not so]' (as the old legal adage had it), the English
parliament's claim to legislate for Ireland would be demonstrated to be invalid in
the present.[140]

Molyneux's exposition of the case for legislative independence

Before considering the substance of Molyneux's case for legislative independence,
it is desirable to say something of the format that he chose for presentation of his
text, without awareness of which the book may come across as marred by
unexplained contradictions and strange shifts of position. Conveniently, the key to
identifying this is provided by the wording of the title, namely *The case of Ireland
... stated*, which indicated Molyneux's intention to put forward his arguments in a
form analogous to the presentation of a civil case in a court of law. As the large
number of titles along the lines of 'The case of ... stated' listed in Wing's *Short*

137 38 Hen. 6, c. 6: *ESI*, ii, p. 645. Special, i.e. having an individual, particular, or limited application:
      OED, s.v., §5. Cf. Lydon, 'Ireland and the English crown', *IHS*, 29 (1995), pp 290–1.
138 Simms, *Colonial nationalism* (Cork, 1976), p. 32; Cosgrove, 'Parliament' in Cosgrove & McGuire
      (eds), *Parliament* (Belfast, 1983), p. 28.
139 See p. 12, n. 46 above.
140 Cf. Domville, 'Disquisition', p. 35. Molyneux's debt to these earlier writings disposes of the claim
      by Pocock, *Constitution* (Cambridge, 1987), p. 238, that reading William Petyt had been what led
      Molyneux to base his case on an appeal to historic origins.

title catalogue, 1641–1700 shows, this form of title was highly popular with later seventeenth-century authors, especially when dealing with political questions. As well as being used for pamphlets of a more general kind, however, the 'The case of ... stated' title was also employed to denote technical documents required in court proceedings, known as 'pleadings', or the 'state of the case', in which lawyers set out in print the various points on which they intended to rely in court.[141] These printed states of the case (required particularly in proceedings before the higher courts and house of lords) started with the strongest or earliest grounds of the case, each of which would in turn have been elaborated in court, before moving to the next point on the list.[142] Perforce, Molyneux's book constituted an amalgam of the general pamphlet and the technical court document. Presenting his case in print rather than before a court also meant that he had to argue each point in detail before moving on to discuss the next item on his list – a procedure succinctly adumbrated in the original wording of his title, namely 'The case of Irelands being bound ... stated and argued'.[143]

Generally too, cases were presented in court by marshalling all the evidence that could be deployed in favour of a particular point, before moving on to discuss the next point entirely afresh – as if everything raised in the previous argument was no longer relevant. Appreciating this convention helps, for example, render explicable the at-first-sight glaring contradictions in the opening third of *The Case*, where Molyneux first argued that the voluntary submission of the Irish to Henry meant the country had not been conquered; then, that the rights Henry had acquired through the conquest of Ireland were insufficient to establish a title to the country; and third, that although Henry had acquired absolute dominion by conquest, his subsequent concessions to the Irish could not be altered without their consent. Unfortunately, this format was not one that made either for easy reading or for consistency.[144] Litigants were at liberty to pursue contrasting and even contradictory points in the hope that one at least might find favour with the jury (in effect, for Molyneux, the English parliament). And, since the objective was to present the full range of arguments which could be mustered in support of a case, originality was not at a premium as it would have been in a more theoretical work, and there was no shame in drawing heavily on the work of others.[145]

141 Of the 361 entries starting 'The case ...' (Wing (ed.), *Catalogue of books* (New York, 1994–8), i, items C847 to C1208) somewhat under half would appear to be routine court documents (identifiable from their categorization as broadsheets); the rest are either amplified presentations of the case in question, or pamphlets dealing more generally with a particular issue.

142 On these documents, see further Baker, *The legal profession* (London, 1986), pp 115–16. For the one prepared for Bishop King's response to the Irish Society's appeal to the English lords in 1698, and the substantial bill for drawing it up and printing it, see *Derry MSS*, ii, pp 183–91, 213–19.

143 See *The Case*, titlepage, app. crit.; a similar alteration has been made to the half-title on p. 1. Argue, i.e. prove with evidence: *OED*, s.v. §3.

144 *The Case*, p 149 showed that Molyneux was not unaware that frequent repetition might exhaust the reader's patience.

145 See Brooks, *Law, politics and society* (Cambridge, 2009), p. 19, and further the discussion of the sources of *The Case*, pp 71–84, below and esp. p. 81.

The fact that the pamphlet comes across as less dry and lawyerly than this description of the conventions of presenting a legal case suggests is owing to the attractive persona that Molyneux projected in his opening pages. Initially appealing to the king as 'the *Common Indulgent Father* of all your Countries' to defend the rights of 'Your Poor *Subjects of Ireland*' along with those of his other kingdoms, Molyneux presented himself as a public-spirited Irish landholder and MP as free from particular interests as such a person could be (*Case*, pp A3r, A4r). Eager to point out to a wise and beneficent English parliament that it had been misinformed as to Ireland's rights, he offered himself as the defender of Irish liberty in default of any more competent spokesman. This professed submission to the wisdom of the English parliament sat uncomfortably, however, with Molyneux's subsequent claim to speak not only for Ireland but 'the whole Race of *Adam*', which also served to highlight his reliance on natural law and natural right, as well as precedent and legal record to establish Ireland's right to legislative independence (*Case*, p. 3).

Setting out in detail how he intended to proceed, Molyneux indicated that he would examine 'the *Right* which *England* may pretend to, for Binding us by their Acts of Parliament, ...' (*Case*, p. 4), under six headings, namely:

(1) The circumstances of Ireland's original annexation to the English crown under Henry II;
(2) Whether Henry's expedition, or any subsequent suppression of rebellions there, could properly be claimed to have been a conquest of Ireland;
(3) What title a conquest would have conveyed to England;
(4) What subsequent concessions had been made to Ireland by her English rulers by way of grants of laws and liberties;
(5) Various judicial decisions, and the opinions of distinguished jurists on the matter;
(6) A summary of the main arguments for and against legislative independence, leading to some general conclusions on Ireland's behalf.[146]

However, as the text evolved, Molyneux moved somewhat away from this original schema by making various lengthy interpolations in his text such as references to matters raised in the woollens controversy pamphlets (cf. *Case*, pp 142–9), and redistributing other matters under different headings – changes indicated, for example, by the two different occasions on which he spoke of having finished the discussion of his fourth topic, namely *Case*, pp 77 and 115.

The foundation of the Irish constitution by Henry II, John and Henry III

Since the English parliament's right to legislate for Ireland was generally held to derive from the fact that Henry II had conquered the country in 1171–2, Molyneux's starting point was to determine what had actually happened when the

146 *The Case*, pp 4–6.

king came to Ireland.[147] What he sought to show was that, far from being the hostile conquest alleged by Coke and others, what had occurred was the voluntary submission of the Irish princes and prelates to Henry (and his heirs) in return for the grant of English laws and customs, including the right to hold parliaments.[148] For evidence he turned to the histories written in Henry's time or shortly afterwards, which most strongly supported the view that his expedition had been entirely peaceful, primarily the Expugnatio Hibernica of Giraldus Cambrensis, supplemented by the works of Roger Hoveden, John Brompton and Matthew Paris.[149] Such accounts demonstrated that far from resting on conquest, the origins of the Irish polity derived from what (with an eye to English political discourse of the revolution era) Molyneux termed the '*Original Compact*' between Henry and the Irish (*Case*, pp 37–8).

Radically shifting ground in keeping with the conventions of presenting a case in court, Molyneux next turned to consider what rights a victorious Henry would have acquired from the conquest of Ireland, an analysis that he warmly acknowledged drew heavily on the *Two treatises of government* (though he stopped just short of openly identifying Locke as its author).[150] While unlawful conquerors would acquire no right whatever, even the rights of a lawful conqueror were – contrary to general belief – extremely restricted, amounting indeed to no more than reimbursement of the expenses of effecting the conquest. Thus even a lawful conquest would not have left the property of the conquered at the victor's disposal, a conclusion which Molyneux (echoing *Treatises*, ii, § 180) described as 'a strange Doctrine … [though] the Practice of the World is otherwise'. Emphasizing that his concern was with the principles involved, rather than what usually happened, he continued: 'we Enquire not now, what is the *Practice*, but what *Right there is to do so*' – a caveat applicable not only to the point at issue but to the interpretation of other parts of *The Case* as well (*Case*, pp 24–5).[151] In demonstrating the inadequacy of claims based on conquest to give title to the property of the Irish, Molyneux also raised – rather obliquely – the notion that in binding themselves to observe English laws and customs, the Irish had implicitly agreed to forfeit their property, should they in the future rebel against Henry or his successors (*Case*, p. 23). Though not developed at length, the implications of this ostensibly casual observation

147 Cf. Coke, *4th Inst.*, p. 349 et seq.; Calvin's case in *7th Rep.*, f. 17v, cited in *The Case*, p. 117, and further Justice Vaughan's verdict in Crawe v. Ramsey (1670): Vaughan, *Reports and arguments* (London, 1714), p. 292.

148 Namely '*an Acquisition of a Kingdom by Force of Arms, to which, Force likewise has been Opposed*', a definition subsequently singled out for censure by the English commons: *The Case*, p. 12 and nn.

149 Molyneux's use of these histories was not as straightforward as has generally been assumed. See further p. 55 below.

150 Cf. *The Case*, p. 27 and app. crit.

151 E.g. in Molyneux's remarks on the Navigation Acts, Cattle Acts and Tobacco Act: *The Case*, pp 102–4. Cf. Archbishop King's comment as to the book being concerned with the principle of legislative independence, not just the rejection of a particular English act applying to Ireland: King to Samuel Molyneux Jnr, 2 Jan. 1719/20.

established a far more coercive hold over the Irish than mere conquest could have done. Under the common law of treason the Irish who subsequently rebelled against Henry and his heirs would forfeit their property and political rights (to say nothing of their lives). Equally significantly, as a result of their ancestors' voluntary compact with Henry they would no longer have had an unlimited right to '*appeal to Heaven*' against the English (such as Locke asserted that Greek Christians had retained against the Turks), but would remain forever complicit in their own subjection.[152]

Molyneux then seemingly undercut his own argument by stating that what was agreed between Henry and the Irish could in no way have compromised the rights of 'the *English* and *Britains*, that came over and Conquered with him' (*Case*, p. 19). Given that he had just demonstrated at length that Henry's expedition could in no way be considered a conquest, on the face of it this was a fairly astonishing claim.[153] As already pointed out, however, this seeming contradiction arose from the conventions of presenting a legal case, namely that when the first question (whether Ireland was actually conquered by Henry) had been properly disposed of, Molyneux was free to focus afresh on his second question, without reference to what had been said already. Considering what the effect of the conquest was on the 'Assisters in the Conquest' (as the marginal heading termed them) had the added advantage of bringing the king's English followers into the story. So long as the narrative simply involved the voluntary submission of the Irish to Henry, it failed to provide a place for these crucial figures, who in the persons of their descendants would be the beneficiaries of property forfeited by the rebellious Irish.[154] What has perhaps diverted attention from the apparent anomaly of speaking of the 'Assisters in the Conquest' was Molyneux's ensuing remark that the vast majority of Ireland's inhabitants were of mixed Irish and British descent and that 'there remains but a meer handful of the Antient *Irish* at this day' (*Case*, p. 20). Decrying this assertion as a 'brazen' denial of Irish identity is, however, somewhat misplaced.[155] The view that the majority of inhabitants of this island were of inextricably mixed British and Irish descent was fairly common in the seventeenth-century in both Ireland and England; notable assertors of it included Camden's *Britannia*; the Irish commons' remonstrance of November 1640; Molyneux's friend the Gaelic antiquary Roderick O'Flaherty; Sir Richard Cox; and Sir Edward Coke himself.[156] Moreover, reference

152 Cf. *Treatises*, ii, §§168, 192.
153 Cf. *The Case*, p. 19, marginal heading: 'None over the Assisters in the Conquest'. Nor did a conqueror acquire rights over 'those of the Country who *Oppos'd him not*': ibid., p. 20.
154 The language employed revealed the tenacity of the conviction among the Anglo-Irish (including Molyneux) that their ancestors had come to Ireland as conquerors. See further Hill, 'Ireland without union' in Robertson (ed.), *A union for empire* (Cambridge, 1995), pp 280–4.
155 Cf. Barnard, 'Protestantism' in Clayton & McBride (eds), *Protestantism* (Cambridge, 1998), p. 213; Simms, *William Molyneux* (Dublin, 1982), p. 105; Hill, 'Ireland without union' in Robertson (ed.), *A union for empire* (Cambridge, 1995), p. 280; and for a different interpretation Smyth, 'Like amphibious animals', *Historical Journal*, 36 (1993), p. 789.
156 Camden, *Britannia* (London, 1637), sect. iii, p. 731. *Commons Jnl [Ire.]*, i, p. 162; O'Flaherty,

to *The second treatise of government* suggests that Molyneux's allusion to this mixed British and Irish ancestry was in intent wholly benign, as serving to establish that no one in Ireland could be denied English rights on the ground that he was not of English descent.[157]

Molyneux's fourth answer dealt with the subsequent concessions which the first three Norman kings had made to the Irish, concessions which under the law of nature and nations even the most absolute of conquerors was obliged not to alter without the consent of the conquered. First of these was the document that had confirmed Henry's grant of parliament to the Irish in the form of a modified version of the Modus Tenendi Parliamentum given to England by William the Conqueror, which by default became for Molyneux the founding document of the English polity in Ireland.[158] Conveniently for him, the Modus Tenendi Parliamenta et Consilia in Hibernia was by then available in print thanks to its publication by his brother-in-law Anthony Dopping in 1692, in an edition which included the early fifteenth-century exemplification of its authenticity by the then governor and council of Ireland.[159] Dismissing John Selden and William Prynne's diplomatic criticism as beside the point, Dopping asserted that not only had the Irish Modus been issued by Henry II but that the medieval roll which had served as his copy-text (formerly owned by his uncle Sir William Domville) was very probably the actual document the king had sent to Ireland. Next (for Molyneux) came the concession made by King John on his second visit to Ireland in 1210, when he left the Irish a grant of English law 'reduced into writing' in the exchequer in Dublin, in a document no longer extant by the seventeenth century but known through its confirmation by Henry III in 1227 (*Case*, pp 52–3).[160] From then on Irishmen enjoyed the full benefits of English laws and liberties, including the right to assent to future laws in parliament. Furthermore, the provision for the consent of the Irish people in the law- making process opened the way to the future divergence of English and Irish law, a divergence which would figure significantly in Molyneux's subsequent arguments in relation to judicial decisions and the case of appeals to the English king's bench.[161]

Ogygia (London, 1685), pp 12, 171 (cited in Cox, *Hibernia Anglicana* (London, 1689), 'Apparatus', fol. cv). Cf. Coke, *4th Inst.*, p. 349.

157 Cf. *Treatises*, ii, §177. Recourse to Locke for clarification on matters relating to conquest was a strategy recommended by Molyneux himelf: *The Case*, pp 26–7.

158 As claimed by M.V. Clarke, *Medieval representation and consent* (New York, 1936), p. 75. Prior to Hakewill's 'discovery' of the Irish Modus in 1614, Sir John Davies' *Reports* had admitted there were no records of what form of government Henry had established in Ireland. Cf. Davies, *Le primer report* (London, 1615), dedic., and the note on the history of the Irish Modus in appendix A below.

159 Cf. *The Case*, pp 30–6.

160 See further Brand, 'Magna Carta in Ireland' in Crooks & Mohr, *Law and the idea of liberty* (Dublin, forthcoming), which speaks of 'some general statement of English law and custom [possibly covering at least some] of the ground of Magna Carta of five years later … Whatever it was, it cannot have been too detailed.' Citation from Bolton, *Declaration*, p. 2.

161 Cf. *The Case*, p. 135.

Even before 1210, however, Ireland's status had been fundamentally altered by Henry's transferring the country as a separate and independent kingdom to his youngest son John, in a parliament held at Oxford in 1177. Crucially, Molyneux asserted, the English lords and commons had not functioned as co-legislators with Henry in effecting this transfer, merely as witnesses to the grant. Though such an interpretation was in accordance with the understanding of the law-making process that Molyneux inherited from Domville (cf. *Case*, p. 166), by the 1690s such a view was already obsolete in England. Accordingly, critics of *The Case* claimed that, on the contrary, the English parliament's involvement in 1177 was incontrovertible evidence of its central role in the establishment of the English polity in Ireland, and thus justified its subsequently legislating directly for the country.[162] Following the 1177 grant, Molyneux continued, Ireland would have remained as a separate and independent kingdom like Scotland, had John not succeeded to the English throne on the death of his brother Richard. Nor, since Henry's donation of Ireland to John as 'an *Absolute Kingdom*' (*Case*, p. 148) had left Richard without rights there, could it be asserted that John inherited any additional right to Ireland on his brother's death. Thus the re-founding of the Irish polity by donation in 1177 both freed the Irish constitution from any residual taint of conquest and affirmed that Ireland's allegiance was due exclusively to the English crown, not conjointly to the English parliament.

The culmination of these early concessions was the granting of a Magna Carta to Ireland by the guardians of the child Henry III in 1216, a Magna Carta that Molyneux (erroneously) boasted was in form even more ancient than the earliest surviving version of Magna Carta in the English statute 9 Hen. 3 (*Case*, p. 45).[163] Extolling Magna Carta as the acme of the ancient fundamental laws of England, Molyneux traced the genealogy of English rights and liberties from the laws of Edward the Confessor through their confirmations by William the Conqueror, Henry I and Henry II, and culminating in the Great Charter of King John (*Case*, pp 58–62). These ancient laws constituted a line of descent similar to that described in Coke's *Institutes* and *Reports*, being 'only so many *Confirmations* of each other, all of them *Sanctions of the Common Laws* and *Liberties* of the People of *England*' (*Case*, p. 59).[164] However, as the reaction of his critics would show, this appeal to the two countries' common heritage of fundamental laws did not awaken the sympathy for Irish rights that Molyneux had hoped for from English Whigs.

---

162 Cf. Atwood, *History*, pp 35–6, 90–1; Clement, *Answer*, pp 49–53. For Domville's view of the law-making process, see *The Case*, p. 166 nn.

163 *Pace* Molyneux, the text of the Magna Carta issued for Ireland in 1216 cannot have been that found in the Dublin Red Book of the Exchequer: *ESI*, i, pp 4–19, which recent scholarship has identified as the unofficial handiwork of an early C.14 Exchequer clerk. Cf. Brand, 'Magna Carta in Ireland' in Crooks & Mohr, *Law and the idea of liberty* (Dublin, forthcoming). Both Bolton, 'Declaration', p. 4, and Domville, 'Disquisition', pp 54–5, cited the English statute 9 Hen. 3 as the text of Magna Carta in force in Ireland, with no mention of a differently worded Irish version.

164 Cf. Coke, *1st Inst.*, proem; *2nd Inst.*, proem. and ch. 2; *8th Rep.*, proem.

With these three foundational documents – viz., Henry II's Modus, supposedly dating from 1171; John's no-longer-extant grant of English law in 1210; and the Irish Magna Carta of 1216 – Ireland now had an independent constitution founded on compact and donation, and dependent only on the king, not the parliament, of England. Under it, Irishmen enjoyed the laws and customs of England, while retaining the rights of free-born Englishmen, especially that of making their own laws for the future through their chosen representatives in parliament, 'that Universal *Law of Nature*, that ought to prevail throughout the whole World, *of being Govern'd only by such Laws to which they give their own Consent by their Representatives in Parliament*' (*Case*, p. 48).[165] Molyneux's emphasis on the exercise of such consent through the people's representatives in parliament should put us on our guard, however, against seeing him as any form of proto-democrat. Like Coke, he accepted that the people participated in parliament through their representatives, even if, as individuals, they did not directly possess the franchise.[166] This emphasis on the importance of the consent of the people for the validation of law was fundamental to Molyneux's case for Ireland's legislative independence. Above all it was the failure to provide for the consent of the Irish people (as exercised through their representatives in parliament) that left the claim of the English parliament to legislate directly for Ireland without moral or legal foundation.[167] Later in the book, Molyneux's sleight of hand would transform what was understood by the term 'People of *Ireland*' from the descendants of the princes and people who had submitted to Henry II into 'the *Protestants of Ireland*', against whom, he asserted, 'the *Irish Papists*' had been guilty of treason on two occasions in the seventeenth century.[168]

Modifications to the Irish constitution effected by subsequent legislation

Molyneux's fourth concern was the extent to which this ancient Irish constitution had been modified by concessions from later English kings, primarily through the numerous re-enactments of English statutes in Ireland between the later thirteenth century and the reign of William III.[169] In describing the process he contrasted

---

165 Cf. Locke's view that the right to consent to the laws by which one was governed was universal, for which he cited the authority of 'the Judicious Hooker', as did Molyneux, *Case*, pp 151–2. See also the criticism of Coke's claim that Ireland was bound by English acts 'Naming Ireland', *Case*, p. 118.

166 In support of this, *Case*, p. 154, cited the English statute 1 Jac. I, c. 1: and a supporting passage from Coke, *4th Inst.*, p. 1.

167 Molyneux developed the theme in more systematic form in *Case*, pp 151–3, asserting it commanded 'the Universall Agreement of all Civilians [i.e. natural law writers]' specifying '*Grotius, Puffendorf, Locke's Treat<ise of> Government, &c.*'.

168 See *The Case*, pp 38, 54, 106, 172, and in particular p. 143, which explicitly identified the '*Protestants of Ireland*' with 'the People of *Ireland* in Parliament Assembled' after 1641 rebellion of '*[t]he Irish Papists*'.

169 Molyneux's version of the ancient Irish constitution should not be confused with the pre-Norman ancient Irish constitution that C.18 antiquarians like Charles Vallancey purported to find in the work of Geoffrey Keating, etc. Cf. Kidd, *British identities* (Cambridge, 1999), p. 150 et seq.

what he termed 'the *Antient Precedents*' extending from medieval times to 1641 with the modern precedents following the Restoration, asserting that if the former '*do not conclude* against us; it will follow that the *Modern* Instances given, *ought not to*' (*Case*, p. 85). In enumerating these re-enactments Molyneux was at pains to emphasize that all English statutes re-enacted in Ireland had only become law in Ireland 'by the *Peoples consent in Parliament*, to which we have had a very *antient Right*, and as full a Right as our next Neighbours can pretend to' (*Case*, p. 77). A crucial turning point was marked by Poynings' parliament of 1494, which had enacted (10 Hen. 7, c. 22) '*That all Statutes* late ... *made in* England, *concerning the Common and Publique Weal of the same, from henceforth be Deem'd effectual in Law, and be Accepted, Used and Executed within this Land of Ireland, in all Points*' (*Case*, p. 69). From then on, even English opinion conceded that Ireland was no longer bound by acts subsequently passed in England, unless specifically named or included by implication through the use of comprehensive words such as 'in all the Dominions of the King'.[170] Also highly significant in defining the constitutional relations between the two countries was what came to be known as Poynings' Law (10 Hen. 7, c. 4). For Molyneux, the latter's importance lay in reaffirming the indissoluble link between Ireland and the English crown, while leaving no role for the English parliament in the Irish constitution – not in the restrictions that Poynings' Law imposed on the power of the Irish parliament to initiate legislation, which would prove so offensive to patriots in the eighteenth century.[171] Henceforth, as he pointed out, no examples – other than statutes declaratory of the existing law – could be found of England's legislating for Ireland up to the Adventurers' Acts of 1642 at the beginning of the Irish war.[172] On the contrary, even where English legislation purported to bind Ireland through comprehensive wording, such as '*All the King's Dominions* or *Subjects*', it had been found necessary to re-enact such statutes in Ireland (*Case*, pp 81–2). Notable examples included the legislation that effected the Reformation (in both Henry VIII's reign and Elizabeth's reign), and acts of recognition of the succession to the crown from Henry VIII to William and Mary (*Case*, pp 127–8).

If the precedent of Irish representatives having occasionally attended the English parliament in medieval times proved that laws passed in the English parliament should now bind Ireland, it was only right, Molyneux asserted, that Ireland should have its representatives there at the present day (*Case*, pp 95–7). However, to conclude from this (in conjunction with the follow-up remark, 'And

---

170 Cf. Coke, *4th Inst.*, pp 349, 351, and see further *The Case*, p. 69 nn. Hale, *Prerogatives of the crown* (London, 1976), p. 38, however, asserted mention by specific name was required to bind Ireland, not merely comprehensive words.

171 From the mid-C.18 commentators vilified Poynings' Law as an unnatural constraint on the Irish parliament's ability to initiate legislation. See Lucas, *A tenth address* (Dublin, [1749]), p. 2; [Jebb], *Guatimozin's letters* (London, 1779), p. 31, and Sir Laurence Parsons' speech of 1799, in *Report of the debates* (Dublin, 1799), p. 100.

172 A claim entirely without foundation, as Molyneux's critics would point out. Cf. Cary, *Vindication*, pp 70–1, and further *The Case*, p. 98 nn.

this, I believe we should be willing enough to embrace; but this is an Happiness we can hardly hope for') that Molyneux was a serious advocate of political union with England is far from convincing.[173] Not only does the context show that he did not in fact accept that these medieval precedents established that 'the Parliament of *England* may *Bind Ireland*' in his own day, but he also emphasized that sending representatives to the English parliament to make laws for Ireland was only a second best solution, to be resorted to when rebellion or civil war made it impossible to hold a parliament here. To regard it as a serious proposal for political union (as recent commentators have done) flies in the face of Molyneux's reiterated emphasis on both the distinct and separate nature of the kingdom of Ireland, and the need for the consent of the Irish people, given through their representatives in an Irish parliament, to make valid laws for the country.[174] Furthermore, his statement (*Case*, p. 98) that sending representatives to England in medieval times had been 'very Troublesome and Inconvenient', would (as Cary, *A Vindication* (London, 1698), p. 106, pointed out) seem equally applicable to reviving the practice in his own time. Although some important Anglo-Irish figures in the 1690s, including William King, did on occasion advocate union as the solution to Ireland's problems, Molyneux's comments on securing consent through the presence of Irish representatives in a union parliament are more credible as a rhetorical challenge to the English parliament to recognize that it could not validly legislate for Ireland without Irish consent, than as a serious proposal for union.[175]

The example of the '*Modern* Instances' against Irish 'Liberty' proved less conclusive than the '*Ancient* Precedents', and Molyneux's counterarguments carried less conviction than his earlier responses. On the positive side, the 1662 Act of Settlement had shown that the Irish parliament possessed the power to set aside English statutes, when it annulled the Adventurers' Acts as a preliminary to the land settlement.[176] On the other hand, the years since the Restoration also afforded the most blatant instances of direct English legislation for Ireland, notably the Navigation Acts, the Irish Cattle Acts and the act prohibiting growing tobacco in

173 Particularly as the autograph manuscript shows that Molyneux interpolated 'an Happiness we can hardly hope for' as a translation of the Latin phrase '*Nobis non licet esse tam beatis*' (loosely translatable as 'we should be so lucky'). Cf. *The Case*, p. 98, app. crit.

174 Simms, *William Molyneux* (Dublin, 1982), p. 106; J. Kelly, 'Origins of the Act of Union', *IHS*, 25 (1987), p. 242; Smyth, 'Like amphibious animals', *Historical Journal*, 36 (1993), p. 792, and Hill, 'Ireland without union' (Cambridge, 1995), p. 277, regard the proposal as a serious call for union, though Hayton concedes it was perhaps merely rhetorical: 'Ideas of union' in Boyce, Eccleshall & Geoghegan, *Political discourse* (Houndsmills, 2001), p. 149.

175 In his unpublished reply to [Toland], *A letter from a gentleman* ([London], 1697), King had spoken of union in rhetorical terms almost identical to Molyneux's (cf. P. Kelly, 'A pamphlet attributed to John Toland', *Topoi*, 4 (1985), p. 88), though his subsequent letter to Southwell, 19 July 1698, stated the matter more straightforwardly. See also Sir Richard Cox to Edward Harley, 28 Oct. 1699: *Portland MSS*, iii, p. 609, and pref. to Burridge, *A short view* (1708).

176 Cf. Pulton (ed.), *A Collection* (London, 1670), p. 1248, and the view of the English attorney general in 1671, as cited in *The Case*, p. 100 nn.

Ireland. Though Molyneux objected that these statutes either no more obliged the
Irish than the French and the Dutch, or had been consistently challenged ever
since, Irish acquiescence in English legislation for Ireland during the Jacobite War,
and subsequent lack of protest from the Irish parliament, were hard to deny. All
Molyneux could offer was the rather lame analogy that accepting a benefit did not
confer authority, in other matters, over a willing recipient. Going over to the
offensive, he pointed out that men would not subject themselves to laws which
were to their detriment, unless constrained by force, 'let the Statesman or Divine
say what they can' (*Case*, pp 112–13).

Judicial decisions

Molyneux's fifth topic was '[*t*]*he Opinions of those Learned in the Laws*', by which
he meant important judicial decisions that corroborated Ireland's claim to
legislative independence. His first example was the judgment in the Merchants of
Waterford's case of 1485, which involved the question whether Irishmen were
bound by the English Staple Act of 1423 restricting woollen exports to the port of
Calais. The collective decision of the English judges had been that Irish subjects
were not constrained by this act, because Ireland had its own parliament,
administration and law courts, *prout in Anglia* (just as in England), and in
particular did not send representatives to parliament in England. Though this
verdict was promptly overturned by Chief Justice Hussey, Molyneux asserted that
the original arguments in Ireland's favour had by no means been fully answered –
as Brooke's *Abridgment* had pointed out.[177] In Pilkington's case of 1439–41, which
involved a dispute over holding office in Ireland by means of deputies, the majority
of English judges had favoured a defendant citing an Irish statute against a
plaintiff relying on an English act. In the third instance, the Prior of Llanthony's
case of 1427–9, the English king's bench had explicitly refused to interfere with a
judicial decision of the Irish parliament, while the prior's subsequent appeal to the
English lords had not proceeded.[178] Also raised in the context of judicial decisions
was the question of whether Ireland's legislative subordination was demonstrated
by the process of appeals on writs of error to the English king's bench, as claimed
by Coke, who had baldly stated that judicial subordination necessarily implied
legislative subordination.[179] Against this, Molyneux argued that English judges
decided such appeals in accordance with Irish rather than English law, and thus the
procedure should be understood as an appeal from Ireland directly to the king in
person rather than to a superior English court.[180] Though Molyneux did not

177 See further *The Case*, p. 100 nn.
178 *The Case*, p. 125. It is unclear whether the English lords disallowed the appeal, or it merely lapsed
     with the end of the parliamentary session.
179 Cf. *The Case*, p. 131 nn for Mayart's exposition of the basis of Coke's reasoning.
180 Coke seriously contradicted himself on this issue; *4th Inst.*, p. 350, also spoke of appeals from the
     king's bench in Ireland in C.13 and C.14 being made *coram rege*, and decided by the English
     council in accordance with Irish law.

explicitly advert to the issue (perhaps because of the Derry appeal), this assertion of Coke's may have afforded an additional reason for his earlier spirited repudiation of Coke's authority for seeking to 'Bind a *whole Nation*' on '*the bare Assertion* of a Judge', in claiming that Ireland was known to be a conquered country '*by Judgment of Law*' (*Case*, pp 116–19).

Matters raised in the Irish woollens controversy pamphlets, and summary

Molyneux's concluding discussion introduced matters that had been raised in the pamphlet controversy over Irish woollens exports in early 1698, sparked off by Toland's *Letter from a gentleman*. First of these was the claim that England had somehow acquired Ireland through purchase by paying for her liberation from James II and the French (*Case*, pp 142–4). His answer, asserting that it had been as much in England's interest to defend Ireland from the French as Ireland's, highlighted his intermittent insensitivity to what might cause offence to English readers, despite the numerous changes which the manuscripts show were made to render his text more innocuous.[181] More significant was the second issue raised, namely the claim by Cary and other opponents of Irish woollen exports that Ireland should be regarded as a mere dependency of England, like her colonies in America, an assertion Molyneux strongly rebutted.[182] This rejection of the colonial analogy reinforced a point that he had made on several earlier occasions, namely that Ireland had as much right to be considered an independent kingdom as Scotland. The only difference he was prepared to concede was that Scotland had remained unlinked to the English crown till 1603, while Ireland had only been fully separated from England between 1177 and 1199. Clearly, therefore, the model to which Molyneux aspired for Ireland's constitutional relations with England was that of Scotland rather than the colonies. While the union of 1707 rendered this analogy irrelevant, it opened the way, however, to reading *The Case* as an account of the proper relations between England and its colonial dependencies and thereby ensured it a welcome in the America of the 1760s and 1770s that it might not otherwise have received.[183]

The work concluded with the recapitulation of the main arguments of the book, under ten numbered headings, which drew heavily on the format of Domville's 'Disquisition' as well as its substantial arguments. These concluding points were

181 Despite other such lapses, Molyneux took considerable pains to obviate possible occasions of offence, including deleting all references to 'our Adversaries' (*The Case*, pp 67, 78, 115,130, 149, 164, app. crit.,) and the allusion to the fable of the stag and the horse (p. 111, app. crit.). See also his claim to Locke, 19 Apr. 1698, to have written 'with that Caution and Submission, that It cannot justly give any offence': *Locke Corr.*, 2422.

182 Challenging this claim was the nearest Molyneux came in the main text of *The Case* to raising the attack on Irish woollen exports directly. For allusions to other matters put forward in the woollens pamphlets of early 1698, see *The Case*, pp 145–8 nn.

183 Cf. *The Case*, pp 55, 84, 93, 108 and note, added in the 1776 and 1782 editions at the first mention of Scotland (*The Case*, p. 55), pointing out that Molyneux had written prior to the 1707 union. For American interest in *The Case*, see further p. 48, n. 230 below.

significant not merely in summing up Molyneux's arguments for Irish liberty, but in some cases clarifying and more fully expounding them. This was most notable in relation to the first point, where he demonstrated that grounding legal obligation on the universal consent of mankind in turn derived from the basic equality of mankind in the state of nature, which ensured that no individual had the right to command another. Also highly significant was his penultimate point denying England's right to tax Ireland without its consent, for which he cited medieval precedents in Ireland's favour underpinned by a definition of property based on Locke: 'Whatever another may *Rightfully* take from me *without my Consent*, I have certainly no *Property* in' (*Case*, pp 170–1).[184] In setting out these concluding points Molyneux also raised a number of what the English commons would interpret as threats that trampling on the rights of the kingdom of Ireland might lead the English there to renounce their allegiance to England. Even more offensive, probably, was the parallel that he drew between the English parliament's overthrow of the Irish constitution and the recent abrogation of the Edict of Nantes (*Case*, p. 172).

Arguments from natural right

At first sight, Molyneux's use of natural-law and natural-rights arguments in *The Case* may appear as isolated instances of appealing to Locke or other authorities to substantiate particular points, such as the insufficiency of conquest as the basis for the English title to Ireland or the universal need for popular consent to the making of laws. More careful consideration would suggest, however, that reliance on natural law, natural rights and the law of nations consistently underlay the work as a whole, and that Molyneux's appeal to precedent, record and history served to flesh out these more abstract arguments and anchor them in the concrete experience of English and Irish history.[185] There is, however, a danger of setting up a false dichotomy through placing too much emphasis on the difference between these two approaches; for Molyneux as for most of his contemporaries, the demands of precedent and record on the one hand and natural law and natural rights on the other were complementary rather than at variance with each other.[186] However, it was only with the spread of Enlightenment ideas in the eighteenth century that the natural-rights aspect of Molyneux's argument came to predominate in the eyes of readers over the emphasis on precedent and record that had focused the attention of their predecessors, a transition not fully apparent till the 1770s.[187] The range of

184 Cf. *Treatises*, ii, §138.
185 Significantly, the first of Molyneux's ten concluding points appealed to natural law and natural right, namely the assertion that England's claim to legislate for Ireland was '*against Reason, and the Common Rights of all Mankind*' (*The Case*, p. 150).
186 Coke on Calvin's case had stated that the 'law of nature is part of the laws of England': *7th Rep.*, ff 4v, 12v.
187 This change was matched by a greatly enhanced Irish interest in Locke's *Treatises* at the same period. Cf. P. Kelly, 'Perceptions of Locke', *Proceedings of the Royal Irish Academy*, 89 (1989), p. 26.

sources on which Molyneux drew for his natural-rights discourse was considerable. These included primarily Locke, but also an older natural-law tradition appealed to by Hooker; allusions to Grotius and Pufendorf; and finally, the common-law tradition of reliance on natural equity and the reason of the law, together with appeals to the birthrights of free-born Englishmen.

For Molyneux (as for Locke) natural rights were dependent on the law of nature rather than being the stand-alone principles derived from the understanding of human nature that they came to be seen as in the eighteenth century. An important aspect of Lockian natural law was its dependence on self-evident truths; as *The Case* (pp 27–8) stated in relation to conquerors being bound by concessions to the conquered: 'the very Proposing it, strikes the Sense and Common Notions of all Men so forcibly, that it needs no farther proof'.[188] Similarly, drawing on Locke and Hooker, Molyneux derived the necessity of universal consent to the making of law from the original foundation of political society, when free and equal human beings in the state of nature agreed to set up rules governing their association for purposes of mutual benefit and security. 'This I take to be a Principle in it self so evident, that it stands in need of little Proof.' Natural equality in turn was deduced from the lack of significant differences between individuals of the state of nature: 'Tis not to be conceiv'd, that Creatures of the same Species and Rank, promiscuously born to all the same Advantages of Nature, and the use of the same Faculties, should be Subordinate and Subject one to another' (*Case*, p. 150). Having grounded the basis of natural equality on this self-evident hypothesis, Molyneux followed Locke in asserting that men's natural right to dispose of themselves persisted into the political state in the form of the right to consent to the laws by which they were governed. And this in turn ensured that lawmakers could only exercise their authority for the common good (*Case*, pp 113–14).

The other intellectual strain that melded with Molyneux's conception of natural law was the parallel he drew between natural law and the idea of natural equity and the reason of the law, as expounded by common lawyers. This specialized reason, held to be only fully accessible to those who had undergone extensive training in the common law, served to elucidate the principles that guided judges in making their decisions in the form of self-evident principles or maxims of law.[189] Molyneux illustrated this by showing how such reasoning had guided the judges in the Merchants of Waterford's case, in reaching the conclusion that they were not bound by the English Staple Act on the basis of the principle: '*Quia non habent Milites hic in Parliamento*; because they have no *Representatives* in the Parliament of *England*' (*Case*, p. 155). He went on to cite Judge Hobart's dictum in the case of Savage versus Day that nothing which was against natural equity could

---

188 Molyneux also embraced the principles of Lockian psychology, as can be seen in the reference to the men acting from the 'desir[e] to *free* themselves from *Uneasiness*': *The Case*, p. 112. Cf. Locke, *An essay concerning human understanding* (Oxford, 1975), bk II, ch. 21, sects 28–40.

189 Cf. Finch, *Nomotechnia* (London, 1614), and Dodrige, *The English lawyer* (London, 1631), esp. pp 242–3.

be lawful, from which Hobart had concluded that any statute which violated the principle of natural equity was therefore *ipso facto* void.[190] In turn Molyneux applied this principle to the condemnation of English statutes binding Ireland, on the ground of their violating of the universal requirement for consent to the making of law. For the English parliament to behave as if Ireland, though the recipient of the English charters of liberties, should not benefit from the rights they conferred was 'so repugnant to all Natural Reason and Equity, that I hope no Rational Man will Contest it' (*Case*, p. 157).

Where Molyneux went beyond Locke was in claiming that not only individuals but also nations might assert the natural right to liberty on an equal basis. The point was first raised in the rhetorical appeal at the beginning of the text proper where Molyneux claimed to speak for 'all *Mankind*' in asserting the inherent right to liberty, explaining that 'on whatsoever Ground any one Nation can Challenge it to themselves, on the same Reason may the Rest of *Adam*'s Children Expect it' (*Case*, p. 3). In the detailed exposition of the universal right to consent to the laws by which a people was governed in *The Case* (pp 153–4), he affirmed that '*there is no Reason that any one Commonwealth of it self, should to the Prejudice of another, annihilate that whereupon the whole World hath Agreed*'. In the way that all individuals were entitled to the same '*Right, Liberty* or *Freedom*' that other men might claim, any one nation had an equally just claim to the rights and liberties that other nations asserted. 'Is *England* a *Free* People? So ought *France* to be. … And the same runs through the whole *Race of Mankind*.'[191] Later Irish thinkers influenced by Molyneux, such as Joseph Pollock, would develop this idea still further by claiming that on grounds of natural equality no one nation had the right to dominate another: 'That no nation, can by conquest, or any other means, acquire a right of perpetual dominion over another …'[192]

Contemporary criticism of *The Case*

As we have already seen, *The Case* gave rise to five printed responses; namely, three immediate answers from Whig critics and two slightly later ones from Tories. Though we have looked at these critics' backgrounds and main lines of riposte, a more general consideration of these contemporary reactions throws light on what they found significant in *The Case* (as opposed to how it has been viewed by later readers and modern commentators). While much of the work of his earliest critics – Cary, Atwood and Clement – was devoted to the refutation of specific points, two main assumptions dominated their broad line of attack. The first was the concept

190 See *The Case*, p. 155, for a supporting citation from Coke's *1st Inst.* f. 97v.

191 The idea that nations had rights under natural law similar to those enjoyed by individuals was also advanced in manuscript by some of Molyneux's Jacobite contemporaries, such as the historians Charles O'Kelly and Nicholas Plunkett. See P. Kelly, 'Nationalism and the historians' in O'Dea & Whelan, *Nations and nationalism* (1996), pp 95, 98–9.

192 [Pollock], *The letters of Owen Roe O'Nial*, p. 72. First published in 1779, this pamphlet was appended to the 1782 edn of *The Case* (with integral pagination).

of an imperial interest uniting England and its colonies, to which all other interests, including those of Ireland, should naturally be subordinate – a view they clearly shared with Locke. The second was the way in which they saw Molyneux's precedents for Irish legislative independence as a challenge to the integrity of England's ancient constitution.[193] Ironically, their common starting point, the conviction that the English parliament had existed since Saxon times in much the same form as it did currently, was a view also shared by Molyneux (*Case*, pp 30, 102, 155). Where Clement and Atwood went further was in seeing an 'English empire' already in existence at the time of Henry II's expedition to Ireland, not in terms of the heterogeneous Angevin monarchy known to history but as an idealized model of what they took to be the proper relations between England and its colonies in their own day. From such a perspective, Henry's expedition to Ireland could only have been authorized and paid for by parliament, just as William of Orange's re-conquest of the country had been in 1689–91, and no land could have been annexed by the king other than as part of the possessions of the English crown.[194] In their eyes, only someone who failed to recognize the immemorial antiquity of the English parliament could have argued that Henry II had established a separate, independent Irish polity, and in doing so revealed himself as a spokesman for absolutism.[195]

All three critics emphasized the significance of the English parliament's determining the choice of sovereign in 1689, thereby effectively confirming Ireland's status as a subordinate kingdom.[196] Similarly all three, particularly Cary, also made much of Englishmen's not forfeiting their birthright of freedoms by going to the colonies, and though Cary cited a medieval precedent for imposing customs dues in Ireland, the others denied England the right to tax Ireland.[197] Importantly, Cary and Clement accused the Irish (and Molyneux in particular) of being misled by the common use of the term 'parliament' into thinking that the Irish legislature was of equal standing with the parliament of England, while Atwood asserted Ireland was merely a palatinate on a par with Wales or Chester.[198] Atwood was also unique in devoting a substantial section to exploring an issue that Molyneux had sought to dispose of by depicting the Irish submission to Henry II as Ireland's 'Original Compact', namely the English monarchs' pre-1171 claims to suzerainty over Ireland and the associated claim by Canterbury to primacy over the Irish church.[199]

---

193 This criticism must have rather shocked Molyneux, who would seem to have regarded his account of Ireland's ancient constitution as supportive of the English ancient constitution and thus welcome to English Whigs. Locke, however, was no supporter of ancient-constitution-type arguments, cf. *Treatises*, ii, §103.

194 A similar view was taken by Molyneux's Tory critic Charles Davenant in *A discourse upon grants and resumptions* (London, 1700), pp 408–9.

195 Atwood, *History*, epist. ded.

196 Cary, *Vindication*, pp 20, 93; Atwood, *History*, epist. ded.; Clement, *Answer*, pp 109–10, 121.

197 Cary, *Vindication*, pp 6, 47; Atwood, *History*, pp 207–8; Clement, *Answer*, pp 71–8.

198 Cary, *Vindication*, pp 1–2; Clement, *Answer*, pp 143–4; Atwood, *History*, pp 59–61.

199 Atwood, *History*, pp 12–39 *passim*.

Clement identified the crucial distinction between Scotland and Ireland being that only the latter was subject to the English privy council.[200] As we have seen, both he and Atwood chose to treat Henry II's donation of Ireland to John in the parliament at Oxford in 1177 as the foundation stone of Molyneux's case for legislative independence. For them the circumstances of the 1177 donation established beyond question that the English parliament had been an essential participant in the foundation of the Irish polity, rather than the mere witness to Henry's grant claimed by Molyneux.[201] And both ridiculed Anglo-Irish pretensions by asserting that were Ireland truly the independent kingdom that Molyneux claimed, James' stand in Ireland in 1689 would not have been the rebellion the Anglo-Irish denounced it as.[202]

A rather similar view was taken by Molyneux's Tory critic Charles Davenant, who called for the outright suppression of Irish woollen exports as a danger to England's most important industry.[203] Such a step would, however, be likely to threaten English security by stirring up Protestant disaffection in Ireland and so give rise to the need for increased military expenditure there. To avoid this, Davenant recommended allowing the resumption of Irish cattle imports rather than encouraging the linen industry, a policy which, though widely advocated, would, he feared, prove a more serious long-term threat than the cattle trade.[204] Davenant's political critique also took into account the dangers of alienating the colonists through harsh treatment.[205] While accepting Henry II's concessions to the native Irish as genuine, he questioned how these rights could be said to have descended to the colonists 'who are now properly the Body-Politick of that Kingdom'.[206] Despite the ancient designation of 'the kingdom of Ireland', the 'English-Irish' (as he termed them) were in reality still only a colony, and as such altogether different from the Scots, who remained independent allies, however much in need of military protection.[207] While political subordination did not impair the rights of Englishmen in Ireland as individuals (including that of taxing themselves), the interests of the empire as a whole required an overarching, directive authority that only the English parliament could provide.[208]

200 Clement, *Answer*, pp 62–3.
201 Atwood, *History*, pp 35–6, 90–1; Clement, *Answer*, pp 49–53.
202 Atwood, *History*, p. 90; Clement, *Answer*, pp 118–21.
203 Davenant's critique of *The Case* comes in sect. III of the *Essay*, 'Of the land of England, and its product'. It was preceded by a far-reaching analysis of the commercial threat presented by Ireland.
204 Davenant, *An essay* (London, 1699), pp 120–30. See further, Hont, *Jealousy of trade* (Cambridge, MA, 2005), pp 220–33.
205 Davenant justified Ireland's legislative subordination even more forcefully in *A discourse upon grants and resumptions* (London, 1700), p. 409.
206 Davenant, *An essay* (London, 1699), p. 112.
207 Ibid., pp 114–16. Like Atwood (cf. p. 21, n. 101 above), Davenant also reversed his benevolent view of the Scots in a 1704 work on the union question.
208 Davenant, *An essay* (London, 1699), pp 110, 115–16. In spite of his virulent attack on the Irish woollen industry and strong support for the 1700 Resumption Act, C.18 Irish writers regarded Davenant as a leading authority on economic matters: P. Kelly, 'The politics of political economy' in Connolly (ed.), *Political ideas* (Dublin, 2000), p. 127.

The approach of Molyneux's other Tory critic, Charles Leslie, was strikingly different: far from attacking the case for Ireland's legislative independence, he objected that Molyneux had not sufficiently defended it. As a leading Irish non-juror, his chief concern was what he saw as the despoliation of the Church of Ireland after 1688, and he accused Molyneux of failing to challenge the Irish parliament's abject compliance with English legislation for Ireland at the time of the revolution and later.[209] Though the 1691 English Act for Abrogating the Oath of Supremacy in Ireland had led to the deprivation of one bishop and several lower clergy, the Irish parliament (including Molyneux) had accepted it without demur in both 1692 and 1695. Leslie also effectively deployed arguments from the *Two treatises of government* to deflate several of Molyneux's claims, though his later writings would show strong disapproval of Locke's book.[210] In conclusion, Leslie asserted that slavery in the form of subjection to the English parliament was God's punishment for the complicity of the Irish parliament in depriving the Irish clergy of their spiritual authority.[211]

Aftermath: the *fortuna* of *The Case*, and its later editions

It remains to say something about the growing reputation that Molyneux's pamphlet acquired during the eighteenth century, though detailed consideration of the book's *fortuna* is beyond the scope of this introduction. With its ten editions to 1782, *The case of Ireland* was one of the most frequently republished Irish political writings of the eighteenth century, enjoying a status comparable to William King's *State of the Protestants* (fourteen editions, 1691–1768); Hugh Reily's *Impartial history of Ireland* (twelve editions, 1695–99) or Thomas Prior's *List of absentees* (nine editions, 1729–83).[212] The book's standing soon came to be symbiotically linked with that of its author, whose reputation was immensely enhanced by the publication of his correspondence with John Locke in 1708 (subsequently reprinted in each of the ten editions of the latter's works to 1820).[213]

Eighteenth-century reissues of *The Case* fell into two well-defined groups, both associated with a period of prolonged political tension between Britain and Ireland in which the question of legislative independence figured prominently, together with isolated editions in 1706 and in 1749. The book's importance in the later eighteenth century came to lie, as Archbishop King predicted in 1720, in the fact that even after the British Declaratory Act (6 Geo. 1, c. 5) had seemingly put paid to Ireland's aspirations to legislative independence, *The Case* would serve to keep

209 Leslie's remarks on the navigation and tobacco acts were quite similar to those of his sometime antagonist Bishop King. Cf. p. 23 above.
210 [Leslie], *Considerations* ([London], 1698), pp 3–5. Cf. Leslie, *The new association* (London, 1703), pt II, supplement, pp 3–10.
211 [Leslie], *Considerations* ([London], 1698), p. 8.
212 For details, see Simms, *Colonial nationalism* (Cork, 1976); P. Kelly, 'William Molyneux', *ECI*, 3 (1988), p. 136; and Power, 'Publishing and sectarian tension', *ECI*, 19 (2004), pp 91–4.
213 Locke, *Some familiar letters* (London, 1708), and comments in *Hibernian Magazine*, July 1782, p. 479. See further, P. Kelly, 'Locke and Molyneux', *Hermathena*, 126 (1979), p. 38.

the claim alive, thus allowing it to 'be prosecuted whenever a favourable Juncture offers'.[214] The first reissue was that of 1706, which had neither place of publication nor printer's name, and is generally thought to have been produced in Dublin, though a less plausible claim has been made for Cork.[215] Its appearance is assumed to have been connected with the debate over the projected union of England and Scotland. As early as 1703 the Scots patriot Andrew Fletcher of Saltoun had referred extensively to *The Case* as a warning of how Scotland might be treated under union, though without naming the book or its author.[216] The 1706 text is a reasonably accurate reprint of the first edition, though none of the latter's extensive marginalia are reproduced. Rather more is known of the next edition in 1719, which was the first of a group of three reissues connected with renewed tensions in Anglo-Irish relations. The difficulties began with the appeal in the Annesley v. Sherlock case to the British house of lords in 1717 that resulted in the 1720 Declaratory Act asserting Britain's legislative and jurisdictional supremacy over Ireland, persisted through the bank crisis of 1720–1, and re-emerged with the controversy over Wood's halfpence in 1723–5.[217] Even before 1719, however, Bishop Evans of Meath had complained that proponents of Irish rights found inspiration in Molyneux's book.[218] The titlepage of the 1719 edition reproduced that of the 1698 edition (bar the imprint), identifying itself as 'Printed in the Year 1719', but again lacked either printer's name or place of publication. Bishop Nicolson of Derry credited its appearance to John Maxwell (brother of the pamphleteer Henry Maxwell), in a letter also containing the first recorded mention of the pamphlet's having been burned by order of the English commons in 1698.[219] The third reprint of *The Case* in 1720 was a London publication from William Boreham, and included in the same volume a reprint of one of the classics of early Irish legal publishing, James Barry's *Case of defective tenures*, first printed in Dublin in 1637. Since there is no apparent connection in terms of subject matter,

---

214 King to Samuel Molyneux Jnr, 2 Jan. 1719/20.

215 For the Cork printing see Falkner Greirson & Co., *Catalogue five* (Dublin, 1967), item 345. Favouring Dublin are the *British Library catalogue* (New York, 1967), xvii, p. 791, and Dix, 'The Case', *Irish Book-Lover*, 5 (1914), p. 117.

216 See Fletcher, *An account of a conversation* [1703] in *Political works* (Cambridge, 1997), pp 193–6, which showed considerable sympathy with Molyneux's arguments, particularly as regards English interpretation of the rights of conquest as well as their recent assault on Irish trade.

217 The Annesley appeal was against the Irish lords' 1716 confirmation of the decision of the Irish court of exchequer in favour of Hester Sherlock. For this and the circumstances leading to the Declaratory Act, see Hayton, 'The Stanhope/Sunderland ministry', *English Historical Review*, 113 (1998), pp 612–13, 625–35.

218 Evans to Archbishop Wake, 19 Mar. 1718/9, cited in Victory, 'The making of the Declaratory Act of 1720' in O'Brien (ed.), *Parliament, politics and people* (Blackrock, 1984), p. 145, n. 45.

219 Nicolson to Archbishop Wake, 1 Sept. 1719: BL Add. MS 6116, no. 115. Nicolson, *The Irish historical library* (London, 1724), p. 138, however, made no mention of the burning of Molyneux's book. A reference to the burning in another letter to Wake in Sept. 1719 suggests the claim was currently circulating at the time: Victory, 'The making of the Declaratory Act of 1720' in O'Brien (ed.), *Parliament, politics and people* (Blackrock, 1984), pp 144–5 and nn.

the decision to link the two works may perhaps be explained by the fact that, in both the Annesley case and the case of tenures, Englishmen appointed as judges in Ireland were considered to have inappropriately favoured English interests over Irish ones.[220] The third item in this group of editions was a Dublin reissue of the conjoint *Case of Ireland* and *Case of tenures* in 1725.[221] This republication arose out of the Wood's halfpence controversy, in the course of which Lord Chancellor Midleton named *The Case* to the lord lieutenant and council in October 1724 as the source of the ideas of independency seditiously elaborated in Swift's *Fourth Drapier's letter*.[222] Shortly later the *Fifth Drapier's letter* hailed Molyneux as one of the 'dangerous Authors, who talk of Liberty as a Blessing, to which the whole Race of Mankind hath an Original Title'.[223] Thus by the mid-1720s Molyneux was established as the champion of Irish liberty in the broad sense, not just a spokesman for legislative independence, and to meet a growing interest in Molyneux the man, the 1725 edition included a crude portrait engraved by Philip Simms.[224]

The 1749 edition of *The Case* was something of an anomaly in associating issues of Dublin municipal politics with the question of Irish legislative independence. Its publication arose from the efforts of the radical politician Charles Lucas to reform Dublin municipal politics by purging it of the corruption that he saw as endemic in oligarchic rule. Lucas drew attention to Molyneux's work in his *Tenth address to the free citizens and free-holders of the city of Dublin* in early 1749, the first printed work to claim overtly that *The Case* had been burned by order of the English commons in 1698.[225] The further embellishment that this outrage was effected at the 'hands of an English hangman', as Wolfe Tone put it in 1792, came in the new preface to the 1770 edition (see below), and together established a narrative that greatly enhanced the reputation of both book and author.[226] The *Tenth address* also included a lengthy summary of *The Case*, interspersed with Lucas' own observations, which made Molyneux's arguments available to a much

---

220   In 1636, the judges had benefited the crown by overturning titles to land granted on terms of 'knight's service' rather than the more onerous 'tenancy in chief', while in 1719 the barons of the exchequer in Dublin had implemented the orders of the English lords in direct contravention of the Irish house.

221   The edition did not sell quickly, being re-advertised in Berkeley's *Querist*, pt II (Dublin, 1736).

222   I am grateful to David Hayton for a copy of Lord Chancellor Midleton's original letter of 31 Oct. 1724 (Surrey History Centre, Brodrick Papers, 1248/6/78–81), which is fuller than the version in Coxe (ed.), *Memoirs* (London, 1798), iii, pp 395–8. Cf. Marmaduke Coghill to Edward Southwell, 31 Oct. 1724: Coghill, *Letters of Marmaduke Coghill* (Dublin, 2005), pp 11–12.

223   Swift, *Prose works* (Oxford, 1961), p. 86. For his earlier admiring reference to Molyneux, see *Fourth Drapier's letter*, ibid., pp 62–3.

224   The engraving was probably based on the portrait of Molyneux attributed to Kneller (cf. plate 4), which had been sent to Dublin after Molyneux's death: Thomas Molyneux to Locke, 15 May 1699: *Locke Corr.*, 2589. For Simms, see Strickland, *A dictionary of Irish artists* (Shannon, 1969), s.v.

225   Lucas, *A tenth address* (Dublin, 1749), p. 10.

226   Wolfe Tone, *Writings of Theobald Wolfe Tone* (Oxford, 1998), i, p. 92; *The Case*, 1770 edn, pref., p. vi.

wider public.[227] This concern to disseminate his message was reflected in the cheaper format of the sixth edition, which sold for less than a quarter of the price of its immediate predecessor.[228] The publishers' advertisement announcing its appearance in October 1749 spoke of *The Case* having been 'condemned to the Flames', as well as its being extolled by Swift as fit to be written in 'Letters of Gold'.[229] But where Swift had hailed Molyneux as the champion of liberty in general, Lucas went further in popularizing his message and transforming him into the radical friend of the people, thereby creating an image of Molyneux that would provide a major plank of his appeal in the age of revolutions: American, Irish and French.

The final surge of eighteenth-century reprintings of *The Case* started in 1770, and was influenced by the growing difficulties between Britain and its colonies in America, as well as the radical, popular politics of the Wilkesite movement in England.[230] The immediate stimulus for its republication in 1770 was probably the culmination of the augmentation crisis in late 1769, with Townshend's entering his protest in the journal of the Irish house of lords, as Sydney had done in 1692.[231] What appeared to the patriot opposition as English determination to undermine the Irish parliament's sole remaining legislative competence in initiating finance led to the production of various other works concerned with the constitutional issue in Ireland at this time, to say nothing of an exchange of vituperative pamphlets.[232] The publication of the 1770 edition of *The Case* in London suggests, however, that those responsible for bringing it out saw the relevance of the pamphlet as extending well beyond the Irish context.[233] Such certainly was the view conveyed by the new five-thousand-word preface, introduced in place of Molyneux's dedication to King William and preface to the reader. Probably written

227 Lucas, *A tenth address* (Dublin, 1749), pp 11–29. Dix's characterization of the 1749 edition as 'curtailed and corrupt' suggests confusion between Lucas' summary and the actual text of the pamphlet. Cf. Dix, 'The Case' in *Irish Book-Lover*, 5 (1914), p. 117.

228 The 1725 edition had been priced at 2s. 2d. (sterling), while those of 1749 and 1782 were sold for 'a British Sixpence' (i.e. 6 ½ d. Irish). However, the 1770 edn (with its new preface) went for 3s. (sterling), and the 1776 edition for 1s. 1d. (Irish). See checklist of printings of *The Case*, pp 82–4.

229 *Faulkner's Dublin Journal*, 30 Sept.–3 Oct. 1749; Swift's comment would not seem to have been made in print; it was also referred to in Seward, *The rights of the people* (Dublin, 1783), p. 48.

230 Cf. Simms, *Colonial nationalism* (Cork, 1976), pp 53–67 passim. Among the distinguished figures known to have owned copies or referred to the book were Franklin, Jefferson, John Dickinson, John Hancock, James Madison and John Adams; no systematic investigation has yet been made of American interest in Molyneux and *The Case* in the revolutionary era. Molyneux does not figure among the most frequently cited European writers identified in Lutz, 'The relative influence of European writers', *American Political Science Review*, 78 (1984), pp 192–3.

231 *Lords Jnl [Ire.]*, iv, pp 539–40. For the crisis, see Bartlett, 'The Townshend viceroyalty' in Bartlett & Hayton (eds), *Penal era and golden age* (Belfast, 1979), esp. pp 93–100.

232 E.g. Howard, *Some questions* (Dublin, 1770); [French], *The constitution of Ireland* (Dublin, 1770); the anonymous *The policy of Poynings' Law* (Dublin, 1770), and the reissue of Harris' *Hibernica: part II* (1770). For examples of the pamphlet literature, see *Baratariana* (Dublin, 1773).

233 The edition proved slow to sell, and Almon re-advertised it at 2s. 6d. (sterling) in his *Narrative of the … debates in the parliament of Ireland* (London, 1776).

by the patriot leader Henry Flood, the preface referred principally to affairs in America and the Wilkesite movement in Britain, together with the extension of ministerial corruption into Ireland.[234] It also specifically raised the augmentation crisis, by alluding to the power over money bills as the sole 'Essential Independency of Legislature' that remained to the Irish parliament and pointed to the detrimental consequences of Ireland's loss of the 'dernier judicial power' – a combination that led Benjamin Franklin to describe it as 'shrewdly written'.[235] Though the publisher was the Irish-born radical printer and journalist John Almon, known to have been in contact with Flood and other patriot leaders from the mid-1760s, it remains a mystery who precisely was responsible for reissuing *The Case* in 1770.[236] The next edition of the pamphlet, published in Dublin in 1773, retained the 1770 preface but also reinstated Molyneux's original prefatory matter. The circumstances of its appearance were even more obscure than those of its immediate predecessor, though the fact that its publisher, John Milliken, would shortly reprint another Almon work may indicate a link with the 1770 edition and the patriot opposition.[237] Not long after the 1773 edition appeared, Molyneux's arguments were enthusiastically taken up by the English pamphleteer and slavery abolitionist Granville Sharp, who claimed to have been converted to belief in Ireland's right to political independence by reading *The Case*.[238] Sharp's work was the prelude to widespread renewed interest in Molyneux over the next seven years on the part of Irish pamphleteers, such as Frederick Jebb in *Guatimozin's letters on the present state of Ireland, and the right of binding it by British acts of parliament, &c.* (1779), which drew heavily on the *The Case*, without, however, identifying its source.

The ninth edition of *The Case* appeared in Belfast in 1776, the year of the declaration of American independence, dropping the new preface and reverting to the original text issued by the author. A brief publisher's advertisement drew attention to events in America (in phrases redolent of Flood's preface), and to the need both to translate the substantial number of Latin extracts in the book and to keep the price low in order to increase its circulation.[239] The final eighteenth-century edition appeared in the summer of 1782 after the 'recovery of Irish independence' with the new Rockingham ministry's hasty bowing to Irish pressure

234 The attribution to Flood came from his fellow Kilkennyman, Deane Swift: T. Swift, *The utility of union* (Dublin, 1800), pref., p. iii. It is accepted by Flood's latest biographer, see further J. Kelly, *Henry Flood* (Dublin, 1998), pp 141–4.

235 Franklin to Samuel Cooper, 14 Apr. 1770: Franklin, *The papers of Benjamin Franklin* (London, 1973), xvii, p. 124.

236 See P. Kelly, 'William Molyneux', *ECI*, 3 (1988), p. 139 and nn.; J. Kelly, *Henry Flood* (Dublin, 1998), pp 93–7, 141–5.

237 E.g. *Another letter to Mr Almon* (Dublin, 1771).

238 Reading Molyneux prompted Sharp to include a substantial addition to the 2nd edn of his *Declaration of the people's natural right in the legislature*, in 1775, entitled *Part II: containing a declaration or defence of the same doctrine ... applied particularly to the people of Ireland; in answer to assertions of several eminent writers ...* (notably Pufendorf and Blackstone).

239 See further note on Latin translations, pp 74–5 below.

by revoking the 1720 Declaratory Act. The revocation had shortly followed Grattan's famous speech of 16 April, long thought to have opened with the invocation, 'Spirit of Swift, Spirit of Molyneux, your Genius has prevailed. Ireland is now a Nation', which has now been shown to have been interpolated in the version revised for publication four decades later.[240] Other sources, however, confirmed that the names of Swift, Molyneux and even Darcy, whose *Argument* had been reissued in 1764, were on the lips of Irish 'patriots' reasserting the nation's right to legislative independence over the previous twenty-four months, while Grattan's earlier speech on the subject on 22 February 1782 drew heavily on *The Case*, though without crediting its author.[241] Subsequently, his by-then rival Henry Flood spoke of Molyneux's pamphlet rising phoenix-like from the flames, in his second speech on simple repeal of 14 June 1782.[242] Molyneux's high standing at this time was shown by the inclusion of his portrait by Robert Home in Trinity's newly completed public theatre in 1783, while in 1784 the Cork painter James Barry depicted him (holding *The Case*) in a fresco for the Society of Arts in London.[243]

The 1782 edition reprinted *The Case* conjointly with a reissue of Joseph Pollock's well-known *Letters to the men of Ireland, from Owen Roe O'Nial* (a work itself much indebted to Molyneux). The Latin extracts were translated afresh, dropping the original Latin, and the edition notably omitted Molyneux's description of the prospect of union with England as 'an Happiness we can hardly hope for'.[244] Though acknowledging that legislative independence was on the threshold of achievement, the editor's advertisement justified republication on the ground that Irishmen needed to be reminded of the principles upon which their liberty depended. Between *The Case* and *O'Nial's letters*, the anonymous editor also printed (pp 62–4) a short paper which he identified as Molyneux's 'Reasons', challenging the English lords' *coram non judice* verdict of 1698, with a note tracing its provenance back to what he asserted was an autograph in Molyneux's hand 'written in the blank leaves of one of his Cases', presented to 'the then Bishop of Meath' (Richard Tenison). Given the number of bishops among the recipients of surviving presentation copies of the book, the claim might at first sight seem credible.[245] However, internal evidence points to the 'Reasons' having drawn up in

240 The reliability of the reporting of Irish parliamentary debates in 1779–82 is discussed in O'Brien, 'The Grattan mystique', *ECI*, 1 (1986) and O'Brien, 'Illusion and reality', *ECI*, 3 (1988); McCormack, 'Vision and Revision', *ECI*, 2 (1987), and P. Kelly, 'William Molyneux', *ECI*, 3 (1988), p. 147.

241 Cf. *Hibernian Magazine*, Sept. 1782, p. 479. For an ironic comment on Grattan's reliance on Swift and Molyneux, see Duigenan, *An Answer* (Dublin, 1798), pp 2, 88–9.

242 *Parliamentary register* (Dublin, 1782), i, p. 425.

243 For Home's portrait, see Strickland, *A dictionary of Irish artists* (Shannon, 1916), pp 37, 65; the Brocas engraving based on it was commissioned for *Autobiography*. For the Barry fresco, entitled *Elysium or Tantalus, or the state of final retribution*, see Pressly, *The life and art of James Barry* (London, 1981), pp 113–15, 295–6.

244 For subsequent comments on the omission, see *The Case*, p. 98 nn.

245 See list of presentation copies, p. 80 below.

England rather than Ireland, particularly in its emphasis on the difficulties the verdict would cause for the English lords themselves.[246] It is also unlikely that Molyneux would have personally transcribed the paper's more than a thousand words into the book rather than used an amanuensis; more probable is that Tenison (ob. 1705), or some subsequent owner of the volume, had the 'Reasons' copied into it, believing the piece to be by Molyneux. However, despite the editor's claim that the paper had never before been printed, the 'Reasons' had already been published in the controversy preceding the 1720 Declaratory Act, as an appendix to *A letter from a member of the house of commons in Ireland*, and identified as the duke of Leeds' protest against the *coram non judice* verdict in 1698.[247] Thus, in the absence of further evidence, the 1782 claim that Molyneux was author of the 'Reasons' remains unconvincing.

Prior to the appearance of the 1782 edition in mid-June, there had been an unsuccessful attempt by the *Hibernian Chronicle* to publish a more lavish, subscription version of *The Case*.[248] This failure by no means indicated a fall-off of interest in Molyneux or his book, and with the outbreak of the French Revolution his reputation as a champion of liberty was again revived. His memory was honoured, along with Locke's, in the 1791 and 1792 Belfast celebrations of the fall of the Bastille, though Irish writers on the revolution did not look to his words to support their arguments in the way they did to Locke's.[249] His influence was further acknowledged by the founders of the United Irishmen, with Wolfe Tone claiming that it was reading *The Case* that had first brought home to him that the root of Ireland's troubles was the link with England.[250] The final eighteenth-century revival of interest in *The Case* came in the debates over union with Britain in 1797–1800, when Molyneux's pamphlet (along with Swift's writings and Locke's *Treatises*) was among the most widely cited authorities on both sides of the question, one champion of union referring to *The Case*'s having become 'the standard of political orthodoxy in Ireland'.[251] Even the achievement of union, however, did not immediately exhaust Molyneux's appeal; early nineteenth-

---

246 See text of 'Reasons' in appendix E below. The items indicating probable composition in England are numbers 6, 8, 10 and 14.

247 Two manuscript versions of the 'Reasons' are found in Marsh's Library (MS Z.3.2.5, items 83 and 84), with an inscription (perhaps in Archbishop King's hand) identifying it as the work of the duke of Leeds, 'as I have heard'. No protest against the verdict is, however, found in the *Lords Journal [Eng.]* for 1698.

248 See further checklist of printings of *The Case*, item 10a, p. 84 below.

249 *Hibernian Journal*, 22 July 1791; 16 July 1792. Cf. P. Kelly, 'Irish writers and the French Revolution' in *La Storia* (Rome, 1990), pp 332–4.

250 Cf. 'Autobiography, 1763–1792' in Wolfe Tone, *The writings of Theobald Wolfe Tone* (Oxford, 1998), ii, p. 284; for other United Irish interest in Molyneux, see Elliott, *Partners in revolution* (London, 1982), p. 27.

251 This claim derives from my unpublished 1986 analysis of authorities cited in over 160 union pamphlets (excluding reported speeches or verse), which covered the bulk of relevant titles subsequently listed in McCormack, *The pamphlet debates* (Dublin, 1996). Citation from Geraghty, *The present state of Ireland* (London, 1799), p. 36.

century Catholic historians such as Plowden, O'Conor and Taaffe all praised his principled stand for Ireland's rights, while a critic of the union named I[saac?] Colles used *The Case* as the platform in 1812 from which to launch his denunciation of its consequences.[252] However, there was no further indication of Molyneux's continuing relevance for contemporary affairs before the 1821 publication of Grattan's final revision of his speech of 16 April 1782, which incorporated the celebrated apostrophe, 'Spirit of Swift, Spirit of Molyneux ...'[253]

Tributes to Molyneux's influence on the 'patriot' tradition continued throughout the nineteenth century, perhaps most notably in R.R. Madden's *History of Irish periodical literature* in 1867. As well as extolling Molyneux in extravagant terms, Madden did much to draw attention to his arguments by providing a fourteen-page synopsis of the work.[254] The perceived importance of *The Case* was also reflected by the inclusion of a page from the printer's copy in Sir John Gilbert's multi-volume *Facsimiles of the national manuscripts of Ireland*, which referred for the first time in print to the author's debt to Domville's 'Declaration'.[255] Not until the end of the century, however, were there any further reprints of the pamphlet, with *The Case*'s appearance in 1892, together with an introduction and life of the author by Canon John O'Hanlon, an edition that was reissued in 1897.[256] No further edition appeared till 1977, when Andrew Carpenter included *The Case* in a limited edition of 350 copies in his Irish Writings from the Age of Swift series.[257] The volume contained a brief introduction by J.G. Simms (whose biography, the first full-length study of Molyneux, would be published five years later), together with an afterword by Denis Donoghue. A French translation from the Groupe de Recherches Anglo-Irlandaises at the University of Caen appeared in 1995, with an illuminating historical introduction by Pierre Gouhier that combined the insights afforded by a different cultural background with a sound grasp of Irish history.[258] In 1999 Mark Goldie reprinted the 1698 edition of *The Case* in his six-volume collection *The reception of Locke's politics*, including for the first time a useful set of explanatory notes, while in 2009 the Dodo Press issued a straightforward reprint of the 1770 edition (which included Henry Flood's new preface in place of Molyneux's dedication to the king and preface to the reader).[259]

---

252 See F. Plowden, *History of Ireland* (Dublin, 1803), ii, p. 23; (the rather more enthusiastic) Taaffe, *Impartial history of Ireland* (Dublin,1809–10), iii, pp 532–3; O'Conor, *History of the Irish Catholics* (Dublin, 1813), p. 150, and Colles, *The Case* (1812).
253 Grattan, *Speeches* (London 1821), p. 45. Cf. p. 50 above.
254 Madden, *History* (London, 1867), i, pp 40–61.
255 Gilbert, *Facsimiles* (Dublin, 1884), ii, intro. p. cix., and pl. xciii.
256 See further checklist of printings of *The Case*, item 12, p. 84 below. For the factors that may have led O'Hanlon to publish, see *DIB*, s.v.
257 Though purporting to have been reprinted from the 1698 edition, Carpenter's actual copy-text was that of the 1719 edn. See further checklist of printings of *The Case*, item 13, p. 85 below.
258 See further checklist of printings of *The Case*, item 14, p. 85 below.
259 See further checklist of printings of *The Case*, items 15 and 16, pp 85–6 below.

THE
CASE
OF
IRELAND's
Being Bound by
Acts of Parliament
IN
ENGLAND,
Stated.

BY.

William Molyneux
of *Dublin*, Esq;

Dublin, Printed by *Joseph Ray*, and are to be Sold at his Shop in *Skinner-Row*. MDCXCVIII.

1. Original issue of the titlepage of the 1698 edition of *The Case*, showing the imprint of Joseph Ray, of Skinner-Row, àDublin, and the date MDCXCVIII.

THE
CASE
OF
IRELAND's
Being Bound by
Acts of Parliament
IN
ENGLAND,
Stated.

BY
William Molyneux,
of *Dublin,* Esq;

Dublin, Printed by and for J. R. And are to be
Sold by Rob. Clavel, and A. and J. Churchil, Booksellers in London. 1698.

2. Second issue of the 1698 titlepage, with imprint for sale by London booksellers,
Robert Clavel and A. and J. Churchill, and the date in Arabic numerals (presumably
prepared for the projected London publication, cf. intro. p. 90)

THE
CASE
OF
IRELAND's

Being Bound by

Acts of Parliament

I N

ENGLAND,

Stated.

BY

William Molyneux,

of Dublin, Efq;

Dublin, Printed by *Joseph Ray,* and are
to be Sold at his Shop in *Skinner-Row.* MDCXCVIII.

3. Cancellans titlepage for the third issue of the titlepage, distinguished from
the first issue by the non-swash 'M' for Molyneux (cf. intro. p. 90).

Wᵐ Molyneux .F.R.S
Member For the Univerſity
1692

4. Portrait of William Molyneux, 1698, attributed to Sir Godfrey Kneller, Bt.,
© National Portrait Gallery, London.

John Lock.

5. Portrait of John Locke, 1696, by Michael Dahl, © National Portrait Gallery, London.

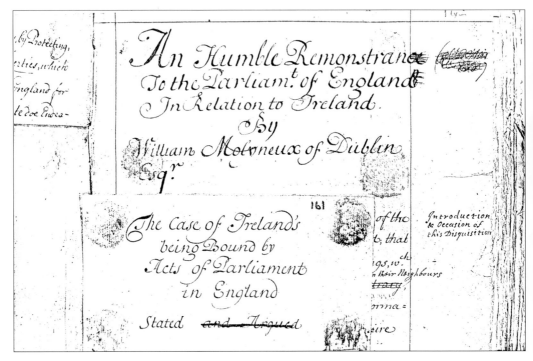

6. Page from the printer's copy MS showing the dismounted label in the hand of Molyneux's amanuensis, changing the half-title from 'An Humble Remonstrance to the Parliament of England' to 'The Case of Ireland's being Bound by Acts of Parliament in England' (*Case*, p. 1). Note the (subsequently deleted) instruction in the printer's hand, reading 'alter this title': MS TCD 891, fols 161–2.

7. (*opposite*) Page from the printer's copy MS showing a deleted interpolation in Molyneux's hand, written around the marginal heading, 'Record out of Mr Petyt of the Antiquity of Parliaments in Ireland'. Note also the printer's mark up for the start of quire 'E' (*Case*, p. 49): MS TCD 891, fol. 186r.

thought adviseable in these latter Days to break in upon Old setled Constitutions. no one knows how fatall the Consequents of that may be .

Teste apud Glouc. 6 Februar.

~~Here we may observe~~ Here we have a free Grant of all the Libertys of England to the People of Ireland. But we know the Libertys of English men are founded on that universal Law of Nature, that ought to prevail throughout the whole World, of being Govern'd only by such Laws to which they give theire own Consent by their Representatives in Parliament.

And here before I proceed farther I shall take Notice, that in the late Raised Controversy, whether the House of Commons were an Essentiall part of Parliament before ye 49th year of Hen. y^3. The Learned Mr Petyt Keeper of the Records in the Tower, in his Book on that Subject. pag. 71. Ded-uces his 9th Argument From the Comparison of the Antient Generale Concilium or Parliament of Ireland instanced An. 38. Hen. 3. with the Parliament in England, wherein the Citizens

and

E Prima / 49 /

Record out Mr Petyt of ye Antiquity of Par-liaments in Ire-land

Pag. 129. lin. 6. after England.

add * * — And in all the Charters and Grants of Libertys and Immunitys to Ireland we still find this, That Holy Church shall be Free. &c. I would fain know what is meant here by the word Free. Certainly if our Church be Free and absolute within it self, our State must be so. likewise; for how our Civil and Ecclesiastical Government is now interwoven, every body knows.

K. Prima
129

8. Interpolated sheet in Molyneux's hand, keyed to show where the passage was to be inserted in the text of printer's copy. Note also the printer's mark up for the start of quire 'K' (*Case*, p. 129): MS TCD 891, fol. 232r.

Textual introduction

Manuscript sources

As already stated, the chief manuscript source on which Molyneux drew was the paper entitled, 'A disquisition touching that great question, whether an act of parliament made in England shall bind the kingdom and people of Ireland without their allowance and acceptance of such an act in the kingdom of Ireland', written by his father-in-law, Sir William Domville, in July 1660. So great indeed was this debt that on its first appearance some contemporaries mistook *The Case* for a mere reissue of Domville's paper.[1] His second most important manuscript source was the earlier paper by Sir Richard Bolton, entitled 'A declaration setting forth how, and by what means, the laws and statutes of England, from time to time, came to be of force in Ireland', written in early 1644, and identified as a source of the pamphlet by Molyneux's brother-in-law, John Madden.[2] The third major manuscript source of *The Case* has only been recently identified among Molyneux's papers, namely a legal opinion drawn up in 1697 entitled 'That the legislative power in Ireland doth belong to the king by the advice of his parliament of Ireland, not of his parliament of England'.[3] However, while Molyneux transcribed large swathes of the 'Disquisition' (often little-changed) into his pamphlet, as well as reformulating ideas and citing precedents put forward by Domville, extended citation from the 'Declaration' was rare, though he drew extensively on Bolton's ideas and precedents, and subsequently made use of the 'Legislative power in Ireland' in much the same fashion, though on a rather lesser scale.[4]

Domville's 'Disquisition' was the source from which Molyneux began work on *The Case*, and it served as the basis of roughly a third of the book. As the colophon to the 1664 manuscript explained, the 'Disquisition' had been drawn up in July

---

1 See p. 24 above. Prior to James Wood's 2015 discovery of Marsh's presentation copy of *The Case* in the Boston Public Library, USA, Molyneux's extensive debt to the 'Disquisition' had been pointed out in Monck Mason's 1814 catalogue of the TCD MSS, though the first reference in print was not till Gilbert, *Facsimiles* (Dublin, 1884). See further p. 52, n. 255 above.

2 See p. 24 above.

3 MS TCD 888/1, ff 127–30; P. Kelly, 'Recasting tradition' in Ohlmeyer (ed.), *Political thought* (Cambridge, 2000), p. 99, n. 53.

4 Specific indications of where Molyneux has drawn on the various manuscript sources are provided in the explanatory notes to the text.

1660 for the then marquess of Ormond, Charles II's chief adviser on Irish affairs, presumably preparatory to deciding the country's church and land settlements, but also perhaps for Ormond's personal guidance as an Irish landowner.[5] Its author, William Domville, who had been appointed Irish attorney general the previous month, was a Dublin-born lawyer with family connections and some property in the country, but who had been educated in England and practised exclusively there in the 1640s and 1650s.[6] Not till later in 1660 did he return to Ireland, where he remained in office until dismissed by James II in 1687, two years before his death. One not insignificant difference between *The Case* and Domville's paper was the fact that the 'Disquisition' was written in England rather than Ireland, as can be seen from the frequent confusion over the appropriateness of 'here' or 'there', 'we' or 'they', and 'our' or 'your' in passages from the 'Disquisition' embodied in Molyneux's holograph.[7] Unravelling the respective importance of Domville and Bolton as sources for *The Case* is complicated by the fact that Domville had himself drawn extensively on the 'Declaration', though there were issues on which the two authors differed substantially – notably the origins of the English polity in Ireland.[8] The version of the 'Disquisition' that Molyneux used in writing *The Case* was the copy still among his papers, written in the hand of his long-term amanuensis, who was later responsible for preparing the printer's copy of the book.[9] This copy of the 'Disquisition' was transcribed from the final version of Domville's paper written in 1664, which was a stylistic revision of the text compiled for Ormond in July 1660, and is now in the Robinson Library in Armagh.[10] However, Domville continued to correct and add to this Armagh manuscript till at least 1682, and not all these minor changes are found in Molyneux's transcript. Thus this transcript must have been made well before Domville's death in 1689, and certainly was not freshly transcribed early in 1698 in preparation for writing *The Case*, as I mistakenly asserted in 1979.[11]

Molyneux's use of Domville as a source for his pamphlet was far from unreflecting; he skilfully adapted the 'Disquisition' to the demands of his argument and the format he had chosen to present it. In places he simply copied Domville's narrative largely as it stood, while in others he combined it with the rather different emphasis found in Bolton's 'Declaration' or in printed sources,

5 Charles' government initially hoped to effect an Irish settlement without holding a parliament here, while Ormond relied on a private act in England (12 Car. 2, c. 7) to restore his Irish properties. See P. Kelly (ed.), 'Sir William Domville', *Analecta Hibernica*, 40 (2007), pp 22–3.
6 See *DIB*, s.v.
7 See *The Case*, app. crit. passim. A further source of confusion in transcription arose from Domville's amanuensis' frequent spelling of England as 'Ingland'.
8 See further p. 56 below.
9 See further p. 65 below.
10 The 'Disquisition' is found in a composite volume of manuscripts (labelled 'Hibernica 64') said in a note on the flyleaf to have been compiled by Walter Harris in the mid-C.18: Robinson Library, P001733040. See further P. Kelly (ed.), 'Sir William Domville', *Analecta Hibernica*, 40 (2007), intro. p. 29.
11 P. Kelly, 'The printer's copy of the MS', *Long Room*, 18–19 (1979), p. 11.

modifying Domville's account in the light of these other works. For example, Molyneux began the substance of his argument by reproducing the bulk of Domville's narrative depicting Henry's expedition to Ireland as a peaceful intervention which led to the Irish submitting voluntarily to him, in return for the grant of English laws and customs and their own parliament.[12] But, while Domville purported to derive this narrative from Giraldus and the other historians whom he listed (cf. p. 31 above), closer examination shows that the Latin extracts he cited did not entirely correspond to the only text of the Expugnatio then in print.[13] In particular, where Domville provided an extract stating that the High King Rotherick O'Connor came in person to do homage to Henry in Dublin, as representative of all the men of Ireland, the other historical accounts to which he referred (including the printed text of the Expugnatio) spoke of a meeting between O'Connor and the English king's envoys at the Shannon. And where Domville stated that no one of any importance in Ireland failed to submit to Henry, all his other sources excepted the men of Ulster.[14] In addition, he also omitted minor exceptions to the submission of the Irish rulers being entirely universal and voluntary found in Roger Hoveden and Matthew Paris (see *Case*, pp 9–10 nn). However, a very similar account of Henry's expedition to Ireland in which O'Connor is said to have submitted in person at Dublin 'as king of all the Irishmen of the land' is found in the 1569 Irish Act for the Attainder of Shane O'Neill (11 Eliz. ses. 3, c. 1), an account described in the most recent assessment of the statute as 'a sustained attempt to diminish the role of conquest in Irish history'.[15] The act also failed to refer to the absence of the Ulstermen, while the kings it listed as having submitted to Henry are the same as those given by Domville, with the addition of 'Donald king of Ossorie' among those submitting from the south of Ireland. Domville cited other passages in confirmation of the peaceful nature of Henry's expedition that are found in the 1569 act, notably 'for the Chronicles make no Mention of any Warr or Chivalry done by King H. 2. all that time he was in Ireland', not subsequently reproduced by Molyneux.[16] Although the 1569 act spoke of using both Giraldus' history and 'a short collection of this his historie',

---

12 For example, Molyneux consistently avoided Domville's occasional lapses in referring to Ireland as 'conquered'. Cf. *The Case*, p. 30 nn.

13 Camden, *Anglica* (Frankfurt, 1603), pp 755–813.

14 Cf. Domville, 'Disquisition', pp 40–3. Differences between Domville's Latin extracts, as cited by Molyneux, and the 1603 text of the Expugnatio are noted in *The Case*, pp 9–10, app. crit. Not all the Latin extracts cited by Domville were reproduced in *The Case*.

15 Domville, 'Disquisition', pp 43–4. Cf. Brady, 'The attainder of Shane O'Neill' in Brady and Ohlmeyer (eds), *British interventions* (Cambridge, 2005), p. 36.

16 Domville, 'Disquisition', p. 43. Cf. Bolton, *Statutes of Ireland* (Dublin, 1621), p. 316. *Pace* McGowan-Doyle, *The book of Howth* (Cork, 2011), pp 91–7, the C.15 text, published by Furnival in 1896 as *The English conquest of Ireland*, could not have served as the main source for the 1569 act, since it had Henry's envoys meet O'Connor at Shannon and excepted the men of Ulster. An intermediate position is found in James Yonge's 'The governaunce of prynces' (1421), an expanded translation of the pseudo-Aristotelian *Secreta Secretorum* (see further Whelan, 'James Yonge' in Seán Duffy (ed.), *Medieval Dublin XIII* (Dublin, 2013)). Ch. 32, which discussed the English title

the latter would seem to have been in English, and thus does not help identify the Latin source used by Domville.

Following the digression discussing the inadequacy of conquest as the basis for a title to newly acquired territory (based on Locke), Molyneux reverted to Domville's narrative of the details of the Irish submission to Henry at Lismore and what the king had granted in return. As already noted, he also followed Domville in citing the Modus Tenendi Parliamenta in Hibernia, which the king had supposedly issued to the Irish (based on the original English Modus of William the Conqueror), as evidence that Henry had granted them a parliament in 1171–2. He fleshed out Domville's account of the subsequent history of the Modus with material from Dopping's preface to the 1692 edition of the work, adding fresh arguments of his own to refute Prynne's diplomatic critique of the document.[17] Where Molyneux turned to Bolton rather than Domville was in claiming that Henry's grant of Ireland to John in 1177 brought about a crucial re-founding of the Irish polity as a separate and independent kingdom, after which the new ruler could only alter laws with the consent of its people. While Domville, who had already claimed that the compact at Lismore established Ireland as a separate and independent kingdom, merely viewed the 1177 grant to John as setting Ireland 'more Eminently apart' through giving her a different ruler to England (and potentially a different line of succession for the future).[18] Molyneux parted company with both sources over the role of the English parliament in the 1177 transfer, in (as we have seen) regarding the English lords and commons merely as witnesses to the grant. Bolton, however, claimed that their active participation in the transfer gave added weight to the transaction, though emphatically denying that this accorded them any role in the future government of Ireland. Although Domville made no reference to the English parliament's being involved in the acquisition of Ireland, he asserted that the phrase '*contra omnes*' in the oath sworn by the Irish at Lismore was specifically directed at the English lords and commons, claiming that it had never been the intention of either the king or the Irish princes that the English parliament should have any share in the government of Ireland.[19]

A further extended debt to the wording of the 'Disquisition' came in Molyneux's account of England's ancient laws from Edward the Confessor to Magna Carta, followed by the description of the subsequent reception of English laws in Ireland up to and including 10 Hen. 7, c. 4, which re-enacted all English acts '*for the Publique Weal*'.[20] From this point (*Case*, p. 70), very little further extended citation of material from the 'Disquisition' is found before the numbered

---

to Ireland, had O'Connor come in person to Dublin, while still excepting the men of Ulster: Steele, *Three prose versions* (London, 1898), pp 184–5.

17 Molyneux's refutation of Prynne's criticism of the Modus was a late interpolation in the printer's copy. See *The Case*, p. 31 app. crit.

18 Harris, *Hibernica: part II* (Dublin, 1750), pp 18–19.

19 Domville, 'Disquisition', pp 41, 44–5, 47.

20 *The Case*, pp 58–70, and nn. Cf. Domville, 'Disquisition', pp 52–7, which in turn cited Selden's *Eadmeri* (London, 1623), p. 171 et seq., and various sources in Coke, esp. *8th Rep.*, ff 18v–20r.

set of conclusions starting on page 150, though in the intervening pages Molyneux continued to make occasional use of short excerpts from the paper. No less than half of Molyneux's ten concluding points were taken directly from those in the 'Disquisition'. For example, Domville's first objection (that it was against the common law for the English parliament to legislate directly for Ireland) became Molyneux's second point, while he divided Domville's second contention (that the English parliament's legislating directly for Ireland was contrary to both statute law and ancient charters) in two, dealing with statutes in his third objection and charters in his fourth.[21] Molyneux's concluding points also drew extensively, however, on matters raised by Bolton, bringing us to the question of the 'Declaration's' overall contribution to *The Case*, and not least the identity of its author.

Although known in the seventeenth century as the work of the Irish lord chancellor, Sir Richard Bolton, 'A declaration setting forth how, and by what means, the laws and statutes of England, from time to time, came to be of force in Ireland', has until recently been believed to have been written by the distinguished Catholic lawyer Patrick Darcy (author of *An argument delivered by Patrick Darcy* … (Waterford, 1643)). The identification of Darcy as author was tentatively put forward by its eighteenth-century editor, Walter Harris, when he published the 'Declaration' together with a brief explanatory preface in 1750.[22] The main evidence that Harris adduced in favour of Darcy's authorship was that both the 'Declaration' and Darcy's *Argument* cited the two statutes 10 Hen. 4 and 29 Hen. 6 in support of legislative independence. Though forcefully rejected by Granville Sharp in 1775 and by Henry Monck Mason in 1820, Harris' re-ascription was not seriously questioned again until the 1990s.[23] As the reasons for rejecting Harris' identification of Darcy and confirming Bolton's authorship of the 'Declaration' are somewhat complex, I shall confine what follows to a summary of the main points, referring those interested in further details to my article on the subject in *Irish Historical Studies* in 2006.[24] The earliest mention of the 'Declaration' occurred in April 1644, when manuscript copies of the work were laid before the Irish lords and commons in an effort to persuade parliament to endorse the principle of legislative independence and so advance the peace negotiations with the Catholic Confederates. The most important manuscript for identifying the author is that found in a commonplace book belonging to Sir Paul Davys, who as clerk of the house of commons had been responsible for having copies prepared for the 1644 debates.[25] Though this version did not name Bolton as the author, the title of the next item in the commonplace book (namely Sir Samuel Mayart's 'Answer to a

21 *The Case*, pp 150–70 passim; cf. Domville, 'Disquisition', pp 58–69 passim.
22 See Harris, *Hibernica: part II* (Dublin, 1750), pp [i]–[ii], 1–21.
23 Sharp, *A Declaration* (London, 1775), p. 80; Monck Mason, *An essay* (Dublin, 1820), p. 31; A. Clarke, 'Patrick Darcy' in Ohlmeyer, *Political thought* (Cambridge, 2000), p. 49 n.
24 See P. Kelly, 'Sir Richard Bolton', *IHS*, 35 (2006).
25 Though Harris claimed this manuscript served as his copy-text, its reading was highly defective, see ibid., p. 6.

declaration') dating from May 1644 and written in the same hand, specifically identified Richard Bolton as having written the 'Declaration'.[26] In addition, some of the key material used in the paper would seem to have derived exclusively from Bolton's archives, particularly the exemplifications of no-longer-extant medieval statutes confirming the need for the re-enactment of English statutes before they applied in Ireland, which Bolton had obtained from the treasury at Waterford.[27]

It was in relation to this material from Waterford that doubt remained, however, whether the two works could have been written by a single author. Where Bolton's gloss to the 1621 *Statutes* referred to the statutes 10 Hen. 4 and 29 Hen. 6 as establishing the principle of legislative independence, the 'Declaration' cited the statutes 19 Edw. 2 and 29 Hen. 6.[28] Comparison of the relevant passages from the two works, however, offers a possible explanation for this apparent anomaly, namely that a reference to 10 Hen. 4 has been accidentally dropped in the process of transcribing the 1621 gloss into the 'Declaration' before the phrase 'and the like statute was made again Ann. 29 Hen. 6' (which occurs in both texts).[29] Moreover, as 19 Edw. 2 contained nothing directly relevant to legislative independence, the intended reference was probably to 17 Edw. 2, which re-enacted the English statutes of Lincoln (9 Edw. 2) and York (12 Edw. 2), that had both legislated (inter alia) for issues exclusively applicable to Ireland, though it did not specifically enunciate the principle that English statutes needed to be re-enacted in Ireland.[30] That Bolton should have felt it necessary to corroborate his 1621 claims by reference to much earlier statutory support for legislative independence is explained by the fact that in 1643 the Catholic Confederates had called for statutory confirmation of the principle in their peace negotiations with the Irish royalists. Since circumstances in England made it impossible for Charles to concede this, Bolton was seeking to satisfy the Confederates by proposing an alternative means of copper-fastening the principle of legislative independence through demonstrating that re-enactment of English acts had been the constant practice since the Irish parliament had begun legislating for the colony, and was thus by implication an integral part of the Irish constitution.[31] Though the

---

26 MS TCD 647, ff 9–22, and 23–45, respectively. The manuscript was subsequently acquired by Molyneux's brother-in-law, John Madden, but probably after the former's death as there are no indications that Molyneux had any knowledge of Mayart's 'Answer'.

27 The different wording of Bolton's references to the exemplifications in 1621 and in 1644 would seem to confirm Mayart's statement (*Hibernica: part II* (Dublin, 1750), p. 91) that the exemplifications were no longer in Waterford by 1644. Cf. appendix B below.

28 Cf. A. Clarke, 'Patrick Darcy' in Ohlmeyer, *Political thought* (Cambridge, 2000), p. 49, n. 33.

29 See relevant extracts set forth in parallel in appendix B below. Instances of the re-enactment of other C.15 statutes after an interval of 40–50 years, such as 32 Hen. 6, c. 1, the adoption of all English statutes against provisors, cited *The Case*, p. 68 (first enacted in 13 Hen. 4), make the accidental omission of a ref. to 4 Hen. 10 rather more probable than the re-enactment of 19 Edw. 2 after an interval of 125 years.

30 For the texts of 17 Edw. 2 and 19 Edw. 2, see *ESI*, i, pp 300–5, 306–7. See further *The Case*, p. 95 nn. Domville, however, made no reference to these acts at all.

31 The first example cited in the 'Declaration' was 13 Edw. 2 (cited in Bolton, *Statues of Ireland*

measure failed to win sufficient support even in the Protestant parliament, the arguments of the 'Declaration' in favour of legislative independence were fully consistent with the position to which Bolton had adhered from his 1621 *Statutes*, through the peace negotiations with the Confederates in 1643–6 and up to his death in 1647.

While no manuscript of Bolton's 'Declaration' survives among Molyneux's papers, it seems likely that the version that he used in preparing *The Case* was also transcribed from a copy owned by Domville. In the composite manuscript volume containing the 1664 version (now in the Robinson Library, Armagh) the text of the 'Disquisition' is immediately followed by Domville's legal opinion on holding inquisitions in the Ormond Palatinate dated 1676, and a copy of Bolton's 'Declaration', all written in the same hand.[32] Not only did Molyneux have his amanuensis transcribe the 1676 opinion in addition to the 'Disquisition' from this source, but the final page of its transcription bears the catchword 'Declaration', which suggests that a (no-longer-extant) copy was also made of the latter. Were this not the case, however, Molyneux would have had little difficulty in obtaining the text, as the 'Declaration' was widely known in the later seventeenth century, and his brother-in-law John Madden, for example, owned three copies.[33] The main contribution of Bolton's 'Declaration' to *The Case* was confined to the final two thirds of the pamphlet, and (as already indicated) involved reproducing his opinions and precedents that he relied on rather than embodying substantial passages from his text.[34] The middle third of *The Case* drew on a combination of Bolton and Domville, particularly in using more detailed accounts found in the 'Declaration' to supplement the treatment of issues that Domville had only briefly alluded to, such as the key constitutional cases of the Merchants of Waterford's (*Case*, pp 89–92) and of John Pilkington (*Case*, pp 125–6).[35] In addition, the discussion of appeals on writs of error from Ireland to the English king's bench (a topic barely touched on by Domville) was also heavily indebted to the 'Declaration', as well as drawing on the third of Molyneux's main manuscript sources, the paper entitled 'Legislative power in Ireland'.[36]

The influence of this legal opinion, drawn up in 1697 (whose full title was 'That the legislative power in Ireland doth belong to the king by the advice of his

(Dublin, 1621) p. 67n.), which re-enacted the English statutes of Merton and Marlborough together with statutes from Edw. I's reign, followed by 19 [recte 17] Edw. 2. See further appendix B below.

32 All three items are in the hand of Domville's habitual amanuensis, and retain an obsolete pagination, indicating they had probably been disbound from an earlier volume. See further intro. to Domville, 'Disquisition', pp 29–30.

33 P. Kelly, 'Sir Richard Bolton', *IHS*, 35 (2006), pp 3–4.

34 The only earlier material from the 'Declaration' concerned the 1177 grant of Ireland to John and an interpolation relating to the latter's 1210 grant of English law to Ireland. Cf. *The Case*, pp 40–1 and 44 app. crit.

35 That is from the start of the account of the re-enactment of Tudor English statutes (which drew heavily on the 'Declaration') to the first of the numbered concluding points (*The Case*, pp 71–150).

36 See MS TCD 888/1, f. 130r.

parliament of Ireland, not of his parliament of England') was largely confined to the final forty pages of the pamphlet, which suggests Molyneux may only have obtained access to it at a late stage in his writing. Two versions of the piece are found in his papers; the first contains extensive corrections and interpolations and was presumably written by the author, while the second is an exceptionally clean scribal copy.[37] There is, unfortunately, no indication as to who the author was, though clearly he was an experienced lawyer, and may indeed have been one of the 'good Friends' whom Molyneux informed Locke he had discussed the composition of his book with.[38] 'Legislative power in Ireland' was seemingly the source of the information about Irish representatives having occasionally attended parliament in England during the Middle Ages that gave rise to Molyneux's ambivalent reflection on the desirability of Ireland's being represented in the English parliament (see pp 36–7 above).[39] And as already stated, the paper also contributed to the discussion of appeals from Ireland to the English king's bench, where Molyneux used it to supplement material derived from Bolton's Declaration, as for example, in providing the reference to the Kelly case in Charles I's reign (*Case*, p. 132).

Printed Sources

As J.G. Simms has shown, Molyneux referred to a range of more than forty different printed authorities in *The Case* (several more than once).[40] Yet one must be careful not to regard these citations as evidence of his personal research, since by far the majority of these references were cited at one, or even two removes from the ostensible original. Credit for the scholarship displayed was frequently owing either to Domville's 'Disquisition' or to Bolton's 'Declaration', though what these two writers themselves cited was often derived from the works of Coke or other legal authorities.[41] To conclude from this that Molyneux was little more than a plagiarist would, however, be seriously misleading. Not only was it was necessary to draw on as wide a range of sources as possible when arguing a legal case, but Molyneux presented his borrowed arguments with skill and acumen. Indeed, his achievement appears all the more impressive, given that the pamphlet was, as he explained to Locke, very much written against the clock in order to have it in print before the end of the English parliamentary session.[42]

---

37 Autograph version, MS TCD 888/1, ff 127–30 (paginated 1–7), and scribal copy, ff 131–7 (last leaf blank).

38 Molyneux to Locke, 19 Apr. 1698: *Locke Corr.*, 2422.

39 Attributed in 'Legislative power in Ireland', f. 129v, to the Close Rolls of 5 Edw. 3, memb. 19 and 23.

40 See Simms, 'Introduction' in *The case of Ireland stated by William Molyneux* (Monkstown, Co. Dublin, 1977), pp 145–8, appendix C. The explanatory notes to *The Case* correct Simms' occasional misidentification of the particular work of an author that Molyneux cited, such as naming Walsingham's *Historia brevis* rather than *Ypodigma Neustriæ* (*The Case*, p. 37), or Dyer's *Abridgement* in place of his *Reports* (*The Case*, p. 116).

41 On occasion, Domville claimed he was citing archival material, when he was in fact copying Coke. Cf. *The Case*, p. 164 nn.

42 See p. 14 above.

Foremost among the (legal) authorities that Molyneux cited were Coke's *Institutes* and *Reports*, Prynne's *Brief animadversions on* [Coke's *4th Inst.*] (1669), Locke's *Two treatises of government* (1690), and the *Modus tenendi parliamenta et concilia in Hibernia* (1692) published by Molyneux's brother-in-law Anthony Dopping. His chief debts to historians were to the Expugnatio Hibernica of Giraldus Cambrensis, and the works of his contemporaries and supposed near contemporaries, Roger Hoveden, John Brompton and Matthew Paris, material that Molyneux had derived from Domville.[43] Molyneux's most extensive resort to a printed source was to Locke's *Two treatises of government* – in places, as we have seen, acknowledged and in others not. As regards more conventional legal literature, his greatest debt was to Coke's *Institutes* and *Reports*, though on occasion Molyneux strenuously rejected Coke's authority and subjected him to more outspoken criticism than any other authority he cited.[44] Next most important was William Prynne's *Animadversions*, though it was with Prynne that he took the greatest liberty in his handling of sources, in referring (*Case*, p. 56) to him for confirmation that Henry II had held a parliament in Ireland, oblivious of Prynne's subsequent qualification that this claim was 'a fabulous untruth'.[45] Other significant printed sources included the *Year Books* for the accounts of the Merchants of Waterford's case and that of John Pilkington (though Molyneux accessed both of these at second-hand through Domville and Bolton), and later legal reports such as those of Judge Hobart. What is easily overlooked because of its sheer obviousness was his very substantial debt to the statutes, both English and Irish.[46] Most of these references were taken from the printed versions, particularly the 1670 edition of Pulton's *Statutes* (possibly acquired by Molyneux as a law student in London), and Bolton's 1621 *Statutes of Ireland*, though very occasionally his statutory references were the fruit of manuscript research.[47] While Dopping's edition of the Irish *Modus* was the most recent work on which Molyneux drew extensively, he also referred to Joseph Keble's 1695 collection of English statutes. Immediately before the start of the conclusion of *The Case* (p. 150), he alluded to matters raised in the pamphlets connected with the Irish woollens controversy published the spring of 1698, though unfortunately failing to specify individual titles.[48] Among these works was almost certainly John Toland's *Letter from a gentleman* (1697), though it is not known whether Molyneux saw the original version published in London, or one of its London or Dublin reprints.[49] While

43 Though as has been shown, pp 55–6 above, the texts that Domville used for these sources were not always what he claimed them to be.
44 See pp 38–9 above.
45 Cf. Prynne, *Brief animadversions* (London, 1669), pp 249, 259. Of the seven allusions to the *Animadversions*, four were in the original text of the holograph, and the remainder added as interpolations in the printer's copy.
46 Cf. index of statutes cited in *The Case*, pp 307–10 below.
47 Pulton (ed.), *A Collection* (London, 1670), see p. 4, n. 12 above; and Bolton's continuation in *A collection of all the statutes* (Dublin, 1678). See also ref. to the MS Red Book of the Exchequer, *The Case*, p. 64.
48 For references to matters raised in these pamphlets of early 1698, see *The Case*, pp 143–8 nn.
49 See intro. pp 11–12, 15–16 above.

The Case may to some extent have been a direct response to the *Letter*, the latter was probably more significant for having launched the pamphlet controversy of early 1698, in which Molyneux's work came to play so signal and ultimately fatal a part.

The final point to be made in relation to Molyneux's printed sources is a negative one. Despite the frequent assertions that *The case of Ireland* was indebted to Patrick Darcy's 1641 *Argument*, there would seem to be no evidence to support this claim.[50] The section of Darcy's *Argument* that dealt with the issue of legislative independence was extremely short, adducing little by way of precedent and reasoned argument in its support.[51] The only area that might have constituted sufficient common ground to demonstrate a specific link between the two works was the question of appeals on writs of error to the English king's bench. However, the only reference common to both authors was Coke's report on Calvin's case, a precedent too widely cited to link Molyneux conclusively to Darcy's *Argument*.[52] More to the point was the absence of any overlap between the other three cases cited by Molyneux in connection with appeals and the three referred to by Darcy. The claim that Molyneux was heavily indebted to Darcy would seem to have originated in Davis' *Patriot parliament*, a work determined to establish continuity between the Protestant patriot tradition of Molyneux, Swift, Grattan and Tone, and the Catholic Confederation of the 1640s and the Jacobite parliament of 1689.[53]

II. THE MANUSCRIPTS OF *THE CASE*

Uniquely for an Irish printed work from the age of the hand press, not only does the author's holograph of *The Case* survive but also the manuscript copy used by the printer to set the book. Although examples are known of printers' copies of various English works from the age of the hand press, no others have yet been discovered for this period in Ireland.[54] What is even rarer, however, is to have access to the complete run of holograph, printer's copy and first edition of a book, not only for what this shows about an individual writer's and printer's practices but for the light which these throw on the nature of printing practices at the time. The provenance of both holograph and printer's copy can be traced in an unbroken line

---

50 Cf. McIlwain, *American Revolution* (New York, 1973), p. 35; Robbins, *Commonwealthman* (Cambridge, MA, 1959), p. 139; Simms, *William Molyneux* (Dublin, 1982), p. 102; O'Malley, 'Patrick Darcy' in Ó Cearbhaill (ed.), *Galway* (Dublin, 1984), pp 106–7; Boyce, *Nationalism* (London, 1991), pp 102–3; Caldicott's intro. to Darcy, *An Argument* (1992), p. 201; and York, *Neither Kingdom* (Washington, DC, 1994), p. 26. The case for Darcy's influence appeared rather more persuasive when he was still believed to have written the 1644 'Declaration'.

51 Cf. A. Clarke, 'Patrick Darcy' in Ohlmeyer, *Political thought* (Cambridge, 2000), p. 48.

52 *The Case*, pp 132–4; Darcy, *An Argument* (1992), p. 271; Bolton, 'Declaration', pp 15–16.

53 Davis, *The patriot parliament* (London, 1893), pp 139–40, 152. Cf. Leerssen, *Mere Irish and Fior-Ghael* (Amsterdam, 1993), p. 343.

54 For this reason a somewhat lengthier description is given of the printer's copy than of the holograph or the first edition.

from Molyneux to the present day. After his death in 1698, they passed with the rest of his papers and books to his son Samuel Molyneux, who transferred them to England where he went to live permanently in 1712. On Samuel's death in 1728 the books were inherited by his wife Lady Elizabeth (Capel), who shortly after her remarriage sold the bulk of the Molyneux library (as accumulated over three generations by Samuel the elder, William, and Samuel the younger), at an auction in London in 1730 lasting for thirteen days, conducted by the bookseller, John Wilcox.[55] Among the buyers recorded in the auctioneer's marked catalogue was Claudius Gilbert (vice provost of Trinity College, Dublin), who acquired among other purchases:

> A Collection of Original Letters sent to and written by William Molyneux D.D. [an error for LL.D., also found elsewhere in catalogue] and the Hon. Samuel Molyneux, relating to writing a Natural History of Ireland; with two large Folio MSS curiously writ, as if designed for the Press …[56]

One of the two manuscripts referred to was almost certainly the printer's copy of *The Case*, written in the distinctive hand of Molyneux's long-standing amanuensis, while the other was probably the latter's transcription of Domville's 'Disquisition'. On Gilbert's death in 1743 his Molyneux purchases were bequeathed along with the rest of his books to Trinity College Library, arriving just too late for inclusion in Lyon's original manuscripts catalogue of 1745.[57] The Molyneux material was, however, subsequently listed in Henry Monck Mason's manuscripts catalogue of 1814, which also identified the 'Disquisition' as a source of *The Case*.[58] Trinity's Molyneux papers were subsequently reorganized in the early 1840s, when the various pieces associated with *The Case* were rebound in a single volume (now TCD MS 890).[59]

The holograph

The holograph manuscript of *The Case* is in MS TCD 890, ff 66r–155r. It contains the complete text of the pamphlet, apart from the preface to the reader which is found only in the printer's copy. Molyneux's initial draft of the main text was written on thirty-seven numbered, folio quires, measuring 30.0 cm by 20.0 cm, with an Arms of Amsterdam watermark.[60] The interpolated sheets (which included

55 For the sale and details of the auction, see P. Kelly, 'The one that got away' in Vaughan (ed.), *The Old Library* (Dublin, 2013). Wilcox's marked catalogue is in the Hyde Collection of the Houghton Library, Harvard University (shelf mark B 1827.578); it recorded prices and most purchasers' names.

56 *Molyneux library catalogue*, p. 78, 'Manuscripts' sect., item 25. See further P. Kelly, 'The one that got away' in Vaughan (ed.), *The Old Library* (Dublin, 2012), p. 98.

57 TCD MS Mun Lib/1/53; Lyon's original catalogue only extended to classis G; the Molyneux papers were included in the subsequently added classis I.

58 TCD MS Mun Lib/1/55/1–6.

59 Information for which I am indebted to the late keeper of manuscripts, William O'Sullivan.

60 Quire 37 was only a single leaf.

the dedication to the king) were also mostly on quired sheets (with a few single leaves), measuring 23.0 cm by 17.5 cm. Some of these have the same Arms of Amsterdam watermark as the main text and others a post-horn watermark also found in the quires of the printer's copy manuscript, while the interpolated quire ff 143–4 has the 'P IOLLY' watermark found in the quires of prefatory matter in the printer's copy.[61] An unusual feature of the holograph is that while Molyneux began by writing on both the recto and verso of the folio quires containing his original text, from quires f. 84 to f. 109 he wrote only on the recto. From f. 110 to f. 121 he reverted to using both sides of the leaf, and maintained this practice for the rest of the manuscript with the exception of ff 129–32 and ff 140–5, and the single leaf f. 155, which were once more written only on the recto. While writers at this time often wrote their initial drafts on the recto leaves of their manuscript so as to leave space for interpolations on the facing verso pages, rather than using the blank versos for this purpose Molyneux added his lengthy interpolations on separate (smaller) quires, such as ff 66–72, 87–8 and 143–4. An explanation for this unusual format may be that in originally transcribing the holograph Molyneux brought together earlier fragmentary drafts, some virtually complete and others in need of further expansion – a hypothesis seemingly corroborated by the fact that fewer changes made in the course of transcription are found in the parts of the holograph written on both recto and verso of the leaves. Subsequently, however, he extensively emended the holograph and added several lengthy interpolations (some on separate sheets), though only at one point have the changes been so intensive as to require the rewriting of a whole page (presumably to facilitate transcribing the printer's copy).[62] In general the handwriting of the holograph is fairly easy to decipher, though certain habits such as Molyneux's occasional leaving the tops of 'a's open and his tendency to render the letters 'C', 'M' and 'L' as capitals can be confusing. Further comment on such details will be found in the note on the transcription of manuscripts (p. 71 below).

The printer's copy

It is necessary to begin by explaining why what until 1976 was described merely as a scribal 'fair copy' of *The Case* (and accordingly considered of little interest) is now identified as the actual manuscript from which the text of Molyneux's pamphlet was set by the printer.[63] The main reason is that the manuscript has been marked up for 'casting off'; that is directions have been inserted to indicate the start of the different sheets of the printed edition, while in the sections

---

61 See p. 66 below.
62 Namely, the material on the Merchants of Waterford's case in ff 119–20 (corresponding to p. 92, n. 2 to p. 95, n. 1. of the text below).
63 The term 'fair copy' originated with Monck Mason's 1814 catalogue, and was repeated in Abbott, *Catalogue* (Dublin, 1900), s.v. MS 890; see also Simms' introduction to the 1977 Cadenus Press edition of *The Case*, p. 13. Interestingly, the *Molyneux library catalogue* had referred to manuscripts 'writ, as if designed for the Press'. Cf. p. 63 above.

corresponding to sheets A, C, D and F, the divisions corresponding to the inner and out formes of the printing process have also been indicated. Such subdivision was unusual by English standards, and perhaps reflected the need to employ additional, less-skilled workers to cope with what by Dublin standards was a large printing job, which needed to be carried out quickly.[64] The fact that a small number of these divisions do not coincide precisely with the signatures of the printed text, confirms that this involved the marking up of the 'takes' by the master printer or foreman before the typesetter began work, rather than reflecting divisions corresponding to pages already set.[65] Although the marks for casting off into sheets and formes provide the main evidence for concluding that the 'fair copy' was the manuscript from which the type was actually set, there is also further corroborating evidence. Instructions relating to the printing are found in three specific places, namely ff 161–2, 192v and 212r–v, while in many other places there are traces of printer's ink, including four distinct inky fingerprints, on ff 164v, 180r, 213v and 225r.[66] There are also a number of miscellaneous marks, mostly in pencil, perhaps indicating where a compositor broke off temporarily in the course of setting the material.[67]

The printer's copy of *The Case* is an elaborately penned manuscript in the hand of Molyneux's long-term amanuensis, which bears out the *Molyneux library catalogue*'s commendation of his work as 'finely writ'.[68] It consists of 175 numbered pages, made up of folded quires with a margin on all four sides ruled in red ink, together with a small number of interpolated sheets, some in Molyneux's hand and some in that of the amanuensis. Also unnumbered are the two quires of prefatory material, namely the titlepage, the dedication to the king, and the preface to the reader.[69] The numbered pages measure 24.0 cm by 18.5 cm, and the margins are ½ ins, except in the case of the outer margins which are 1½ ins in order to accommodate marginal headings, source references and occasional comments as found in the 1698 edition.[70] The interpolated sheets in the hand of the amanuensis also measure 24.0 cm by 18.5 cm, while those in Molyneux's hand are only 18.0 cm by 12.0 cm. The paper used for the main text and the interpolated sheets has the

64 For a detailed description of the marking-up process, see Moxon, *Mechanick exercises* (London, 1962), pp 240–4; and further Gaskill, *A new introduction* (Oxford, 1974), pp 40–2.

65 In three instances the discrepancy between the 'takes' and the material as actually set has subsequently been corrected in pencil.

66 TCD MS 890, ff 162r, 192v, 212v; the brief instructions are noted in app. crit. for *The Case*, pp 1, 60 and 94.

67 For a more detailed consideration of the printer's copy, see P. Kelly, 'The printer's copy', *Long Room*, 18–19 (1979), pp 7–9.

68 E.g. folio lot no. 98 (Molyneux's compendium of parliamentary journals, now TCD MS 622); *Molyneux library catalogue*, p. 9. Unfortunately, it has not been possible to establish his identity.

69 The prefatory quires have similar margins to the main text, though ruled in grey pencil rather than red ink; the smaller interpolated sheets lack margins.

70 Margin measurements are given in inches, as these are the units that would have originally determined their width.

same post-horn watermark as that of the 1698 edition. An interpolated sheet (f. 71) bearing this watermark has a deleted note on the back reading '999 Common Paper for the Ordinary Sale'.[71] The two quires of prefatory material were written on a superior-quality paper with the Arms of Amsterdam and the legend 'P IOLLY' as the watermark. The reference to 'the Ordinary Sale' suggests Molyneux may have considered using this superior paper for the presentation copies. No such paper has, however, been found in those that have so far come to light, which are merely large paper copies (with an identical tooled-calf binding) printed on the same paper as the copies for sale.[72]

Unfortunately, however, the printer's copy is no longer complete; at some stage, pp 149–58, and 161–72 (which correspond to p. 151, n. 2 to p. 160, n. 3, and pp 162, n. 1 to p. 172, n. 6 of this edition) have become detached from the manuscript. Whether this was due to a mishap at the printers, or the pages were mislaid after being returned to the author, is not known. However, collation of these pages of the printed text with the holograph reveals only a small number of substantive changes from the final (i.e. corrected) reading of the latter. Although it is conceivable that Molyneux may have made emendations to these missing pages, which he subsequently rejected, it is fortunate that the losses should only have occurred where there are so few differences between the reading of the holograph and that of the first edition. Apart from the interpolations added on separate sheets, the printer's copy contains numerous interpolations and deletions in the original text, slightly more than half of which are in Molyneux's own hand. Some of these changes are also found in the holograph, showing that Molyneux continued to amend it even after the transcription of the printer's copy. Also added in the margins of the printer's copy are the vast majority of the marginal headings, reference notes, and occasional comments found in the margins of the first edition. Much, however, of this marginal material was copied from the holograph, while some of the holograph's marginalia can in turn be traced back to Domville's 'Disquisition'.

III. THE FIRST EDITION OF 1698

As can be seen from the apparatus criticus, the reading of the first edition of *The Case* differs in several places from the final, i.e., corrected, text of the printer's copy. Leaving aside trivial errors by the printer, most of the changes are fairly minor – altering singulars to plurals (or vice versa), amending the use of prepositions, inserting definite articles or single words for the sake of clarity, and more occasionally adjusting the division into paragraphs. Substantive changes amount to around half a dozen, such as altering the reference at the end of the dedication from 'our Brethren of England' to 'our Friends ...', or restoring the

---

71 See further p. 68 below.
72 See list of presentation copies, p. 80 below.

phrase towards the foot of p. 109 marked out (probably in error) by the printer. The restricted nature of these changes suggests that while Molyneux exercised oversight of the printing, the imperative to get the work into circulation before the end of the English parliamentary session pre-empted him from more extensive alteration of the text.

The printing history of the 1698 edition is somewhat complicated. Not only is it found in three issues but it was also subject to in-press correction, with sheets D and G being found in two different states.[73] The printer, Joseph Ray, who had served his apprenticeship in England, had an earlier connection with Molyneux as printer to the Dublin Philosophical Society in the 1680s.[74] By the standards of Dublin printing in the 1690s, *The Case* was a substantial piece of work, and it may well have taxed Ray's capabilities to produce it in the little more than two weeks from the original dating of the preface on 26 March to the appearance of the completed and bound work around the middle of April 1698.

The most notable feature of the first edition of *The Case* is that it is found with three different states of the titlepage. The earliest is distinguishable by the swash 'M' in Molyneux, and the imprint '*Dublin*, Printed for Joseph Ray, and are to be Sold at his Shop in Skinner-Row. MDCXVIII.' This was the version of the pamphlet that went on sale in Dublin, and was used by Molyneux for presentation copies. Sheets D and G were both reissued correcting a series of minor errors on pages 34, 37, 41 and 48 in D, and pages 83, 90 and 94 in G. The changes made in G would seem to be earlier than those in D, as the corrected version of G occurs in the majority of presentation copies along with the original version of sheet D. Two in-press corrections are also found: the first, on p. 15, line 16, corrected 'his Prerogative' to 'their Prerogative' in most but not all printed versions (a correction strangely enough also found in the printer's copy manuscript), while similarly an error in the marginal heading on p. 45, line 1, reading 'concessiom' has been corrected to 'concessions' in some copies. All except one of the copies examined have also been corrected by hand to read 'Jornal' in place of 'Jornal/-lensis' on p. 11, lines 11–12.

The second issue of the titlepage was substantively different from the first, with an imprint reading '*Dublin*, Printed by and for *J.R.* And are to be Sold by *Rob. Clavel*, and *A.* and *J. Churchil*, Booksellers in *London*, 1698'.[75] It may be assumed that this was the titlepage intended for the English publication of *The Case*, the appearance of which Molesworth managed to forestall before 21 May.[76] This London titlepage is found both as a cancellans, and as integral to quire A. It is not

73 For details, see further checklist of printings, p. 78 below.

74 See Pollard (ed.), *A Dictionary* (London, 2000), s.v. Joseph Ray.

75 Though the Churchills were Locke's publishers, and had distributed copies of *The Case* for Molyneux in Apr. 1698 (cf. p. 14 above), the latter's business dealings with them went back to 1688: Arber, *Term Catalogues* (London, 1903), i, p. 216. Robert Clavel had brought out William King's *State of the Protestants* in 1691 and continued to act for him throughout the decade.

76 See pp 14, 17 above.

known how many copies were intended to be issued of the London edition, though Methuen informed Galway that the English customs had seized a hundred copies of the pamphlet (presumably with this titlepage) on 24 May.[77] Finally the third version of the titlepage lacks a swash 'M' for Molyneux, and has the original Dublin imprint, with some copies having an accidental space between the M and D of the date 'MDCXCVIII'. This second Dublin version of the titlepage would seem to be an attempt to make good the losses of the proposed London issue, and like the latter is found with its titlepage sometimes as a cancellans and sometimes as integral to quire A. Molyneux's note, referred to above, reading '999 Common Paper for the Ordinary Sale' suggests that the initial print run was roughly a thousand copies, which would have been normal for a pamphlet of this kind in the late seventeenth century. It is not known whether the considerable interest that the pamphlet generated led to the printing of further copies, though it is unlikely that Ray had the resources to keep the type for its fourteen quires standing for any considerable length of time.

IV. THE CHOICE OF COPY-TEXT

As there is no evidence that the second or any subsequent edition of *The Case* was set from a version corrected by the author, or embodied authorial corrections, the choice of copy-text for this edition has been straightforward, namely the first edition of 1698. The specific copy which has served as the basis for the text is that in the Trinity College Library, shelf mark OLS B-9-141 (formerly 190.s.135). This has been collated with the three other copies of the 1698 edition in the library, as well as the five copies in the National Library of Ireland; the two copies in the Gilbert Library, Dublin; the two copies in Marsh's Library, Dublin; and the two copies in the Royal Irish Academy Library. In all, some three dozen copies of the 1698 edition have been examined for textual variants. I am conscious that this represents only a tiny proportion of the thousand or so copies envisaged for the first edition, and that it is possible that further in-press variants may yet come to light. None of the copies inspected contained any form of printed errata list.

V. PRESENTING THE TEXT OF *THE CASE*

Deciding how best this edition of *The Case* should be presented on the page has involved finding the appropriate balance between maintaining the formal features of the first edition and meeting the requirements of readers for a diverse range of background information, while still producing an easily readable text. The extensive marginalia of the 1698 edition (in the form of headings indicating topics under discussion, and Molyneux's notes and references to sources) needed to be correlated with the editorial apparatus showing variants in the manuscripts, the

77 See p. 17, n. 80 above.

explanatory notes providing background information, as well as translations of the numerous passages in Latin, required by modern readers. Since relegating the apparatus and explanatory notes to the back of the book would have greatly reduced their utility for readers, it has been decided to present this editorial material, together with the English translations, on the same page as Molyneux' s text, while maintaining a clear distinction between the original text and editorial annotation. This has been achieved by reproducing the pagination and general layout (though not the lineation) of the text of the first edition, including retaining the marginalia in the outer margin of the pages. Doing so has made it possible to locate the English translations in the otherwise blank inner margins,[78] thus enabling the editorial apparatus and explanatory notes to be placed below the text at the foot of the page. It must be emphasized that the ensuing text is in no way intended as a quasi-facsimile reproduction of the first edition of *The Case*.[79] Not only is it a fresh critical edition, with editorial amendments and correction of the errors in the 1698 text, but the format adopted for its presentation is considered the most suitable for meeting the needs of both general readers and scholars concerned with the evolution of Molyneux's work.

The text of *The Case*, reproducing the pagination of the 1698, is presented below, accompanied by:

1.   Molyneux's marginal headings, printed in bold in the outer margins
2.   Molyneux's marginal notes and references, printed in the outer margins
3.   Translations of passages in Latin, which are printed within square brackets in the inner margins, keyed (where necessary) to the relevant Latin extract by asterisks
4.   The apparatus criticus, which is printed subjacent to the text
5.   The explanatory notes, which are printed below the apparatus criticus

The printed text of *The Case*, and the marginal headings and notes

1.   The page numbers of the 1698 edn are indicated at the top of each reproduced page, within square brackets, e.g. [17].
2.   The titlepage: relative type sizes, styles and layout have been reproduced.
3.   A complete list of Molyneux's marginal headings has been inserted at the beginning of the text, as these serve to bring out the structure of *The Case* as the author conceived it. No such list featured, however, in the published text.
4.   Ligatures: printer's ligatures, such as 'st' have been ignored, except for 'æ' in Latin passages (which generally reproduces MS practice).

---

78 Thanks to the skill of the typesetter, all translations have been accommodated within the relevant inner margins, other than where a Latin extract itself extends to a further page.

79 Consideration was initially given to presenting a continuous text of *The Case* that incorporated both the marginalia and the translations in the main body of the text, and placed the apparatus and explanatory notes at the foot of the page. This option, which would have involved breaking up the text with marginal headings and references, was rejected as unnecessarily confusing for readers, even if the marginalia were printed in a different font.

5. Minor errors in the copy-text have been corrected, and the erroneous reading noted in the subjacent apparatus. This includes occasional errors in references to statutes, both English and Irish.

6. Use of the long 'ʃ' has not been reproduced. Long 'ʃ's at beginning of words have been rendered as lower case, other than at the beginning of a sentence or of proper nouns.

7. The double quotation marks commencing each line of the lengthy Latin extracts on pp 29, 33, 47–8, 49–51 and 52–3 have not been reproduced.

8. The gaps between paragraphs in the main text of *The Case* have been closed up, though those in the dedication and preface to the reader have been retained.

9. The following features should be noted as regards the reproduction of italicization in the 1698 edn (except for titlepage): swash capitals in italic type have been ignored; occasional use of italic colons with roman type has been ignored; the practice of setting the apostrophe and following 's' of the possessive form of italicized words (esp. proper nouns) in roman type, e.g. '*Ireland*'s', has not been reproduced; the 1698 edn does not use italic numerals, nor generally speaking, italic punctuation.

10. Catchwords have been ignored, except where the catchword differs from the first word of the following page. Such differences may help provide indications as to how the 1698 edn was set by the printers.

11. The few corrections of minor printer's errors introduced in the revised states of sheets D and G of the 1698 edition (cf. list of printings of *The Case*, p. 80) are noted in the apparatus, as are the small number of other in-press corrections.

The recording of variant readings in the manuscripts of *The Case*

Basic Principles

1. Variant readings in the manuscripts recorded in the subjacent apparatus represent substantive differences from the copy-text in either William Molyneux's holograph or the copy transcribed for the printer. Two sets of pages, however, are missing from the printer's copy (cf. intro. p. 66), corresponding to p. 151, n. 2 to p. 160, n. 3 and p. 162 , n. 1 to p. 172, n. 6 of the present text, thus making it possible to record only variants in the holograph for these pages.

2. Variants are noted in all instances where the final (i.e. corrected) manuscript reading differs from the printed text, other than the minor exceptions described in (5) and (9) below. Such changes – especially if substantive – may represent Molyneux's amendments at proof stage.

3. Substantive changes within the manuscript texts are also recorded.

4. Minor variations or accidental differences in the manuscripts have not in general been noted. This particularly applies to the printer's copy, where the

accidental dropping of a word, or the writing of it twice, have not been corrected by Molyneux or his amanuensis.

5. Variations in the use of contracted forms of sovereigns' names etc. are not noted (such variants are particularly common in references to statutes, *Year Books* and other records).

6. In order to illustrate manuscript practice, the actual contractions employed in the manuscript are reproduced when noting variant readings (e.g. 'ye Parlmt of Engld'), with the exception that superscript abbreviations are printed on line.

7. Catchwords in manuscripts have not been noted. Catchwords are employed in the printer's copy, but only occasionally in the holograph.

8. The foliation and/or page numbers of manuscripts have not been noted, except in the app. crit. to indicate where page(s) of addenda have been inserted. Such adscititious material is identified by the appropriate foliation number(s).

9. Ampersands in Latin citations do not reproduce manuscript practice, which consistently employs 'et' in both the holograph and the printer's copy.

10. The apparatus also lists variants in the citations from Giraldus' Expugnatio Hibernica in *The Case* (pp 9–10), from the reading of the text in *Anglica, Hibernica ... a veteribus scripta*, ed. William Camden (Frankfurt, 1603). These variants establish that the extracts come from an abbreviated manuscript version of Expugnatio Hibernica, not from the 1603 edition, which *The Case* (p. 16) implies was the text used by Molyneux. See further intro. pp 55–6.

Additional observations relating to the manuscripts

1. Molyneux's handwriting is reasonably easy to decipher, though his habit of occasionally leaving the top of 'a's open can lead to confusion with 'u's. That of the amanuensis of the printer's copy is extremely clear.

2. The vast majority of changes in the printer's copy (other than corrections of minor errors of transcription) are in Molyneux's hand. Substantive changes in the hand of the amanuensis are identified by the siglum '*aman.*' A very small number of corrections in heavy black ink have been made in a hand which is neither that of Molyneux nor that of his amanuensis. These are probably to be identified as the work of the person who 'marked up' the printer's copy in preparation for setting the type.

3. The marking up of the printer's copy by 'casting off' into quires, and occasionally formes, is not noted in the apparatus (see further intro. pp 64–5), though the very few printer's instructions relating to changes in wording are shown.

4. Most of the marginal headings, marginal notes, and marginal source references in the printer's copy have been added by Molyneux himself, usually in emphatic style rather than his normal cursive. Attention is drawn in the notes to the marginalia in the hand of the amanuensis, as well as to the small number of marginalia copied from the holograph. It has not been

thought necessary to indicate which marginalia in the holograph come from Domville's 'Disquisition' (though many of those in the passages based on Domville can be traced back to the 'Disquisition').

5. Most of the underlining to italicize material in the holograph was added at various stages subsequent to the original writing. While much of this interpolated italicization was reproduced in the printer's copy, some italicization was dropped, and further italicization added. Finally, additional italicization was introduced in the printed text, mostly for proper nouns and adjectives, etc. and is thus probably attributable to the printer. The extent of changes in italicization at these various stages is such that recording them in the apparatus has not been considered practicable.

The system for the recording of variant readings from the manuscripts in the apparatus criticus

Variant readings and changes in MSS

1. A superscript footnote indicator number in the main text indicates that a variant reading is recorded at that point.
2. In the apparatus the keyword, or keywords, of the printed text are given after the appropriate footnote number, followed by a right-hand square bracket which marks off the variant reading and the appropriate siglum or sigla (in bold) to denote the source(s). All other readings are to be taken to agree with the printed text (though not necessarily its spelling or capitalization).
3. Where more than one variant is recorded for a given keyword, or keywords, the earliest version comes immediately following the square bracket, with the other reading(s) marked off from the first siglum by an upright line, thus '|'.
4. The following conventions are used to indicate variant readings:
   — The caret ‹∧› is employed after a word to indicate the absence of punctuation in one version, where that word is followed by the punctuation mark shown for another reading.
   — *not in* – indicates that the keyword(s) noted in the present text are not found in an earlier version.
5. The following conventions are used to indicate changes in MSS:
   — [abc] – the letters 'abc' are deleted in the MS.
   — `abc´ – the letters 'abc' have been interpolated in the MS.
   — a̱ḇc̱ – the letters 'abc' are doubtful in MS reading.
   — […] abc – the letters 'abc' are preceded by an illegible deletion.
   — [[abc]]cde – the letters 'abc' have been deleted by the superimposition of the letters 'cde'.
   — [[…]]abc – the letters 'abc' have been superimposed on deleted letters which are now illegible.
   — <abc> – the letters 'abc' have been supplied editorially.
   — {abc} – the letters 'abc' have been deleted editorially.

— Editorial comment, such as an indication that an interpolation is written in the margin or added on a separate sheet, is given in italics within parentheses before the source siglum in bold.

— Where an unfinished word is deleted and what was intended is clear from the surrounding material, the word is completed within angular brackets, e.g. '[con<cern>]'. Where a conjectural completion is offered, the deleted letters are repeated (within parenthesis) and followed by '*perhaps for*' and the conjectural reading, e.g. '([co] *perhaps for* [co<ncern>])'.

Sigla indicating the source of variant readings

1. **H** denotes Molyneux's holograph (MS TCD 890, ff 66–155).
2. **PC** denotes the printer's copy (MS TCD 890, ff 156–246).
3. **I** denotes the 1698 edn.
4. **ed** denotes an editorial emendment of the reading of the copy-text.
5. **Domville** denotes the reading of Domville's 'Disquisition', cited to indicate the basis for an editorial amendment.

In the case of the heavily amended holograph page (f. 120r – dealing with Hussey's verdict in the Merchants of Waterford's case), which has been rewritten as fair-copy (f. 119r–v) by Molyneux, the additional sigla **H orig** and **H f/copy** are used to indicate the original holograph version and the holograph fair-copy readings respectively (see *Case*, pp 92–5, app. crit.).

Examples

1. (*The Case*, p. 3, n.1) 'that] [the least] `that´ **H**' means that where the text as printed reads 'that', the words 'the least' were deleted in the holograph, and 'that' interpolated in their place.
2. (*The Case*, p. 45, n. 8) '*Dat.*] *Dat.* **H & PC** | *Dat*∧ **I**' means that where the word '*Dat*' in the text as printed is followed by a full stop, as is the case in the holograph and the printer's copy, the reading of the 1698 edition has no punctuation mark.
3. (*The Case*, p. 119, n. 2) 'constitute] make **H** | [make] `constitute´ **PC**' means that where the printed text reads 'constitute', the holographs reads 'make'; 'make' was deleted in the printer's copy, and 'constitute' interpolated in its place.
4. (*The Case*, p. 59, n. 4) '4 *marginal ref.*] *in* **H** | (*manu aman.*) **PC**' means that the marginal reference source in the printed text '**(a) Selden Notæ & specileg. ad eadmerum, pag. 171.**' is found in the holograph, and is written in the hand of the amanuensis in the printer's copy.
5. (*The Case*, p. 88, n. 1) '*Rome*] Ro[[man]] me **H**' means that where the printed text reads 'Rome', the 'me' of 'Rome' in the holograph has been super-imposed on three indistinct letters, which apparently read 'man'.

6. (*The Case*, p. 89, n. 3) '*Privy* … well] [[C<ouncil>]] Privy Council … `as well' H' means that where the text as printed reads '*Privy Council in England*; which appears as well', in the holograph 'Privy' is superimposed on 'C', which from what follows was clearly intended for 'Council', and 'as well' was subsequently added by interpolation.

7. (*The Case*, p. 39, n. 5) 'Patriæ] Patriæ **ed** | Patrio **H, PC & I** | (Patriæ **Domville, 12**)' indicates that the reading 'Patriæ' in the printed text has been preferred for editorial reasons (namely the reading of Domville's 'Disquisition', p. 12) to 'Patrio' as found in the holograph, printer's copy and 1698 edn.

Explanatory notes

The explanatory notes serve to identify works cited in the text, provide information about lesser known individuals, documents, institutions and events, and clarify the meaning of obscure words, or unusual usage of common words. The notes also point to cross references in Molyneux's text, draw attention to the use of sources, especially manuscripts, and illustrate objections raised in the five contemporary responses to *The Case* (intro. pp 20–3). Attention is also drawn to the more significant changes in the manuscripts, as noted in the apparatus criticus. In addition, the notes indicate the passages that the commons committee of inquiry into *The Case* in June 1698 identified as 'denying the Authority of the Parliament of *England* over *Ireland*' (intro. p. 18). N.B. Cross–references to *The Case* continue to be to the 1698 pagination (printed at the top of the page).

Translation of material in Latin

When the ninth edition of *The Case* appeared in Belfast in 1776, the editor sought to extend its circulation by 'procur[ing] the *Latin* quotations to be carefully translated … in order to make it level to the understanding of all'.[80] Over two hundred years later the need for translations of the numerous passages cited in Latin remains as pressing, and they appear in the inner margins.[81]

The translations in general reproduce the fairly free versions in the Dublin edition of 1782 (which are superior to those of its 1776 predecessor).[82] Editorial amendments have only been made where the 1782 version is significantly misleading.[83] The most frequent changes have been to render *miles* as 'knight' rather than 'esquire'; *vicomes* as 'sheriff' rather than 'viscount';[84] *gratanter* as

---

80 *The Case*, 1776 edn, publisher's advertisement.

81 The 1782 edn prints only the English translation of the extracts cited, omitting the Latin original.

82 The 1782 translation's shortcomings can be seen from its translation of the title of Bartolomaeus Anglicus' encyclopedia *De proprietatibus rerum* (On the properties of things) as 'Concerning the Rights of States'. Cf. *The Case*, p. 43 nn.

83 Editorial changes to the 1782 translation are not listed in the app. crit.

84 Cf. Selden's objection to the authenticity of the Irish Modus on the ground that it employed the term '*vicecomes*', though sheriffs were not introduced in Ireland till King John's reign: *The Case*, pp 31–2 nn.

'freely' rather than 'cheerfully'; *magnates* as 'magnates' rather than 'grandees'; and *ministri* as 'officers' rather than 'magistrates'. Though strict consistency might seem desirable in translating apparently technical terms such as *fidelitas* as 'fealty', or *subjectio* as 'submission'; and *homagio* as 'homage', medieval usage by historians and chroniclers was fairly fluid, and I have not sought to impose greater consistency than the 1782 translator.[85] Nor has the 1782 use of italics for proper names etc. been followed.

In a few places Molyneux himself translated parts of the Latin passages that he cited. Although these versions may sometimes seem rather impressionistic (even by comparison with the 1782 translation), unless his wording is seriously misleading no further translation is provided.

Transcriptions from manuscript in the appendices

The expansion of abbreviations, handling of the long 'ſ', and omission of catchwords follow the method for recording manuscript variants set out on p. 70 above. Occasional missing letters, or link words which have had to be added editorially, are printed within angular brackets, e.g. '<not>'.

---

85 This is particularly significant in relation to whether the Irish submission to Henry II involved feudal homage, cf. *The Case*, p. 9 and nn.

Marginal headings in *The Case*[1]

This complete list of Molyneux's marginal headings serves to elucidate the structure of *The Case* as the author conceived it.

1 Italics in the headings, as printed in the text of *The Case*, are not reproduced.

---

2   Inconvenient – i.e. dangerous, cf. p. 171 nn. below.

Checklist of printings of *The Case*[1]

1. 1698 edition. Dublin. 8vo.[2]

Titlepage	[within double rules] | THE | CASE | OF | IRELAND' s | Being BOUND by | Acts of Parliament | IN | ENGLAND, | Stated. | [rule] | BY | *William Molyneux*, |of *Dublin*, Eſq; | [rule] | *Dublin*, Printed by *Joseph Ray*, and are | to be Sold at his Shop in *Skin-*| *ner-Row*. MDCXCVIII.
Collation	8o. A–M8.
Pagination	(16) + 1–174 + (175–6 blank).
Contents	A1r: title (verso blank). A2r: [two rules] 'TO THE | KING.' | signed A5r: 'William Molyneux.' A5v, blank. A6r: [two rules] | 'PREFACE | TO THE | READER.' signed, A8r, '*Dublin, Febr.* 8. | 1697/8 | W. MOLYNEUX. [RULE]. A8v, blank. B1r, [two rules] 'The CASE | OF | Ireland's | Being Bound by | Acts of Parliament | IN | ENGLAND, | STATED.' M7v, [rule] 'FINIS.' | [rule].
Additional details	Post-horn watermark (see intro. pp 65–6). Published shortly before 16 April 1698 (see intro. p. 14). Price '00–02–06', recorded on titlepage of copy belonging to 'Jn Lindon, 1698', RIA: shelf mark MR/16/N21.
Three states of the titlepage	(1a) as above; (1b) Imprint reads '*Dublin*, Printed by and for *J.R.* And are to be | Sold by *Rob. Clavel*, and *A.* and *J. Chur-* | *chil*, Bookſellers in *London*. 1698.'; and (1c) Cancellans reset version of 1a, with non-swash *M* for *Molyneux*, and imprint 'MDCXCVIII.'[3] For the different states, see further intro. p. 67 above.

1   A full bibliographical description is provided for the first three edns to 1719; less detail is given for later edns, in particular attention is no longer drawn to use of the long 'ſ' or line endings in titles.
2   The description of the 1698 edn draws on unpublished work generously made available by the late Mary Pollard.
3   The NLI copy, shelf mark Dix 1698 (12), has a cancellans titlepage with a swash 'M' for Molyneux.

Sheets D	• (p. 34) D1v, line 12 ends	'no-'	'noſtrum'
and G	• (p. 37) D3r, line 1⁴	'Cashal'	'Cashel'
variant	• (p. 41) D5r, catchword	'Brother'	'Bro-'
states			
(original,	• (p. 48) D8v, catchword	'land,'	'land'
revised)	• (p. 83) G2r, line 30	'Wisemnn'	'Wiseman'
	• (p. 90) G5v, line 1	'Yeat-Books'	'Year-Books'
	• (p. 94) G7v, line 5	'reciv'd'	'receiv'd'⁵

In-press   p. 15, line 16, 'this Prerogative' emended to 'their Prerogative'. N.B.
emendation The printer's copy has been similarly emended: '[this] `their'.
Uncorrected copy, RIA, Halliday Pamphlets, 7(1).

Misprints   • p. 11, lines 11–12 'Jorna-/lenſis' corrected in MS to 'Jornal' *all*
and in-press *copies seen, except one.*
corrections   • p. 45, line 1, marginal heading, 'Concessiom' *corrected to*
'Concessions' *in several copies.*
• p. 88, marginal note, line 8, 'Or[space]dinatio' *uncorrected all copies*
seen.
• p. 125, line 16 'the of Prior *Mollingar' uncorrected all copies seen.*
• p. 157, line 22 'diſuſs'd' (recte discuss'd) *uncorrected all copies seen.*

Presentation The following presentation copies are known:
copies
• John Locke – Bodleian Library, Oxford: shelf mark Locke 9. 79a.
• Thomas Molyneux – Gilbert Library, Dublin: shelf mark GC3
Shelf 1 (30).
• Bishop William King – NLI: shelf mark LO 2589 Bd (rebound,
and presented to the Earl of Charlemont, 1818)
• Bishop Foy of Waterford – NLI: shelf mark Thom 32341.
• Elie Bouhéreau – Marsh's Library, Dublin: shelf mark R 2.5.3.
• William Robinson – Marsh's Library, Dublin: shelf mark L 3.9.24.
• Archbishop Narcissus Marsh – Boston Public Library, Boston,
U.S.A.: shelf mark XG. H698.M73C
• Copy inscribed 'From the Author' – TCD: shelf mark RR. nn. 5.
• Sir Thomas Southwell – BL: shelf mark G.4794.
• Lord Chancellor [John Methuen] – sold 20 March 2012 at
Penzance Auction Rooms, Penzance.⁶

4   This change also resulted in the '18.' at end of line 2 of marginal ref. (a) being transferred to the
beginning of line 3.
5   The changes to sheet G were made before those in sheet D, see intro. p. 67.
6   See Baker, 'An English view of the Anglo-Irish constitution in 1670' in *Collected papers on English*
legal history (Cambridge, 2013), ii, p. 921, n. 78.

In addition, Molyneux is said to have presented copies to the lord justices Galway and Winchester, while the 1782 edn referred to a copy of *The Case* presented to the bishop of Meath (Richard Tennison). See intro. pp 14–15 above. The presentation copies are in large format, but on the similar paper to the ordinary copies, see further intro. p. 50

2. 1706 edition. [?Dublin]. small 4vo.

Titlepage	| THE | CASE | OF | IRELAND' s | Being BOUND by | Acts of Parliament | IN | ENGLAND, | Stated. | [rule] | BY | *William Molyneux* of *Dublin*, Eſq; | [rule] | Printed in the Year, M.DCC.VI.
Collation	[A1], A2, Aa2, [A3], [A4]; A–H4; Hh, [Hh2]; I–X4; Y, [Y2].
Pagination	(10) + 1–68 + 65–171 (repeat 65–68 = Hh1r–Hh2v).
Contents	Text lacks all marginalia and notes, otherwise straightforward reprint of 1698 edn, closely following its formal features. Misprints of 1698 edition all corrected; p. 65 reads 'Satutes of Marton' for 'Statutes of Merton'.
Additional details	No place of imprint, no printer's name: assumed to be Dublin by *British Library Cat.* and Dix, 'The case … stated', *The Irish Book-Lover*, 5 (1914), p. 117, while Falkner Greirson & Co., *Catalogue* (Dublin, 1967), item 345, suggests Cork.
Variant titlepage	Reading '*Mollyneux*', noted in *ESCT* as in Gilbert Library, Dublin, not as described.

3. 1719 edition. [probably London]. 12vmo.

Titlepage	[within double rules] | THE | CASE | OF | IRELAND' s | Being BOUND by | Acts of Parliament | IN | ENGLAND, | Stated. | [rule] | BY | *William Molyneux* of *Dublin*, Eſq; | [rule] | Printed in the Year 1719. (Reproduces third state of 1698 titlepage, without imprint, and non-swash 'M' for Molyneux.)
Collation	A–D12, E8.
Pagination	(10) + 102.
Misprints	Misprint on p. 56, lin. ult., renders 'Seat of the Monarchy' (1698 end., p. 94, l. 17) as 'State … Monarchy' (1719, p. 56, lin. ult.).
Additional details	Advertised among books sold by J. Peele 'at the Sign of *Locke's Head*' in 2nd edn of *Lord Shaftesbury's letters to Lord Molesworth* (London, 1721). Bishop Nicolson of Derry attributed the publication to John Maxwell, intro. p. 46.

4. 1720 edition. London. 8vo.

Titlepage　　The Case of Ireland's Being Bound by Acts of Parliament in England, Stated. By William Mollyneux of *Dublin*, Esq; To which is added, The Case of Tenures Upon the Commission of Defective Titles, Argued by all the Judges of *Ireland*. With their Resolutions, and the Reasons of their Resolutions. London: Printed for W. Boreham at the *Angel* in *Pater-Noster-Row*. 1720.

Collation　　A–P8, Q4, R2.

Pagination　　xv + ( ) + 236.

Additional details　　*The case of tenures* (originally published 1637) has separate titlepage [L3r]. For the inclusion of *The case of tenures*, see intro. pp 46–7.

5. 1725 edition. Dublin. Small 6mo.

Titlepage　　The Case of Ireland's Being Bound by Acts of Parliament in England, Stated. By William Molyneux, of *Dublin*, Esq; To which is added, the Case of Tenures Upon the Commission of Defective Titles, Argued by all the Judges of *Ireland*. With their Resolutions, and the Reasons of their Resolutions. *Dublin*: Printed by *Pressick Rider* and *Thomas Harbin*, for *Pat. Dugan*, Bookseller, on *Cork-Hill*, 1725.

Collation　　A–R6.

Pagination　　(2), + vi, + (4), + 192.

Additional details　　Facing titlepage, engraved portrait of Molyneux (tipped in), signed 'P[hilip]. Simms Sc.' See further intro. p. 47, n. 224. Advertised in list of books for sale in Berkeley, *The querist* (Dublin, 1736) at *2s. 2d.* as 'Mullineaux's Case of Ireland, with Case of Tenures'. *ESTC* lists variant titlepage in Spencer Library, University of Kansas, with imprint '1705'. As the Rider-Harbin partnership only functioned in 1724–6 (Pollard, *A Dictionary* (London, 2000), s.vv.), this date is presumably a misprint.

6. 1749 edition. Dublin. 4to.

Titlepage　　The Case of Ireland's Being Bound by Acts of Parliament in England Stated. By William Molyneux, of Dublin, Esq; Dublin: Printed for, and Sold by Augustus Long, under *Welsh's* Coffee-house in *Essex-street*; and Henry Hawker, at *Homers*-Head, in Dame-street, Booksellers. MDCCXLIX.

Collation　　[A]2; B – G4; H2.

Pagination　　(4) + 9–60.

Additional details　　Advertised in *Faulkner's Dublin Journal*, 30 Sept.–3 Oct. 1749, at 'a British Sixpence' (6 ½d. Irish). Probably published by Charles Lucas, intro. pp 47–8.

7. 1770 edition. London. 8vo.

Titlepage   The Case of Ireland Being Bound by Acts of Parliament in England, Stated. By William Mollyneux of Dublin, Esq; With a New Preface. London: Printed for J. Almon, opposite Burlington-House in Piccadilly, and M. Hingeston in the Strand, near Temple-Bar. MDCCLXX.

Collation   a8, b4; B – I8; K2.

Pagination   (4) + v–xxiv + 132.

Additional details   Omits dedication to the king, and preface to the reader. New preface, attributed by T. Swift, *The utility of union* (Dublin, 1800), pref. p. iii, to Henry Flood: intro. pp 48–9. Price 3s. (sterling) in *List of books and pamphlets printed for J. Almon* ... [1770], appended to NLI copy of 1770 edn, shelf mark J. 32341/MOL/1770.

8. 1773 edition. Dublin. 4to.

Titlepage   The Case of Ireland Being Bound by Acts of Parliament in England, Stated. By William Mollyneux, of Dublin, Esq. With a New Preface. Dublin: Printed for J. Milliken, in College-green. MDCCLXXIII.

Collation   [ ]4, a – b4, B – O4, P2.

Pagination   (4) + xxi–xxiv <sic> + v–ix + (1) –108.

Additional details   Contains the new preface attributed to Flood, together with Molyneux's preface to the reader *followed* by his dedication to the king. Advertised in the *Hibernian Journal*, 6–9 Sept. 1773, at 1s. 7 ½d. (Irish), 'sewed'.

9. 1776 edition. Belfast. 6mo.

Titlepage   The Case of Ireland's Being Bound by Acts of Parliament in England, Stated. By William Molyneux, of Dublin, Esq; Belfast: Printed for John Hay, Junr. Bookseller, in Bridge-Street. M,DCC, LXXVI.

Collation   A4, B–I6, [K1]

Pagination   8 + 97 + (98).

Additional details   Publisher's advertisement on [A2] (see further intro. p. 49). Prints translation of Latin extracts, in parentheses after the Latin. Advertised in the *Belfast Newsletter*, 22–5 Oct. 1776, at 1s. 1d. (Irish), 'stitched in blue paper'.

10. 1782 edition. 8vo. Dublin

Titlepage   The Case of Ireland's Being Bound by Acts of Parliament Made in England, Stated. By William Molyneux, of Dublin, Esq. Also, A small Piece on the subject of Appeals to the Lords of England, by the same Author, Never Before Published. To Which are Added, Letters to the Men of Ireland, By Owen Roe O'Nial. Dublin: Printed in the Year M,DCC,LXXXII. [Price 6 ½*d*. (Irish).]

Collation   A–Q8.

Pagination   (7) + 8-94.

Additional details   Editor's advertisement on verso of titlepage. Separate titlepage for *Letters to the men of Ireland*, on p. 65. Owen Roe O'Nial was the pseudonym of Joseph Pollock, of Newry. The additional item attributed to Molyneux is printed on pp 62–4, see further intro. pp 50–1. A superior translation has been provided of the Latin extracts, and the original Latin omitted. Publication announced in the *Hibernian Journal*, 17–19 June 1782. The numerous advance notices (which spoke of thousands of copies) and subsequent advertisements for *The Case* in the *Journal* 10 May–17 July, suggest that the edition was published by its proprietor Thomas Walker.

10a. Projected subscription edition of early summer of 1782, to commemorate the recovery of Irish parliamentary independence

Proposal advertised in the *Hibernian Chronicle* on 16 and 20 May 1782.

11. 1892 edition. 12mo. Dublin

Titlepage   The Case of Ireland's Being Bound by Acts of Parliament in England, Stated. By William Molyneux, of Dublin, Esq. A New Edition, with Preface and Life of the Author, by Very Rev. John Canon O'Hanlon, P.P., M.R.I.A. Dublin: Sealy, Bryers & Walker. 1892.

Collation   a–c12, A–G12, H1.

Pagination   (frontispiece) + i-xlvi + 1-121, + (122 blank).

Additional details   Appendix (pp 116–21) with Molyneux's 'Reasons' against the Order of the English house of lords, together with the 1782 editor's covering note (printed from no. 10 above). Frontispiece is a Brocas engraving of Molyneux (see further intro. p. 50, n. 243). Translations of the Latin extracts are provided in footnotes.

12. 1897 edition. 12mo. Dublin.

Identical reprint of 1892 edition.

13. 1977 edition. 12mo. Monkstown, Co. Dublin

Titlepage   The Case of Ireland Stated by William Molyneux. Reprinted from the first edition of 1698. With an introduction by J.G.Simms, Trinity College, Dublin, and an afterword by Denis Donohue, University College, Dublin. Being the Fifth Volume of Irish Writings from the Age of Swift. Dublin: The Cadenus Press, 6 Richmond Hill, Monkstown [Co. Dublin]. MCMLXXVII.

Pagination   1–148 + (149) + (150 with printer's colophon giving copy no. in MS).

Additional details   Frontispiece is a P. Simms engraving of Molyneux, 1725. Limited edition of 350 copies, ed. Andrew Isdall Carpenter. Despite the claim to have been reprinted from the 1698 edn, the actual copy-text was the 1719 edn. See further, Archives of the Cadenus Press, TCD Library, shelf mark Press A CAD / ARCH 1977 / CADENUS PRESS archives 8.

14. French translation of no. 13, 1995. Caen, France

Titlepage   William Molyneux, *Discours sur la sujétion de l'Irlande aux lois du Parlement d'Angleterre*. Traduit sous la direction de Jacqueline Genet et Élizabeth Hellegouar'ch. Présentation historique de Pierre Gouhier. Caen: University of Caen, Groupe de Recherches Anglo-Irlandaises, 1995.

Pagination   (10) + 11–155 + (156), + (157, legal deposit).

Additional details   Translation of no. 13 above, including Simms' introduction and Donohue's afterword, together with new preface and historical introduction. Reproduces frontispiece and titlepage of no. 13 above.

15. Reprint of 1698 edn in Goldie, *The reception of Locke's politics* (London, 1999), i, pp 211–82

Pagination   Facsimile of 1698 titlepage (p. 211), editor's pref. (p. 212), text of *Case* (pp 213–82).

Additional details   First edition to contain explanatory footnotes, together with a brief appendix on the use of Locke in the answers to Molyneux by [Clement], *An Answer* (London, 1698); Cary, *A Vindication* (London, 1698), and [Leslie], *Considerations* (London, 1698), pp 282–4. The Latin extracts have been replaced by the 1782 English transl., printed within square brackets.

16. Reprint of 1770 edn. Dodo Press. Gloucester, UK.

Pagination   Titlepage and Flood's 1770 preface [pp 1–17], text of pamphlet (pp 1–75), Molyneux's reference notes (pp 76–8).

Additional details   No editor identified.

THE

CASE

OF

IRELAND's

Being BOUND by

Acts of Parliament

IN

ENGLAND,

Stated.[1]

BY

William Molyneux,
of Dublin, Esq;

Dublin, Printed by *Joseph Ray*, and are to be
Sold at his Shop in *Skinner-Row*.
MDCXCVIII.

---

1 Stated] Stated and Argued **H** | Stated [and Argued] **PC**

Titlepage for variant forms of 1698 titlepage, see checklist of printings, p. 79 above. **Titlepage, 14** *Stated* – Molyneux had originally intended to continue '*and Argued*' (cf. app. crit.), i.e. proved with evidence: *OED*, s.v. 3. See further intro. p. 40.

TO THE

5

KING.

10

SIR,

15

THE Expedition Your MAJESTY[1] Undertook into *England*, to Rescue these
20
Nations from Arbitrary Power, and those Unjust Invasions that were made

---

1 KING … MAJESTY] King[s Most Excellent Majesty] … [Glorious] Expedition … you`r Majesty´ **H**

A2r, 3–9 *To the King* – the decision to address the work to William, rather than the English parliament
(cf. *Case*, p. 1, app. crit.), was made on the recommendation of unnamed friends in Dublin: Molyneux to
Locke, 19 Apr. 1698: *Locke Corr.*, 2422. **A2r, 16–A2v, 2** *Expedition … Liberties* – cf. William's Declaration
of 20 Sept. 1688, setting forth his intentions in coming to England (Williams, *Constitution* (Cambridge,
1970), pp 15–6). However, *Case*, p. 115 claimed that, unlike England and Scotland, Ireland had not
benefited in terms of political rights from the Glorious Revolution.

on our Religion, Laws, Rights and Liberties, was an Action[1] in it Self so *Great*, and of such Immense
5 Benefit to our Distressed Countries, that 'tis Impossible to give it a Representation so *Glorious* as it Deserves. Of all Your
10 Majesty's Kingdoms, none was more Sensible of the Happy Effects thereof,[2] than Your *Kingdom of Ireland*, which from the
15 Depth of Misery and Despair,[3] is Raised by your Majesty to a Prosperous and Flourishing Condition. And we presume most humbly
20 to Implore the Continuance of Your Majesty's Graces[4] to us, by Prote-

---

1 Religion ... Action] [Laws Libertys and Rights] `Religion ... Libertys´ [is] `was´ a `n´ [Subject] Action
H   2 thereof] [of your Majestys Actions] `thereof´ **H**   3 and Despair] *not in* **H**   4 Raised ...Graces]
raised [up] ... [do] `presume´... [Counten̲] Graces ([Counten̲] *perhaps for* [Counten̲<ance>] **H**

A2v, 14–18 *Ireland ... Condition* – Ireland's rapid recovery after the Jacobite War, as evidenced by
expanding woollen exports to the Continent, was the subject of considerable envy in England from the
mid-1690s: intro. pp 9–10, 15–16.

cting and Defending[1] those *Rights* and *Liberties* which we have Enjoy'd under the Crown of *England* for above Five Hundred Years, and which some of late do Endeavour to Violate.[2] Your most Excellent Majesty is the *Common Indulgent*[3] *Father* of all your Countries;[4] and have an *Equal* Regard to the *Birth-Rights* of all Your *Children*; and will not permit the *Eldest*, because the *Strongest*, to Encroach on the Possessions[5] of the *Younger*: Especially considering with what Duty, Loyalty, and Filial Obedience, we have ever behav'd our selves to Your Majesty:

---

1 Protecting … Defending] [preserving inviolable to us] [`Sheltering´] `Protecting … Defending´ H
2 Endeavour … Violate] [have] `do´ indeavour[d] … infringe H   3 *Indulgent*] *not in* H   4 Countries]
[Dominions] `Countrys´ H   5 Possessions] Possession H

A3r, 2–5 *Rights … Years* – the essence of Ireland's constitutional claim as an independent kingdom having
a parliament, courts, administration, &c. *prout in Anglia* [just as in England] since the establishment of
English government under Henry II. See further the verdict in the Merchants of Waterford's case, *Case*,
p. 91.   A3r, 6–7 *which … Violate* – namely, England's various constitutional interventions since 1641, and
more particularly since the 1688 Revolution. See further *Case*, pp 105–15.   A3r, 9–17 *the Common …
Younger* – cf. *Case*, p. 147. While the image of the king as the common father of his people was long
established (and even employed by William himself: Boyer, *The history of King William the Third* (London,
1703), iii. p. 507), Molyneux probably derived the idea of the magistrate preventing the eldest brother from
despoiling his juniors from Locke, *Treatises*, ii, §202.

Insomuch that I take leave[1]
to Assert, That Your
Majesty has not in all Your
Dominions a People more
5   *United* and *Steady* to
Your Interests, than the
Protestants of Ireland:
Which has[2] manifestly
Appear'd in all our Actions
10   and Parliamentary
Proceedings, since Your
Majesty's Happy Accession
to the Throne.[3] To Relieve
the Distress'd, has ever been
15   the Peculiar *Character* of
Your Majesty's *Glorious*
Family. The *United*
Provinces have found
this in Your *Famous*
20   *Ancestors*: And all *Europe*
has been Sensible of this
in Your *Royal Person*. To
this End more particu-

---

1 take leave] dare venture **H**   2 People ... has] `People´ ... your [Majestys] ... Brittish Protestants ... `has´ **H**   3 – A4r, n.1 To Relieve ... People.] *not in* H

A3v, 5 *Steady* – persistently devoted to: *OED*, s.v. 6a.   **A3v, 10–13** *Parliamentary ... Throne* – given the failure of the 1692 parliament, the problems over ratifying the Treaty of Limerick, difficulties in raising finance, and the intense factional struggles of 1695–7, this claim was unlikely to have carried weight with William. Cf. his remark to Lord Galway, 16 July 1698, 'I should be very glad not to be obliged, for a good while to have another parliament in Ireland': Grimblot (ed.), *Letters* (London, 1848), ii, p. 85. **A3v, 17–20** *The United ... Ancestors* – earlier members of the House of Orange had played a leading role in Dutch politics since the king's great-grandfather, William the Silent, had led the revolt against Spain in the later C.16: Blom & Lambert, *A History* (Providence, RI, 1999), pp 132–81 *passim*. **A3v, 20–22** *all Europe ... Person* – William had been the animating spirit of the Grand Alliance, which had successfully concluded the Nine Years War against France in the Treaty of Ryswick, 20 Sept. 1697: Baxter, *William III* (London, 1966), pp 288–91, 358–9.

larly You came into these
Kingdoms, as Your Majesty
has been pleas'd to Declare:
And   as   You   have
5   Establish'd the *Rights and
Liberties of England on a
Foundation that, we hope,
can *never be shaken*; So we
doubt not but Your Sacred
10   Majesty will have a Tender
Care of Your Poor *Subjects
of Ireland*, who are *Equally*
Your Subjects, as the rest of
Your People.[1]

15

Pardon I most Humbly
beseech Your Majesty, my
Presumption, in Appealing
to You[2] on this Occasion:
20   Nothing but the *Dignity* and
Weight of the Subject, can

---

1 People.] *end of passage not in* H *begun A3v, n.3 above*   2 Pardon … You] [May it please your Majesty,]
Pardon … You`r Majesty´ … You[r Majesty] H

A4r, 2–14 *Your Majesty … People* – cf. the aspirations in William's declaration of 20 Sept. 1688, given
constitutional force in the Declaration of Rights of Feb. 1689, and enacted into law as the Bill of Rights
(1 W. & M., ses. 2, c. 2) in Nov. 1689. Despite a similar settlement in the Scottish Claim of Right, June
1689 (*English historical documents* (London, 1956), viii, pp 635–9), attempts to introduce an Irish bill of
rights had been defeated by the administration in 1695 and again in 1697. See further *Osborough*, 'The
Failure', *Irish Jurist*, n.s. 33 (1998), pp 394–402.

Excuse my Boldness
herein: But if That be
Consider'd, it Deserves the
Regard of the *Greatest*
5 *Prince*; 'Tis no less than the
Rights and *Liberties* of one
of His Kingdoms, on which
their Religion, their
Property, their *All*
10 Depends; and which they
have Enjoyed for Five
Hundred Years past. This,
I think, I have clearly
shewn in the following
15 Leaves: I am sure, if my
Management thereof, were
suitable to the *Justice* of our
Cause, our *Friends*[1] of
England can no longer
20 Doubt it.

1 Friends] Brethren **H & PC**

A4v, 8 *their Religion* – the only mention of religion in *The Case* not added as an afterthought.

At Your Majesty's Feet
therefore, I throw it; and
with it[1] the Unworthy
Author thereof,

5

*(May it please Your
Majesty)*

Your Majesty's

10

Most Dutiful, Loyal,

and Obedient

15 *Subject and Servant,*

William Molyneux.[2]

20

---

1 with it] `with it´ **H**    2 William Molyneux] W. M. / `Dublin March 26. / 1698´ (*perhaps add. later*) **H** |
William Molyneux / [Dublin March / 26. 1698.] **PC** (*cf. change listed A8r, n. 1 below*)

———————————————————

———————————————————

5

PREFACE[1]

TO THE

10

READER.

15

I Have nothing to Offer
in this *Preface, more
than to let the Reader*
know, how Unconcern'd
20 *I am in any of those
Particular Inducements,
which might* seem

A6r–A8r *Preface … Reader* – no holograph version survives of the preface, see further intro. p. 63.

at this Juncture to have Occa-
sion'd the following Discourse.

I have not any Concern *in*
5 Wooll, *or the* Wooll-Trade.
I am no wise Interested in the
Forfeitures, *or* Grants. *I am*
not at all Solicitous, whether
the Bishop, *or* Society *of*
10 Derry *Recover the Land they*
Contest *about.*

So that, I think, I am as
Free *from any* Personal
15 Prejudice *in this Cause, as 'tis*
possible to Expect any Man
should be, that has an Estate
and Property *in this King-*
dom, and who is a Member
20 of Parliament *therein. I hope*
therefore *'tis* *a* Pub-

A6v, 4–11 *I have … about* – these disclaimers cannot be accepted at face value. Not only was Molyneux actively involved in the preparation of the bishop of Derry's case in the autumn of 1697 (intro. p. 12, n. 46), but he also encouraged his Armagh tenants in the manufacture of linen: *Locke Corr.*, 2131. **A6v, 9–10** *Society of Derry* – the Honourable the Irish Society was the company that managed the London Livery Companies' plantation in Co. Derry. See further, intro. p. 12. **A6v, 17–20** *Estate … Parliament* – Molyneux had been elected second representative for Dublin University in 1692, and again in 1695. For his property, see intro. 6, n. 21.

lick Principle *that has mov'd me to this Undertaking: I am sure, I am not Conscious to my Self of any other Intention.*

5

I have heard it has been said, That perhaps I might run some Hazard *in Attempting this Argument; But I am not at all Apprehensive of any such Danger: We are in a Miserable Condition indeed, if we may not be Allow'd to* Complain, *when we think we are Hurt; and to give our Reasons with all* Modesty *and* Submission. *But were it otherwise, it would not in the least Affect, or Discourage me in an Attempt, where I think my Cause Good, and my Country*

10

15

20

A7r, 7–11 *I might … Danger* – cf., however, Molyneux to Locke, 19 Apr. 1698: 'till I either see how the Parliament at Westminster is pleasd to take [*The Case*], or till I see them Risen, I do not think it adviseable for me to go on tother side of the Water.': *Locke Corr.*, 2422. His concern persisted until mid-July: Simms, *William Molyneux* (Dublin, 1982), p. 120.

Concern'd, and where I am
fully perswaded, the True
Interest *of* England *is as*
Deeply Engaged, as the Pro-
5   testant Interest *of* Ireland.

The Great and Just
Council *of* England *freely*
Allows all Addresses of this
10   *sort.*[1] *To* Receive *and* Hear
Grievances, *is a great part of*
their Business; and to
Redress *them, is their Chief*
Glory. *But this is not to be*
15   *done, till they are laid before*
them, and fairly Stated for
their Consideration.

This I have endeavour'd
20   *in the following Paper.*
What Success it may
have, I am not very

---

1 *sort.*] sort. **PC** | sort∧ **I**

A7v, 2–5 *the True … Ireland* – cf. similar claim in Bishop King's May 1698 paper on the consequences of the *coram non judice* decision in his appeal before the English lords: TCD MS 2331. **A7v, 4–5** *the Protestant … Ireland* – a common later C.17 phrase describing the Anglo-Irish. Cf. [King], *The state of the Protestants* (London, 1691), pp 13, 57, 63, 87, 120, 162. It is equivalent to the term 'the *English Interest* of Ireland', *Case*, p. 160. **A7v, 7–14** *The Great … Glory* – Molyneux frequently employed this synonym for the English parliament, and cited (*Case*, p. 48) Petyt, *The antient right* (London, 1680), p. 71, on '*the Ancient Generale Concilium, or Parliament of Ireland*'. For redress of grievances as a major function of parliament, see Coke, *4th Inst.*, p. 11, and preamble to the 1694 English Triennial Act (6 & 7 W. & M., c. 2).

*solicitous about. I have Done
what I thought was my
Duty, and Commit the
Event to* GOD Almighty,

5 *and the* Wise Council of
England.

10 *Dublin, Febr. 8.*[1]
1697/8

W. Molyneux.[2]

15

———————————

20

1 Febr. 8] [March 26] `Febr. 8´ **PC**   2 W. Molyneux] [Will] W. Molyneux **PC** | (*end of passage not in*
***H** begun A6r, n. 1*)

A8r, 10 *Febr. 8* – the antedating of the Preface from the original 26 Mar. 1698 (cf. app. crit.) is one of the
most important revelations provided by the manuscripts of *The Case*, see further intro. p. 14.

The CASE

OF

IRELAND's

Being Bound by

Acts of Parliament

IN

ENGLAND,

STATED.[1]

I HAVE ever been[2] so fully perswaded of the strict[3] Justice of the Parliament of *England*, that I could never think that any of Their Proceedings,[4] which might seem to have the least Tendency to Hardship on their Neighbours,[5] could arise from any thing but want of Due Information, and a right State of the

Introduction, and Occasion of this Disquisition.

---

1 The CASE ... Stated.] An Humble Remonstrance / To the Parliament of England / In Relation to Ireland. / by W: M: of D. Esq[r] **H** | `The Case ... Stated [and Argued].´ *manu aman., on label pasted over* [An Humble Remonstrance / To the Parliamt: of England / In Relation to Ireland. / By / William Molyneux of Dublin / Esq[r]] [`alter this Title´] (*final del. interpolation in margin in printer's hand*) **PC** **2** ever been] been ever **H** | [been] ever `been´ **PC** **3** strict] [`the great´] the [great] `strict´ ([`the great´] *in margin*) **H** **4** Proceedings] Proceedings [and de] ([de] *perhaps for* [de<liberations>]) **H** **5** Hardship ... Neighbours] the Contrary **H** | [the Contrary] `Hardship ... Neighbours´ **PC**

4–16, headtitle *THE CASE ... STATED* – cf. app. crit. for the original headtitle 'An Humble Remonstrance to the Parliament of England In Relation to Ireland'. For the significance of the change, see intro. p. 14. **1, 31** *State* – i.e. statement, meaning account, or description: *OED*, s.v. state, vi. 37a.

Business under their Consideration.
The want of which, in Matters
wherein another People[1] are chiefly
Concern'd, is no Defect in the
5 Parliament of *England*, but is highly
Blameable in the Persons whose
Affair is Transacting, and who
permit that Illustrious Body of
Senators to be Mis-inform'd,
10 without giving them that[2] Light
that might Rectifie them.

I could never Imagine that those
Great *Assertors* of their *Own*
Liberties and *Rights*, could ever
15 think of making the least Breach in
the *Rights* and *Liberties* of *their*
Neighbours, unless they thought
that they had *Right* so to do; and
this they might well surmise, if their
20 Neighbours quietly see their
Inclosures Invaded, without
Expostulating the Matter at least,[3]
and shewing Reasons, why they
may think that Hardships are put
25 upon them therein.

The Consideration hereof has
Excited me[4] to undertake this Disquisition,[5] which I do with all Imaginable Diffidence of my own
30 Performance, and with the most[6] pro-

---

1 in ... People] [is no fault of theirs when other] `in ... wherein´ ... People [of] **H**  **2** that] [the least] `that´
H **3** *Expostulating* ... least] [ex] [at least] expostulating ... least **H** **4** me] me [`at this juncture´] **H**
5 undertake ... Disquisition] address [the] this Paper to that Great Assembly **H** | [Address this ... Assembly]
`undertake ... Disquisition´ **PC**  **6** all ... the most] [that] `all Imaginable´ ... [that] `the most´ **H**

2, 5–11 *highly ... Rectifie them* – the reality, however, was very different, as may be seen from the English
lords' refusal to allow the bishop of Derry's counsel even to raise the question of their competence in Irish
chancery appeals: intro. p. 16. **2, 19–21** *their Neighbours ... Invaded* – cf. *Case*, p. 66. Comparisons of
political rights with private property were commonplace in the later C.17. See further Nenner, *By colour
of law* (Chicago, 1977), pp 36–40. **2, 22** *Expostulating* – complaining of: *OED*, s.v. expostulate, 2.
2, 27 *Excited* – induced: *OED*, s.v. excite, 3. **2, 27** *Disquisition* – a treatise or discourse in which a subject
is investigated and discussed, or the results of an investigation set forth at some length: *OED*, s.v. 2. The
term had been used by Domville in the title of his paper on English legislative competence in Ireland, on
which much of *The Case* was based.

found Respect and Deference to
that August Senate.[1] The present
Juncture of Affairs, when the
Business of *Ireland* is under the
5 Consideration of both Houses of
the English[2] Parliament*, seems to
require this from some Person; and
seeing all Others silent, I venture to
Expose my own Weakness, rather
10 than be wanting at this time *to my
Country*.[4] I might say indeed *to
Mankind*; for 'tis the Cause of the
whole Race of *Adam*, that I Argue:
Liberty seems the Inherent Right of
15 all *Mankind*; and on whatsoever
Ground any one Nation can
Challenge it to themselves, on the
same Reason may the Rest of
Adam's Children Expect it.[5]

20 If what I Offer herein seems to
carry any Weight, in relation to my
own Poor Country, I shall be
abundantly happy in the Attempt:
But if after all, the Great Council of
25 *England* Resolve the[6] contrary, I shall
then believe my self to be[7] in an
Error, and with the lowest Submission ask Pardon for my Assurance.[8]
However, I humbly presume I shall
30 not be hardly Censur'd

3*Bishop of *Derry* in the House of Lords, and Prohibiting Exportation of our Woollen Manufacture in the House of Commons.

1 Senate] [As<sembly>] `Senat´ H   2 the English] `the English´ H   3 *marginal note*] *in* H | (*manu aman.*) PC
4 Person ... *Country*] [body] `Person´ ... `at ... time´ ... Country [at ... Time] H   5 any ... it] [the People of England] `any ... can´ ... [sons dem] `Children´ `expect it´ ([dem] *perhaps for* [dem<and>]): `expect it´ *add in line*) H   6 the] [to] the H   7 to be] *not in* H   8 Assurance] [Presumption] [`Folly´] `Assurance´ H

3, 3–6 *the Business ... Parliament* – the woollens controversy, the Derry appeal, and the forfeited Jacobite estates were not the only Irish issues to be raised in the 1697–8 session (cf. *Case*, p. A6v). Also important were compensation for losses in the siege of Derry; the size of military forces in Ireland; the appeal in the earl of Meath's case; and the Irish parliament's attempt to pass an amended version of the English Act of Security (7 & 8 Will. 3, c. 27). Though unsuccessful, this attempt was condemned by the English commons, together with Molyneux's *Case*, 27 June 1698: intro. p. 18.   **3, 14–19** *Liberty ... Expect it* – in extending Locke's principles to demonstrate that one nation did not have the right to dominate another, Molyneux was breaking significant new ground in English political discourse. See further, *Case*, pp 150–4, and intro. p. 42. Atwood, *History*, p. 4, insinuated that in contending for rights of nature antecedent to government Molyneux revealed himself as an adherent of Robert Filmer.   **3, 17** *Challenge* – assert one's right to, or lay claim to: *OED*, s.v. 5.   **3, 24–8** *But if ... Assurance* – cf. manuscript comment in copy of 1770 edn (RIA, shelf mark HP 360/18): 'Was it for Molyneux to use this Language?' Assurance – hardihood, or presumption: *OED*, s.v. 10.

by them, for offering to lay¹ before
them a fair State of our Case, by such
Information as I can procure;²
especially when at the same time I

5   declare my Intention of a Submissive
Acquiescence in whatever they
Resolve for or against what I Offer.

Subject of
this Enquiry.

The Subject therefore of our
present Disquisition³ shall be, *How*

10 *far the Parliament of* England *may*
think it Reasonable to intermeddle
with the Affairs of Ireland, *and*
Bind us up by Laws made in their
House.

15 ⁴And seeing the *Right* which
England may pretend to, for Binding
us by their Acts of Parliament, can
be founded only on the *Imaginary*
Title of Conquest or *Purchase⁵*, or on

20 *Precedents* and *Matters of Record;⁶*
We shall Enquire into the following
Particulars.

(1.) *First*, How *Ireland* became⁷
a Kingdom *Annex'd* to the Crown

25 of *England.* And here we shall at
large give a faithful Narrative of the
First Expedition of the Britains into
this   Country,   and   King

---

1 lay] [give] lay **H.** 2 a fair … procure] such … can **H** | `a fair … by´ … `procure´ **PC** 3 Disquisition] [Enquiry]
`Disquisition´ **H**  4 – 6 And … Record] [In order to this] `And … Record´ (*interpolation in margin*) **H** 5 or
Purchase] *not in* **H** | `or Purchase´ **PC**  6 Record] *end of interpolation begun n. 4 above* **H**  7 became] `be´came **H**

4, 2 *State … Case* – the term, 'state of the case' (or 'state of the plea'), denoted the printed document setting forth the
plaintiff or defendant's pleadings, required in certain trial proceedings: *OED*, s.v. state, vi. 37a. See further intro. p. 29.
4, 8–14 *The Subject … House* – the first passage from *The Case*, denounced by the English commons committee of
inquiry as 'denying the Authority of the Parliament of *England* …', 27 June 1698: *Commons Jnl [Eng.]*, xii, p. 324. See
further, intro. p. 18. *Intermeddle* – concern oneself with (cf. *Case*, p. 126), rather than the obsolete sense of 'interfere in
what is none of one's business': *OED*, s.v. 2, 3. **4, 15–22** *And seeing … Particulars* – passage denounced by English
commons committee: *Commons Jnl [Eng.]*, xii, p. 325. *Imaginary* – supposed, or purported: *OED*, s.v. 6. **4, 19** *or*
Purchase – this phrase was a subsequent interpolation, cf. app. crit. See further the discussion, *Case*, pp 142–5, whether
England could be said to have somehow 'purchased' Ireland through paying for the suppression of rebellions there, a
point strongly asserted in [Toland], *A Letter* (London, 1697), pp 2–3. **4, 23–6, 11** *First … Whole* – these six questions
provided the structure of *The Case*, see intro. p. 30. *Question 1* was answered, *Case*, pp 6–12; *question 2*, pp 12–17;
question 3, pp 18–28; *question 4*, pp 28–77, and pp 77–115 (since Molyneux spoke twice of having answered the fourth
head or question); *question 5*, pp 115–42; and *question 6*, pp 142–71.

Henry the Second's Arrival here, such as our best Historians give us.

(2.) *Secondly*, We shall Enquire, Whether this Expedition, and the English[1] Settlement that afterwards follow'd thereon, can properly be call'd a *Conquest* ? Or whether any Victories obtain'd by the English, in any succeeding Ages in this Kingdom, upon any *Rebellion*, may be call'd a *Conquest* thereof ?[2]

(3.) *Thirdly*, Granting that it were a *Conquest*, we shall Enquire what *Title* a Conquest gives[3].

(4.) [4]*Fourthly*, We shall Enquire what *Concessions* have been from time to time made to *Ireland*[5], to take off what even the most Rigorous Assertors of a Conquerour's Title do pretend to. And herein we shall shew by what Degrees the English Form of Government, and the English Statute-Laws,[6] came to be received[7] among us:[8] And this shall appear, to be wholly by the *Consent* of the People and Parliament of *Ireland*.[9]

---

1 the English] the [the] `English´ **H.**   2 Or ... thereof ?] [and herein I am humbly of opinion, it cannot be so [called] termed] `Or ... `upon ... rebellion´ ... thereof?´ (*interpolation largely in margin*) **H**   3 gives] gives [wh] [and whether future concessions may not destroy the Title of Conquest even whatever it is; and How far this is the case of Ireld.] [`which I conceive is very little [as we shall see hereafter] `or nothing in our Case´´] **H**   4 – 8 *Fourthly* ... among us] `4 [Granting that Ireland is a Conquered Country] {`(4)´} we ... pretend to´ `And ... among us´ (*interpolation add. on separate sheet* f. 74r, `And ... among us´ *add. later at end of line*) **H**   5 to *Ireland*] [thereto] `to Ireland´ **H**   6 and ... Statute-Laws] *not in* **H** | `and ... Statute-Laws´ **PC**   7 received] setled **H** | [setled] `received´ **PC**   8 among us] *end of interpolation begun at n. 4 above* **H**   9 And ... *Ireland*.] *not in* **H** | `And ... Ireland.´ **PC**

5, 2 *our ... Historians* – especially Giraldus Cambrensis, Roger Hoveden, John Brompton and Matthew Paris, on whom Molyneux drew, *Case*, pp 10–44   5, 20 *Title* – a legal right to the possession of a property: *OED*, s.v. 6, 7.

[1](5.) *Fifthly*, We shall Enquire
into the Precedents and Opinions
of the Learned in the Laws,[2]
relating to this Matter, with
5   Observations thereon.[3]

(6.) *Sixthly*, We shall Consider
the Reasons and Arguments that
may be farther Offered on one side
and t'other; and shall Draw some
10   General Conclusions from the
Whole.[4]

Britain's first
Expedition
into *Ireland*.

As to the First, We shall find
the History of the First Expedition
of the[5] *English* into *Ireland*, to be
15   briefly thus: In the Reign of King
Henry the Second, *Dermot*
Fitzmurchard, commonly called
Mac-Morrogh, Prince of *Leinster*,
who was a Man Cruel and
20   Oppressive, after many Battels with
other Princes of *Ireland*, and being
Beaten[6] and put to Flight by them,
Apply'd for Relief to King *Henry*
the Second, who was then busied in
25   *Aquitain*; the King was not then in
such Circumstances as to afford
him much Help: However thus
much he did for him,

---

1 – 3 (5.) *Fifthly* ... thereon] [(([[4]]5) Wee shall enquire into some Precedents, Records, and matters of History, that may give us some Light in this Affair. `and first those that are against Irelands being subject to the English Parliamt; and next those yt are for its being so bound'] `(5) We ... thereon´ (*final interpolation add. on sheet f. 74r*) **H** **2** Learned ... Laws] Judges **H** | [Judges] `Learned ... Laws´ **PC**
3 thereon] *end of interpolation begun n. 1 above* **H** **4** *Sixthly* ... Whole.] [(6) `and lastly´ We shall consider the *Reasons* [that are Offerd,] Why Ireland ought `not´ to be bound by the Parliamt: of England, and the Reasons that are offerd, why it ought to be so bound.] `(6) We ... `shall´ ... Whole´ (*final interpolation add. on sheet f. 74r*) **H** **5** First ... Expedition of the] `first ... of the´ **H** **6** Beaten] [worsted] beaten **H**

6, 3 *the Learned ... Laws* – notably, Sir Edward Coke on binding Ireland by 'Express Words' (*Case*, pp 116–22) and the verdicts in the Merchants of Waterford's case (pp 90–4), Pilkington's case and that of the Prior of Llanthony, (pp 122–6). Cf. app. crit., for substitution of 'Learned in the Laws' for 'Judges'. **6, 13–14** *the History ... Ireland* – for a modern account, see Flanagan, *Irish society* (Oxford, 1989), chs 3–4. **6, 16–18** *Dermot ... Leinster* – Diarmait Mac Murchada, king of Uí Chennselaig, termed by Giraldus 'Prince of Leinster', see further Giraldus, *Expugnatio Hibernica* (Dublin, 1978), p. 285, n. 3.

By Letters Patents he granted
License to all his Subjects throughout his Dominions, to Assist the
said Prince to Recover his
5 Dominions. These Letters Patents
are to be seen in *Giraldus
Cambrensis,[1] who was Historiographer and Secretary to King Hen.
II. and Accompanied him in his
10 Expedition into Ireland, and from
him it is that we have this Relation.
The Irish Prince brought[2] these
Letters into England, and caused
them to be Read in the Audience of
15 many People; Beating up, as it were,
for Voluntiers and free Adventurers
into Ireland. At length, Richard Earl
of Strigul (now, Chepstow in
Monmouthshire) Son of Earl
20 Gilbert, call'd Strongbow, Agreed
with him, to Assist him in the Recovery of his Country, on Condition
that Dermot should give him his
Eldest Daughter in Marriage, and
25 his Kingdom of Leinster after his
Death. About the same time Robert
Fitz-Stephen, Governour of
Abertefie[3] in Wales, Agreed likewise
with Dermot to help him, on
30 Condition that he would grant to
him and Maurice Fitzgerald in Fee

* Giraldus
Cambr. Hib.
Expug. Lib. I.
C. 1,

1 marginal ref.] in H | (manu aman.) PC   2 in his ... brought] `in ... Expedition´ ... [Narrative] `Relation'
... [brings] `brought´ H   3 Abertefie] Abertefie ed | Aberlefie H, PC & I (Aberteivi: Giraldus, Expugnatio
Hibernica (Dublin, 1978), p. 29)

7, 1–3 By Letters ... Dominions – see further, Case, p. 16.   7, 7–10 Historiographer ... Ireland – despite the
claim in his prefatory remarks to have witnessed many of the events he recounted, Giraldus did not
accompany Henry II's expedition to Ireland in 1171, though he visited the country in 1183–4, and again
with Prince John in 1185–6. He did not become a royal clerk until the late 1180s: Giraldus, Expugnatio
Hibernica (Dublin, 1978), pp xii–xx, 3, 277. The designation 'historiographer' echoed Domville's description
of Matthew Paris, cf. Case, p. 28.   7, 15–16 Beating ... Volunties – to beat up for recruits: OED, s.v.
beat, 27.   7, 17–20 Richard ... Strongbow – Richard FitzGilbert de Clare, earl of Pembroke and lord of
Strigoil, known as Strongbow, chief of the Normans who came to Ireland in 1169, did not himself arrive
till 1170, when he married Diarmait Mac Murchada's daughter, Aífe. Though his claim to Pembroke was
not recognised by Henry II, following their reconciliation in 1171 the king acknowledged him as Earl of
Strigoil. See further Flanagan, Irish society (Oxford, 1989), chs 3–4.   7, 26–8 Robert Fitz-Stephen ...
Abertefie – Robert Fitz-Stephen, governor of Aberteivi (Cardigan), and according to his nephew Giraldus
the first Norman leader to reach Ireland: Giraldus, Expugnatio Hibernica (Dublin, 1978), p. 31.

the City of *Wexford*, with two
Cantreds or Hundreds[1] of Land
near adjoining.

These Adventurers afterwards

5 went over, and were successful in
Treating with the *Irish*, and Taking
Wexford, *Waterford*, *Dublin*, and
other Places. Whereupon Earl
Richard Strongbow married *Dermot*'s

10 Daughter, and according to Compact, succeeded him in his Kingdom.

Hen. II.   A little[2] after the Descent of
comes into   these Adventurers, King *Henry* II.
Ireland.   himself went[3] into *Ireland* with an

15 Army, in *November* 1171.[4] and
finding that his Subjects of *England*
had made a very good hand of their
Expedition, he obtain'd from Earl
Richard Strongbow a Surrender of

20 *Dublin*, with the Cantreds
adjoining, and all the Maritime[5]
Towns and Castles. But *Strongbow*
and his Heirs were to Enjoy the
Residue of *Dermot*'s Principality.

Irish **submit**   25   King *Hen.* II Landed at *Water-*
to him.   *ford* from *Milford* in *Pembrookshire*,
and staying there some few days,

---

1 in Fee ... Hundreds] `in fee´ ... `or Hundreds´ **H**   2 little] [while] `little´ **H**   3 went] went over **H** | went [over] **PC**
4 1171] 1171 ed | 1172 **H, PC & I** (*see further Case*, 8nn)   5 Maritime] Maritime **H** | Maritine **PC & I**

8, 2 *Cantreds* – an Irish land measure, equated, as Molyneux's interpolation shows (cf. app. crit.), with the
English hundred: *OED*, s.v. cantred.   **8, 4–11** *These Adventurers ... Kingdom* – see *Case*, pp 15–16 for
rejection of the claim that the adventurers' victories over the Irish amounted to a conquest of the country.
Treating with – dealing with *in the sense of* taking successful action with regard to *as opposed to* negotiating
with: Johnson, *Dictionary*, s.v. treat, 3.   **8, 13–12, 14** *King Henry ... April 1172* – start of material derived
from Domville's 'Disquisition', pp 40–3, with occasional minor differences. Giraldus' dating Henry's arrival
in Ireland to 1172 rather than 1171 (cf. app. crit.) was, as A.B. Scott points out, a simple error. It perhaps
arose from confusion as to whether the murder of Thomas Becket had taken place in Dec. 1170 or 1171.
See further Giraldus, *Expugnatio Hibernica* (Dublin, 1978), xix, pp 74, 92, 280.   **8, 13–15** *Henry ... Army*
– Molyneux was notable for consistently avoiding reference to Henry's acquisition of Ireland as a 'conquest'
or speaking of his 'having conquered' Ireland. Even Domville, while insisting that the Irish submission to
Henry was entirely voluntary, occasionally used such terms. Cf. *Case*, p. 30 nn.   **8, 25–10, 6** *King Hen.* II
... *non exhiberet* – this account of the submission of the secular rulers was not taken directly from
Expugnatio Hibernica, bk I, chs 31–3 (as *Case*, p. 16 seemingly implies), but presented the 'revisionist'
summary of Giraldus' narrative found in the 1569 Act for the Attainder of Shane O'Neill (11 Eliz. sess. 3,
c. 1), as set out by Domville, 'Disquisition', pp 40–3. See further intro. p. 55. *Milford* – Millford Haven:
Domville, 'Disquisition', p. 40.

[*][Dermod, King of Cork, came to him and]

[**][also made his submission to the King.]

[***][and by professions of fealty and submission, obtained peace from the King.]

(says *Giraldus Cambrensis*) *Rex Corcagiensis Dormitius advenit ei, & tam¹ Subjectionis vinculo quam fidelitatis Sacramento Regi² Anglorum se sponte submisit.*[*] *He freely Swore Fealty and Subjection to the King of England.*

From thence he went to *Lismore*, and thence to *Cashel*, where *Dunaldus* King of *Lymerick, se quoque fidelem Regi exhibuit.*[**] The like did all the Nobility and Princes in the South of *Ireland*.

Afterwards he marched to *Dublin*, and there the Princes of the Adjacent Countries came to him, *& sub Fidelitatis & Subjectionis obtentu a Rege Pacem impetrabant.*³[***] Thus *Cambrensis* in his *Hibernia Expugnata*; and there he mentions the several Princes that came in, vizt. *Macshaghlin* King of *Ophaly*, *O Carrol* King of *Uriel* (now *Lowth*) *O Rourk* King of *Meath*, *Rotherick O Connor* King of *Connaught*, and O.E.D.², s.v. *Monarch* as it were of the whole Island, with divers others, *qui ⁴firmissimis fidelitatis & subjectionis vinculis Domino Regi innodarunt & in*

5

10

15

20

25

---

tam] statim [forthwith] Giraldus, *Expugnatio Hibernica* (Frankfurt, 1603), p. 776. 2 Sacramento Regi] sacramento necnon ⸱ obsidibus datis firmiter astrictus, annuo regni suo tributo, se Anglorum regi [firmly bound both by an oath and the giving of ostages, he submitted to the king of England, and agreed to pay a yearly tribute from his kingdom] ibid., p. 776. 3 Rege ... mpetrabant] rege piissimo pacem obnixe postulantes et impetrantes [humbly sought and obtained peace from the most worthy ⸱f kings] ibid., p. 776. 4 – 10, 1 qui firmissimis ... Monarchâ] Qui pace similiter impetrata, Regio Domino, constituto Regni ⸱o Tributo, firmissimis de fidelitatis innodarunt. Sic itaque praeter soles Ultones, subditi per se singuli. Sic et in singulari ⸱otherico Conactiæ Principe, & tamquam Hibernensium capite, & insulae Monarchâ [Who likewise having obtained peace, ⸱nd agreed to a tribute from their kingdoms, bound themselves by the most solemn ties of fealty to the king. So that in this way ⸱l, with the exception of the Ulster rulers, submitted to the king. And in particular, Rotherick Prince of Connacht, and as it ⸱ere chief of the Irish, and monarch of the whole isle] ibid., p. 776.

⸱ 1–10, 6 *Rex ... exhiberet* – differences from the wording of the 1603 text of the Expugnatio are noted in the app. crit. ⸱ 1–2 *Rex ... Dormitius* – Diarmait mac Carrthaig, king of Cork: Giraldus, *Expugnatio Hibernica* (Dublin, 1978), p. 311, n. 149. ⸱ 5–6 *Swore ... Subjection* – Giraldus' assertion that the Irish leaders submitted under the bond of tenurial homage was not ⸱nfirmed by other contemporary accounts. More probable was a looser recognition of Henry as liege lord, not dissimilar to ⸱e Irish submission to a provincial king or high king. See Flanagan, *Irish society* (Oxford, 1989), pp 172–3, 227–8. 9, 9–10 ⸱unaldus ... Lymerick – Domnall Ua Briain, married (like Strongbow) to a daughter of Diarmait Mac Murchada: Giraldus, ⸱xpugnatio Hibernica (Dublin, 1978), p. 311, n. 151. 9, 22–4 *Macshaglin ... Meath* – namely Máelsechlainn Ua Faeláin of Uí ⸱aeláin; Ua Cerbaill of Airgialla, and Ua Ruairc of Bréifne: Giraldus, *Expugnatio Hibernica* (Dublin, 1978), p. 312, n. 156. ⸱ 24–10, 6 *Rotherick ... exhiberet* – in the full text of Giraldus, rather than submitting in person Ruairí Ua Conchobair merely ⸱tered into an agreement with Henry's emissaries at the Shannon: Giraldus, *Expugnatio Hibernica* (Dublin, 1978), pp 94–6. ⸱e further intro. p. 55.

singulari Rotherico Conactiæ Principe
tanquam Insulæ Monarchâ subditi
redduntur universi, nec alicujus fere in
Insula vel nominis vel ominis erat qui
5 *Regiæ Majestati & Debitam*[1] *Do-*
mino Reverentiam, non exhiberet.[*]

The same Relation we have
from *Roger Hoveden* (Annal. Pars
poster. fol. 301.) About the Kalends
10 of *November* 1172.[2] (saith he) King
Henry II. of *England*, took Shipping
for *Ireland* at *Milford*, and Landed
at *Waterford, & ibi venerunt ad eum*
Rex Corcagiensis, Rex de Lymerick,
15 *Rex de Oxerie,*[3] *Rex Midiæ, & fere*
omnes Hiberniæ Potentes.[**] And a
little afterwards in the same place
speaking of King *Henry* the
Second's being at *Waterford, ibidem*
20 *venerunt ad Regem Angliæ omnes*
Archiepiscopi, Episcopi, & Abbates
totius Hiberniæ, & receperunt eum in
Regem & Dominum Hiberniæ
jurantes ei & heredibus suis
25 *Fidelitatem & Regnandi*[4] *super eos*
Potestatem in perpetuum & inde
Dederunt ei Chartas suas. Exemplo
autem Clericorum predicti Reges &
Principes Hiberniæ receperunt simili
30 *modo Henricum Regem Angliæ in*

[*][who by the most
solemn ties of fealty
and subjection bound
themselves to the King,
and, in the single
person of Roderick,
King of Connaught, as
being monarch of the
whole island, were all
reduced to the state of
subjects: Indeed there
were few persons of
rank or consequence in
the island, who did not
do homage to his
Majesty as their liege
Lord.]

[**][and there he was
met by the Kings of
Cork, Limerick,
Ossory, Meath, and
almost all the great
men of Ireland.]

---

1 *Majestati & Debitam*] Maiestati, vel sui præsentiam, vel debitam [to his majesty, either in his presence or <through representatives> did homage] ibid., p. 776.   2 1172] `1172´ **H**   3 *Oxerie*] *Oxerie* ed | *Oxenie* **H, PC & I** (Oxerie *mistranscribed as* Oxenie *in* **H** *from* **Domville, 6**)   4 *Regnandi*] Regnandi **H & PC** | Regandi **I**

10, 3–4 *nec alicujus … erat* – this claim as to no one of consequence having failed to submit to Henry ignored Giraldus' earlier exception of the rulers of Ulster (*præter solos Ultonienses*): Giraldus, *Expugnatio Hibernica* (Dublin, 1978), pp 94–6.   10, 8 *Roger Hoveden* – Hoveden, or Howden, (ob. 1201) was a royal clerk, well placed to have obtained information from those who had accompanied Henry's expedition to Ireland: Flanagan, *Irish society* (Oxford, 1989), p. 230.   10, 15–20 *fere … ad Regem* – Molyneux (following Domville, 'Disquisition', pp 42) omitted Hoveden's important exception of Ruairí Ua Conchobair (*praeter regem de Conacta*), as well as his earlier statement that the Irish princes had come to Waterford at Henry's order (*per mandatum ipsius*): Hoveden, 'Annalium' in Savile (ed.), *Rerum Anglicarum* (London, 1596), fol. 301r.

[*][In this place the King of England was met by all the Archbishops, Bishops, and Abbots of all Ireland, who received him to be King and Lord of Ireland, swearing allegiance to him and his heirs, and that he should have the power of governing them for ever; and upon this they gave him their charters. After the example of the Clergy, the Kings and Chiefs of Ireland, mentioned above, received Henry King of England, in like manner, to be Lord and King of Ireland, and became his subjects, and swore allegiance to him and his heirs against all men.]

[**][the Archbishops and Bishops received him to be King and Lord, swore allegiance, and did him homage.]

[***][He received from each individual Archbishop and Bishop of Ireland letters with seals appended in the manner of charters, confirming their subjection to him and his heirs, and testifying that they in Ireland had received him and his heirs as their Kings and Lords for ever.]

5

10

15

20

25

Dominum & Regem Hiberniæ, & sui devenerunt, & ei & Heredibus suis Fidelitatem contra omnes[1] Juraverunt.[*]

Matthew Paris likewise in his History speaking of King *Hen.* II. being in Ireland, saith *Archiepiscopi & Episcopi ipsum in Regem & Dominum receperunt, & ei Fidelitatem & Homagium Juraverunt.*[**]

John Brampton Abbot of *Jornal* in his *Historia Jornalensi,*[2] pag. 1070. speaking of *Hen.* II. hath these words, *Recepit ab unoquoque Archiepiscopo & Episcopo Hiberniæ Literas cum Sigillis suis in modum Chartæ pendentibus, Regnum Hiberniæ sibi & Hæredibus suis Confirmantes, & Testimonium perhibentes ipsos in Hibernia eum & Heredes suos sibi in Reges & Dominos in perpetuum Constituisse.*[***] All the *Archbishops,* *Bishops* and *Abbots* of *Ireland* came to the King of *England,* and Received him for King and Lord of *Ireland,* swearing Fealty to him and his Heirs for ever. The Kings also and Princes of *Ireland,* did in like manner Receive *Henry*

---

1 *omnes*] omnes Homines **H**   2 Jornal … *Jornalensi*] *Jornal[ensi]* … *Jornalanensi* **H** | Jornalensis … Jor[alanensi]'nallensi' **PC** | Jornal (*alt. by hand from* Jornalensi) … *Jornalensis* **I**

11, 5–10 *Matthew … Juraverunt* – cf. *Historia Maior*, anno 1171 (Paris, *Historia Maior* (London, 1641), p. 126). A monk at St Albans, 1220–59, and protégé of Henry III, Paris' account of Henry II in Ireland drew mainly on Hoveden and Ralph de Diceto (on whom, see *Case*, p. 37 nn), by way of Roger of Wendover. See further *ODNB*, s.vv.   **11, 11–12** *John Brampton … Jornalensi* – this substantial chronicle running from the conversion of the Saxons to the accession of John was not compiled till the mid–C.14. It was wrongly credited to John Brompton, abbot of Jervaulx, who acquired the text a century later: *ODNB*, s.v. Domville cited it from Twysden, *Historiæ Anglicanæ* (London, 1652).

King of *England*, for Lord of
Ireland, and became his Men, and
did him Homage, and swore Fealty
to him and his Heirs against all
5 Men. And he received Letters from
them with their Seals pendent in
manner of Charters, confirming the
Kingdom of *Ireland* to him and his
Heirs; and Testifying, that they in
10 *Ireland* had Ordain'd him and his
Heirs to be their King and Lord of
Ireland for ever. After which, he
return'd into *England* in *April*
following, *vizt. April* 1172.[1]

Ireland 15   [3]I come now to Enquire into our
whether ever   Second Particular proposed, *Viz.*
Conquer'd.[2]   Whether *Ireland* might be properly
said[4] to be *Conquer'*d by King *Henry*
the Second, or by any other Prince in
20 any succeeding Rebellion.[5] And here
we are to understand by *Conquest*, an
*Acquisition of a Kingdom by Force of
Arms, to which,*[6] *Force likewise has
been Opposed,* if we[7] are to understand
25 Conquest in any other sense, I see
not of what[8] Use it can be made
against *Irelands* being a Free Country.
I know *Conquestus* signifies a Peace-
able Acquisition, as well as an Hostile

---

1 1172] 1172 **ed** |1173 **H, PC & I** (*for source of Molyneux's error, see* Case, 8nn.)   **2** *marginal heading*
Conquer'd.] Conquer'd **ed** | Conquer'd∧ **I** (*NB other marginal headings end with a full stop rather than a
question mark*)   **3** – p. 13, n. 3 I come … here] ['And' Now] 'I come… here' (*interpolation in margin, cont.
on separate sheet* f. 77r) **H**   **4** said] said [so] **H**   **5** Rebellion] Rebellion [or] **H**   **6** which ∧] which ∧ **ed.** |
which, **H, PC & I**   **7** we] (*interpolation cont.* f. 77r) **H**   **8** of what] 'of' what ['of'] **H**

12, 14 *April 1172* – Molyneux's assumption that Henry departed from Ireland in Apr. 1173 (cf. app. crit.)
rested on Giraldus' error in dating the king's arrival to Oct. 1172 rather than 1171, see above p. 8 nn.
Neither Giraldus, *Expugnatio Hibernica* (Dublin, 1978), p. 105, nor Domville, 'Disquisition', p. 45, gave a
date for the year Henry left Ireland.   **12, 15–20** *our Second … Rebellion* – the beginning of the reply to the
second of the six questions posed, *Case*, pp 5–6.   **12, 15–17, 30** *I come … England* – though starting from
the reference to the peaceful nature of Henry's expedition in Domville, 'Disquisition', pp 40–4, this
discussion of whether the expedition amounted to a hostile conquest was largely new material (based on
Locke).   **12, 21–4** *Conquest … Opposed* – passage denounced by English commons committee: *Commons
Jnl [Eng.]*, xii, p. 325.

[*][after the conquest]
[**][conqueror and lord of Ireland]

Subjugating of an Enemy. *Vid. Spelman's Glos.* And in this sense *William* the First is[1] call'd the *Conquerour*, and many of our Kings have used the Epocha *post Conquestum.*[*] And so likewise *Henry* the Second stiled himself *Conquestor & Dominus Hiberniæ*;[**] but that His Conquest was no violent Subjugation of this[2] Kingdom, is manifest from what foregoes: For here[3] we have an Intire and Voluntary Submission of all the Ecclesiastical and Civil States[4] of *Ireland*, to King *Henry* II. without the least Hostile Stroke on any side; We hear not in any of the Chronicles of any Violence on either[5] Part, all was Transacted with the greatest Quiet, Tranquility, and Freedom, imaginable. I doubt not but the Barbarous People of the Island at that time were struck with Fear and Terror of King *Hen.* II's Powerful Force which he brought with him; but still their Easie and Voluntary[6] Submissions Exempts them from the Consequents of an *Hostile Conquest*, whatever they are;[7] where there is no Opposition, *such a Conquest* can take no place.

---

1 a Peaceable … is] [an] `a peacable´ … [obtaining] Subjugating … [was] is **H**    2 his Conquest … this] [this] `his Conquest´ … th[[e]]is **H**   3 here] *end of interpolation begun p. 12, n. 1 above*   4 all … States] `all´ … [E] [[s]] States **H**    5 any … either] the [least] `any´ … [any] `either´ **H** | [the] `any´ … either *(manu aman.)* **PC**   6 Easie … Voluntary] `easy and´ Voluntary [and easie] **H**    7 whatever … are] `whatever … are´ **H**

13, 2 *Spelman's Glos.* – cf. *Spelman*, 1687, s.v. Conquestus: 'William I is called the Conqueror because he conquered England, i.e. acquired … it, not because he subdued it.'   **13, 5** *Epocha* – variant form of epoch: *OED*, s.v.   **13, 9–31** *His Conquest … place* – cf. Domville, 'Disquisition', pp 42–3.   **13, 22–5** *the Barbarous … Force* – see further Matthew Paris' account of King John's army terrifying Irish petty kings, cited *Case*, p. 44. For Grotius (and Hobbes), surrender in the face of a superior force constituted a conquest rather than a voluntary submission. Cf. intro. p. 23, n. 111.   **13, 26–9** *but still … Hostile Conquest* – passage denounced by English commons committee: *Commons Jnl [Eng.]*, xii, p. 325. Cf. Coke, *7th Rep.*, f. 17v, on Calvin's case (1608), and Hale, *The Jurisdiction* (London, 1976), pp 3–4. For the consequences of conquest, see further *Case*, pp 18–27.

I have before taken Notice of *Henry* the II's using the Stile of *Conquestor Hiberniæ;*[*] I presume no Argument can be drawn from hence, for *Ireland*'s being a Conquer'd Country; for we find that many of the Kings of *England* have used the Æra of *post Conquestum;*[**] *Edward* the Third was the first that used it in *England*, and we frequently meet with *Henricus post Conquestum Quartus,*[***] &c. as taking the *Norman* Invasion of *William* the First, for a *Conquest*. But I believe the People of *England* would take it very ill to be thought a *Conquer'd Nation*, in the sense that some impose it on *Ireland*: And yet we find the same Reason in one Case, as in t'other, if the Argument from the King's Stile of *Conquestor*[†] prevail. Nay, *England* may be said much more properly to be *Conquer'd* by *William* the First, than *Ireland* by *Henry* the Second: For we all know with what Violence and Opposition from *Harrold*, K. *William* obtain'd the Kingdom, after² a Bloody Battel nigh *Hastings*. Whereas *Henry*

Mr. Selden will not allow that ever *H.2.* used this Stile. *Tit. Hon. Par.* 2. C.5 Sect.26.

[*][Conqueror of Ireland]

[**][after the Conquest]

[***][Henry the Fourth since the Conquest]

[†][Conqueror]

---

1 *Edward … Quartus*] so *Henricus … tertius*, or *Quartus* **H** | [so] `*Edward … with´ … [tertius*, or] *Quartus* **PC** 2 after] [even] after

Marginal note *Mr Selden … C.5. Sect. 26* – cf. Selden, *Titles of honour* (London, 1672), p. 614: 'this style in it agrees not with anything I have seen of him'. For *Dopping* (ed.), *Modus* (Dublin, 1692), pref. p. A3v, however, the use of the style *Conquestor Hiberniæ* was important corroboration of the authenticity of the Irish Modus. See further *Case*, pp 34–5. **14, 15–25** *I believe … Henry the Second* – passage denounced by English commons committee: *Commons Jnl [Eng.]*, xii, p. 325. **14, 22–4** *England … William the First* – cf. Locke, *Treatises*, ii, §177. Refusal to accept that there had been a Norman conquest arose from the view that England would thus have been subject to the imposition of new laws by the conqueror, thereby severing continuity with the free institutions of the Saxon past. See further Pocock, *Constitution* (Cambridge, 1987), pp 393–409.

the Second receiv'd not the least Opposition in *Ireland*, all came in Peaceably, and had large Concessions made them of the like

5 Laws and Liberties with the People of *England*, which they gladly Accepted, as we shall see[1] hereafter. But I am fully satisfy'd, that neither King *William* the First, in his

10 Acquisition of *England*, or *Henry* II. in his Acquest of *Ireland*, obtain'd the least Title to what some would give to *Conquerours*. Tho' for my own part, were they *Conquerours* in a

15 sense[2] never so strict, I should enlarge their[3] Prerogative very little or nothing thereby, as shall appear more fully in the Sequel of this Discourse.

20 [4]Another Argument for *Henry* the Second's *Hostile*[5] *Conquest* of *Ireland* is taken from the Opposition which the Natives of *Ireland* gave to the first

25 Adventurers, *Fitz-Stephens*, *Fitzgerald*, and *Earl Strongbow*, and the Battles they fought in assisting *Mac-Morogh* Prince of *Leinster*, in the Recovery of his Principality.

1 see] see [more fully] H   2 a sense] `a sense´ H    3 their] their H | [this] `their´ PC | their *in-press corr. from* this I   4 Another] Another *preceded by del. unfinished para.* [An other [thing] `Objection´ we are to obviate is taken from ] H    5 Hostile] `Hostile´ H

15, 2–6 *all came … England* – Cary, *Vindication*, pp 5–7, demanded evidence for these concessions in the form of charters or specific grants, though Mayart, 'Answer' (Dublin, 1750), pp 122–4, asserted that Henry II granted English law to the Irish by right of conquest.   15, 11 *Acquest* – acquisition: the legal meaning of acquest is 'property acquired other than by inheritance', and is thus virtually indistinguishable from the legal meaning of conquest: *OED*, s.vv. acquest, 1 and 3; conquest, ii, 5.   15, 14–18 *were they … Sequel* – for the very limited rights acquired even by just conquerors, see *Case*, pp 18–25.   15, 17–19 *as shall … Discourse* – see further *Case*, pp 18–27.   15, 22–6 *the Opposition … Strongbow* – as the Act for the Attainder of Shane O'Neill (11 Eliz., ses. 3, c. 1) stated to be the basis of the third of Queen Elizabeth's five titles to Ireland. Cf. Ussher, *Of the religion* (London, 1631), p. 18; Temple, *The Irish rebellion* (London, 1646), p. 3.

'Tis certain there were some
Conflicts between them and the
Irish; in which the Latter were
constantly beaten; but certainly[1] the
5   Conquests obtain'd by those
Adventurers, who came over only
by the King's *License* and
Permission, and not at all by his
particular *Command* (as is manifest
10   from the words of the Letters
Patents of License recited by
Giraldus Cambrensis, Hib. Expug.
pag.760. *Edit. Francof.* 1603. *Angl.*
Norm. Hiber. Camd.[2]) can never[3] be
15   call'd the Conquest of *Henry* the
Second, especially considering that
Henry the Second himself does not
appear to have any[4] Design of
Coming into *Ireland*, or Obtaining
20   the Dominion thereof, when he
gave to his Subjects of *England*[5] this
License of Assisting *Mac-*
Morrogh. But I conceive rather the
contrary appears, by the
25   Stipulations between *Mac-*
Morrogh and the Adventurers, and
especially between him and
Strongbow, who[6] was to succeed
him in his Principality.[7]

---

1 certainly] [whether] `certainly´ **H**   2 760. *Edit. ... Camd.*] *not in* **H** | `760. Edit ... Camd´ **PC**   3 never]
`never´ **H**   4 any] [the least] `any´ **H**   5 to ... *England*] `to ... England´ **H**   6 who] which **H & PC**
7 Principality.] Principality. [Moreover] **H**

16, 9–14 *as is ... Camd.* – Giraldus, *Expugnatio Hibernica* (Dublin, 1978), p. 289, n. 14, queries the
authenticity of the wording of the licence, as given by Giraldus.

From what foregoes, I presume it Appears that *Ireland* cannot properly be said *so to be Conquer'd* by *Henry* the Second, as to give the

5 Parliament of *England* any Jurisdiction over us; it will much more easily Appear, that the *English Victories* in any succeeding *Rebellions* in that Kingdom, give no

10 *Pretence* to a *Conquest*; If every Suppression of a Rebellion may be call'd a *Conquest*, I know not what Country will be excepted.[1] The Rebellions in *England* have been

15 frequent; in the Contests between the Houses of *York* and *Lancaster*, one side or other must needs be Rebellious. I am[2] sure the Commotions in King *Charles* the

20 First's time, are stiled so by most Historians.[3] This Pretence therefore of *Conquest*[4] from *Rebellions*, has so little Colour in it, that I shall not insist longer on it: I know *Conquest*

25 is an hateful Word to English Ears, and we have lately seen a Book* undergo a severe[6] Censure, for offering to broach the *Doctrine of Conquest*[7] in the *Free Kingdom of*

30 *England*.

Suppressing Rebellions, whether a Conquest.

[5]*Bishop of *Salisbury*'s Pastoral Letter.

---

1 Suppression … excepted] [Quelling] `Subpresion´ … [exempt] excepted **H**    2 I am] [Or if] I am **H**    3 are … Historians] cannot be Excused from being so **H** | [cannot… so] `are … Historians´ **PC**   4 of Conquest] `of Conquest´ **H**    5 *marginal note*] Bishop of Salisbury **H** | Bishop of *Salisbury*'s Pastoral Letter' (Bishop of *Salisbury manu aman.*) **PC**    6 severe] severe but just **H** | severe [but just] **PC**    7 the Doctrine … Conquest] [that] `the´ … `of Conquest´ **H**

17, 7–8 *English Victories … Conquest* – as asserted in [Toland], *A Letter* ([London], 1697), p. 2; the marginal heading, 'Suppressing Rebellions … a Conquest', may have been an indirect reference to Toland's work.   **17, 10–18** *If every … Rebellious* – Clement, *Answer*, pp 24–5, denied any parallel with England, on the ground that civil war differed from rebellion. Davenant, *An Essay* (London, 1699), pp 109–14, asserted that while Henry II's grant of English law and their own parliament had been forfeited by the frequent rebellions of the Irish, these rights had not devolved on the present day 'English-Irish'.   **17, 18–21** *the Commotions … Historians* – the now classic formulation of this view in Clarendon's *History of the Great Rebellion* was not published till 1702. For earlier royalist accounts, see MacGillivray, *Restoration historians* (The Hague, 1974), chap. 2.   **17, 23** *Colour* – show of reason, pretext: *OED*, s.v. 12.   **17, 26–30** *we have … England* – see Luttrell's *Parliamentary Diary*, 21–4 Jan. 1692/3, for the commons debates leading to the burning of Burnet's *Pastoral Letter* (1692): Luttrell, *The parliamentary diary* (Oxford, 1972), pp 378–83. The details on p. 381 indicated the procedures likely to have been followed had *The Case* (as subsequently unfoundedly claimed) suffered a similar fate. See further intro. pp 19–20, 46–7.

What Title is obtain'd by Conquest.

But, to take off all Pretence from this Title by *Conquest*, I come in the third Place to enquire, *What Title Conquest gives by the Law of* 5 *Nature and Reason.*[1]

No Title gain'd by an Unjust Conquest.

And in this particular I conceive, that if the Aggressor or Insulter invades a Nation *Unjustly*, he can never thereby have a Right 10 over the Conquered: This I suppose[2] will be readily granted by all men: If a Villain with a Pistol at my Brest, makes me convey my Estate to him, no one will say that 15 this gives him any Right: And yet just such a Title as this has an *Unjust* Conquerour, who with a Sword at my Throat[3] forces me into Submission; that is, forces me to 20 part with my *Natural Estate*, and Birth-right, of being govern'd only[4] by Laws to which I give my *Consent*, and not by his Will, or the Will of any other.

What Title by a Just Conquest.

25 Let us then suppose a *Just* Invader, one that has *Right* on his side to Attack a Nation in an Hostile manner;[5] and that those who

---

1 *Reason.*] Reason. [And this I find [`I find´] losed already to my Hand in an Incomparable <Treatise>] (*cf. ref. to Locke's* Treatises, *p. 27 below*) **H**   2 And ... suppose] [And this I humbly conceive] `And ... conceive´ ... [Invader] Insulter ... [People or] Nation ... [otherwise I] `this I suppose´ **H**   3 Right ... Throat] Right [to my Estate] ... [brest] `throat´ **H**   4 only] `only´ **H**   5 a Nation ... manner] [an] a Nation ... Manner [by force of Arms] **H**

18, 3–5 *in the third ... Reason* – the start of the reply to the third of the six questions posed, *Case*, pp 5–6. Accepting that 'the People of Ireland are a free People ...', Cary, *Vindication*, p. 7, dismissed Molyneux's discussion of conquest as irrelevant.   **18, 3–28, 16** *to enquire ... this Kingdom* – as acknowledged *Case*, p. 27, this account of the implications of conquest was largely based on Locke, *Treatises*, ii, ch. 16, 'Of Conquest'. Molyneux did not, however, consider Locke's assertion in sect. 175 that conquest alone could never serve as a legitimate basis for government. See further, intro. pp 43–4.   **18, 7–19** *if the Aggressor ... Submission* – based on *Treatises*, ii, §176, lines 1–11. Clement, *Answer*, pp 26–7, asserted that Molyneux depicted Henry as an unjust invader forcing the Irish into submission with his sword at their throats.   **18, 20–4** *Natural ... other* – cf. Locke's view that the right to consent to the laws by which one was governed was universal, for which he cited the authority of 'the Judicious Hooker', as did Molyneux, *Case*, pp 151–2. For the concept of rights as property in the broad sense, see *Treatises*, ii, §87, and Laslett's intro., pp 101–2.

oppose him are in the *Wrong*: Let us then see what Power he gets, and over whom.

First, 'Tis plain he gets by his Conquest no Power over those who *Conquered with him*;[1] they that fought on his side, whether as private Soldiers or Commanders, cannot suffer by the Conquest, but must at least be as much Freemen, as they were before: If any lost their Freedom by the *Norman Conquest*, (supposing King *William* the First had *Right* to Invade *England*) it was only the *Saxons* and *Britains*, and not the *Normans* that Conquered with him. In like manner supposing *Hen.* II. had *Right* to Invade this Island, and that he had been opposed therein by the Inhabitants, it was only the *Antient*[2] *Race* of the *Irish*, that could suffer by this Subjugation; the *English* and *Britains*, that came over and Conquered with him, retain'd all the Freedoms and Immunities of *Free-born* Subjects; they nor their Descendants[3] could not in reason lose these, for being Successful and Victorious; for so, the state of both[4]

None over the Assisters in the Conquest.

---

1 by his ... *him;*] `by ... Conquest´ no [new] Power [by his Conquest] ... him, [and were sharers] **H**  2 *Antient*] Milesian **H** | [Milesian] `Antient´ **PC** 3 came ... Descendants] `came ... and´ ... the[ir] ... `nor ... descendants´ **H** 4 both] (*only as catchword* **I**)

19, 4–11 *'Tis plain ... before* – cf. Locke, *Treatises*, ii, §§177, 185. To speak of 'those *who Conquered with him*' conflicted strikingly with Molyneux's reiterated denials that Henry had conquered Ireland, but see further intro. p. 32. **19, 17–19** *supposing ... Island* – since Molyneux took the foundation of the English polity in Ireland to have been purely consensual, the status of Henry's title to invade was presumably immaterial to him. For Atwood, *History*, pp 13–20, however, Henry's just right derived from earlier English titles to Ireland asserted by Arthur, Edgar and William the Conqueror. On these claims, see Flanagan, *Irish society* (Oxford, 1989), pp 41–9.

Conquerours and *Conquered* shall be[1] equally *Slavish*. Now 'tis manifest that the great Body of the present People of *Ireland*,[2] are the Progeny

5 of the *English* and *Britains*, that from time to time have come over into this Kingdom; and there remains but a meer handful of the Antient *Irish* at this day; I may say,

10 not one in a thousand:[3] So that if I, or any body else, claim the like Freedoms with[4] the Natural Born *Subjects of England*, as being Descended from them, it will be

15 impossible to prove the contrary. I conclude therefore, That a *Just*[5] *Conquerour* gets no Power, but only over those who have *Actually Assisted* in that *Unjust* Force that is

20 used against him.[6]

None over the Non-Opposers.[7]

[8]And as those that joyned with the Conquerour in a Just Invasion, have lost no Right by the Conquest; so neither have those of the

25 Country who *Oppos'd him not*: This seems so reasonable at first Proposal, that it wants little Proof. All that gives Title in a *Just*[9] Conquest, is the *Opposers* using *Brutal Force*,

30 and[10] quitting the Law of

---

1 shall be] [are] shall be **H**   2 present … *Ireland,*] `present´… Ireland, [I may say 999/1000] **H**   3 I may … thousand] `I may … thousand´ (*cf. previous note*) **H**   4 like … with] `like´ Freedoms [of] [with] `with [us]´ **H**   5 a *Just*] [J] `a Just´ **H**   6 I conclude … against him.] `I conclude … against him.´ **H**   7 *marginal heading* Non-Opposers.] Non-Opposers. ed | Non-Opposers∧ **I**   8 – p. 21, n. 2 And … Enslave him.] `And … Enslave him.´ (*interpolation in margin*) **H**   9 *Just*] `Just´ **H**   10 Force, and] Force, [those therefore and] and **H**

20, 3–10 *the great … thousand* – this apparent marginalization of the native Irish has long puzzled commentators. However, the notion that the Irish were of mixed British and Irish descent was fairly widespread in C.17, see further intro. p. 32.   **20, 10–15** *if I … contrary* – passage denounced by English commons committee: *Commons Jnl [Eng]*, xii, p. 325. Cf. Locke, *Treatises*, ii, §177: 'And if I, or any Body else, shall claim freedom, as derived from [the Normans], it will be very hard to prove the contrary.'   **20, 29** *Brutal Force* – i.e. literally the force of brutes or beasts, as a result of abandoning reason through resort to aggression. Cf. *Treatises*, ii, §181.

Reason, and using the Law of
Violence; whereby the Conquerour
is[1] entitled to use him as a *Beast*;
that is, Kill him, or Enslave him.[2]

5 Secondly, Let us consider what
Power that is, which a *Rightful
Conquerour* has over the Subdued
Opposers:[3] And this we shall find
extends little farther than over the
10 *Lives* of the *Conquer'd*; I say, *little
farther* than over their Lives; for
how far it extends to their *Estates*,
and that it extends not at all to
Deprive their *Posterity* of the[4]
15 *Freedoms* and *Immunities* to which
all *Mankind* have a *Right*, I shall
shew presently. That the *Just
Conquerour* has an Absolute Power
over the *Lives* and *Liberties*[5] of the
20 Conquer'd, appears from hence,
Because the Conquer'd,[6] by putting
themselves in a *State of War* by
using an Unjust Force, have thereby
forfeited their *Lives*. For quitting
25 *Reason*, (which is the Rule between
Man and Man) and using *Force*
(which is the way of *Beasts*) they
become liable to be destroy'd by
him against whom they use
30 *Force*, as any savage wild *Beast*

**Just Conquerour
intitled to the
Lives of the
Opposers.**

---

1 the Conquerour is] [I am] `the ... is´ H **2** Enslave him.] [take him captive] Enslave him. (*end of
interpolation begun p. 20, n. 8 above*) H **3** which ... *Opposers*] `which´ ... `Opposers´ H **4** Deprive ...
the] Depriv[[ing]]e ... the[ir] H **5** and *Liberties*] `and Libertys´ H **6** Because ... Conquer'd] [that]
because `the Conquerd´ H

21, 5–22, 1 *Let us ... Being* – based on *Treatises*, ii, §181.

that is Dangerous to his Being.

And this is the Case of *Rebels* in a settled Commonwealth, who forfeit their Lives on this Account. But as for forfeiting their Estates, it depends on the Municipal Laws of the Kingdom. But we are now Enquiring what the Consequents will be between[1] two Contesting Nations.

Which brings me to Consider how far a Just Conquerour has Power over[2] the *Posterity* and *Estates* of the Conquer'd.

As to the *Posterity*, they not having Joyn'd or Assisted in the *Forcible Opposition* of the Conquerours *Just* Arms, can lose no Benefit thereby. 'Tis unreasonable any Man should be punish'd but for his own fault. Man being a free Agent, is only Answerable for his own Demerits;[4] and as it would be highly Unjust to Hang up the Father for the Sons Offence, so the Converse is equally Unjust, that the Son shou'd suffer any Inconvenience for the Fathers Crime.[5]

Just Conquerour how far impower'd over the Posterity[3] of the Opposers.

5

10

15

20

25

---

1 between] [of] `between´ **H** 2 over] [of] over **H** 3 Posterity] Posterity [and Estates] **PC** 4 Demerits] [faults] `Demerits´ **H** 5 Crime] [Demerits] `Crime´ **H**

22, 2–7 *the Case … Kingdom* – an important qualification suggesting that the right of victims of aggression to 'appeal to Heaven' to recover their freedom and property (recognized in *Treatises*, ii, §192) would not extend to the Irish, who had voluntarily submitted to Henry II. See further next paragraph but one. 22, 7 *Municipal Laws* – the laws of a particular state, as distinguished from the law of nations, or of nature: *OED*, s.v. municipal, 1a. 22, 15–24, 27 *As to … Subdued* – this discussion of rights over the property of the conquered was based on *Treatises*, ii, §182–9. 22, 23 *Demerits* – offences, blameworthy acts: *OED*, s.v. 2b. 22, 27 *Inconvenience* – danger or injury, rather than incommodity or discomfort: *OED*, s.v. 4, 7.

A Father hath not in himself a
power over the Life or Liberty of
his Child, so that no Act of his can
possibly forfeit it.[1] And tho we find[2]
5　in the Municipal Laws of particular
Kingdoms, that the Son loses the
Fathers Estate for the Rebellion or
other Demerit of the Father,[3] yet
this is Consented and Agreed to, for
10　the Publick Safety, and for deterring
the Subjects from certain Enormous Crimes that would be highly
prejudicial to the Commonwealth.[4]
And to such Constitutions the
15　Subjects are bound to submit,
having consented to them,[5] tho' it
may be unreasonable to put the like
in Execution between *Nation* and
Nation[6] in the *State of Nature*: For
20　in Settled Governments, Property
in Estates is Regulated, Bounded
and Determined by the Laws of the
Commonwealth, consented to by
the People, so that in these, 'tis no
25　Injustice for the Son to lose his
Patrimony for his Fathers Rebellion
or other Demerit.[7]

---

1 A Father ... it.] `A Father ... it.´ (*interpolation in margin*) **H**　2 find] find it otherwise **H** | find [it
otherwise] **PC**　3 that the ... Father] *not in* **H** | `that ... Father´ **PC**　4 Consented ... Commonwealth]
consented [to] ... to [by the Commonwealth] for ... [Body Politick] `Commonwealth´ **H**　5 having ...
them] *not in* **H** | `having ... them´ **PC**　6 *Nation ... Nation*] [Kingdom] `Nation´ ... [Kin<gdom] Nation
H　7 For ... Demerit.] `For ... `in Estates´ ... Demerit.´ (*interpolation on separate sheet* f. 82r) **H** | `for ...
Demerit´ (*interpolated between paras, manu aman.*) **PC**

23, 1–4 *A Father ... forfeit it* – taken almost verbatim from *Treatises*, ii, §189, lines 2–4.　23, 19–27 *For in
... Demerit* – this significant interpolation (cf. app. crit.) brought out how the loss of property as
punishment for rebellion was the consequence of the rebels' (or rebels' ancestors') consent to the original
establishment of government. Founding the Irish polity on the compact between Henry II and the Irish
princes provided therefore a far more secure title for Anglo-Irish property than Henry's supposed conquest
of Ireland. See further intro. pp 31–2.

How far over
their Estates.

If therefore the *Posterity* of the Conquer'd are not to suffer for the Unjust *Opposition* given to the Victor by their *Ancestors*, we shall

5 find little place for any Power of the Conquerours over the *Estates* of the Subdued. The *Father* by his Miscarriages and Violence can forfeit but his own Life, he involves

10 not his *Children* in his Guilt or Destruction. His *Goods*, which *Nature* (that willeth the Preservation of all *Mankind* as far as possible) hath made to belong to

15 his *Children* to sustain them, do still continue to belong to his[1] *Children*. 'Tis true indeed, it usually happens that *Damage* attends[2] Unjust Force; and as far as the *Repair* of this

20 *Damage* requires it, so far the Rightful Conquerour may invade the *Goods* and *Estate* of the Conquer'd; but when this Damage is made up, his Title to the Goods

25 ceases, and the Residue belongs[3] to the *Wife* and[4] *Children* of the Subdued.

It may seem a strange Doctrine, that any one should have a Power

30 over the *Life* of another Man[5], and

---

1 his ... his] [the] `his´ Children {to} [keep] to sustain ... [the] `his´ **H** 2 attends] commonly attends all **H** | [commonly] attends [all] **PC** 3 belongs] belong **H & PC** 4 *Wife* and] `Wife and´ **H**  5 any ... Man] [Conquest should give a Title to the] `any ... over´ ... Life [and] of [ye Conquered] `an other Man´ **H**

24, 1–7 *If therefore ... Subdued* – the rights of innocent wives and children did not, however, confer any entitlement on the dispossessed Irish of C.17, whose ancestors had forfeited their lands through treason subsequent to the original agreement with Henry II; see previous paragraph. Locke, however, considered a wife to have an absolute right to her own property: *Treatises*, ii, §183. **24, 12–16** *Nature ... Children* – paraphrased from *Treatises*, ii, §182, lines 5–9. Locke had earlier identified '*the preservation of Mankind*' as '*the fundamental Law of Nature*': ibid, ii, §§16, 134–5. **24, 28** *strange Doctrine* – the phrase was Locke's, cf. *Treatises*, ii, §180.

not over his *Estate*; but this we[1] find
every day, for tho' I may *Kill* a Thief
that sets on me in the High-way, yet
I may not *take away his Money*; for
5 'tis the *Brutal Force* the Aggressor
has used, that gives his Adversary a
Right to take away his *Life*, as a
noxious Creature. But 'tis only
Damage sustain'd,[2] that gives Title
10 to another Mans *Goods*.

It must be confess'd that the
Practice of the World is otherwise,
and we commonly see the Conqueror (whether *Just* or *Unjust*) by
15 the Force he has over the Conquer'd,
compels them with a Sword at their
Brest to stoop to his Conditions,
and submit[3] to such a Government
as he pleases to Afford them. But
20 we Enquire not now, what is the
Practice, but what *Right there is to
do so*. If it be said the Conquer'd
submit by their own *Consent*: Then
this allows *Consent* necessary to give
25 the Conquerour a Title to Rule[4]
over them. But then we may Enquire whether Promises[5] Extorted
by *Force* without *Right*, can be
thought *Consent*, and how far they

Practise of
Conquerors
otherwise.

---

1 we] [will] we **H**   **2** *sustain'd*] sustain **H & PC** | sustain **I**   **3** stoop ... Submit] [submit] stoop ...
submitt **H**   **4** to Rule] `to rule´ **H**   **5** Promises] [Covenant or] Promise **H** | Promise´s´ **PC**

25, 2–10 *for tho'* ... *Goods* – reproduced *Treatises*, ii, §182, lines 22–27.   **25, 13–26, 15** *the Conqueror* ... *by
Force* – based on *Treatises*, ii, §186.   **25, 19–22** *But we* ... *do so* – this qualification was of considerable
significance for Molyneux's general position, see further intro. p. 31.

are *Obligatory*; And I humbly conceive they *Bind not at all*. He that *forces* my Horse from me, ought presently to *Restore* him, and

5 I have still a *Right* to retake him: So he that has *forced* a Promise from me, ought presently to *Restore* it, that is, quit me of the *Obligation* of it, or I may chuse whether I will[1]

10 perform it or not: For the *Law of Nature* obliges us[2] only by the *Rules* she prescribes, and therefore cannot oblige me by the *Violation* of her[3] Rules; such is the Extorting

15 any thing from me by *Force*.

From what has been said, I presume it pretty clearly appears that an *Unjust* Conquest gives *no Title* at all; That a *Just* Conquest

20 gives Power only over the *Lives* and *Liberties* of the *Actual Opposers*, but not over their *Posterity or Estates*, otherwise than as before is mentioned; and not at all over those that

25 did *not Concur* in the Opposition.[4]

[5]They that desire a more full Disquisition of this Matter, may find it at large in an Incomparable *Treatise*[6] concerning the *True Original*,

---

1 will] may **PC**   **2** obliges us] [layin<g>] obleidges **H**   **3** her] [t]he´r´ **H**   **4** that an *Unjust…* Opposition.] [the Little or No Title gaind by Conquest] [`that Conquest gives´] `that [Conq<uest>] an unjust Conquest… Opposition.´ (*final interpolation in margin*) **H**   **5** They] *no new para.* **H**   **6** at large … *Treatise*] [Discusd] at … [Discourse] `*Treatise*´ **H**

26, 7 *presently* – immediately: *OED*, s.v. 3.   **26, 29–27, 1** *the True … Government* – cf. subtitle of Locke's *Second treatise*, viz. *An essay concerning the true original, extent, and end of civil government*.

Extent and End of Civil Government, Chap. 16.[1] This Discourse is said to be written by my Excellent Friend, *JOHN LOCKE*, Esq; Whether it be so or not, I know not;[2] This I am sure, whoever is the Author, the Greatest Genius in *Christendom* need not disown it.

But granting that all we have said in this Matter is *Wrong*, and granting that a Conquerour, whether *Just* or *Unjust*, obtains an *Absolute* Arbitrary *Dominion* over the Persons, Estates, Lives, Liberties and Fortunes of all those whom he finds in the Nation, their Wives, Posterity, *&c.* so as to make perpetual *Slaves* of them and their Generations to come. Let us next Enquire whether *Concessions* granted by such a Victorious *Hero*, do[3] not bound the Exorbitancy of his Power, and whether he be not Obliged strictly to Observe these Grants.

And here I believe no Man of Common Sense or Justice, will Deny it; None that has[4] ever Consider'd the Law[5] of Nature

Marginal note: Concessions granted by a Conquerour, whether Obligatory

---

1 Chap. 16.] Chap 16. [to which I acknowledge my self beholding in a Great Measure for what I have deliverd on this Head] **H**   2 Whether … not;] `whether … not´ **H**   3 do] [may] `do´ **H**   4 None … has] `None´ … [have] `has´ (`None´ *perhaps add. later* **H**)   5 Law] Laws **H & PC**

27, 3 *my … Friend* – cf. Locke's reference to his pride in Molyneux's friendship in *An Essay* (2nd edn, London, 1694), bk II, ch. ix, sect. 8. For a more bald attribution to Locke, see *Case*, p. 153. Goldie, *The reception of Locke's politics* (London, 1999), i, p. 212, credits Molyneux as the first writer to identify Locke in print as author of *Two treatises*. **27, 4–5** *Whether … I know not* – this interpolation (cf. app. crit.) betrayed misgivings at revealing Locke's authorship of *Two treatises*. For Locke's reaction to Molyneux's disclosure, see intro. p. 19. While acknowledging Locke's authority on the subject of Conquest, both Cary, *Vindication*, p. 103, and Clement, *Answer*, p. 30, accused Molyneux of distorting his arguments. **26, 9–19** *But granting … to come* – this apparent concession did not represent a denial of the argument Molyneux had just articulated but reflected the conventions of presenting a case in court, which he had adopted as the format for his book. Having marshalled all that could be said on the subject of conquest, he now moved on to consider the fourth of the six questions posed *Case*, pp 5–6, namely what concessions had been made to the Irish subsequent to Henry II's expedition. See further intro. p. 29. **27, 20–4** *Concessions … Grants* – it was generally held under both common law and the law of nations that a conqueror was free to impose new laws on the (Christian) conquered, but once having done so could only alter them with the consent of the conquered. Cf. extract from Coke, *7th Rep.*, ff 17v–18r, cited *Case*, p. 122.

and Nations, can possibly hesitate on this matter; the very Proposing it, strikes the Sense and Common Notions[1] of all Men so forcibly, that
5   it needs no farther proof. I shall therefore insist no longer on it, but[2] hasten to consider how far this is the Case of *Ireland*: And that brings me naturally to the fourth Particular[3]
10   propos'd, *vizt*. To shew by Precedents, Records, and History,[4] what Concessions and Grants have been made from time to time to the People of *Ireland*, and by what steps
15   the Laws of *England* came to be introduced into this Kingdom.

[*][King Henry (saith he) before he left Ireland, called an Assembly at Lismore, where the Laws of England were freely received by all, and confirmed by the solemnity of an oath.]

[5]What Concessions have been made from the Crown of *England* to the Kingdom of *Ireland*.

By Henry II.

We are told by[6] *Matth. Paris*, Historiographer to *Hen*. III. that[7] *Henry* the Second, a little before he
20   left *Ireland*, in a Publick Assembly and Council[8] of the *Irish* at *Lismore*, did cause the *Irish* to Receive, and swear to be Govern'd by the Laws of *England*: *Rex Henricus* (saith he)
25   *antequam ex Hibernia Rediret apud Lismore Concilium Congregavit ubi Leges Angliæ sunt ab omnibus gratanter receptæ, & Juratoriâ cautione prestitâ Confirmatæ*, Vid. Matth.
30   Paris, ad An. 1172. Vit. H.2.[*]

---

1 and ... Notions] `and ... Notions´ H    2 insist ... but] `insist ... but´ H   3 fourth Particular] [`4th. Partissular?`] (*in margin beside line*) H   4 by Precedents ... History,] `by ... History´ H    5 *marginal heading*] What ... [time to time] `the Crown ... Ireland´ **PC**   6 We ... by] [We have seen before from] `We ... by´ H   7 that] [How] that H   8 Assembly ... Council] Council ... Assembly H

28, 17–37, 23 *We are ... Paris* – cf. *Historia maior* (1641 edn), p. 126. This discussion of the Irish Modus as evidence for Henry II's establishing a parliament in Ireland was prompted by Domville, 'Disquisition', pp 46–7, with extensive additions by Molyneux, drawn partly from Dopping's 1692 edn of the Irish Modus. Given the lack of other documentary substantiation of Henry's grant of English law and government to the Irish, the authenticity of the Modus was fundamental to Molyneux's case. See further intro. p. 33.   **28, 17–24** *Matth. ... England* – Cary, *Vindication*, p. 9, asserted that if Molyneux accepted that statutes were part of the laws which the Irish accepted from Henry II, he must logically concede that subjection to the English parliament was part of 'the original Contract'. The designation 'Historiographer to *Hen*. III' came from Domville, 'Disquisition', p. 44.

And not only thus, but if we
may give Credit to Sir *Edward Cook*,
in the 4th Instit. Cap. 1. and 76. and
to the Inscription to the *Irish*
5   *Modus Tenendi Parliamentum*, it
will clearly Appear, that *Henry* the
Second did not only settle the Laws
of *England* in *Ireland*, and the
Jurisdiction Eclesiastical there, by
10   the *Voluntary Acceptance* and
Allowance of the Nobility and
Clergy, but did likewise Allow them
the Freedom of *Holding of
Parliaments* in *Ireland*, as a separate
15   and distinct Kingdom from
England; and did then send[1] them a
Modus to Direct them how to
Hold their Parliaments there. The
Title of which *Modus* runs thus:

20

   *'Henricus Rex Angliæ Conquestor
& Dominus Hiberniæ, &c.*[2]
*Mittit hanc formam Archi-
episcopis, Episcopis, Abbatibus,*
25   *Prioribus, Comitibus, Baronibus,
Justiciariis, Vicecomitibus, Majoribus, Praepositis, Ministris*[3] *&
omnibus Fidelibus suis Terræ
Hiberniæ Tenendi Parliamentum.*[4]

---

1 send] send **H & PC** | sent **I**   2 &c.] `&c.´ **H**   3 Ministris] `ministris´ **H**   4 *Parliamentum*] Parliament [[a]]um **H**

29, 4–5 *the Inscription … Modus* – that was the exemplification recounting the seizure of the Irish Modus at Clane, Co. Kildare, in 1418, given in full, *Case*, p. 33. Cary, *Vindication*, p. 10, objected to Molyneux's citing Coke, who wrote five hundred years later, as evidence for what was done by Henry II.   **29, 12** *Clergy* – Molyneux omitted the important qualification in Domville, 'Disquisition', p. 46: 'without the Accesse of any pretended Coordinate Power of the Lords, and Commons of England'. Cf. *Case*, p. 166 nn.

In primis Summonitio Parliamenti præcedere debet per Quadraginta Dies.[*]

[*][Henry King of England, Conqueror and Lord of Ireland, &c. sends this form of holding parliaments to the Archbishops, Bishops, Abbots, Priors, Earls, Barons, Justices, Sheriffs, Mayors, Seneschals, Officers, and all his loyal subjects of Ireland. Imprimis, the calling of a parliament ought to be forty days before <it meets>.]

5   And so forth.

This *Modus* is said to have been sent into *Ireland* by *Hen*. II. for a Direction to Hold their
10 Parliaments there. And the sense of it agrees for the most part with the *Modus Tenendi Parl.* in *England*, said to have been Allowed by *William* the *Conquerour*, when he
15 obtain'd that Kingdom; where 'tis alter'd, 'tis[1] only to fit it the better for the Kingdom of *Ireland*.

I know very well the Antiquity[2] of this *Modus*, so said to be Trans-
20 mitted for *Ireland* by *Hen*. II. is question'd by some Learned Antiquaries, particularly by Mr. *Selden* (a)[3] and (b) Mr. *Pryn*,[4] who deny also the English *Modus* as well as this.[5] But
25 on the other hand, my Lord Chief Justice *Cook*, in the 4th Instit. pag. 12. and 349. does strenuously Assert them both. And the late Reverend and Learned Dr. *Dopping* Bi-

(a) *Tit. Hon.* Par. 2 C.5. *Sect.* 26. *Edit. Lond. An.* 1672
(b) Against *Cook's* 4th Instit. C.76.

---

1 'tis] is **H** | `t´is **PC**   2 Antiquity] [Credit] `Antiquity´ **H**   3 *marginal ref.*] *in* **H** | (*manu aman.*) **PC**
4 *marginal ref.*] *in* **H** | (*manu aman.*) **PC**   5 who ... this] `who ... this´ **H**

30, 8–15 *Hen. II. ... Kingdom* – characteristically Molyneux omitted Domville's phrase: 'when he Conquerd that Kingdome', after '*Hen.* II.', and read 'obtain'd' for Domville's 'Conquered'. Cf. Domville, 'Disquisition', p. 46. For the history of the Irish Modus, see appendix A below.   **30, 23–6** *Mr. Pryn ... Instit.* – cf. Prynne, *Brief animadversions* (London, 1669), p. 249: 'this mistake of [Coke's] I have at large refuted before [ibid., p. 7], ... and proved the Modus to be a spurious late Imposture.'   **30, 27** *Assert* – champion or vindicate: *OED*, s.v. 2,5.

shop of *Meath*, has Published the
Irish Modus, with a Vindication of
its Antiquity and Authority in the
Preface.

5   ¹There seems to me but two
Objections of any Moment raised
by Mr. *Pryn* against these *Modi*.
The One relates both to the *English*
and *Irish Modus*; the other chiefly
10   strikes at the *Irish*. He says the
Name *Parliament*, so often found in
these *Modi*, was not a name for the
great Council of *England*² known so
early as these *Modi* Pretend to. I
15   confess I am not prepared to
Disprove this Antiquary in this
Particular: But³ to me it seems
reasonable enough to Imagine that
the Name *Parliament*, came in with
20   *William* the *Conqueror*. 'Tis a Word
perfectly French, and I see no
reason to doubt it's Coming in with
the *Normans*. The other Objection
affects our *Irish Modus*, for he tells
25   us, That *Sheriffs* were not establish'd
in *Ireland* in *Henry* II's. time, when
this *Modus* was pretended to be
sent hither, yet we find the Word
Vicecomes therein. To this I can only
30   Answer,   That   *Hen.*   II.

1 – p. 32, n. 5 There ... Time.] *not in* **H** | `There ... [be] `me´ ... [[o]]Objections ... Time.´ (*interpolation on separate sheet* f. 177r–v) **PC**   **2** for the ... *England*] `for ... England´ **PC**    **3** Particular: But] Particular `:´ [[b]]But **PC**

31, 5–32, 18 *There ... Time* – despite Prynne's objection that there were no sheriffs in Ireland in Henry II's time, Dopping's pref. had dismissed his arguments as irrelevant to the authenticity of the Irish Modus. Molyneux's riposte was a last moment addition to the text (cf. app. crit.); his etymology of 'parliament' probably derived from Lambarde, *Archeion* (Cambridge, 1635), p. 240 (a work cited *Case*, pp 136–8). **31, 27** *pretended* – claimed: *OED*, s.v. 7.

intending to Establish in *Ireland*[1] the
English form of Government, as the
first, and Chief step thereto, he sent[2]
them Directions for Holding of
5 Parliaments, Designing afterwards
by degrees and in due time[3] to settle
the other Constitutions, agreable to
the Model of *England*. If therefore
England had then *Sheriffs*, we need
10 not wonder to find them named in
the *Irish Modus*, tho they were not
as yet establish'd amongst us, for they
were designed to be appointed soon
after, and before the *Modus* could
15 be put regularly in execution; and
accordingly we find them establish'd
in some Counties of *Ireland*[4] in *King
Johns* Time.[5]

This *Irish Modus* is said to have[6]
20 been in the Custody of Sir
Christopher Preston at *Clane* in
Ireland, An.6. *Hen*.5. And by Sir
John Talbot, Lord Lieutenant of
Ireland, under King *Hen*.5. It[7] was
25 Exemplified by *Inspeximus* under the
great Seal of *Ireland*, and the
Exemplification was sometimes in
the Hands of Mr. *Hackwel of Lincolns*
Inn, and by him was Communicated[8]
30 to Mr. *Selden*. [9]The Tenor of which
Exemplification runs thus.

---

1 in *Ireland*] `in Ireland´ **PC**   2 sent] [gave] `sent´ **PC**   3 by degrees ... time] `by ... time´ **PC**   4 of *Ireland*] `of Ireland´
PC   5 Time.] *end of interpolation begun p. 31, n. 1 above*   6 have] `have´ **H**   7 at *Clane ... Hen*.5. And ... *Hen*.5 it] at
Clane ... Hen.5. And ... *Hen*.5 it ed | of *Clane ... Hen*.4. and ... *Hen*.4. It **H, PC & I**   8 by ... Communicated] by him
... Communicated [by him] **H**   9 – p. 35, n. 1 `The Tenor ... body of it.´ (*interpolation on separate quire* ff 87r–88r) **H**

32, 7 *Constitutions* – institutions of government: *OED*, s.v. 3b.   **32, 19–33, 27** *This Irish ... Summonitio* – Domville,
'Disquisition', p. 47, based the original of this passage on Coke, *4th Inst.*, p. 12. Selden and Coke read 'Clare' for 'Clane',
though Domville, 'Disquisition', p. 47, and Dopping, *Modus* (Dublin, 1692), pref., p. A3r have 'Clane' (both presumably
following Domville's roll).   **32, 21–2** *Sir Christopher ... Hen. 5* – Talbot's account showed this episode to have been a
manoeuvre in the factional struggle between Butlers and Talbots rather than the simple forestalling of treason, depicted
in the exemplification below: Crooks, 'The background to the arrest', *Analecta Hibernica*, 40 (2007), pp 5–9. The mistaken
reference to Henry IV rather than Henry V (cf. app. crit.) derived from Hakewill's 1614 transcript (cf. Steele (ed.), *A
Bibliography* (Oxford, 1910), p. clxxxviii), and was perpetuated in Selden, *Titles of honour* (London, 1672), p. 614, and
Coke, *4th Inst.*, p. 12.   **32, 25** *Exemplified ... Inspeximus* – i.e. an officially attested copy was made, embodying a recital
that the earlier document had been inspected and confirmed: *OED*, s.vv. exemplify 7, and *inspeximus*.   **32, 28–9** *Mr.
Hackwel ... Inn* – the antiquary William Hakewill MP had championed parliamentary rights in the commons, 1601–28;
his *Manner of holding parliaments* (1641) included a translation of the English Modus: *ODNB* s.v. Archbishop Ussher had
addressed a (no longer extant) letter to him, impugning the authenticity of the Irish Modus: Prynne, *Brief animadversions*
(London, 1669), p. 7.   **32, 30** *Tenor* – in legal usage, the actual wording of a document: *OED*, s.v. I, 1a.

[*][Henry, by the grace of God, King of England and France, and Lord of Ireland, to all whom these presents shall come, greeting. We have examined the tenor of several articles, written in a parchment-roll found in the custody of Christopher Preston, Knight; at the time of his being lately arrested in the town of Clane, by the Deputy of our trusty and beloved John Talbot of Halomshire, Knight, the Lieutenant of our territory of Ireland, in our own presence, and before our council in the said territory, at the town of Trim, on the ninth day of January last past) in these words:]

[**][The method of holding parliaments. Henry King of England, conqueror and Lord of Ireland, sends this form to the Archbishops, &c]

[***][And to all his loyal subjects of the Land of Ireland a Summons for holding a Parliament]

Henricus Dei Gratia Rex Angliæ & Franciæ, & Dominus Hiberniæ, *omnibus ad quos presentes Literæ pervenerint salutem, Inspeximus Tenorem Diversorum Articulorum in quodam Rotulo Pergameneo Scriptorum cum* Christophero Preston,[1] *Milite Tempore Arrestationis suæ apud Villam de* Clane,[2] *per Deputatum Dilecti & Fidelis nostri Johannes Talbot de* Halomshire *(Chivaler locum nostrum Tenentis Terræ nostræ Hiberniæ, nuper factæ inventorum ac coram nobis & Concilio nostro in eadem terra[3] nostra apud Villam de* Trim. *Nono die Januarii ultimo præterito[4] in hæc verba,*[*]

5

10

15

20

"Modus Tenendi Parliamenta Henricus Rex Angliæ, Conquestor & Dominus Hiberniæ[5], Mittit hanc formam[6] Archiepiscopis,[**] &c. and so as before, *"Et omnibus Fidelibus suis Terræ Hiberniæ Tenendi Parliamentum Imprimis Summonitio,* &c."[***] and

25

1 Christophero Preston] Christophero [`dę´] `de´ Preston ([`dę´] *interpolated in line and del. probably because unclear for transcription of* PC) H   2 Clane] Clane ed | Clare **H, PC & I** (Clane **Domville, 47**)   3 *Terra*] *Terra* **H & PC** | *Terræ* **I**   4 *præterito*] præterito **H & PC** | *præteriti* **I**   5 *Hiberniæ*] *Hiberniæ* **H & PC** | *Hibernia* **I**   6 *formam*] formam [&c] **H**

33, 11–13 *Johannes Talbot … Hiberniæ* [transl. *John Talbot … Ireland*] – Sir John Talbot, Baron Furnevalle, or Talbot de Halomshire (the feudal honor of Hallamshire in Yorkshire), was lord lieutenant of Ireland, 1414–19; he later became 1st earl of Shrewsbury: *Complete Peerage*, s.v. Furnevalle and Shrewsbury. The deputy who arrested Kildare and Preston, 26 June 1418, was his brother Sir Thomas: Crooks, 'The background to the arrest', *Analecta Hibernica*, 40 (2007), pp 5–6.

then follows the *Modus*, agreeable in most things with that of *England*, only fitted to *Ireland*. Then the Exemplification concludes:

Nos autem tenores Articulorum prædictorum de Assensu præfati Locum tenentis & Concilii prædicti tenore præsentium duximus Exemplificandum & has Literas nostras fieri fecimus Patentes. Teste Præfato Locum nostrum tenente apud Trim. 12 die¹ Januarii Anno Regni nostri sexto.[*]

Per ipsum Locum tenentem & Concilium.[**]

[*][Now we have thought proper by the tenor of these presents to cause an exemplification to be made of the tenor of the aforesaid articles, by and with the consent of our above-named Lieutenant and of our council named above, and have ordered these our letters patent to be made. Witness our aforesaid Lieutenant at Trim, on the 12th January in the sixth year of our reign.]

[**][By the Lieutenant and Council.]

Now we can hardly think it credible, (says the Bishop of *Meath*)² that an *Exemplification* could have been made so solemnly of it by King *Henry* the Fifth,³ and that it should refer to a *Modus* transmitted into *Ireland* by King *Henry* II. and Affirm that it was produced before the Lord Lieutenant and Council at *Trym*, if no such thing had been Done: This were to call in question the Truth of all former Re

---

1 *die*] die **H & PC** | *diæ* **I**   2 (says … *Meath*)] `(says … Meath)´ **H**   3 Fifth] Fifth **ed.** | Fourth **H, PC & I**

34, 7–10 *tenores … tenore* [transl. *tenor … tenor*] – the term is perhaps used here in two different senses: in line 8, meaning 'effect, or substance', and in line 9 'the actual wording': *OED*, s.v. I, 1a.   **34, 19–22, 2** *Now … of it* – based on Dopping, *Modus* (Dublin, 1692), pref., p. A3r. Richardson, 'The Preston exemplification', *IHS*, 3 (1942–3), p. 189, points out that while exemplification confirmed the existence of the copy of a document at a given time, it could throw no light on the authenticity of the original text.

cords and Transactions, and make the Exemplification contain an Egregious Falshood in the body of it.[1]

5 The Reverend Bishop of *Meath*, in his fore-cited Preface does believe that he had obtain'd[2] the very Original Record, said by my Lord *Cook* to have been in the
10 Hands of Sir *Christopher Preston*: It came to that Learned Prelates Hands amongst other Papers and Manuscripts of Sir *William Domviles*,[3] late Attorney General in
15 this Kingdom, who in his Life-time, upon an occasional Discourse with the Bishop concerning It, told him that this Record was bestow'd on him (Sir *W. Domvile*) by Sir *James*
20 *Cuffe*, late Deputy Vice-Treasurer of *Ireland*, that Sir *James* found it among the Papers of Sir *Francis Aungier*, Master of the Rolls in this Kingdom; and the present Earl of
25 *Longford* (Grandson to the said Sir *Francis Aungier*) told the Bishop, that his said Grandfather had it out of the Treasury of *Waterford*.

---

1 of it.] *end of interpolation begun p. 32, n. 9 above*   2 obtain'd] `obtaind´ H   3 *Domviles*,] Domviles, [which] **H**

35, 5–28 *The Reverend … Waterford* – based on Dopping, *Modus* (Dublin, 1692), pref. p. A2v. Aungier had arrived in Ireland in 1609 and died in 1632 (*Complete Peerage*, s.v.); Cuffe was his son-in-law. Both Domville and Lord Longford were grandsons of Archbishop Thomas Jones (A. Clarke, *Prelude to Restoration* (Cambridge, 1999), p. 177), a relationship that may account for Domville's acquiring the *Modus*.
35, 24–8 *the present … Waterford* – the treasury at Waterford is also identified, *Case*, p. 65, as the repository of the exemplifications of the two lost constitutional statutes, 10 Hen. 4 and 29 Hen. 6.

¹Whilst I write this, I have this
very Record now before me, from
the Hands of the said Bishop of
Meath's Son, my Nephew, *Samuel*
5 *Dopping*; and I must confess it has
a Venerable Antient Appearance,
but whether it be the True Original
Record, I leave on the Arguments
produced for its Credit by the said
10 Bishop.²

Parliaments very early in Ireland.

This I am sure of, that whether
this be the very Record Transmitted
hither by King *Henry* the Second,
or not; yet 'tis most certain from the
15 Unanimous Concessions of all the
fore-mentioned Antiquaries, *Cook*,
Selden, *Pryn*, &c. That we have had
Parliaments in *Ireland* very soon
after the Invasion of *Henry* II. For
20 *Pryn* confesses that³ (*a*) King *Hen.*
II. after his Conquest of *Ireland*,
and the General Voluntary
Submission, Homages, and Fealties
of most of the *Irish* Kings, Prelates,
25 Nobles, Cities and People, to him,
as to their Soveraign Lord and
King, *Anno* 1170, (it should be
1172.) held therein a General
Council of the Clergy

⁴(*a*) Against the 4th Instit. c.76: p.249.

---

1 Whilst] [`The Exemplification of Hen. ye 2ds Irish Modus under the Broad Seale of Ireld in Hen. ye 4th time, said to be in the Hands of Mr Hakewell of Lincolns Inn´] (*del. interpolation in margin*) Whilst **H**
2 and I must ... Bishop] [And tho it have a venerable Antient Appearance, yet I `must confess I´ dare not Venture to Assert that this was the very Original Record. for first] and I must ... Bishop **H** 3 *Pryn* ... that] [thus says Pryn, Certain it is] `Pryn ... that´ **H** 4 *marginal ref.*] in **H** | (*manu aman.*) **PC**

36, 1–5 *Whilst ... Dopping* – Anthony Dopping (ob. 1697) was doubly related to Molyneux by marriage, being both the first cousin of his wife, Lucy Domville, and the husband of his sister Jane; their son Samuel was born in 1671. **36, 6** *Venerable ... Appearance* – cf. Dopping, *Modus* (Dublin, 1692), pref. p. A3r. For the subsequent history of the roll, see further appendix A below. **36, 20–37, 23** *Pryn confesses ... Paris* – as p. 36, marginal ref. (a) stated, this material (including the two marginal refs on p. 37) was taken from Prynne, *Brief animadversions* (London, 1669), p. 249, which contained the erroneous ref. to Expugnatio Hibernica, book II in place of book I (cf. p. 37 app. crit.). Prynne cited the concluding phrase, 'Leges Angliæ ... confirmatæ' (pp 37, 14–15) from Paris, *Historia maior* (London, 1641), p. 126. **36, 28–37, 10** *held therein ... to come* – this reference to Henry's church reforms (like that in Domville, 'Disquisition', pp 44–5) avoided mention of the specific abuses that commentators, such as Stanihurst, *De rebus in Hibernia* (Antwerp, 1584), pp 128–9, had regarded as justifying Henry's conquest of Ireland in fulfilment of the papal mandate in *Laudabiliter* (1155).

at *Cashel*[1], wherein he Rectify'd many Abuses in the Church, and Establish'd sundry Eclesiastical Laws, agreeable to those in the Church of *England*; *Ecclesiæ illius statum ad Anglicanæ Ecclesiæ formam Redigere Modis omnibus elaborando*[*]; To which the *Irish* Clergy promis'd Conformity, and to observe them for[2] time to come, as *(a)* Giraldus *Cambrensis*[5] who was then in *Ireland*, and other *(b)* Historians relate:[6], *Et ut in singulis Observatio similis Regnum Colligaret utrumque* (that is *England* and *Ireland*) *passim omnes unanimi voluntate communi Assensu, Pari desiderio Regis imperio se subjiciunt, omnibus igitur hoc modo Consummatis, in Concilio habito apud Lismore Leges Angliæ ab omnibus sunt gratanter*[7] *receptæ, & juratoriâ cautione praestitâ Confirmatæ*,[**] says *Math. Paris.*

Can any Concession in the World be more plain and free than this? We have heard of late much Talk in *England* of an *Original Compact* between the *King* and *People of England*;[8] I am sure 'tis not possible to shew a more fair *Origi-*

[*][Labouring by all means to reduce the state of that Church to the form of the English Church]

[**][And that in every particular the same observances might unite both kingdoms; (that is England and Ireland), they all every where, with perfect unanimity, by common consent, and with equal willingness, submit to the King's pleasure; every thing, therefore, being settled in this manner, in an assembly held at Lismore, the laws of England were freely accepted by all, and established with the solemnity of an oath]

5
10
15
20
25
30

[3][a] *Topograph*[4] *Hibern.* l. 3, c.18. *Hib. Expug.* l.I. c.33, 34. [b] *Hoveden Annal pars-post.* p.302. *Brampton Chr. Col.* 1071. *Knighton. de Even. Angl.* l. c.c. 10. col. 2394, 2395. *Pol. Virg. Hist. Angl.* l.13. *Radul. de Diceto. Walsingham,* &c.

Original Compact for Ireland.

1 *Cashel*] Cashel H | Cashell PC | Cashall I original state D3r   2 and ... for] [for] and ... for H   3 *marginal ref. (a)*] in H | (*manu aman.*) PC   4 *Topograph*] Topograph H & PC | Togograph I   5 Hib. Expug. l.I.] Hib. Expug. l.I. ed | Hib. Expug. l.II. H, PC & I   6 *marginal ref. (b)*] in H | (*manu aman.*) PC   7 *gratanter*] gratanter H & PC | gratantur I   8 between ... England] `between ... England´ H

37, marginal ref. (a) *Topograph ... c. 33,34.* – *Topographia Hiberniæ* merely described the state of the Irish church (Giraldus (Mountrath, 1982), pp 112–15), while *Expugnatio Hibernica* provided an account of the council and its decrees (chs 34–5 in Giraldus (Dublin, 1978), pp 98–101).   **37, marginal ref. (b)** – *Hoveden ... Walsingham, &c.* For Hoveden and Brompton, see *Case*, pp 10–11 nn. Though Henry Knighton's *De Eventibus Angliae* dated from the end of C.14, Ralph de Diceto's later C.12 *Ymagines Historiarum* drew on contemporary documents and significant personal contacts. The only work of the late C.14–early C.15 chronicler Thomas Walsingham to mention the Council at Lismore was *Ypodigma Neustriæ* in Camden (ed.), *Anglica, Normannica, Hibernica* (Frankfurt, 1603), pp 447–8. The *Historia Anglica* of the Italian humanist Polydore Vergil (who lived for many years in England) was written in the early C.16. See further *ODNB*, svv.   **37, 11** *who ... Ireland* – Giraldus did not come to Ireland till 1183, see *Case*, p. 7 nn.   **37, 19–22** *in Concilio ... Confirmatæ* – this grant of English laws at Lismore was entirely apocryphal; the council held there in 1172 was purely ecclesiastical. See Brand, 'Ireland and the literature' in Brand, *The making of the common law* (London, 1992), p. 449, n.72.   **37, 22–3** *says ... Paris* – see Paris, *Historia maior* (London, 1641), p. 126.   **37, 26–38, 1** *We have ... Compact* – speakers in the convention debates on the succession to the throne in 1689 had referred to the 1689 Bill of Rights as England's original compact; cf. Grey (ed.), *The Debates* (London, 1769), ix, p. 477; x, p. 75.

nal Compact between a King and
People, than this between Henry
the Second, and the *People* of
Ireland, That they should Enjoy the[1]
5 *like Liberties and Immunities, and be*
Govern'd by the same Mild Laws,
both Civil and Ecclesiastical,[2] *as the*
People of England.

From all which, It is manifest[3]
10 that there were no Laws Imposed
on the People of *Ireland*, by any
Authority of the Parliament of
England; nor any Laws introduced
into that Kingdom by *Henry* the
15 Second, but by the *Consent* and
Allowance of the People of *Ireland*:
For both the Civil and Ecclesiastical State were settled there *Regiæ*
sublimitatis Authoritate, solely by
20 the Kings Authority, *and their own*
good Wills, as the *Irish*[4] Statute, 11
Eliz. c.1. expresses it. And not only
the *Laws* of *England*, but the
manner of *Holding Parliaments* in
25 *Ireland* to make Laws of their own
(which is the *Foundation* and
Bulwark of the Peoples *Liberties*
and *Properties*[5]) was Directed and
Established there by *Henry* the
30 Second, as if he were Resolved

---

1 the] *not in* **H & PC**   2 *both… Ecclesiastical*] `both … Eclesiastical´ **H**    3 From … manifest] `from …
which´ … manifest [from hence] **H**   4 State … *Irish*] [[Es]]State … `Irish´ **H**   5 *Properties*] Property **H**

38, 9–43, 15 *From all … Europæ* – based on Domville, 'Disquisition', pp 47–9 and 38.   38, 9–11 *From all*
… Ireland – passage denounced by English commons committee: *Commons Jnl [Eng.]*, xii, p. 325.
38, 21–2 *the Irish … 11 Eliz., c. 1.* – viz. the Act for the Attainder of Shane O'Neill, 1569 (recte 11 Eliz.
ses. 3, c. 1). Cf. Cary, *Vindication*, p. 15: 'What the Irish Statutes express, I think hath no great Weight …'.

that no other Person or Persons should be the Founders of the Government of *Ireland*, but himself and the *Consent* of the People, who

5 submitted themselves to him against all Persons whatsoever.

Let us now see by what farther Degrees[1] the Government of *Ireland* grew up Conformable to

10 that of *England*.

About the Twenty-third year of *Henry* the Second, (which was within Five years after his Return from *Ireland*) he created his younger

15 Son[2] *John, King of Ireland*, at a Parliament held at *Oxford*. Soon after *King John* being then about Twelve Years of Age, came into Ireland, from *Milford* to *Waterford*,

20 as his Father had formerly done. The *Irish* Nobility and Gentry immediately repaired[3] to him; but being Received by him and his Retinue with some Scorn and

25 Derision, by reason of their long[4] rude Beards, *quas more Patriæ*[5] *grandes habebant & prolixas*[*], (says *Giraldus Cambrensis, Hib. Expug. Cap.35.*) they took such Offence

King *John* made King of *Ireland*.

[*][which they wore of great length and size, after the manner of their country]

---

1 by ... Degrees] [what Concessions] by ... [stops] `Degrees´ **H**   2 younger Son] `younger´ Son [`younger´] **H**   3 Nobility ... repaired] `Nobility ... Gentry´ ... [repaird] `repared´ **H**   4 some ... long] [levity] `some scorn´ ... `long´ **H**   5 Patriæ] Patriæ **ed** | Patrio **H, PC & I** | (Patriæ **Domville, 12**)

39, 4 *and the ... People* – added by Molyneux to Domville, 'Disquisition', p. 47.   **39, 6** *against ... whatsoever* – an emphatic reiteration (in English) of the phrase *contra omnes* cited from Hoveden (*Case*, pp 10–11), implying that the fealty sworn by the Irish to Henry II held good even against the English lords and commons. Cf. Domville, 'Disquisition', p. 44, and his citation from Matthew Paris.   **39, 11–16** *About ... Oxford* – Domville, 'Disquisition', p. 47, identified '*Brampton Historia Jornalensi, ad annum 1177*' as his source. Both Mayart's 'Answer' (Dublin, 1750), pp 26–7, and Atwood's *History*, pp 35–6, made much of Henry's recognising the need for parliamentary backing in creating John King of Ireland, as did Hale, *The Prerogatives* (London, 1976), p. 32. See further intro. pp 34, 44, 56. Atwood, *History*, pp 34–5, cited Hoveden and Brompton as evidence that those who received lands in Ireland on this occasion did homage to both Henry 'and his Son John'.   **39, 15** *King of Ireland* – although the early chroniclers (and Molyneux) used the terms 'king' or 'lord' of Ireland interchangeably, strictly speaking John was created only lord of Ireland in 1177. The kingly title was not adopted till 1541 in 33 Hen. 8, ses. 1, c. 1. Prior to this, the official designation was 'the Lordship of the Kingdom of Ireland', see further Lydon, 'Ireland and the English crown', *IHS*, 29 (1995), pp 281–2.   **39, 19** *Milford* – Millford Haven: Domville, 'Disquisition', p. 48.   **39, 28–9** *Giraldus ... Cap. 35* – Molyneux's sole citation from Book II of *Expugnatio* (ch. 36 in 1978 edn).

thereat, that they departed in[1] much Discontent; which was the occasion of the young Kings staying so short a time in *Ireland*, as he did this his first time of being here.

And here, before we proceed any farther, we shall observe, That by this Donation of the *Kingdom* of *Ireland* to *King John*, *Ireland* was most eminently[2] set apart again, as a *Separate* and *Distinct Kingdom* by itself from the Kingdom of *England*; and did so continue, until the Kingdom of *England* Descended and came unto *King John*, after the Death of his Brother *Richard* the First, King of *England*, which was about Twenty two years after his being made King of *Ireland*; during which space of Twenty two years, both whilst his Father *Henry* the Second, and his Brother *Richard* the First, were living and Reigning, King *John* made divers Grants and Charters to his Subjects of *Ireland*, which are yet in being in this Kingdom; wherein he stiles himself *Dominus Hiberniæ*,[*] (the constant Stile[3] till *Henry* the Eighth's

By this *Ireland* made an Absolute separate Kingdom.

[*][Lord of Ireland]

---

1 in] with **H & PC**   2 eminently] [Distinctly] `eminently´ **H**    3 Stile] [Titl<e>] `stile´ **H**

40, 8–9 *this Donation … John* – see intro. p. 56. The significance of John's title by donation is discussed further, *Case*, pp 41–2, 53–4.

[¹][Lord of Ireland and Count of Mortain]

time) and in others, *Dominus Hiberniæ & Comes Meritoniæ*.[¹] By which Charters both the City of *Dublin*, and divers other Corporations enjoy many Priviledges and Franchises to this day. But after the said¹ Grant of the Kingdom of *Ireland* to King *John*, neither his Father *Henry* II. nor his Brother King *Richard* I. Kings of *England*, ever stiled themselves, during their Lives, *King* or *Lord* of *Ireland*; for the *Dominion* and *Regality* of *Ireland* was wholly and separately vested in K. *John*, being absolutely Granted unto him without any Reservation. And he being Created King in the Parliament at *Oxford*, under the Stile and Title of *Lord of Ireland*,² Enjoy'd all manner of *Kingly Jurisdiction*, *Preheminence*, and *Authority Royal*, belonging unto the *Imperial State* and *Majesty of a King*, as are³ the Express words of the *Irish* Statute, 33 *Hen.* VIII.c.I. by which Statute the Stile of *Dominus*[⁂] was changed to that of *Rex Hiberniæ*[⁂⁂].

Let us then suppose that *Richard* the First, King *John*'s Elder

[⁂][Lord]

[⁂⁂][King of Ireland]

---

1 to this ... said] [un]to ... `sd´ H    2 *being ... Ireland*] `being ... Oxford´ ... *Ireland* [*being ... Oxford*] H   3 *and Majesty ... are*] as majesty ... `are´ H | [as.] `and´ ... are PC

41, 2–4 *By which ... Dublin* – John's Dublin charter of 1192, granted as *Dominus Hiberniæ et Comes Meritoniæ*, is reproduced in Gilbert (ed.), *Facsimiles* (Dublin, 1879–84), iv, pt ii, pl. lxv.   **41, 12–16** *the Dominion ... Reservation* – this claim was strongly rejected by Clement, *Answer*, pp 50–3, who accused Molyneux of ignorance of feudal law under which the grantor (and his heirs) remained the feudal superior of the grantee, as demonstrated by John's arraignment for treason by the barons of England during Richard's reign (in 1194, cf. Warren, *King John* (London, 1981), p. 32).   **41, 20–7** *all manner ... Hiberniæ* – as defined in the 1541 act establishing the kingly title. Clement, *Answer*, p. 48, queried the value of so late an act as evidence for events in John's reign.   **41, 28–42, 10** *Let us ... England* – discussion of this hypothetical line of descent highlighted the basis of John's sovereignty by donation, and resolved any remaining doubts as to England's current title to Ireland resting on conquest. See further, *Case*, pp 54–5, and intro. p. 34. An apparently contradictory line of argument, resting on John's title by conquest, is developed, (*Case*, p. 122), to demonstrate that the English parliament had no right to alter the laws which John granted to the Irish, without the latter's consent.

Brother, had not died without Issue, but that his Progeny had sat on[1] the Throne of *England*, in a Continued Succession to this Day: Let us suppose likewise the same of King *John*'s Progeny, in relation to the Throne of *Ireland*; where then had been the *Subordination* of *Ireland* to the *Parliament*, or even to the *King* of *England*? Certainly no such thing could have been then pretended: Therefore if any such *Subordination* there be, it must arise from something that followed *after*[2] the Descent of *England*, to King *John*; for *by* that *Descent England* might as properly be *Subordinate* to *Ireland*, as the converse; *Ireland* being vested in the Royal Person of King *John*, Two and Twenty years before his[3] Accession to the Crown of *England*, and being a more *Ancient Kingdom* than the Kingdom of *England*. As the English Orators in the Council of Constance, *An.* 1417 (*a*) confess'd and alledged, as an Argument in the Contest between *Henry* the Fifth's Legates, and those[5] of *Charles* the Sixth King of *France*, for *Precedence: Satis Constat* (say

[4](*a*) *Seldens Tit. Hon. Par.* I. C.8 Sect. 5. *Usher* Archbishop of *Armagh*, of the Religion of the Antient *Irish, Cap.* 11.

---

1 on] in **PC**   2 that ... *after*] [subsequent to] `that ... after´ **H**    3 his] [the] his **H**    4 *marginal ref.*] *in* **H** | (*manu aman.*) **PC** | (Archbi-/bishop **I**)    5 as an ... those] `as an Argument´ ... [the Legates] those **H**

42, 8–43, 15 *Subordination ... Europæ* – based on Domville, 'Disquisition', pp 49 and 38.   **42, 24–43, 15** *As the English ... Europæ* – as indicated in the marginal ref., this passage was based on Ussher, *Of the religion* (London, 1631), p. 127; the Latin was transcribed verbatim from Ussher's footnote, together with the reference to the manuscript in the Royal Library. For the printed acts see Schelstrate (ed.), *Acta Constantientis Concilii* (Antwerp, 1683). The Council of Constance, 1414–18, ended the Great Schism in the papacy, begun in 1378: Strayer, *Dictionary* (New York, 1982), iii, pp 645–51.   **42, 25** *Orators* – ambassadors, or envoys: *OED*, s.v. 4.

[*][It is perfectly clear (say they) according to Albert the Great, and Bartholomew, Concerning the Properties of Things, that, the whole world being divided into three parts, Europe, Asia and Africa (for America was not then discovered): Europe is divided into four kingdoms, those of Rome, Constantinople, Ireland, (now transferred to the English), and Spain. Hence it follows, that the King of England and his Kingdom, are among the most distinguished and most ancient Kings and kingdoms of all Europe.]

they) (*b*)[1] *secundum Albertum Magnum & Bartholomeum de Proprietatibus Rerum, quod toto Mundo in tres partes Diviso, scilicet in Europam, Asiam & Africam* (for *America* was not then Discovered) *Europa in quatuor Dividitur Regna scilicet, Primum Romanum, Secundum Constantinopolitanum, Tertium Regnum Hiberniæ* (*quod jam translatum est in Anglos*) *& Quartum*[2] *Regnum Hispaniæ. Ex quo patet, quod Rex Angliæ & Regnum suum sunt de Eminentioribus*[3] *Antiquioribus Regibus & Regnis totius Europæ.*[*] The *Antiquity* and *Precedence* of the King of *England*, was allow'd[4] him wholly on the Account of his Kingdom of *Ireland*.

Perhaps it will be said, That this *Subordination* of the Kingdom of *Ireland*, to the Kingdom of *England*, proceeds from *Ireland*'s being Annex'd to, and as it were united with the Imperial Crown of *England*, by several Acts of Parliament both in *England* and *Ireland*, since King *John*s time. But how farr this Operates, I shall Enquire more fully[5] hereafter; I shall only at present Observe, that I conceive little

(*b*) *Act. Concil. Constant. Ses.* 28. *MS. in Bib. Reg.* not in the Printed Acts.

Ireland in what sense Annex'd to England.

1 *marginal ref.*] *in* H | *but add. manu WM* PC   2 *Primum … Quartum*] [*Romam Constantinopolim*] `*primum … Constantinopolitanum, tertium*´ … [*ad*] `*in*´ … `*quartum*´ H & PC   3 *Eminentioribus*] Eminentioribus [*et*] H & PC   4 allow´d] allowd H & PC | allo´wd I   5 since King … fully] `since … time´ … `more fully´ H

43, 1–3 *Albertum Magnum … Rerum* – it is unclear which of Albert the Great's works Molyneux had in mind. Neither the 1495 edn of Bartholomaeus Anglicus' widely cited C.13 encyclopaedia, *On the properties of things* (Cf. Strayer, *Dictionary* (New York, 1982), iv, p. 448), nor the 1975 transl., refer to the antiquity of either the Spanish or Irish kingdoms in the division of the world into Europe, Asia and Africa found in book xiv, ch. 1, §50.   **43, 2–3** *de Proprietatibus Rerum* [transl. *Concerning … Things*] – the 1776 and 1782 edns translated Bartholomaeus' title as 'Concerning the Rights of States'.   **43, 19–44, 10** *this Subordination … Lord* – notably in Poynings' Act (10 Hen. 7, c. 4), 1494, and its various C.16 confirmations and amendments. See further, *Case*, p. 127.   **43, 24** *Imperial … England* – cf. the concept of untrammelled sovereignty owing subordination to no earthly superior, set forth in the 1533 English act against appeals to Rome (24 Hen. 8, c. 12), and *Case*, p. 128. Clement, *Answer*, p. 56, accused Molyneux of seeking to draw an unsustainable distinction here between the imperial crown of England and the kingdom of England.

more is Effected by these Statutes Than that *Ireland* shall not be *Alien'd* or *Separated* from the King of *England*, who cannot hereby

5 dispose of it, otherwise than in *Legal Succession* along with *England*; and that whoever is *King of England*, is *ipso facto King of Ireland*, and the Subjects of *Ireland* are oblig'd to

10 Obey him as their Liege Lord.

To proceed therefore. After both Crowns[1] were united, on the Death of *Richard* the First without Issue, in the Royal Person of King *John*:

15 He, about the Twelfth Year of his Reign of *England*, went again into *Ireland, viz.* the Twenty Eighth[2] day of *June*, 1210. and *Math. Paris* tells us, pag. 230.[3] *Cum Venisset ad*

20 *Dublinensem Civitatem Occurrerunt ei ibidem plus quam* 20 *Reguli illius Regionis qui omnes Timore maximo perterriti*[4] *homagium ei & Fidelitatem fecerunt. Fecit quoque*

25 *Rex ibidem,* Construere Leges & Consuetudines Anglicanas, *ponens Vicecomites aliosque Ministros, qui populum Regni illius* juxta Leges Anglicanas Judicarent.[5][*]

Marginal note (left): King *John* comes a second time into *Ireland.* The People submit to him.

Marginal note (right): [*][After his arrival at the city of Dublin, there met him more than twenty petty Princes of that country, who struck with the greatest fear, did him homage, and swore allegiance. There also the King caused them to establish the laws and customs of England, appointing Sherrifs, and other Officials, to govern the people of that kingdom according to the English laws.]

---

1 To proceed ... Crowns] [After both] (*new para.*) To ... [Kingdoms] Crowns **H**   2 Twenty Eighth] 8th **H & PC**   3 230.] 230. **ed** | 220. **H, PC & I**   4 perterriti] perterriti **H]** p[[re]]erterriti **PC** | preterriti **I**   5 Judicarent.] Judicarent. [(*new para.*) And the Pat. Rol. 11. Hen. 3. in Angl. tells us that K. John] **H**

44, 3 *Alien'd* – alienated: *OED*, s.v. alien, vb.   **44, 7–10** *whoever ... Liege Lord.* The question of whom to obey once the English Convention had settled the throne on William and Mary (13 Feb. 1688/9) and James II had arrived in Ireland (12 Mar. 1688/9) deeply divided Irish Protestants. Returning exiles in 1690 argued that those who remained behind and recognized James' authority should be indicted for treason: NLI MS 2055, f. 6.   **44, 11–29** *After both ... Judicarent* – based on Domville, 'Disquisition', p. 49. Where Molyneux gave an (abbreviated) extract from Matthew Paris, *Historia maior* (cited from Prynne, *Brief animadversions* (London, 1669), p. 249, n. f), Domville cited passages from the 'Aid Roll 120 Johannis in the Pipe Roll Office' and 'Patent Roll 18 H. 3'.   **44, 24–9** *Fecit ... Judicarent* – this presumably referred to John's lost charter of 1210, which is discussed in Brand, 'Magna Carta in Ireland' in Crooks & Mohr (eds), *Law and the idea of liberty* (Dublin, forthcoming). See further intro. p. 34, n. 163. Atwood, *History*, p. 92, argued that John's legislation of 1210 was proof that Henry II did not allow Ireland a parliament, since otherwise its consent would have been necessary to validate John's grant. The record in Rot. Pat. 18 Hen. 3, m. 17, n. 21 (cited in Domville, 'Disquisition', p. 49), however, spoke of the Lord John ordaining the observance of the laws of England *'communi omnium in Hibernia consensu'* [with the consent of all men in Ireland] (cf. *Case*, p. 54), which (as Vaughan, *Reports and arguments* (London, 1714), p. 294, pointed out) misled Coke, *4th Inst.*, pp 12, 349, into believing that an Irish parliament had sat in 1210, an error copied by Bolton, 'Declaration', p. 13.

His Son King *Henry* the Third came to the Crown the Nineteenth of *October* 1216. and in *November* following he Granted to *Ireland* a

5 *Magna Charta*, Dated at *Bristol* 12 *November*, the First Year of his Reign. 'Tis Prefaced, *that for the Honour of God, and Advancement of Holy Church, by the Advice of his Council of England*, (whose

10 names are particularly recited) He makes the following *Grant to Ireland*;[3] And then goes on Exactly Agreeable to the *Magna Charta* which he granted to *England*;[4] only in ours we have *Civitas*

15 *Dublin*,[*] & *Avenliffee*,[**] instead of *Civitas London*,[***] and *Thamesis*[†] with other Alterations of the like kind where Needful. But ours is Eight years older than that which he granted to *England*, it

20 not being till the Ninth Year of his Reign, and ours is the First Year. This *Magna Charta* of *Ireland* Concludes thus, *Quia vero sigillum nondum Habuimus*[6] *presentem Cartam Sigillis*

25 *Venerabilis Patris nostri Domini Gualt. Apost. Sedis Legati & Willelmi Mareschalli Comitis Pembrooke Rectoris nostri & Regni nostri fecimus Sigillari. Testibus*[7] *omnibus prænominatis & alijs*

30 *Multis Dat.*[8] *per Manus Predictorum*

Concessions[1] *from Hen. III.*[2]

[*][City of Dublin]
[**][Avenliffey]
[***][City of London]
[†][Thames]

---

1 *marginal heading* Concessions] Concession **H** |Concessions **PC** | Concessions *in-press corr. from* Concessiom **I**   2 – p. 46, n. 1 His Son … *Dublin*] `His … Dublin´ *(interpolation on separate sheet f. 72r–v keyed to* **PC** *p. 43.*) **H** | `His Son … Dublin´ *(interpolation on separate sheet f. 184r–v: a somewhat similar interpolation (manu WM) has been del. p. 48, n. 2)* **PC**   3 Prefaced … to *Ireland*] Prefaced [by the] … *[Privy] Council* … `to Ireland´ **H**   4 *England*;] England, [not till the 9th year of his Reigne. So that ours is [older than the English Magna Charta.] `8 years older than the English Magna Charta.´] *(but cf. following sentence)* **H**   5 This … *Ireland*] th[[e]]is [Iris<h>] … of Ireland **H**   6 *Habuimus*] Habuerimus **H** | Habui[[erimus]]mus *(manu aman.)* **PC**   7 *Testibus*] [An Antient Coppy] Testibus **H**   8 Dat.] Dat. **H & PC** | Dat∧ **I**

45, 4–6 he Granted … Reign – cf. text in *ESI*, i, pp 4–19. Modern scholarship, however, identifies the text of Magna Carta Hiberniæ in the Red Book of the Exchequer (see below) as the unofficial handiwork of an early C.14 exchequer clerk. See further intro. p. 34, n. 163. Interestingly, Atwood, *History*, p. 99, had also argued that the 1216 Irish Magna Carta must be spurious, though on the ground that it followed the wording of the English statute, 9 Hen. 3, rather than the original Magna Carta of 1215. See further following two notes.   **45, 12–21** Exactly … First Year – though no contemporary version survived, the Irish Magna Carta of 1216 was based on the revised version of John's Great Charter, issued by the regents of Henry III in 1216. The English reissue of 9 Hen. 3 (1225) was the classic text of the charter, which became the first item in the English statute book. For further discussion of the charters, see *Case*, pp 61–2, 156–8.   **45, 21–46, 7** This Magna … Dublin – the Red Book of the Exchequer was the most important source for Irish statutes prior to the inception of the Statute Rolls in 1427; it was destroyed in the Four Courts in 1922: *ESI*, i, intro. p. ix; H. Wood, *A Guide* (Dublin, 1919), p. 125. Cf. *Case*, p. 61 nn. **45, 25–7** Gualt. .. Pembrooke – Cardinal Guala Bicchieri was the second papal legate sent to help John regain control of England after the king's submission to the pope in 1213; arriving in 1216, he remained till 1218. William Marshall, earl of Pembroke (one of John's most prominent supporters) assumed the role of regent and guardian of the kingdom after the king's death, himself dying in 1219. See *ODNB*, s.vv.

Domini Legati & Willelmi Marescalli. Apud Bristol Duodecimo die Novembr. Regni nostri Anno Primo.[*] An Antient Coppy
5 of this *Magna Charta of Ireland* is to be found in the *Red Book* of the *Exchequer Dublin.*[1]

In *February* following in the First Year likewise of his Reign, by
3(*a*) Pryn against the 4th Inst. c.76. p.250.
10 Advice of all his Faithful Counsellors in *England*, to gratify[2] the *Irish* (says (*a*) *Pryn*) for their eminent Loyalty to his Father and Him, he[4] granted them out of his
15 *Special Grace*, that they and their Heirs for ever should enjoy the *Liberties* granted by his Father and Himself to the Realm of *England*; which he Reduced into Writing,
20 and sent Seal'd thither under the Seal of the Popes Legat, and W. Earl Marshal his Governour, because he had then no Seal of his own. This as I conceive Refers to
25 the foremention'd *Magna Charta Hiberniæ.* The record as Recited by Mr. *Pryn*, here follows.[5]

[*][Because we have not hitherto had a seal, we have caused the present Charter to be sealed with the seals of the venerable father, Lord Walter, Legate of the Apostolic See, and of William Mareschall, Earl of Pembroke, our Governor, and Governor of our Kingdom. Witness all who are mentioned above and many others. Given under the hand of the aforesaid Lord Legate, and William Mareschall, at Bristol, on the 12th day of November in the first year of our reign.]

---

1 *Dublin.*] *end of interpolation begun p. 45, n. 2 above*   2 In ... gratify] His son K. Hen. ye 3d. in the first ... [to gratify] by Advise ... to gratify **H** | [His ... ye 3d.] `In ... following´ in ... `likewise´ ... to gratify **PC** 3 *marginal ref.*] *in* **H** | (*manu aman.*) **PC**   4 he] *not in* **H** | `he´ **PC**   5 This ... follows.] as the ensuing record testifys **H** | [as ... testifys] `this ... `forementiond´ ... follows´ **PC**

46, 9–11 *by Advice ... Counsellors* – Clement, *Answer*, pp 59–62, took 'Counsellors' to refer to the privy council (as did Molyneux in connection with the *Ordinatio pro statu Hiberniæ, Case,* p. 89), and argued that for Ireland to be subject to the English privy council was inconsistent with the status of an 'Independent Kingdom'. *Gratify* – reward: *OED*, s.v. 1.

¹'Rex Archiepiscopis, Epis-
copis, Abbatibus, Comitibus,
Baronibus, Militibus & Libere
Tenentibus, & omnibus

5 Fidelibus suis per Hiberniam
Constitutis, Salutem: Fidelitatem
vestram in Domino Com-
mendantes quam Domino Patri
nostro semper Exhibuistis &

10 nobis estis diebus nostris
Exhibituri: Volumus quod in
signum Fidelitatis vestræ, tam
præclaræ, tam Insignis
Libertatibus Regno Nostro

15 Angliæ a Patre nostro & nobis
Concessis, de gratia nostra &
Dono in Regno nostro Hiberniæ
gaudeatis² vos & vestri Hæredes
in perpetuum.³ Quas Distincte

20 in Scriptum Reductas de
Communi Consilio omnium
Fidelium nostrorum vobis Mittimus Signatas Sigillis Domini
nostri G. Apostolicæ Sedis Legati

25 & Fidelis nostri Com. W.
Maresc. Rectoris nostri & Regni
nostri quia Sigillum non-

*Pa. I H.III. m. 13.
intus.*

---

1 *marginal ref.*] *in* **H** | (*manu aman.*) **PC**   2 gaudeatis] gaudeatis **ed** |guadeatis **H, PC & I**   3 in
perpetuum] imperpetuum **H & PC**

47, 1–48, 5 *Rex ... 6 Februar.* – cf. Prynne, *Brief animadversions* (London, 1669), p. 250, extract (3).

dum habuimus, easdem processu temporis de Majori Consilio proprio Sigillo Signaturi.'[*]

5   Teste apud Glouc. 6 Februar.[1][**]

Here we have[2] a free Grant of all the *Liberties of England* to the[3] *People* of *Ireland.* But we know the *Liberties* of Englishmen are Founded on that Universal *Law of Nature*, that ought to prevail throughout the whole World, *of being Govern'd only by such*[4] *Laws to which they give their own Consent by their Representatives in Parliament.*

And here, before I proceed farther, I shall take Notice, That in the late Raised Controversie, *Whether the House of Commons were an Essential part of Parliament*, before the 49th year of *Henry* the Third; The Learned Mr. *Petyt*, Keeper of the Records in the *Tower*,[5] in his Book on that Subject, pag. 71. Deduces his 9th Argument *From the Comparison of the Antient* Generale Concilium, *or Parliament of Ire-*

Record out of Mr. Petyt of the Antiquity of Parliaments in Ireland.

[*][The King to the Archbishops, Bishops, Abbots, Earls, Barons, Knights, and Freeholders, and all our faithful subjects settled in Ireland, greeting. Commending your loyalty in the Lord to the King our father, and that which we know, you will always show to us; our will and pleasure is, that of our grace and favour to our kingdom of Ireland, you and your heirs for ever should enjoy, in testimony of your unshaken and distinguished loyalty, the liberties granted to our kingdom of England by our father and ourself. Which liberties reduced to writing, with the common consent of our faithful subjects, we send to you sealed with the seals of our Lord Walter, Legate of the Apostolic See, and of our trusty Earl, William Mareschall, our Governor, and that of our kingdom, because we have as yet no seal; determined in process of time, with farther advice, to ratify the same liberties with our own seal.]

[**][Given at Gloucester, the 6th of Feb.]

---

1 6. Februar.] `6. Februar.´ *(perhaps add, later)* **H**   2 Here we have] [And] [[h]]Here we may observe **H** | [Here ... observe] `Here we have´ *(preceded by del. interpolation in margin, manu WM, add. after marginal note* Record ... Ireland) [So likewise we find in the Red Book of the *Exchequer. Dublin.* the Coppy of the *Magna Charta* of *Ireland* granted by Hen. ye 3d. and Dated at Bristol the 12th of *Novembr.* ye 1st year of his Reigne: it agrees in all things with the *Magna Charta* which he granted to England, only ours is 8 years more Antient. Hen. 3d. began his Reign the 19. Octob. 1216 so that in Novembr following he granted this Charter to Ireland. and afterwards in Febr. he farther made the Grant in the record here recited.'tis also to be noted that this *Magna Charta Hiberniæ* concludes as the foregoing Record, *et Quia sigillum nondum habuimus*] *(cf. interpolation p. 45, n. 2 to p. 46, n. 1)* **PC**   3 of all ... to the] [to the] of all ... to the **H**   4 are Founded ... *of* ... *such*] [consist in] `are ... of´ ... [by] `only by such´ **H**   5 Keeper ... Tower] `Keeper ... Tower´ **H**

48, 19–23 *late Raised ... Henry the Third* – now known as the 'Brady controversy', cf. Pocock, *Constitution* (Cambridge, 1987), ch. 8. Ironically, despite his refusal to commit himself on the origins of the English commons, Molyneux was accused by Atwood, *History*, dedic., of aping Brady's views; 49 Hen. 3 referred to the parliament of 1265, the first occasion of the summons of both knights of the shire and burgesses. 48, 25 *his Book ... Subject* – *The antient right of the commons of England asserted ...* (London, 1680).

land, instanced cAn. 38. *Hen.* III.
with the Parliament in England,
wherein the Citizens *and* Burgesses
were; which was Eleven years before
5 *the pretended beginning of the*
Commons in England.

For thus we find it in that
Author.

'As great a Right and Privilege
10 surely was and ought to be allow'd
to the *English* Subjects, as to the
Irish, before the 49th of *Hen.* III.
And if that be admitted, and that
their (the *Irish*) *Commune Concilium*,
15 or Parliament, had its Platform
from ours (the English) as I think
will not be Deny'd by any that have
consider'd the History[1] and Records
touching that Land (*Ireland*) we
20 shall find the ensuing Records,
cAnn. 38 *Hen.* III. clearly evince
that the Citizens and Burgesses
were then a part of their (the *Irish*)
Great Council or Parliament.'

25 [2]'That King being in *partibus*
[*][in parts beyond   *Transmarinis*[*] and the Queen being   *Rot. 38 H.III,*
the sea]   left Regent, she sends Writs (or a   *in 4. Hibernia*

---

1 History] Historys **H & PC**   2 *marginal ref.] in* **H** | (*manu aman.*) **PC**

49, 1 *An. 38. Hen. III.* – 1253. Cf. Prynne, *Brief animadversions* (London, 1669), p. 259, as cited *Case,*
pp 56–7. Richardson & Sayles, *Irish parliament* (Philadelphia, 1952), pp 69–70, argue against the regular
attendance of the Irish commons before the early C.14.   **49,** 5 *pretended* – alleged (but without the
implication of falsely so): *OED,* s.v. 7.   **49,** 15 *Platform* – pattern, or model: *OED,* s.v. 3a.   **49,** 20 *the*
ensuing – 'the two ensuing': Petyt, *The antient right* (London, 1680), p. 71.   **49,** 26–7 *the Queen ... Regent*
– Eleanor of Provence, wife of Henry III, served as regent with the king's brother, Richard of Cornwall
(see *Case,* p. 51), in 1253–4: *British chronology,* p. 34.

Letter)[1] in the Kings Name, directed *Archiepiscopis, Episcopis, Abbatibus, Prioribus, Comitibus, Baronibus, Militibus, Liberis Hominibus,* Civibus & Burgensibus, *Terræ suæ Hiberniæ;*[*] telling them that, *Mittimus Fratrem Nicholaum de Sancto Neoto, Fratrem Hospitii Sancti Johannis Jerusalem in Anglia ad partes Hiberniæ ad exponendum vobis*[**] (together with *J. Fitz-Geoffery*[2] the Kings Justice)[***] the State of his Land of *Vascony,* endanger'd by the Hostile Invasion of the King of *Castile, qui nullo Jure sed potentia sua Confisus Terram nostram Vasconiæ per ipsius Fortitudinem, a manibus nostris Auferre & a Dominio Regni Angliæ segregare Proponit*[†]. And therefore *universitatem Vestram Quanta possumus Affectione Rogantes quatenus nos & jura nostra totaliter indefensa non deserentes nobis in tanto periculo quantumcunque poteritis de* Gente & Pecunia *subveniatis*[‡]; which would turn to their Everlasting Honour; concluding, *His nostris Augustiis taliter Compatientes, quod nos & Herædes no-*

[*][To the Archbishops, Bishops, Abbots, Priors, Earls, Barons, Knights, Freemen, Citizens, and Burgesses of his Land of Ireland]

[**][We send Brother Nicholas of Saint Neots, Friar of the Hospital of Saint John of Jerusalem in England, into Ireland]

[***][to explain to you]

[†][who regardless of every law but that of force, attempts by violence to wrest from us, and from the sovereignty of the kingdom of England, our territory of Gascony]

[‡][entreating the whole body of you with the greatest earnestness and affection to support us and our just rights, which at present are entirely defenceless, with men and money to the utmost of your power, not forsaking us in so great a danger]

---

1 (or a Letter)] `(or a Letter)´ **H**   2 *J. Fitz-Geoffrey*] [John] J. Fitz-Geoffrey **H**

[*][that we and our heirs
may have the most
pressing obligations to
you and your heirs,
should you thus
sympathize with us in
these our straits.
Witness the Queen,
and Richard Earl of
Cornwall, at Windsor,
17th of Feb.]

[**][By the Queen<'s
command>]

*stri vobis & Hæredibus vestris sumus
non immerito Obligati. Teste Regina,
& R. Comite Cornubiæ, apud
Windesor, 17 die Februar.*[*]

Per Reginam.[**]

Thus far Mr. *Petyt.*

Here we have a Letter from the
Queen Regent[1] to the *Parliament*
in *Ireland,* in an humble manner
beseeching them for an Aid of
Men and *Money* against the King
of *Castiles* Hostile Invasion of
Gascony; from whence we may
perceive that[2] in those days, no
more than at present, *Men* and
Money could not be Rais'd but by
Consent of Parliament. I have been
the more particular in Transcribing
this Passage out of Mr. *Petyt,* to
shew that we have as Antient and
Express an Authority for our
present Constitution of Parliaments
in *Ireland,* as can be shewn in
England. And I believe it will not be
thought Adviseable in these latter
Days, to break in upon
Old Settled Constitutions: No

---

1 from … Regent] `from … Regent´ H   2 that] that [even] H

51, 13–15 *King … Gascony* – the threat of an attack on Gascony during Henry's negotiations with Alfonso
X in early 1254 was exploited to supplement royal revenues in Ireland and England: Powicke, *Henry III*
(Oxford, 1947), i, pp 234–6. **51, 17–19** *Men … Parliament* – a reference to article 4 of the 1689 Bill of
Rights (1 W. & M., ses. 2., c. 2) is more likely than to the claim raised by the Irish commons in 1692 and
1695 to the 'sole right' of introducing money bills, which Molyneux did not support. See further intro. p. 6,
n. 20. **51, 26–52, 2** *I believe … may be* – presumably an allusion to how the necessity of restoring the
constitution after the innovations of James II's reign had given rise to the revolution of 1688. For further
comments on the dangers of oversetting established constitutions, see *Case,* pp 160, 174.

one knows how fatal the Consequents of that may be.

To return therefore where we
Digress'd. *Henry* the Third, about
the Twelfth year of his Reign, did
specially Impower *Richard de
Burgh*, then *Justice of Ireland*, at a
certain day and place, to summon
all the Archbishops, Bishops,
Abbots, Priors, Earls, Barons,
Knights, Freeholders and Sheriffs of
each County, and before them to
cause to be Read the Charter of his
Father King *John*, whereunto his
Seal was Appendant, whereby he
had granted unto them the *Laws*
and *Customs* of *England*, and unto
which they swore Obedience: And
that he should cause the same Laws
to be observed and Proclaimed in
the several Counties of *Ireland*, that
so none presume to do contrary to
the Kings Command. The Record I
have taken out of Mr. *(a)* *Pryn*,[1] in
these words:

"Rex Dilecto & Fideli suo
Richardo de Burgo Justic' suo
Hibern. Salutem. Mandamus
vobis   firmiter   præ-

Marginal notes:

Farther
Concessions
from *Hen. III.*

5

10

15

20

(a) Against
Cook's 4th
Instit. p. 252.

25

[2] *Claus. 12 H.III
in 8 de Legibus &
Consuetudinibus
Observandis in
Hibern.*

30

---

1 *marginal ref.*] Against ye 4th ... p. 252. **H** | (b) Against ... p. 252. (*manu aman.*) **PC**   2 *marginal ref.*] *in*
H | (*manu aman.*) **PC**

52, 3–4 *To return ... Digress'd* – that is, from the discussion of the presence of the Commons in parliament
to the account of concessions by English rulers in the form of grants of laws in Ireland, see *Case*, p. 48.
52, 4–63, 22 *about the Twelfth ... be so* – based on *Domville*, 49–55. Henry III's letter of instruction was
dated 8 May [1227], see *Case*, p. 53.   **52, 8** *Justice* – Justiciar, or viceroy: *OED*[2], s.v. 9.   **52, 23–5** *The Record
... words* – 'I shall render you the Charter verbatim as I have taken it out of the Roll.': *Domville*, 50. In fact
Domville transcribed his text from Coke, *4th Inst.*, 351.

[*][The King to his trusty and beloved Richard de Burgh, Justiciar of Ireland, greeting. We command and strictly charge you, that at a 5 certain time and place, you cause to appear before you the Archbishops, Bishops, Abbots, Priors, Earls, Barons, Knights, Freeholders, and Bailiffs 10 of every county; and cause to be read before them the Charter of the Lord John our Father, to which his seal is annexed, and which he 15 caused to be made and sworn to by the great men of Ireland, concerning the observing of English laws and customs in Ireland. And command 20 them on our behalf, that for the future they strictly hold and follow those laws and customs, which are contained in the aforesaid Charter, And cause the same to 25 be proclaimed and observed in every county in Ireland. And none shall presume to go against this our command. Witness ourself, at Westminster, the 8th of May in the 12th year of our reign.]

cipientes quatenus certo die & Loco faciatis venire coram vobis Archiepiscopos Episcopos Abbates Priores Comites & Barones Milites & libere Tenentes & Ballivos singulorum Comitatum & coram eis Publice legi faciatis Chartam Domini J. Regis Patris nostri cui Sigillum suum appensum est quam fieri fecit & jurari a Magnatibus Hibern. de Legibus & Consuetudinibus[1] Angliæ Observandis in Hibernia. Et præcipiatis eis ex parte nostra quod Leges illas & Consuetudines in Charta prædicta contentas de cætero firmiter teneant & observent & hoc idem per singulos Commitatus Hiberniæ clamari faciatis & teneri prohibentes firmiter ex parte nostra & super foris facturam nostram nequis contra hoc Mandatum nostrum venire præsumat, &c. *Teste Me ipso Apud Westm' 8 die Maii An. Reg. nostri 12.*'[*]

---

1 Consuetudinibus] Consuetudinibus **H & PC** | Consuetudinis **I**

53, 26 *præsumat* – Molyneux omitted the ensuing words given by Prynne excepting the death and chattels of murdered Irishmen from the protection of the law ['*eo excepto, quod nec de morte, nec de catallis Hibernensium occisorum nihil statim ex parte nostro*']. This passage posed the question whether the benefits of English law, granted by the Norman kings, were restricted solely to princes and ecclesiastics or extended to the general populace. However, cf. *Case*, pp 129–30.

By what foregoes, I presume it plainly appears, that by three several Establishments under the three first Kings of *Ireland* of the *Norman*
5 *Race*, the *Laws and Liberties of the People of England, were granted to the People of Ireland*. And that neither of these three Kings[1] Established those Laws in *Ireland* by any *Power*
10 of the *Parliament* of *England*, but by the free *Consent, Allowance* and *Acceptance* of the *People of Ireland*.

Hen. II. first introduced the Laws of *England* into *Ireland*, in a
15 Publick Assembly of the *Irish* at *Lismore*, and Allowed them the *Freedom* of *Parliaments* to be held in *Ireland*, as they were held in *England*.

20 King *John* at the *Request*, and by the *Consent* of the *Irish*, did appoint the Laws of *England* to be of Force in *Ireland*; and tho' he did not this till the Twelfth year of his
25 Reign of *England*, yet he did it not as *King of England*, but as *Lord* of *Ireland*: for the Crown of *England* came to him by *Descent*

[1]Recapitulation.

---

1 Kings] *not in* **H** | `Kings´ **PC**   2 *marginal heading*] *in* **H** | (*manu aman.*) **PC**

54, 1–12 *By what … Ireland* – passage denounced by English commons committee: *Commons Jnl [Eng.]*, xii, p. 325.   **54, 4–5** *Norman Race* – Domville, 'Disquisition', p. 50, continued 'the first [Henry II] by Conquest, The second [John] by Donation or Creation, the third [Henry III] by Descent and Inheritance'. **54, 25–55, 4** *he did … descend to him* – emphasizing that John's 1210 grant of English law to the Irish was made not by right of conquest but by virtue of the donation of the lordship by his father. See further intro. p. 34. Coke, *7th Rep.*, ff 17v–18r, however, claimed that the feudal suzerainty based on conquest, which Henry II retained over John and the lordship, descended in primogeniture to Richard I, subsequently passing together with the English crown to John, who thus had titles to Ireland 'by two discents [i.e. donation and also conquest]'.

from his Brother *Richard*, who had
no *Regal Power* in *Ireland*; and
what his Brother had not, could not
descend to him.

5   *Henry* the Third in the first year
of his Reign gave *Ireland* a *Magna
Charta*; and[1] in the Twelfth year of
his Reign did provide, That all the
Laws of *England* should be observ'd
10 in *Ireland*; and that the Charter
granted to the *Irish* by his Father
King *John* under his Seal, when he
was in that Kingdom, should be
kept inviolably.

15   And from the Days of these
three Kings, have *England* and
Ireland been both Govern'd by the
lik[2] Forms of Government under
one and the same Supreme Head,
20 *the King of England*; yet so, as both
Kingdoms remain'd Separate and
Distinct in their several Jurisdictions
under that *One Head*, as are the
Kingdoms of *England* and *Scotland*
25 at this day, without any *Subordination* of the One to the Other.
    It were endless to mention all
the[3]

---

1 in ... and] *not in* H | `in ... and´ **PC** 2 the like] [one an<d>] the Like **H** 3 the] (*catchword* **I**, *but no
corresponding* the *at start of p. 56*)

55, 15–26 *And from ... Other* – passage denounced by English commons committee: *Commons Jnl [Eng.]*,
xii, p. 325. 55, 23–4 *as are ... Scotland* – for further comparisons with Scotland, see *Case*, pp 84, 95, 108,
115, 147. Clement, *Answer*, pp 62–3, pointed out the crucial difference that Scotland, unlike Ireland, was
not subject to the authority of the English privy council. 55, 25–6 *at this ... Other* – followed by a
footnote in 1776 and 1782 edns: 'This work was Published before the Union between England and
Scotland.'

(a) Fourth Instit.
(b) Against the
4th Instit.
(c) Placita
Parliamentaria.

**English Laws
Established in
Ireland.**

**Law of
Parliament.**

Records and Precedents that might be quoted for the Establishment of the Laws of *England* in *Ireland*; I shall therefore enter no farther into that Matter, but therein refer to Lord Chief Justice *Cook*, (a) *Pryn*, (b) *Reyly*, (c) &c.

If now we Enquire, *What were those Laws of England that became thus Established in Ireland ?* Surely we must first reckon[1] the Great *Law of Parliaments*, which *England* so justly Challenges, and all *Mankind* have a *Right* to. By the *Law*[2] of *Parliament*, I mean that Law whereby all Laws receive their Sanction, *The Free Debates and Consent of the People, by Themselves, or their Chosen Representatives.* That this was a main Branch of the English Law Established in this Kingdom[3], and the very Foundation of our Future Legislature, appears manifest from Parliaments being so early convok'd in *Ireland*, as the fore-mention'd Precedents express.[4]

[5]Mr. *Pryn* acknowledges one in *Hen.* II's time, (*pag. 259.* against the 4th *Instit.*) but makes a very false

---

1 Surely ... reckon] [Surely, amongst the Rest, we shall not forget] `surely we [surely] ... reckon´ H
2 *Law*] [Great] Law H 3 *Chosen ... Kingdom*] `chosen´ ... [Part] `main Branch´ ... [amongst us] `in ... Kingdom´ H 4 express.] expres. [for tho [Mr Pry<n>] some Imagine, that we had no Parliamts in Ireland before] H 5 Mr. *Pryn*] *no new para.* H

56, 10–58, 15 *Surely ... slender* – Domville, 'Disquisition', pp 51–2, merely referred to 'all the Laws and Customes of England ... such as were generally used over the whole Kingdom ... which is the common Law of England'. For the important addition of what Molyneux termed 'the Great Law of Parliaments' (*Case*, p. 48), see further intro. pp 34–5. 56, 27–9 *Mr. Pryn ... Instit.* – this assertion was the most cavalier treatment of sources in *The Case*, see intro. p. 61.

Conclusion, that there appears no Footsteps of a Parliament afterwards, till the third year of *Edward* the Second, because the

5 Acts of that Parliament are the first that are Printed in our Irish Statute-Book: For so we may argue the Parliaments of *England* to be of later Date than pretended,[1] when

10 we find the first Printed Acts in *Keeble* to be no older than the 9th of *Hen.* III. Whereas 'tis most certain, that Parliaments have been held in *England* some Ages before that.[2]

15 After this *Great Law of Parliaments*, we may reckon the *Common Law* of *England*, whether it relates to Regulating and Setling of *Property*,[3] and Estates in Goods or

20 Land, or to the *Judiciary* and *Executive* parts of the Law, and the Ministers and Process thereof, or to *Criminal* Cases. These surely were all Establish'd in this Country, by

25 the three first Kings of *Ireland* of the *Norman* Race.[4]

Let us now consider the state of the *Statute Laws* of *England* under

Common Law.

Statute Law.

---

1 Acts ... pretended] [Statutes] `Acts´ ... For [who] ... `than pretended´ **H**   2 Whereas ... that.] *not in* **H** | `Whereas ... that.´ **PC**   3 Regulating ... *Property*] [Meum or <Tuum>] regulating ... Property **H** 4 These ... Race.] [These certainly were all Establishd by these three first Kings in Ireland, and if] `these ... `in ... Country´ ... Race.´ **H**

57, 2 *Footsteps* – vestiges, or traces: *OED*, s.v. 4.   **57, 6–7** *our* ... *Statute–Book* – though a limited edition of Irish statutes had been printed at Sir Henry Sidney's direction in 1572, Bolton, *Statutes of Ireland* (Dublin, 1621) was the first widely available collection. See further *Quinn*, 'Government printing', *Proceedings of the Royal Irish Academy*, 49 (1942–3), pp 54–7, 73–6. **57, 9** *pretended* – claimed: *OED*, s.v. 1. **57, 11–14** *Keeble ... before that* – i.e. Keble (ed.), *Statutes at large* (London, 1695), the most up-to-date collection available in 1698; 9 Hen. 3 was the earliest statute in the English statute book, namely Magna Carta in its 1225 issue, see further *Case*, p. 61 nn. The reference (*Case*, p. 30) to 'the *Modus* ... in *England* said to have been allowed by *William* the *Conquerour*' shows that Molyneux accepted that parliaments went back to Saxon times. See further, *Case*, pp 155–6.

these three Kings, and their Predecessors: For by the Irish Voluntary
Submission to, and Acceptance of
the Laws and Government of
5   *England*, we must repute them to
have submitted themselves to these
likewise; till a Regular Legislature
was Establish'd amongst them,[1] in
pursuance of that Submission and
10   Voluntary Acceptance.

      And here we shall find, that in

Statute-Law of
***England* from**
the Norman
Conquest to
Hen. III.

those Times, *viz.* from the *Norman*
Conquest to *Henry* the Third's time
inclusive, the Statute-Laws of
15   *England* were very few and slender.
'Tis true, that before the 12th of
Hen. III. we find amongst the
English[2] Historians frequent mention
of the Laws of *Edward the Confessor*,
20   *William the Conquerour*, *Hen.*I.
*Hen.*II. *King John*, and *Hen.* III. All
which are only *Charters*, or several
Grants of *Liberties* from the King;
which nevertheless had the force of
25   Acts of Parliament, and laid as great
Obligations both upon Prince and
People, as Acts of Parliament do at
this day: Whereof we may read
several Proofs in the *Princes Case*,
30   *Cook*'s 8th *Report*. But these were

---

1 them] them [selves] H   2 'Tis ... English] ''tis ... that' ... [our] 'the English' H

58, 16–63, 14 *Tis true ... day* – this account of England's ancient laws closely followed Domville,
'Disquisition', pp 52–5. Such laws and charters (regarded as so many confirmations of each other)
constituted the core of the ancient constitution, as conceived of by Coke. See further, intro. pp 34–5.
58, 15 *slender* – limited in extent: *OED*, s.v. 8.   58, 17–18 *the English Historians* – Domville, 'Disquisition',
p. 52, read 'our Antient Historians' (cf. app. crit.), a phrase employed by Prynne, *Brief animadversions*
(London, 1669), p. 7, to denote medieval chroniclers.   58, 19–28 *the Laws ... day* – these so-called laws
of early kings were in reality private compilations from the reigns of Henry I and Henry II, some
embodying fragments of genuine legislation, others entirely apocryphal: Richardson & Sayles, *Law and
legislation* (Edinburgh, 1966), *passim*. By 1688 their authenticity had been subjected to criticism by scholars
such as Spelman and Brady: Pocock, *Constitution* (Cambridge, 1987), pp 45–63.   58, 22 *several* – sundry,
or various: *OED*, s.v. 2c.   58, 29 *the Princes Case* – the relevant point in the Prince's case (1606) was that
royal charters granted in, or with the consent of, parliament, had the force of statute (and thus could only
be amended in parliament), the first instance cited being Magna Carta (9 Hen. 3): Coke, *8th Rep.*, ff 18v–
20r.

[ˣ][long used and approved of through the whole land, and under which they and their ancestors had been born and raised]

[ˣˣ][and ratified and confirmed through the whole kingdom, had been formerly set forth and established in the reign of his grandfather, King Edgar. Nevertheless from the death of the same King Edgar, until the coronation of the holy King Edward, (which was 67 years),the aforesaid laws had slept and were allowed to lapse. But after King Edward was raised to the throne of the realm, by the advice of the barons of England, he revived that law which had been allowed to sleep, and after its revival, he improved, adorned and confirmed it: and thus confirmed, it was called the law of the holy King Edward; not because he was the establisher of it, but because he improved and restored it]

only so many *Confirmations* of each other, and all of them *Sanctions of the Common Laws* and *Liberties* of the People of *England*, *ab Antiquo Usitatæ & comprobatæ per totam terram & in quibus ipsi & eorum Patres nati & nutriti sunt*,[ˣ] as the words of the Manuscript *Chronicle of Litchfield* express it.[1]

5

10

15

20

25

30

The Laws of *Edward the Confessor*, held in so great Veneration[2] in Antient Times, *& per universum Regnum corroboratæ & confirmatæ, prius inventæ & Constitutæ fuerunt Tempore Regis Edgari Avi sui. Verum tamen post mortem ipsius Regis* Edgari, *usque ad Coronationem Sancti Regis* Edwardi (which was 67 years) *prædictæ Leges Sopitæ sunt & penitus intermissæ. Sed postquam Rex* Edwardus *in Regno sublimatus fuit Consilio Baronum Angliæ Legem illam sopitam Excitavit, Excitatam*[3] *Reparavit, Reparatam Decoravit, Decoratam Confirmavit; & confirmatæ vocantur* Lex Sancti Regis Edwardi, *non quod* ipse primus eam ad invenisset; sed quod Reparavit, Restituitque[ˣˣ] (*a*) as the said *Litchfield* Chronicle has it. These Laws

Law of *Edward* the Confessor.

[4](*a*) *Selden Notæ & specileg. ad eadmerum*, pag. 171.[5]

---

1 *ab Antiquo Usitatæ*... it.] `ab ... it.´ (*interpolation largely in margin*) H | 2 Veneration] [Reverence] 'veneration' H   3 *Excitatam*] Excitatam H | *Excitam* PC & I   4 *marginal ref.*] *in* H | (*manu aman.*) PC
5 171.] 171. H & PC |171ₐ I

59, 2 *Sanctions* – solemn ratification of a law by supreme authority: *OED*, s.v. sanction.   **59, 4–9** *ab Antiquo ... express it* – as identified in the marginal ref., Domville's source was Selden's commentary on Eadmer's early C.12 chronicle. The extracts have in places been somewhat condensed from Selden's text.   **59, 10–29** *The Laws ... Restituitque* – the laws of Edward the Confessor (perhaps the most famous of these legal apocrypha) had been produced in the reign of Henry I: Richardson & Sayles, *Law and legislation* (Edinburgh, 1966), pp 47–9. The obligation introduced in the coronation oath of 1307 to maintain the 'Laws and Customs ... [of] King St. Edward' was dropped in the new oath of 1689: Pocock, *Constitution* (Cambridge, 1987), p. 43.

of *Edward the Confessor* were transcribed by *Ingulphus Abbot of Croyland* under *William the Conqueror*, and are annexed to his History.

Of *Wil.* Conq. 5 ¹The Laws of *William the Conqueror* are but a *Confirmation* of the Laws of *Edward the Confessor*, with some small *alterations*, as the very Letter of those Laws themselves

²(*b*) *Leges W.* I.
Cap. 63. *apud*
Selden in notis ad
eadmerum p. 192.

10 express it. (*b*) *Hoc quoque præcipimus ut omnes habeant & teneant Leges Edwardi Regis in omnibus Rebus adauctis his quas constituimus ad Utilitatem Anglorum.*[*]

Of *Hen.* I. 15 The Laws of *Henry* I. which are in the *Red Book of the Exchequer*, in the custody of the Kings *Remembrancer* in *England*, are but a summary confirmation both of the Laws of

20 *Edward the Confessor* and *William the First*, as the Charter itself expresses it,

³(*c*) *Vid. Selden ut*
supra.

(*c*) *Lagam Regis* Edwardi *vobis Reddo cum illis emendationibus quibus Pater meus emendavit Consilio Baronum*

25 *suorum.*[**]

Of *Hen.* II. The Laws of *Henry* II. called *Constitutiones Clarendoniæ*, and the *Assize of Clarendon* in the 2*d* part of

[*][This likewise we command, that all hold and observe the Laws of King Edward in all things, with those additions which we have established for the benefit of the English.]

[**][I restore you the laws of King Edward along with those amendments which it received from my father by the advice of his Barons.]

---

1 The Laws] The Laws *preceded by printer's instruction in margin* Begin here **PC**   2 *marginal ref.*] *in* **H** | (*manu aman.*) **PC**   3 *marginal ref.*] *in* **H** | (*manu aman.*) **PC**

60, 2–4 *Ingulphus ... History* – though Ingulph of Croyland had acted as secretary to William I (cf. Atwood, *History*, pp 44–5), the chronicle attributed to him has long been shown to be spurious: *ODNB*, s.v. Ingulph. **60, 5–10** *The Laws ... express it* – the apocryphal laws of William the Conqueror (found both in Latin and French versions) were said to have been granted at the request of his barons: Richardson & Sayles, *Law and legislation* (Edinburgh, 1966), pp 121–5.   **60, 15–16** *The Laws ... Exchequer* – though Henry I was the first significant post-Conquest legislator, these laws too were largely apocryphal: Richardson & Sayles, *Law and legislation* (Edinburgh, 1966), pp 42–5. The English Red Book of the Exchequer was, like its Irish counterpart, an important repository of early legislation; an edn by Hubert Hull appeared in 1896. **60, 22** *Lagam* – a code of laws: Baxter & Johnson, *Medieval Latin* (Oxford, 1934), s.v. *laga*.   **60, 26** *The Laws of Henry II* – while the constitutions of Clarendon of 1164 represented genuine legislation, the assizes were a largely apocryphal creation of the late 1170s, embodying three genuine articles from 1166: Richardson & Sayles, *Law and legislation* (Edinburgh, 1966), pp 93–5, 125–7.

Cooks Inst. p. 6. are all but confirmations and vindications of the King's just Prerogative against the Usurpations of the Pope and

5 Clergy: As we find at large in *Chron. Gervasii. Doroborn* p. 1387. Edit. Lond. an. 1652.[1]

The Laws of *King John*, called The *Great Charter of King John*,

10 granted in the 17*th* Year of his Reign, upon the Agreement made between him and his Barons at *Running-Mead* between *Staines* and *Windsor*, was but a *Confirmation*

15 of the Laws of *Edward the Confessor* and *Henry the First*, as (*d*) *Mat. Paris* relates it. *Anno Regis* Johannis 17. *venientes ad Regem magnates petierunt quasdam Libertates & Leges*

20 *Regis* Edwardi *cum aliis libertatibus sibi & Regno Angliæ & Ecclesiæ Anglicanæ concessis confirmari prout in Charta Regis* Hen I. *ascriptæ continentur.*[1] The same Historian gives

25 us also at large both *Charta Libertatum*[**]; and *Charta de Foresta*[***], which are not extant in the Rolls of those times, nor to be found in any till the 28*th* of *Edward* I. and that

30 but by *inspeximus*.

Of K. *John.*

[1][In the 17th year of King John, the magnates came to the King, and requested that certain laws and liberties of King Edward, together with other liberties granted to them and to the kingdom and church of England, should be confirmed, as they are contained in writing in the Charter of King Henry I.]

[**][the Charter of Liberties]

[***][the Charter of the Forest]

[2](*d*) *Mat. Paris ad an.* 1215. *pag.* 253, *&c.*

---

1 1652] *blank in MS* H | `1652´ **PC**   2 *marginal ref.*] *in* H | (*manu aman.*) **PC**

61, 6–7 *Chron. ... 1652* – Gervase's chronicle dated to the late C.12 and early C.13; it was printed in Twysden, *Historiæ Anglicanæ* (London, 1652). See further *ODNB*, s.v. Gervase of Canterbury. (Domville, 'Disquisition', p. 54, read 'nuper Edita' [lately published]).   **61, 9–62, 27** *The Great ... England* – this account of Magna Carta and its reissues was based on Coke, *1st Inst.*, proem, *2nd Inst.*, proem and ch. 1, which spoke of more than thirty-two confirmations of Magna Carta following 1216. While it was accepted that there were substantial differences between the reissues of Hen. III and the original 1215 charter (cf. ref. to Paris' *Historia Maior*), at a more profound level the various issues of the charter were thought of as essentially the same, just as Magna Carta itself was held to be a confirmation of the charter of Hen. I: Thompson, *Magna Carta* (Minneapolis, 1948), pp 244–5.   **61, 24–30** *The same ... inspeximus* – a separate Charter of the Forest (differing from the forest clauses in the 1215 charter) was granted when Magna Carta was reissued for the second time in 1217: Holt, *Magna Carta* (Cambridge, 1992), p. 385. The text of Magna Carta in the English statute book, though held to be that of 9 Hen. 3 (1225), in fact derived from the confirmation of 25 Edw. 1 (1297): Coke, *2nd Inst.*, p. 3; Baker, *Reinvention* (Cambridge, 2017), pp 6–10.

Of *Hen. III.*

The Laws of *Henry* III. contain'd in *Magna Charta* and *Charta de Forresta*, both which are called *Magnæ Chartæ Libertatis Angliæ*[*], and were establish'd about the *9th* Year of *Henry* III. are for the most part but[1] *declaratory* of the common municipal Laws of *England*, and that too no *new* declaration thereof; for King *John* in the 17*th* year of his Reign had granted the like before,[2] which was also call'd *Magna Charta*. (a) And by the English Statute 25 *Ed.*I.*1*. it is Enacted, That the *Great Charter*, and the *Charter of the Forrest* be taken as the *Common Law of England*.

By what foregoes, I conceive, it is very clear, That all the *Charters* and *Grants of Liberties* from *Edward the Confessor's* time down to the 9*th* of *Henry the Third* were but *Confirmations* one of another, and all of them *Declarations*, and Confirmations of the *Common Law of England*. And by the several Establishments, which we have formerly mention'd, of the Laws of *England* to be of force in *Ireland*:

[*][the Great Charters of the Liberties of England]

[3](a) *Cook's* Pref. to the 2d Inst.

5

10

15

20

25

30

---

1 the most ... but] [[bu<t>]]the ... but **H**   2 before] `before´ **H**   3 *marginal ref.*] *in* **H** | (*manu aman.*) **PC**

62, 8 *common ... Laws* – 'the principal grounds of the Common Laws': Domville, 'Disquisition', p. 55. *Municipal* – the laws of a particular state, as opposed to the law of nations, or of nature: *OED*, s.v. 1a. **62, 20–7** *all the Charters ... England* – cf. Coke, *2nd Inst.*, proem.

First, in the 13*th* of *Henry* II.
Secondly, in the 12*th* of King *John*.
Thirdly, in the 12*th* of *Henry* III.
All those Laws and Customs of
5 *England*, which by those several
Charters were *Declared* and
Confirmed to be the Laws of
England, were establish'd[1] to be of
force in *Ireland*. And thus *Ireland*
10 came to be govern'd by one and the
same *Common Law* with *England*;
and those Laws continue as part of
the municipal and fundamental
Laws of both Kingdoms to this day.

15 It now remains that we enquire,
How the *Statute Laws* and *Acts of
Parliament* made in *England since*
the 9*th* of *Henry the Third* came to
be of force in *Ireland*; And whether
20 all or any of them, and which, are in
force here, and when and how they
came to be so.

And the first Precedent that
occurs in our Books, of Acts of Par-
25 liament in *Ireland* particularly mentioning and confirming special Acts
of Parliament in *England*, is found
in a Marginal Note of Sir *Richard*
Bolton's formerly Lord Chief Baron

**Engl. Statutes
since the 9th.
Hen. III.
introduced in
Ireland.**

---

1 establish'd] [Declared] Established **H**

63, 1–3 *13th ... Henry III* – i.e. Henry II's Modus of 1172; John's missing charter of 1210, and Henry III's
reissue of the Irish Magna Carta in 1227. See further, *Case*, pp 28, 45, 52. **63, 26** *special* – having an
individual particular, or limited application: *OED*, s.v. 5. **63, 28–65, 27** *a Marginal ... 139 years* – this
passage was based on the editorial note to 10 Hen. 7, 22 in Bolton, *Statutes of Ireland* (Dublin, 1621), p. 67.
Caldicott's claim (Darcy, *An Argument* (1992), pp 217, 271, nn.) that it was directly cited from the 1644
Declaration, which Molyneux specifically identified as the work of Bolton, ignores both the explicit
reference to the 1621 *Statutes* in 'Thus far the Note' (*Case*, p. 65), and the *Declaration*'s citation of 19 Edw.
2 rather than 10 Hen. 4. **63, 29–64, 1** *Chief Baron ... Exchequer* – the alteration of Bolton's designation
from Lord Chancellor (cf. app. crit.) in the printer's copy is puzzling; however, Bolton was similarly
designated Chief Baron in 'Legislative power in Ireland', f. 129r.

of the *Exchequer* in[1] *Ireland*, affixed
in his Edition of the *Irish Statutes*
to Stat. 10 *Hen.7. Cap.* 22. to this
purport, That in 13 *Edw.*II. *by*

5 *Parliament in this Realm of* Ireland
the Statutes of Merton, *made the*
20th of *Hen.*III.[2] *and the Statutes of*
Marlbridge, *made the 52 of* Henry
the Third; *The Statute of* West-

10 minster *the First, made the 3d of*
Edward *the First*; *The Statute of*
Gloucester, *made the 6th of* Edward
the First; *And the Statute of* Westminster *the Second, made the 13th of*

15 Edward *the First, were all confirm'd*
in this Kingdom, and all other Statutes
which were of force in England, *were*
referr'd to be Examin'd in the next
Parliament; *and so many as were*

20 *then Allow'd and Publish'd, to stand*
likewise for Laws in this Kingdom.
And in the 10th[3] *of* Henry *the Fourth,*
it was Enacted in this Kingdom of
Ireland, That the Statutes made in

25 England should not be of force in
this Kingdom, unless they were
Allow'd and Publish'd in this
Kingdom by Parliament. *And the*
like Statute was made again in the

30 *29th of* Henry *the Sixth. These*
Statutes are not to be found in the

Statutes of
Merton. Marlbr.
Westm. Gloucest.

Vid. Lib. Rubr.
Scaccar. Dubl.

---

1 Chief … *Exchequer* in] High Chancellor of **H** | [High Chancellor] `Cheif Baron´ of **PC**    2 Hen. III] Hen. ye 3d. **H & PC** | Hen. II **I**    3 10th] 20th **H** | [20] `10´th **PC** (*broken numeral* `1´ *in Bolton,* Statutes of Ireland *(Dublin, 1621), p. 67, looks like* `2´; *since Henry died in the fourteenth year of his reign (1413), there was no year* 20 Hen. 4)

64, 4–13 *13 Edw. II … Edward the First* – that is in 1320, cited from note in Bolton, *Statutes of Ireland* (Dublin, 1621), p. 67. Cf. *ESI*, i, pp 281–2. For a slightly different form of this passage, see Domville, 'Disquisition', p. 56.   **64, 20,** *marginal ref. Lib. … Dubl.* – namely the Red Book of the Exchequer of Ireland, see further *Case*, p. 45 nn.   **64, 22** *10th … Henry the Fourth* – while no statute survived from this regnal year, Richardson & Sayles, *Irish parliament* (Philadelphia, 1952), pp 348–9, list two parliamentary sessions for the appropriate months of 1408–9. The authenticity of 10 Hen. 4 was accepted by Hale, *The Prerogatives* (London, 1976), p. 38.   **64, 22–65, 6** *And in … Waterford* – as in Bolton, *Statutes of Ireland* (Dublin, 1621), p. 67, except that 'he [Bolton] had' read 'I have'.   **64, 28–30** *the like … Henry the Sixth* – no such clause is found in the version of 29 Hen. 6 (1450) in *ESI*, ii, pp 251–91. Though familiar with Bolton's *Statutes* and his 1644 'Declaration', Domville failed to refer to these key missing statutes; whether due to doubt as to their authenticity or for some other reason is impossible to discover.

Rolls, nor any Parliament Roll *of*
that time; *but he* (Sir Richard
Bolton.) *had seen the same Exemplify'd*
under the Great Seal, and the
5 Exemplification *remaineth in the*
Treasury of the City of Waterford.
Thus far the Note. ¹If we consider
the frequent Troubles and Dis-
tractions in *Ireland*, we shall not
10 wonder that these, and many other
Rolls and Records, have been lost in
this Kingdom: For from the third
year of *Edward* the Second, which
was *Anno* 1310.² through the whole
15 Reigns of *Edward* III. *Richard* II.
Henry IV. and *Henry* V. and so³ to
the Seventh year of *Henry* the
Sixth, *Anno* 1428⁴. which is about
118⁵ years, there are not any
20 *Parliament Rolls* to be found, (*a*)
yet certain it is, that divers
Parliaments were held in *Ireland* in
those times.⁶ (*b*) The same may be
said from *Henry* the Second's
25 coming into *Ireland*, *Anno* 1171. to
the third year of *Edward* the Second,
Anno 1310. about 139⁷ years.⁸
⁹Perhaps it may be said, That if
there were such Statutes of *Ireland*
30 as the said Acts of the 10th¹⁰ of

(*a*) Annals of
Ireland, at the
End of *Camden's*
Britan. Edit.
1637. page 196,
197, &c.
(*b*) *Ibid.* p. 160.
Pryn against the
4th Instit. Chap,
76.

---

1 – 6 If we … times.] [`And´] `If … times.´ (*interpolation in margin*) H   2 which … 1310.] *not in* H |
`which … 1310.´ PC    3 through … so] `through … so´ H   4 *Anno* 1428] *not in* H | `An. 1428´ PC
5 118] 119 H | [119] [`[[[146]]5[`460´] `11[[9]]8´ PC   6 times.] *end of interpolation begun* n. *1 above*
7 1171] 1171 … 139 ed | 1172 … 138 H, PC & I (*see further* pp 8, 9–12, 6 nn *above*)   8 The same …
years.] *not in* H | 'The same … years.' PC   9 – p. 68, n. 1 Perhaps … foregoes.] *not in* H | `Perhaps …
foregoes.´ (*interpolation, manu WM, on separate quire* ff 196–7) PC   10 10th] [[2]]10th PC

65, 1 *Rolls … Parliament Roll* – the Irish statute rolls only started in 1427; even subsequently, however,
many statutes failed to reach the rolls: Richardson & Sayles, *Irish parliament* (Philadelphia, 1952),
pp 224–6. **65, 3–6** *seen … Waterford* – by 1644 it was thought these exemplifications were no longer
extant, see intro. p. 58, n. 27. *Exemplify* – make an officially attested copy of: *OED*, s.v. 7. **65, 7** *Thus …*
Note – cf. *Case*, pp 63, 15–65, 2; only three such lengthy editorial notes, or glosses, commenting on a
particular statute are found in Bolton, *Statutes of Ireland* (Dublin, 1621). **65, 7–23** *If we … times* – this
interpolation in the holograph (cf. app. crit.) drew on Bolton, 'Declaration', p. 4. The only parliament
Camden recorded for 1172–1310 was that at Kilkenny in 1294: Camden, *Britain* (London, 1637), sect. iii,
p. 160.

Henry the Fourth, and the 29th of
Henry the Sixth; As they shew, that
the Parliaments of *Ireland* did think
that English Acts of Parliament
5   could not[1] bind *Ireland*; yet they
shew likewise, that even in those
days the Parliaments of *England* did
claim this Superiority; or else, to
what purpose were the said Acts
10   made, unless in denial of that
Claim[2] ?

All which I hope may be readily
granted without any prejudice to
the Right of the Irish Parliaments:
15   There is nothing so common, as to
have one Man claim[3] another Mans
Right: And if bare *Pretence* will give
a *Title*, no Man is secure: And it
will be yet worse, if when another so
20   *Pretends*, and I insist on *my Right*,
my Just Claim shall be turn'd to
my Prejudice, and to the
Disparagement of my Title.

We know very well that many of
25   the Judges of our Four Courts have
been from time to time sent us out
of *England*; and some of them
may easily be supposed to

---

1 did ... not] did [not] ... not **PC**   2 did ... Claim] [pretended to] `did claim´ ... [but] unles ...
[pretended Right] `Claim´ **PC**   3 claim] [`*unjustly´ pretend to*] `claim´ **PC**

66, 3–5 *the Parliaments ... Ireland* – Clement, *Answer*, pp 67–9, considered that such claims by the Irish
parliament carried little weight in England. He also conjectured that had these supposedly crucial statutes
been then known in Ireland, they would surely have been cited in the Merchants of Waterford's case, (on
which see *Case*, pp 89–91). **66, 8–11** *to what ... Claim* – Cary, *Vindication*, p. 27, objected: 'nor do I find
by any Record you produce, that that Assembly, or any other, had the power to refuse the Laws transmitted
to them from time to time out of England'. The point is also raised in Caldicott's intro. to Darcy, *An
Argument* (1992), p. 220. **66, 17** *Pretence* – assertion of a right, or title: *OED*, s.v. 1a. **66, 24–67, 3** *many
of ... England* – such had been the position taken by the majority of Irish judges in the face of the
commons' questions in 1641: Darcy, *An Argument* (1992), pp 221–2, 242–3.

come over hither *Preposses'd* with an Opinion of our Parliaments being subordinate to that of *England*. Or at least, some of them may be

5 *Scrupulous*, and desirous of full *Security* in this Point; and on their Account, and for their Satisfaction, such Acts as aforesaid, may be devised, and Enacted in *Ireland*. But

10 then, God forbid, that these Acts should afterwards be laid hold of[1] to a clear other intent than what they were framed for; and instead of Declaring and Securing our Rights,

15 should give an Handle of Contest, by shewing[2] that our Rights have been question'd of Antient Time.[3]

[4]In conclusion of all, If this *Superiority* of the Parliament of

20 *England* have been *Doubted* a great while ago, so it has been as great a while ago Strenuously *Opposed*, and Absolutely *Denied* by the Parliaments of *Ireland*. And by the

25 way, I shall take Notice, That from whencesoever this Antient *Pretence* of *Ireland's Subordination* proceeded in those days, it did not arise from the *Parliament* of *Eng-*

---

1 laid ... of] [constru'd] `laid ... of´ **PC**   2 Declaring ... shewing] `Declaring and´ ... give [our Adversarys] ... shewing [them] **PC**   3 Time.] Time. [On the upshot of all, If the Parliament of England have a great while ago laid aside Claim to this Superiority] **PC**   4 In conclusion] *no new para.* **PC**

67, 6 *Security* – assurance, freedom from doubt: *OED*, s.v. 2.   **67, 18–68, 8** *In conclusion ... foregoes* – passage denounced by English commons committee: *Commons Jnl [Eng.]*, xii, p. 325. Cf. Bolton, 'Declaration', p. 21: 'most certain it is, that there is not any statute extant, either in *England* or *Ireland*, whereby it is enacted, that any statute made in *England* should be of force in *Ireland*, before the same were approved, and enacted in the Parliament of *Ireland*.'   **67, 20** *Doubted* – perhaps in sense of *redoubted*, i.e. apprehended, or stood in awe of: *OED*, s.v. doubt, 1.

land itself: For we have not one single Instance of an English Act of Parliament *Expresly Claiming* this Right of Binding us: But we have several Instances of Irish Acts of Parliament, *Expresly Denying* this *Subordination*, as appears by what foregoes.[1]

Afterwards by a Statute made in *Ireland* the 18th of *Hen.* VI. *Cap.*1. All the Statutes made in *England* against the *Extortions* and *Oppressions* of *Purveyors*,[2] are Enacted to be *holden and kept in all Points, and put in Execution in this Land of Ireland.*

And in the 32d year of *Henry* the Sixth, *Cap.*1. by a Parliament in *Ireland*, 'tis Enacted, *That all the Statutes made against* Provisors *to the Court of* Rome, *as well in* England *as in* Ireland, *be had and kept in force.*

After this, in a Parliament at *Drogheda* the 8th of *Edward* IV. *cap.*1.[3] it was Ratify'd, that the *English* Statute against *Rape*, made the 6th of *Richard* the Second,

---

1 foregoes.] *end of interpolation begun p. 65, n. 9 above*   2 *Purveyors*] *Purveyors* [and] **H**   3 cap.1.] `cap.1.´ **H**

68, 10–70, 21 *18th of … Otherwise* – based on Domville, 'Disquisition', pp 56–7.   **68, 13** *Purveyors* – officials who requisitioned goods and services for the crown: *OED*, s.v. 3.   **68, 20** *Provisors* – people seeking papal grants to succeed to benefices on the death of the current holder: *OED*, s.v. 1.   **68, 24–69, 11** *in a Parliament … March* – 8 Edw. 4, c. 1 (1469): *ESI*, ii, pp 617–19.

should be of Force in *Ireland* from the 6th day of *March* last past: *And that from henceforth the said Act, and all other Statutes and Acts*

5 *made by Authority of Parliament within the realm of* England, *be Ratify'd and Confirm'd, and Adjudged by the Authority of this Parliament in their force and*

10 *Strength, from the said sixth day of March.* We shall hereafter have occasion of taking farther Notice of this Statute upon another Account.

Lastly, In a Parliament held at

15 *Drogheda* the 10th of *Henry* the Seventh, *cap. 22.*[1] it is Enacted, *That all Statutes*[2] *late* (that is, as the (*a*) Learned in the Laws expound it, *before that time) made in* England,

20 *concerning the Common and Publique Weal of the same, from henceforth be Deem'd effectual in Law, and be Accepted, Used and Executed within this Land of Ireland in all Points, &c.*

25 (*b*) And in the 14th year of the same Kings Reign, in[5] a Parliament held at *Tristle-Dermot*, it was Enacted, That all Acts of Parliament

All English Statutes before the 10th of Hen. VII. in force in Ireland.

[3](*a*) *Cook's* 4th Instit. *Cap.* 76. p. 351.
[4](*b*) *Vid.* Irish Stat.

---

1 In ... *cap. 22.*] [at] `in´ ... `cap. 22´ **H**   2 Statutes] *Statutes* [made within ye P<arliament>] **H** | Estatutes **PC**   3 *marginal ref.*] *in* **H** | (*manu aman.*) **PC**   4 *marginal ref.*] *in* **H** | (*manu aman.*) **PC**   5 in] [at] *in* **H**

69, 4–7 *all other ... Confirm'd* – as in Bolton, *Statutes of Ireland* (Dublin, 1621), pp 42–3. The version in *ESI*, iii, p. 619, however, reads 'of all manner of rapes' after 'England', thus calling into question Molyneux's claim of a general re-enactment of English legislation in 1469. Cf. Monck Mason, *An Essay* (Dublin, 1820), 33 n.   **69, 11–13** *We shall ... Account* – see further *Case*, pp 78–80.   **69, 14–24** *In a Parliament ... Points, &c.* – the so-called 'Poynings' parliament' of 1494, which also passed the eponymous act forbidding the introduction of legislation in the Irish parliament without the prior approval of the king and English council.   **69, 17–19** *late ... time* – Coke, *4th Inst.*, p. 351, referred to an English ruling, 10 Jac. [1] (1613), that *late* in this act meant *before*, thus extending the reception of English legislation under 10 Hen. 7, c. 22, back to Magna Carta and including all subsequent English public acts to 1494. This opinion had been sought from the chief justices and chief baron in preparation for James' forthcoming Irish parliament: *12th Rep.*, pp 110–11. Cf. Domville, 'Disquisition', p. 56.   **69, 20–1** *Publique Weal* – general good, or public welfare: *OED*, s.v. weal, 3.   **69, 25–70, 8** *in the 14th ... Towns* – 14 Hen. 7, sole act (1498): Bolton, *Statutes of Ireland* (Dublin, 1621), p. 69 (not mentioned by Domville). *Tristle-Dermot* is now Castle Dermot, Co. Kildare.

made in *England* for Punishing
Customers, *Controulers*, and *Searchers*,
for their Misdemeanors; or for
Punishment of *Merchants* or

5   *Factors*, be of Force here in *Ireland*,
Provided they be first Proclaim'd at
Dublin, *Drogheda*, and other
Market Towns.

Thus we see by what Steps and

10 Degrees all the Statutes which were
made in *England* from the time of
Magna Charta, to the 10th of
Henry the Seventh, which did concern the Common Publick Weal,

15 were Receiv'd, Confirm'd, Allow'd,
and Authoriz'd to be of Force in
Ireland; all[1] which was done by
Assent of the *Lords Spiritual* and
Temporal, and the *Commons* in the

20 *Parliament of Ireland* Assembled,
and *no Otherwise*.

**English Statutes
Declaratory of the
Common Law in
force in *Ireland*.**

We shall next Enquire, Whether
there are not other Acts of the
English Parliament, both *before* and[2]

25 *since* the 10th of *Henry* the Seventh,
which were and *are* of Force in
Ireland, tho' not Allow'd of[3] by
Parliament in this Kingdom. And
we shall find, That by the Opini-

---

1 all] `all´ **H**   2 both … and] `both … and´ **H**   3 were… of] `were and´ … of [particular] **H**

70, 29–71, 6 *the Opinion … Law* – probably an allusion to Bolton, 'Declaration', pp 4, 6–9, whose listing of Tudor and Stuart statutes re-enacted in Ireland is closely followed below. The distinction was explicitly drawn in Domville, 'Disquisition', p. 58. Mayart, 'Answer' (Dublin, 1750), pp 40, 100, dismissed the distinction between declaratory and innovative laws as of no significance.

on of our best Lawyers, *there are divers such*; but then they are only such as are *Declaratory* of the *Antient*[1] *Common Law* of *England*, and not *introductive* of any *New Law*: for these become of Force by the first *General Establishment* of the *Common Laws* of *England* in this Kingdom, under *Henry* the Second, King *John*, and *Henry* the Third; and need no particular Act of *Ireland* for their Sanction.

As to those English Statutes since the 10th of *Henry* the Seventh, that are *Introductive* of a *New* Law, it[2] was never made a Question whether they should Bind *Ireland*, without being Allow'd in Parliament here; till of very late years this Doubt began to be moved; and how it has been Carried on and Promoted, shall Appear more fully hereafter.

I say, *Till of very late years*; for the *Antient* Precedents which we have to the contrary, are very numerous. Amongst many, we shall[3] mention the following Particulars.

English Acts introductive of a New Law, not of force in *Ireland*.

---

1 *such ... Antient*] `such´ ... `Antient´ **H**   2 English ... it] [[A]]English [Acts] Statutes ... [there] it **H**
3 Amongst ... shall] [[is not]]Amongst ... [may] shall **H**

71, 21–3 *how it ... hereafter* – see further *Case*, pp 99–115.

In the 21th of *Henry* the 8th an
Act was made in *England* making it
Felony in a Servant that runneth
away with his Masters or Mistresses
5   Goods. This Act was not receiv'd in
Ireland till it was Enacted by a
Parliament held here in the 33d of
Henry the 8th. c.5. Ses. 1.

In the 21*th* of *Henry* VIII. c. 19.
10   there was a Law made in *England*,
That all Lords might Distrain on
the Lands of them holden, and
make their Avowry not naming the
Tenant, but the Land. But this was
15   not of force in *Ireland* till Enacted
here in the 33*d* of *Henry* VIII. C.7.[1]
Ses.1.

An Act was made in *England*,
anno 31. *Henry* VIII. That Joint
20   Tenents[2] and Tenents in Common
should be compelled[3] to make
Partition, as Coparceners were
compellable at Common Law. But
this[4] Act was not Receiv'd in *Ireland*
25   till Enacted here *An.* 33. *Henry*
VIII. c.10.

---

1 C. 7] C.7. **H & PC** | C. 1 I   2 Joint Tenents] Joynt [under] Tenents **PC**   3 compelled] Compellable
H   4 But this] [[thi<s>]]But this **H**

72, 1–74, 13 *In the 21th … c.3 Ses. 2* – all the original (i.e. not subsequently interpolated) references to
Tudor and Stuart re-enactments which Molyneux listed in the holograph (cf. app. crit.) to 10 Car. 1 (1635)
are found in Bolton, 'Declaration', pp 9–10.   **72, 11–13** *Distrain … Avowry* – *distrain* – levy distress to
compel the defaulter by detention of the thing seized to pay money, esp. rent: *OED*, s.v. 8; *avowry* – the
plea whereby one who distrained for rent acknowledged the act and justified it: ibid. s.v. 5.
72, 22 *Coparceners* – joint heirs, or more usually, heiresses: *OED*, s.v. Cf. *Case*, pp 86–7, 133–4.

Anno 27. *Henry* VIII.c.10. The Statute for Transferring Uses into Possession was made in *England*; but not admitted in *Ireland* till 10. *Car*.1. C.1. Ses.2.¹

In² like manner, the English Statute 32. *Henry* VIII³ c.1. directing how Lands and Tenements may be dispos'd by Will, &c. was not of force in *Ireland* till 10. *Car*.2. C.2. Ses.2.⁴

The Act of Uniformity of Common Prayer and Administration of the Sacraments was⁵ made in *England* the 1st of *Eliz*. c.2. but was not establish'd in *Ireland* till the 2*d*. of *Eliz*. c.2. And so that of *England* 14. *Car*.2. c.14. was not receiv'd in *Ireland* till 17. & 18. *Car*.2. c.6.⁶

The Statute against Wilful Perjury made in *England* 5. *Eliz*.c.9. was not Enacted in *Ireland* till 28⁷ *Eliz*. c.1.

So the English⁸ Act against Witchcraft and Sorcery made 5 *Eliz*. c.16.

---

1 10. Car. I. C.1. Ses.2.] 10. Car. I. C.1. Ses.2. **ed.** | 10. Car. C.1. Ses.2. **H & PC** | 10. Car. I. Ses.2. **I**   2 In] [So] In **H**   3 32 *Henry* VIII] 32 ... VIII **ed.** | 33 ... VIII **H, PC & I**   4 10. *Car*. 2. C. 2. Ses.2.] 10. *Car*. 2. C. 2. Ses.2. **ed.** | 10. *Car*. C. 2. Ses.2. **H & PC** | 10. *Car*. 2. Ses.2. **I**   5 was] `was´ **H**    6 And ... *Car*. 2. c.6.] `and ... Car. 2. c.6.´ (*perhaps add. later at foot of MS page*) **H**   7 till 28] [[2]]till 28 **H**   8 English] `English´ **H**

And another Act[1] against Forgery 5
Eliz. c.14. were neither of them in
force in *Ireland* till the 28*th* of Her
Reign, Cap. 2 and 3.[2]

5   The English Statute[3] against
Pirates was made the 28th of
*Hen.*8. c.15. but not in *Ireland* till
the 12th of King *James*, c.2.

       In *England* an Act was made the
10   27th of *Eliz.* c.4. against Fraudulent
Conveyances; but it was not in[4]
force in *Ireland* till Enacted here the
10th of *Charles*, the 1st.[5] c.3. Ses.2.

      [6]In the 15th year of King *Charles*
15   the 1st. in a Parliament held at
Dublin there were Six English
Statutes made Laws of this Kingdom, with such Alterations as best
fitted them to the State thereof, *viz.*

20   21 *Jac.* c.14. For pleading the
General Issue in Intrusions brought
by the King, by Chap.1. of the Irish
Statutes.

          31 *Eliz.* c.2. For Abridging of[7]
25   Proclamations on Fines, by Chap. 2.

---

1 Act] *not in* **H & PC**   2 Cap. 2. ... 3.] Cap. 2. ... 3. **ed** | Cap. 3. ... 4. **H, PC & I**   3 Statute] Statute **H & PC** | Statutes **I**   4 in] of **H & PC**   5 *Charles,* the 1st.] *Charles,* the 1st. **ed.** | Charles, **H, PC & I** 6 – p. 76, n. 3 In the 15th ... *Swearing*] `In the 15th ... Swearing´ (*interpolation on f. 113r–v; f. 114 (the second leaf of this quire) is blank and unfoliated*) **H**   7 of] *not in* **H & PC**

74, 14–75, 10 *In the 15th ... Chap. 9* – the remaining references to Tudor and Stuart statutes re-enacted in Ireland were subsequent interpolations in the holograph (cf. app. crit.). *Intrusion* – occupying an estate or ecclesiastical benefice without proper title: *OED*, s.v. 3a.

2 and 3 *Edw.* 6. c.8. Concerning Offices before the Escheator, by Chap. 4.[1]

5 31 *Eliz.* c.1. Discontinuance of Writs of Error in the Exchequer Chamber, by Chap. 5.[2]

8 *Eliz.* c.4. and 18 *Eliz.* c.7. concerning Clergy, by Chap.7.

24 *Hen.* 8. c.5. Concerning
10 Killing a Robber, by Chap.9.

There are Six[3] English Statutes likewise passed in the time of King *Charles* the 2d. upon and soon[4] after the Restoration, some of which
15 were not passed into Laws in *Ireland* till a year, two or three, afterwards: As will appear by consulting the Statute Books. (*a*)

And in the First year of *William*
20 and *Mary*, Ses.2. c.9.[5] an Act passed in *England* declaring all *Attainders and other Acts made in the late pretended Parliament under King* James *at* Dublin *void*: But was not
25 Enacted here in *Ireland* till[6] the 7th year of K. *William* c.3. And this was thought requisite to be done upon mature consideration thereon before

(*a*) Irish Stat. 13 *C. 2. c.2.* 13 *C.2. c.3.* 14 & 15 *C.2. c.1.* 14 & 15 *C.2. c.*19. 17 & 18 *C.2. c.3.* 17 & 18 *C.2. c.*11. English Stat. 12 *C.2. c.*12. 12 *C.2. c.3.* 12 *C.2. c.*14, 12 *C.2. c.*24. 12 *C.2. c.*33. 16 & 17 *C.2. c.5.*

---

1 Chap. 4] Chap. 5 **PC**   2 Chamber ... Chap. 5.] `Chamber ... Chap. 5´ (*perhaps add. later, manu aman.*) **PC**   3 Six] [five] `six´ **H & PC**   4 upon ... soon] [soo<n>] upon ... soon **H**   5 First ... Ses.2.c.9.] [7th of Ki[[l]]ng William our Present King c.3] `1st ... Ses.2.c.9´ **H**   6 not ... till] `not´ ... not till **H** | not ... [not] till **PC**

75, 19–26 *in the First ... K. William c. 3* – see further, *Case*, p. 109 and nn.

²*For we had two
several Acts
transmitted to us at
different times, to
this very purpose.
One we rejected in
the Lord *Sydneys*
Government,
t'other we pass'd
under the Lord
Capell.

the King and Council of *England*,¹*
notwithstanding that the English
Act does *particularly name Ireland*,
and was wholly design'd for, and
relates thereto.

The like may we find in several
other Statutes of *England* passed
since his present Majesties
Accession to the Throne, which
have afterwards been passed here in
Ireland, with such Alterations as
make them practicable and
agreeable to this Kingdom. Such as
are amongst others, the Act for
Disarming Papists. The Act of
Recognition. The Act for taking
away *Clergie* from some Offenders.
The Act for taking *Special Bail* in
the Country, &c. The Act against
Clandestine Mortgages. The Act
against *Cursing and Swearing*.³

These, with many more, are to
be found in our Statute Books in
the several Reigns of *Henry* the 8th.
Edward the 6th. Queen *Elizabeth*,
King *James*, King *Charles* the 1st
and 2d. and King *William*.⁴ But it is
not to be found in any

1 of England] `of England´ H   2 *marginal note (indicated by asterisk)* For ... the Lord ... the Lord] For ...
Lord ... Lord (*manu aman.*) PC   3 *Swearing*] *end of interpolation begun p. 74, n. 6 above*   4 King Charles
the 1st ... *William*] [and] King Charles `the 1st ... William´ H

76, 2–5 *not withstanding ... thereto* – for the significance of English acts naming Ireland, see *Case*,
pp 80, 85, 118–20.   76, 15–16 *Act of Recognition* – the Irish act of recognition (4 W. & M., §1) differed
considerably from the English statute, 2 W. & M., ses. 1, c.1, esp. in explicitly conceding that Ireland was
a dependent kingdom.   76, 27–77, 9 *it is ... Ireland* – as in Bolton, 'Declaration', p. 10, except for the
interpolation of 'introductive of a new Law' (cf. app. crit.).

Records in *Ireland*, that ever any Act of Parliament introductive of a new Law[1] made in *England* since the time of King *John*, was by the
5 judgment of any Court received for Law, or put in Execution in the Realm of *Ireland* before the same was Confirmed and Assented to by Parliament in *Ireland*.

10 And thus I presume we have pretty clearly made out our *Fourth Enquiry* forementioned: and shewn plainly *the several steps by which the English form of Government, and the*
15 English Statute Laws *were[2] received in this Kingdom*; and that this was wholly by the *Peoples consent in Parliament*, to which we have had a very *antient Right*, and as full a
20 Right as our next Neighbours can pretend to or challenge.

I shall now consider the **Objections** Objections and Difficulties that are **Answer'd,** moved on this Head drawn from
25 Precedents, and Passages in our Law-Books that may seem to prove the contrary.

---

1 introductive ... Law] `introductive ... *new law´* **H**   2 *English form...* English Statute ... *were*] [Statute] English form ... English Statute ... [caɱ<e>] were **H**

77, 10–21 *And thus ... challenge* – passage denounced by English commons committee: *Commons Jnl [Eng.]*, xii, p. 325. As noted, *Case*, p. 4 nn, the hasty completion of *The Case* left Molyneux with two conclusions to his 'Fourth Enquiry', cf. *Case*, p. 115. *Challenge* – assert one's right to, or lay claim to: *OED*, s.v. 5. **77, 25–6** *our Law-Books* – as on *Case*, pp 122, 136, it is clear from what follows that this refers to English law books not Irish ones.

Objection from
the Stat. of Rape.

First¹ 'tis urg'd, That in the Irish
Act concerning Rape passed *anno* 8
Edward 4, c.1. 'tis² expressed, That a
Doubt was conceiv'd whether the

5 English Statute of the 6th of
Richard the 2d. c.6. ought to be of
force in *Ireland* without a
Confirmation thereof in the
Parliament of *Ireland*. Which shews

10 (as some alledg)³ that even in those
days it was held⁴ by some, That an
Act of Parliament in *England* might
bind *Ireland* before it be consented
to in Parliament here.

15 But I concieve this Gloss is rais'd
meerly for want of Expressing the
Reason of the said Doubt⁵ in the
Irish Statute of the 8th of *Edward*
the 4th. c.1. which we may

20 reasonably judge was this. By the
Statute of *Westminster* the 2d. c.34. a
Woman that eloped from her
Husband and lived with the
Adulterer, or a Wife that being first⁶

25 Ravish'd did afterwards consent, and
lived with the Ravisher, she should
loose her Dower. This Statute of
Westminster the 2d, was made of
force in *Ireland* by an Act passed here

---

1 First] [And] first **H**   2 'tis] [there] 'tis **H**   3 (as ... alledg)] `(say our Adversarys)´ **H** | ([say ...
Adversarys] `as ... alledge´) **PC**   4 it ... held] held [Ques] ([Ques] *perhaps for* [Ques<tionable>) **H** | `it
was´ held **PC**   5 Gloss ... Doubt] [Construction proceeds meerly from the Want] `Glos of our
Adversarys´ is raised for ... `expressing´ ... Doubt[s being expresd] **H** | Glos [of our Adversarys] ...
`meerly´ ... Doubt **PC**   6 Wife ... first] [Woman] `Wife´ ... `first´ **H**

78, 1–80, 9 *the Irish ... past* – further discussion of the implications of 8 Edw. 4, c. 1 had been indicated,
Case, p. 69. Cf. Bolton, 'Declaration', p. 6; Domville, 'Disquisition', pp 68–9.   **78, 10–17** *some alledg ...
Doubt* – the deletion of the two references to 'our Adversarys' (cf. app. crit.) showed Molyneux's concern to
avoid potentially offensive language. See further intro. p. 39, n. 181.

the 13th of *Edward* the 2d, as we[1]
have seen before, pag. 68, 69.
Afterwards by the English Statute
of the[2] 6th of *Rich.* the 2d. c.6. there
5   was a farther addition made to the
said Statute of *Westminster* the 2d.
to this effect, That a Maiden or
Wife being Ravished, and afterwards consenting to the Ravishers,
10   as well the Ravisher as she that was
Ravished shall be disabled to claim
all Inheritance or Dower after the
death of her[3] Husband or Ancestor.

On this account the Doubt was
15   here raised in *Ireland* in the 8th of
Edward the 4th. c.1. Whether this
latter English Statute of the 6th of
Richard the 2d. c.6. were not in
force in *Ireland* by virtue of the Irish
20   Statute[4] of the 13th of *Edward* the
2d. which confirmed the Statute of
Westminster the 2d. c.34. And for
setling this Doubt the said Statute
of the 8th of *Edward* the 4th c.1.
25   was passed in *Ireland,* and we find
very good reason for the said
Doubt. For the English Statute of
the 6th of *Richard* the 2d. c.6.
contained but a small addition[5]

---

1 *Ireland* ... as we] Ireland [as we] ... as we **H**   **2** of the] *not in* **H & PC**   3 her] their **H**   **4** Irish
Statute] [Stat<ute>] Irish Statute **H**   **5** contained ... addition] [was] [was but an Addition] 'contained ...
small' Addition **H**

to the Statute of *Westminster* the 2d
c.34. and we see that even this
addition itself was judged not to be
of force in *Ireland* till Enacted here.

5   For the said[1] Irish Statute of the 8th
of *Edward* the 4th. c.1. makes the
said Statute of the 6th of *Rich.*2d.
c.6. of Force in *Ireland* only from
the 6th of *March*, then last past.

10   'Tis urg'd secondly, That tho'
perhaps such Acts of Parliament in
England which do not *Name Ireland*,
shall not be construed to Bind
Ireland, yet all such English Statutes

15   as *mention*[2] *Ireland*, either by the
General Words of *all his Majesty's*
Dominions, or by *particularly*
Naming of *Ireland*, are and shall[3] be
of Force in this Kingdom.

20   This being a Doctrine first
broach'd Directly (as I conceive) by
Will. Hussey, Lord Chief Justice of
the Kings Bench[4] in *England*, in the
first year of Henry the *Seventh*, and

25   of late Revived by the[5] Lord Chief
Justice *Cook*, and strongly urged, and
much rely'd upon in these latter
Days; I shall take the Liberty of
Enlarging   thereon,   tho'

---

1 said] `sd´ H    2 *mention*] [Name] `mention´ H   3 are ... shall] [sh<all>] are ... shall H   4 Kings Bench] `Kings Bench´ (*interpolated in blank space in MS*) H   5 the] *not in* H & PC

80, 14–19 *such English ... Kingdom* – notably in Calvin's case which involved the right of *post-nati* (Scots born after the Union of the Crowns in 1603) to inherit property in England: Coke, *7th Rep.*, ff 1r–28v. Consideration of the status of the king's subjects in dominions other than the kingdom in which they were born naturally raised the question of Ireland. Cf. Black, 'Constitution', *University of Pennsylvania Law Review*, 124 (1976), pp 1175–6.   **80, 20–8** *Doctrine ... Days* – that is, Hussey's verdict in the Merchants of Waterford's case, 1485, as interpreted by Coke; see further, *Case*, pp 89–93, 116–22. After 1660 Calvin's case came to be regarded as of key significance for England's relations with Ireland and her overseas plantations (cf. Vaughan, *Reports and arguments* (London, 1714), p. 292), and was accordingly raised in the bishop of Derry's appeal, 1698.

I venture thereby to swell this Pamphlet to a size[1] greater than I desire or design'd.

First therefore, As[2] to such
5   English Statutes as seem to comprehend *Ireland*, and to Bind it, under the *General Words of all his Majesty's Dominions* or *Subjects*, whatever has been[3] the Opinion of
10   Private and Particular Lawyers in this Point, I am sure the Opinions of the Kings of *England*, and their Privy Council, have been otherwise: 'Tis well known since[4] *Poyning's*
15   Act in *Ireland*, the 10th of *Henry* the Seventh, no Act can pass in our Parliament here, till it be first Assented to by the King and Privy Council of *England*, and
20   Transmitted hither under the Broad Seal of *England*: Now the King and his Privy Council there, have been so far from surmising that an Act of Parliament of *England*, mentioning[5]
25   only in General *All the King's Dominions*, or *Subjects*[6], should Bind *Ireland*, that they have clearly shewn the contrary, by frequently Transmitting to *Ireland*, to be pass'd
30   into Laws here, English[7] Sta

Object. English Statutes comprehending Ireland by general Words.

1 size] [[B]]size ([[B]] *perhaps for* [[B<ulk>]]) H   2 As] [Whatever] as H   3 or ... been] `or subjects´ ... [was] 'has been' H   4 since] [[th<at>]]since H   5 mentioning] [conc̦] mentioning ([conc̦] *perhaps for* [conc<erning>]) H   6 or *Subjects*] 'or subjects' H   7 to be ... English] [[[A<cts>]]English] to be... English H

81, 1–2 *this Pamphlet ... greater –* when Robert Hooke had objected to Molyneux's describing one of his works as a pamphlet in 1686, the latter explained that he had taken the term to designate 'small stich'd volumes', and that no slight had been intended: Hoppen, *The common scientist* (London, 1970), p. 115. **81, 10–13** *Private ... otherwise –* specifically, Sir Edward Coke, cf. *Case*, pp 118–20. Striking confirmation of Molyneux's conjecture as to the very different attitude of the king and English council is provided by Charles I's instructions to Ormond on negotiating with Confederates, 9 Jan. 1642/3. See further intro. p. 25. **81, 14–19** *Poyning's Act ... England –* 10 Hen. 7, c. 4, as amended by 3 & 4 Phil. & M., c. 4. Broad Seal should read Great Seal; cf. lengthy account in Bolton, 'Declaration', pp 8–9. For Molyneux, the significance of Poynings' Law lay in confirming Ireland's fundamental, indissoluble connection with the English crown, while at the same time excluding the English parliament from any role in the Irish law-making process. See further, *Case*, pp 127, 159–62, 166–7 below. By mid-C.18, however, Poynings' Law came to be seen as an unwarrantable restriction on the independence of the Irish parliament, see further intro. p. 36, n. 171.

tutes, wherein the *General Words of all the Kings Dominions* or *Subjects*[1] were contain'd; which would have been to no purpose, but meerly *Actum Agere*[*], had *Ireland* been Bound *before* by those English Statutes.

[*][to do what had already been done]

Of this I shall give the following Examples, amongst many others.

Act against Appeals to Rome.

The Act of Parliament in *England* against *Appeals to Rome*, 24 *Hen*.8. c.12. by express words extends to all his Majesties Dominions, yet the same was not in force, nor receiv'd in *Ireland*, till it was Enacted by Parliament there, the 28th of *Hen*.8. c.6.

Acts of First Fruits and Faculties.

(a) Title in the English Statues is, *No Imposition shall be paid to the Bishop of Rome.*

In like manner the Statutes[2] made in *England* concerning *First Fruits*, 26 *Hen*.8. c.3. and the *Act of Faculties*, (*a*) 25 *Hen*.8. c.21.[3] though each of them by express words comprize *All his Majesties Subjects and Dominions*[4], were not receiv'd as Laws in *Ireland*, till the former was Enacted there, 28 H.8. c.8.[5] and the latter the 28 *Hen*.8. c.19. [6]and so

5

10

15

20

25

---

1 or *Subjects*] `or subjects´ **H**   2 Statutes] Statute[s] **H**   3 c.21] [4.] `21.´ **H** | [[[3]]4.] `21.´ **PC**   4 *Subjects … Dominions*] [Dominions] `Subjects´ **H** | Subjects `and Dominions´ **PC**   5 28 H.8. c.8.] 28 H.8. c.8. **ed** | 28 H.8. c.4. **H, PC & I**   6 – p. 83, n. 3 and so … *Dromore*] `And … Dromore´ (*interpolation in margin*) **H**

82, 10–83, 31 *The Act … Dromore* – the original submission to Henry II established an ecclesiastical government independent of England as well as a secular one (cf. *Case*, p. 36–7 above). See further, *Case*, pp 128–9.   **82, 10–27** *The Act … 28 Hen. 8. c.19* – based on Domville, 'Disquisition', pp 66–7. The remainder of the paragraph dealing with Hacket's suspension was a subsequent interpolation (cf. app. crit.).

the Statute Restoring[1] to the
Crown all Jurisdiction Ecclesiastical
made in *England, Anno* I *Eliz.* c.1.
and therein giving Power to Erect
5 an Ecclesiastical *High-Commission-*
Court in *England* and *Ireland,* yet
was not of Force in *Ireland* till
Enacted there, *Anno* 2 *Eliz.* c.1.
And tho' the said English Act, in
10 relation to Erecting such an High-
Commission-Court, was Repeal'd
17 *Car.*1. c.11 and the Repeal confirm'd the 13 *Car.*2. c.12; And the
late Bill of Rights, 1 *W.* and *M.*
15 *Ses.*2. c.2. in *England,* has damn'd all
such Courts. Yet the Act in *Ireland*
2 *Eliz.* c.1. remains still in force
here; and so it was lately declar'd
here by the Lord High-Chancellour
20 *Porter,* Lord Chief Justice *Reynel,*
Lord Chief Baron *Hely,* Mr. Justice
Cox, Mr. Justice *Jeffreyson,* in the
Case of Dr. *Thomas Hacket,* late
Bishop of *Down,* who was depriv'd
25 of the said Bishoprick by such a
Commission, for great Enormities;
the Commissioners being Dr.
Dopping late Bishop of *Meath,* Dr.
King, the present Bishop of *London-*
30 *Derry,* and Dr *Wiseman,*[2] late
Bishop of *Dromore.*[3]

High-
Commission-
Court.

---

1 Restoring] [concerning] restoring **H**   2 *Wiseman*] Wiseman **H & PC** | *Wisemnn* **I original state G2r**
3 Dromore.] *end of interpolation begun p. 82, n. 6 above*

83, 13–31 *the late Bill … Dromore* – a reminder that Ireland had failed to benefit from the revolution as
England and Scotland had done, and that the Irish administration had recently blocked an Irish bill of
rights. Cf. *Case,* A4r nn. Bishop Hacket's deprivation had been effected in 1694 for, among other things,
non-residence in Ireland since 1681. See Osborough, 'The Failure', *Irish Jurist,* n.s. 33 (1998), pp 395–7,
which points out that this is the only surviving mention of Hacket's appeal.

By the same
Reason *Scotland*
may be bound.

And[1] truly I see no more Reason for Binding *Ireland* by the English Laws under the *General Words of all his Majesties Dominions or Subjects*, than there is for Binding *Scotland* by the same; for *Scotland* is as much his *Dominion*, and *Scotsmen* as much his *Subjects* as *Ireland* and *Irish-men*: If it be said, That *Scotland* is an Antient *Separate* and *Distinct* Kingdom from *England*; I say, So is *Ireland*: The Difference is, *Scotland* continued *separate* from the Kings of *England* till of *late*[2] years, and *Ireland* continued *separate* from *England* but a very *little while* in the Person of King *John*, before the Death of his Father, and of his Brother *Richard* the First,[3] without issue. But then 'tis to be considered, that there was a *Possibility*, or even a *Probability*, that *Ireland* might have continued *separate* from the Crown of *England*, even to this very[4] day, if *Richard* the First had left behind him a Numerous Progeny.[5]

---

1 And] [And indeed if we consider [the] Reason [of the] in this Case we shall see,] (*new para.*) And **H**
2 continued ... *late*] [has been annexed to the] `continued ... from ye´ ... [but L] till of late ([L] *perhaps for* [L<ately>]) **H**    3 the First] [2d] `1st´ **H**   4 very] `very´ (*perhaps add. later in margin*) **H**   5 Progeny.]
Progeny. And were it to my Purpose, I could shew, [how much] `that it were equally if not´ more reasonable [it [is] `were´] to make Scotland subordinate to the Parliament of England, than to make Ireland so. for we know [with] what submission Tribute Homage and Fealty many of the Scots Kings have paid to the Kings of England in antient and Latter times, of which our Historys are full. (*cont. in margin*) and at the Latter end of Reylys Placita Parliamentaria we have an Advertisement that that Laborious Collector had in his hands Extracts from ye Records in ye Tower of London shewing *the Homage and Dependency of Scotland on England.* **H** | [And ... (*as final reading of* **H**) ... *England.*] (*del. by cross-hatching*) **PC**

84, 1–21 *And truly ... issue* – passage denounced by English commons committee: *Commons Jnl [Eng.]*, xii, p. 325.   **84, 13–16** *Scotland ... Ireland* – Clement, *Answer*, p. 109, objected that Ireland was never an 'intire Kingdom' until the English conquered the country and gave it laws and a constitution.   **84, 23–8** *Ireland ... Progeny* – cf. *Case*, pp 41–2. See app. crit. for significant deleted passage considering England's medieval claims to suzerainty over Scotland.

Secondly, As to such English Statutes as particularly *Name Ireland*, and are therefore said to be of Force in this Kingdom, tho' never

5 Enacted here; I shall consider only the more *Antient Precedents* that are offered in Confirmation of this Doctrine: For as to those of *later Date*, 'tis these we complain of, as

10 bearing hard[1] on the *Liberties* of this Country,[2] and the *Rights* of our Parliaments, and therefore *these* ought not to be produced as Arguments against us. I presume, if

15 I can shew, that the *Antient* Precedents that are produced, *do not conclude* against us; it will follow that[3] the *Modern* Instances given, *ought not to conclude* against us; that

20 is to say plainly, These *ought* not to have been made as they are, as wanting Foundation both from Authority and Reason.

The *Antient* Precedents of
25 English[4] Statutes, particularly *Naming Ireland*, and said to be made in *England* with a Design of Binding *Ireland*, are chiefly these three:[5]

English
Statutes
naming *Ireland*.

---

1 bearing hard] Incroachments **H** | [Incroachments] `bearing hard´ **PC**  2 of … Country] `of … Country´ **H** 3 the Antient … that] `the´ Antient[ly] … that [neither] **H**  4 English] `English´ **H**
5 and … three] [are chiefly these three] and `said to be´ … three [insisted on by [the] our] **H**

85, 15–18 *Antient … Instances* – the ancient precedents binding Ireland, discussed, *Case*, pp 85–102, were all medieval; while the modern instances, *Case*, pp 102–16, were post-1641.

1. *Statutum Hiberniæ*[*], 14 *H*.3.   [*][the Statute of Ireland]

2. *Ordinatio pro Statu Hiber-*
niæ[**], 17 Edw.1.   [**][the Ordinance for Ireland]

5

3. And the Act that all *Staple*
Commodities passing out of
England or *Ireland*, shall be
carried to *Callis*, as long as the
Staple is at *Callis*, 2. *Hen*.6.
c.4. on which *Hussey* delivered his Opinion, as we shall see
more fully hereafter.

10

15   These Statutes, especially the
two first, being made for *Ireland*, as
their Titles import, have given
occasion to think that the
Parliament of *England* have a *Right*[1]
to make Laws for *Ireland*, without
the *Consent* of their Chosen
Representatives. But if we Enquire
farther into this matter, we shall
find this Conclusion not fairly
Deduced.[2]
[3]First, The *Statutum Hiberniæ*,
14 *Hen*.3. as 'tis to be found in the
Collection of English Statutes, is[4]
plainly thus: The Judges in *Ireland*

20

25

---

1 *Right*] [Power and] Right **H**   2 this ... Deduced] [it otherwise] `this ... deduced´ (*add. at end of MS line*) **H**   3 First] *marginal heading* Statutum Hiberniæ **PC**   4 is] [[[n]]was] is **H**

86, 1–13 *1. Statutum ... hereafter* – these three acts reputedly binding Ireland were considered in greater detail by Bolton, 'Declaration'; namely, *Statutum Hiberniæ*, pp 4, 10–11; *Ordinatio pro Statu Hiberniæ*, pp 11–12, and the Staple Act, pp 7–8. They were not mentioned by Domville. The two first acts were cited as instances of English statutes binding Ireland in Craw v. Ramsey (1673): Vaughan, *Reports and arguments* (London, 1714), p. 293.   86, 9 *Callis* – i.e. Calais, then in English possession, and incidentally the place of origin of the Molyneux family, see intro. p. 2.   86, 13 *more fully hereafter* – see further *Case*, pp 90–4.   86, 29–87, 28 *The Judges ... An. Reg. 14* – see Pulton, *A Collection* (London, 1670) (to which Molyneux referred in *Case*, p. 87), pp 7–8. Bolton, 'Declaration', pp 4, 10–11, cited *Statutum Hiberniæ* as an instance of a declaratory statute, while the note in *The statutes at large of England* (London, 1811), i, p. 15, described *Statutum Hiberniæ* as 'merely a Writ to the Justice of Ireland'. *Statutum Hiberniae* is now dated to 20 Hen. 3: *ESI*, i, p. 293.

conceiving a Doubt concerning Inheritances[1] devolved to Sisters or Coheirs, *viz.* Whether the younger Sisters ought to hold of the Eldest

5 Sister, and do Homage unto her for their Portions, or of the Chief Lord, and do Homage unto him; therefore *Girald Fitz Maurice*, the then[2] Lord Justice of *Ireland*, dispatcht

10 four Knights to the King in *England*, to bring a Certificate from thence of the *Practice* there used, and what was the *Common-Law* of *England* in that *Case*. Whereupon

15 *Hen.*3. in this his Certificate or Rescript, which is called *Statutum Hiberniæ*[*], meerly informs the Justice what the *Law* and *Custom* was in *England*, *viz.* That the Sisters

20 ought to hold of the Chief Lord, and not of the Eldest Sister.[3] And the close of it commands, that *the foresaid Customs that be*[4] *used within our Realm of* England *in this Case, be*

25 *Proclaimed throughout our Dominion of* Ireland, *and be there observ'd. Teste meipso apud* Westminst, 9.Feb. *An. Reg.*14.[**]

From whence 'tis manifest, that

30 this *Statutum Hibernia* was no

[*][the Statute of Ireland]

[**][Witness ourself, at Westminster, the 9th of February in the 14th year of our reign.]

---

1 Inheritances] [an] Inheritances **H**   2 *Fitz Maurice*, the then] Fitz Ma[[r]]uri[[is]]ce then **H**   3 and *Custom ... Sister*] `and Custom´ was `in England ... Sister´ **H**   4 *that be*] [[be]] that be **H**

87, 3–7 *Whether ... unto him* – directly cited from 14. Hen. 3: Pulton, *A Collection* (London, 1670), pp 7–8.
87, 8–12 *Girald Fitz Maurice ... there used* – recte Maurice Fitz Gerald, Justiciar (i.e. governor) of Ireland, 1232–45. For the use of such certificates, see intro. p. 27, n. 134.   **87, 10** *four Knights* – 'certaine knights': Pulton, *A Collection* (London, 1670), p. 7.   **87, 26–8** *there ... An. Reg. 14* – Pulton, *A Collection* (London, 1670), p. 8, translated the ending and read 'straitly kept and' for 'there'.

more than a Certificate of what the *common Law of England* was in that Case, which *Ireland* by the *Original Compact* was to be governed by. And

5 shews no more, that therefore the Parliament of *England* may bind *Ireland,* than it would have proved, that the Common Wealth of *Rome*[1] was subject to *Greece,* if, after *Rome*

10 had received the Law of the *Twelve Tables,* they had sent to *Greece* to know what the Law was, in some Special Case.

Ordinatio pro Statu Hiberniæ.

The Statute call'd *Ordinatio pro*

15 *Statu Hiberniae,*[*] made at *Notingham* the 17th of *Edward* the First, and to be found in *Pultons* Collection *pag. 76. Edit. Lond.* 1670. was certainly never Received, or[2] of

20 Force, in *Ireland.* This is Manifest from the very first Article of that Ordinance, which Prohibits the *Justice of Ireland or others the Kings Officers, there to Purchase Land in*

25 *that Kingdom, or within their respective Balliwicks without the Kings Licence, on pain of Forfeitures.*[3] But that this has ever been Otherwise, and that the Lords

30 Justices, and other Offi-

[*][the Ordinance for Ireland]

---

1 *Rome*] Ro[[man]]me **H**   2 Received, or] `Received or´ **H**     3 *in that ... Forfeitures*] [in Ireland] in that ... `respective´ ... `on ... forfeiture´ **H** | in that ... forfeiture **PC**

88, 8–13 *the Common ... Case* – the earliest collection of ancient Roman written law: Berger, *An encyclopaedic dictionary, Transactions of the American Philosophic Society,* n.s. 43:2 (1953), p. 55. For a similar comparison, cf. Bolton, 'Declaration', p. 19.   **88, 14–17** *The Statute ... First* – though still attributed to the reign of Edward I in *The statutes at large of England* (London, 1811), i, p. 129, the Ordinance of Nottingham has since been shown to date to 17 Edw. 2 (1323): *ESI,* i, p. 300.   **88, 17–18** *Pultons ... 1670* – a copy of this edn of Pulton's *A collection of sundrie statutes,* which had presumably belonged to William Molyneux, was listed in the *Molyneux library catalogue,* p. 77. See intro. p. 4, n. 13.   **88, 21–7** *first Article ... Forfeitures* – Cary, *Vindication,* pp 57–8, pointed out that the *Ordinatio* has seven other sections regulating matters in Ireland, including purveyance, pardoning felonies, and official fees.

cers here have Purchas'd Lands in *Ireland*, at their own Will and Pleasure, needs no Proof to those who have the least knowledge of this[1] Country. Nor does it appear by any Inquisition, Office, or other Record, that any one[2] ever Forfeited on that Account.

Moreover this *Ordinatio pro Statu Hiberniæ*[*], is really in itself *No Act of Parliament*, but meerly an Ordinance of the *King* and his *Privy Council* in *England*; which appears as well from the Preamble to the said Ordinance, as from this Observation[3] likewise, That King *Edward* the First held no Parliament in the 17th year of his Reign: Or if this were a Parliament, this *Ordinatio pro Statu Hiberniæ*, is the only Act thereof that is Extant: But[4] 'tis very improbable, that only this *single Ordinance* should Appear, if any such Parliament were call'd together.[5]

Thirdly, As to the *Staple-Act*, 2 *Hen.*6. c.4. which expresly names *Ireland*,[6] and *Hussey's* Opinion thereon. The Case, as we find it in the

Staple-Act.

[*][the Ordinance for Ireland]

5

10

15

20

25

---

1 here … this] there … that **H** | [t]here … [that] `this´ **PC**   2 any one] [they] `any One´ **H**   3 *Privy* … Observation] [[C<ouncil>]]Privy Council … `as well´ … [conside<ration>] Observation **H**   4 thereof … But] `thereof´ … [which] `But´ **H**   5 only … together] [a Parliamt should be Cald together, and enact no More than this single Ordnance] `only … together´ **H**   6 which … *Ireland*] *not in* **H** | `which … Ireland´ **PC**

89, 15–21 *Ordinance … Extant* – taking the reference to the king and council in the 1288 *Ordinatio* to be to the privy council made clear how greatly Molyneux's picture of parliament in medieval times was determined by C.17 practice and institutions. His error was pointed out by Cary, *Vindication*, p. 59. (However, the meeting of the great council following Easter 1289 is now considered as a parliament: *British chronology*, p. 509.)   89, 22–5 *'tis very … together* – insisting that *Ordinatio pro Statu Hiberniæ* was a statute in regular form, Cary, *Vindication*, pp 64–5, alluded to various other examples of a single legislative act emanating from a parliament, notably the Magna Carta of 9 Hen. 3 (1225).   89, 26–28 *Staple-Act … Ireland* – (1423–4), see *The statutes at large of England*, i, p. 615.   89, 29–91, 23 *The Case … in Angl.* – the Merchants of Waterford's case (1485) was briefly mentioned by Domville, 'Disquisition', pp 67–8, while Bolton, 'Declaration', p. 7, provided a more detailed account which Molyneux used to amend his original holograph version, (cf. app. crit.).

Merchants of
***Waterford*'s Case.**

Year-Books[1] of *Mich.*2. *Rich.*3.
fol.11. and *Mich.*1 *Hen.*7.fol.3. is
in short thus:[2] The Merchants of
Waterford having[3] Ship'd off some
5   Wooll, and consign'd it to *Sluice* in
Flanders, the Ship by stress of
Weather was put in at *Callis*, where[4]
Sir *Thomas Thwaits*, Treasurer of
Callis, seized the said Wooll as
10   forfeited, half to himself, and half to
the King, by the said Statute;
hereupon[5] a Suit was commenced
between the said Merchants and the
said[6] Treasurer, which was brought
15   before all the Judges of *England* into
the *Exchequer* Chamber: The
Merchants pleaded the King's
License to the Citizens of *Waterford*
and their Successors, for carrying
20   Wooll where they pleased; and[7] the
Questions before the Judges were[8]
two, Viz. *Whether this Staple-Act
Binds Ireland*; And Secondly,
Whether the King could grant his
25   License *contrary to the Statute, and
especially where the Statute gives half
the Forfeiture to the Discoverer*[9].

The first Point only relates to
our present purpose; and herein we
30   find the foresaid Year-Book of 2

---

1 Year-Books] Year Books **H & PC** | Yeat Books **I** *original state* G5v   2 *Mich.* 2 ... thus] `Mich. 2. ...
`fol 11´... Mich. I.´ Hen, [ye 7. ye first year of his Reign in Mich. Term] `7. fol.3.´ [was] `is´ ... thus
(*followed by superscript indicator* (a) *for del. marginal ref.* [(a) Mich. 2 ... fol.11b. ... fol.3.b.´)] **H**   3 having]
`having´ **H**    4 *Sluice* ... where] [some other Place beyond seas and not to Callais, thereupon] `Sluice ...
where´ **H**   5 half ... hereupon] `half ... Statute´. [and] `hereupon´ **H**   6 the said] [Sr <?Thomas
Thwaits>] `the said´ **H**    7 The Merchants ... and] `the merchants ... and´ (*interpolation in margin*) **H**
8 the Judges were] the[m seem to be] `Judges were´ **H**   9 *Discoverer.*] Discoverer. [the] **H**

90, 14–16 *brought ... Chamber* – cases raising particularly complex issues were heard by all the judges sitting
together in the exchequer chamber, see further Hemmant, *Select cases* (London, 1933), i, pp ix–xiv, xix–xx.
90, 22–3 *Whether ... Ireland* – the precedent of a medieval English act regulating Irish trade in wool was
particularly relevant to the current controversy over the regulation of Irish woollen exports by the English
parliament. Cf. Cary, *Vindication*, pp 49–50.

[*][And there (in the Exchequer Chamber) with regard to the first question they declared that in the Kingdom of Ireland they have parliaments and courts in every respect as in England: And by their own parliament they make and change laws, and are not bound by statutes made in England; because they have not Knights in Parliament here, (and is this not an unanswerable reason?) but this is to be understood only concerning the affecting of lands and property in that kingdom: For their persons are the King's subjects; and as subjects they shall be bound, when out of that territory, not to do any thing contrary to the statutes (of England), like the inhabitants of Calais, Gascony, Guienne, &c. whilst they were subjects. And they shall be obedient to the <jurisdiction of the> Admiralty of England as touching any thing committed on the high seas. And in like manner there shall be a writ of error from a judgement given in Ireland, to the King's Bench here in England.]

5

10

15

20

25

*Rich.*3. fol.12. to Report it thus: *Et ibi* (in the Exchequer Chamber) *quoad Primam Questionem Dicebant quod Terr. Hibern. inter se habent Parliament. & omnimodo Cur. prout in Angl. & per Idem Parliamentum faciunt Leges & Mutant Leges & non Obligantur per Statuta in Anglia*[1], *quia non hic habent Milites Parliamenti* (and is not that an unanswerable Reason ?) *sed hoc intelligitur de terris & rebus in terris illis tantum efficiendo; sed Personæ eorum*[2] *sunt Subject. Regis & tanquam Subjecti erunt Obligati ad aliquam rem extra Terram illam faciend. contra Statut. sicut habitantes in Calesia, Gascoignie, Guien, &c. dum fuere Subjecti; & Obedientes erunt sub Admiral. Angl. de re fact. super Altum Mare; &*[3] *similit. Brev. de Errore de Judicio reddit. in Hibern. in Banco Reg. hic in Angl.*[*]

I have *verbatim* transcribed this Passage out of the foresaid Year-Book, that I might be sure to omit nothing that may give the Objection its[4] full weight. And all that I can answer to it, is this:

---

1 *& non ... Anglia*] `et non ... Anglia´ (*interpolation in margin*) **H**    2 *eorum*] illæ **H** | [illæ] `eorum´ **PC**
3 *Mare, &*] *Mare. [&c] et* **H**   4 its] it **H & PC**

91, 1–23 *Et ibi ... in Angl.* – an accurate transcription from the Year Book 2, Rich. 3., fol. 12r, case 26. Cf. Brooke, *La grande abridgement* (London, 1573), ii, p. 123; s.v. parliament, sect. 98.   **91, 21–3** *Brev. ... in Angl.* – the question of appeals on writs of error to the English king's bench is discussed, *Case*, pp 131–9. **91, 19–21** *Obedientes ... Altum Mare* [transl. *obedient ... high seas*] – from 1575 Ireland had its own admiralty jurisdiction, subject to appeal to the English court, which continued, however, to assert some direct authority in Ireland: Costello, *The court of admiarlity, 1575–1893* (Dublin, 2011), pp 1, 11.

1. That[1] when the foresaid Case came a second time under the Consideration of the Judges in the *Exchequer* Chamber in *Mich.* 1.

5 *Hen.*7. fol.3. we find it Reported thus: *Hussey the* [2]*Chief Justice said, That the Statutes made in* England *shall bind those of* Ireland, *which was not much gain-said by the other*

10 *Judges, notwithstanding that some of them were of* a contrary[3] Opinion *the last Term in his Absence.* How the Presence and Opinion of the Chief Justice came to influence them now,

15 I leave the Reader to judge.[4]

2.[5] That *Brook* in Abridging this Case of the first of *Hen.*7. fol.3.[6] Title *Parliament*, Sec.90. adds, *Tamen*[7] *Nota* [however, bear

20 in mind], *That Ireland is a Kingdom by it self, and hath Parliaments of its own*; intimating thereby,[8] That therefore *Hussey's Opinion* herein was *Unreasonable*.

25 3.[9] That 'tis manifest, if *Hussey* mean by his[10] words, That *All* Acts of Parliament in *England* shall bind *Ireland*, it is directly contrary to

---

1 1. That] That (*no new para.*) **H** | `1st´ That (*no new para.*) **PC** 2 – p. 95, n. 1 Chief Justice … *Naming Ireland*.] *The original page (f. 120r) in* **H** *has been so heavily amended that WM also inserted a faircopy sheet (f. 119r–v) to facilitate the transcription of* **PC**. *Variant readings are accordingly noted for both the original and faircopy versions of this passage, as* **H orig** *and* **H f/copy** *respectively.* (*NB Minor errors in transcribing the faircopy are not noted.*) 3 contrary] a[n other] `Contrary´ **H orig** 4 How … judge.] `How the Chief Justices Presence and opinion came to [overawe] `influence´ them´ … judge. [*but certain it is that the words here*]´ (*interpolation partly in margin*) **H orig** | How … (*as printed text*) … `of … Justice´ … Judge. **H f/copy** 5 2.] *not in* **H orig & f/copy** 6 of the … fol.3.] `of … fol.3.´ **H orig** 7 *Tamen*] *not in* **H orig** 8 *Kingdom* … thereby] Realm … `thereby´ **H orig** 9 3.] *not in* **H orig & f/copy** 10 his] [these] `his´ **H orig**

92, 1–12 *the foresaid … Absence* – Atwood, *History* , pp 187–8, pointed out that Molyneux had overlooked the reference in Year Book 1, Hen. 7, fol. 2v, to the change of sovereign requiring the recommencement of the case (a requirement ended in 1547 by the act, 1 Edw. 6, c. 7). Johnston, 'The English legislature', *Law Quarterly Review* (1924), p. 101, suggests that Hussey's reversal of the earlier verdict may reflect this former Yorkist judge's desire to ingratiate himself with the Tudor regime. **92, 6–95, 2** *Chief … Ireland* – Molyneux revised the corresponding page of the holograph so extensively at this point as to require making a fair copy (cf. app. crit.). The most significant changes occurred in the discussion of parliamentary control of the trade of non-English subjects, *Case*, p. 94, a matter of considerable significance for the current English efforts to regulate the Irish woollen trade. **92, 16–24** *That Brook … Unreasonable* – cf. Brooke, *La grande abridgement* (London, 1573), ii, p. 122: 'the opinion of the Chief Justice [Hussey] that English statutes bind them in Ireland, which was in manner agreed by other Justices', continuing, 'Tamen Nota …', as below.

the Judges Opinion in the second of
Richard the Third, before recited;
for *within* the Land of *Ireland*, they
are all positive, That the Authority

5   of the Parliament of *England* will
not Affect us.[1] They seem at the
utmost reach[2] to extend the Jurisdiction of the English Parliament
over the Subjects of *Ireland*[3], *only* in

10   relation to their Actions beyond
Seas, out of the Realm of *Ireland*,
[4]as they are the *King of England's
Subjects*; but *even This* will Appear
Unreasonable,[5] when we consider,

15   that by the same Argumentation,
Scotland it self may be bound by
English Laws, in relation to their
Foreign Trade, as they[6] are the *King
of Englands Subjects*. The Question

20   is, Whether *England* and *Ireland* be
two Distinct Kingdoms, and whether
they have each their Respective
Parliaments; neither of which will
be deny'd by any Man: And[7] if so,

25   there can be no Subordination on
either side, each is compleat in its
own Jurisdiction, and ought not to
interfere with t'other in any thing.
[8]If *being the King of England's*

30   *Subjects*, be a Reason why

---

1 for *within* … us.] *not in* **H orig** (*but cf. p. 94, n. 4*) | For … [reach] `affect´ us **H f/copy** 2 They … reach]
[for there they] `they [only] seem´ [restrain their sentence only only] `at the utmost reach [they seem]´ **H
orig** 3 Subjects of *Ireland*] [Irish] Subjects of Ireland **H orig** 4 – p. 94, n. 7 as they … Nations.] `as they
… Nations.´ (*interpolation in margins of* ff 120r *and* 121v) **H orig** 5 *even* … Unreasonable,] how
unreasonable even this is will appear **H orig** 6 in … as they] [as they] in … as they **H orig** 7 neither …
And] For **H orig** 8 – *p. 94, n. 7* If *being* … Nations.] (*del. in* **PC** *by cross-hatching: deletion cancelled by stet
in margin, manu WM*)

93, 3–6 *for within … Affect us* – passage denounced by English commons committee: *Commons Jnl[Eng.]*,
xii. 325. The app. crit. shows it to have been added as an afterthought.   **93, 16–19** *Scotland … Subjects* –
this perhaps referred to the English commons' resolution of 21 Jan. 1695/6 against the Darien
Company: *Commons Jnl [Eng.]*, xi, p. 407. See further Horwitz, *Parliament* (Manchester, 1977), p. 178.
93, 20–8 *Whether … thing* – passage denounced by English commons committee: *Commons Jnl [Eng.]*, xii,
p. 325. Cary, *Vindication*, pp 1–2, and Clement, *Answer*, pp 143–4, accused Molyneux of having been
misled by the common use of the term 'parliament' into thinking that the Irish legislature was of equal
importance to the English one.

we ought to submit to Laws, (in
relation to our Trade abroad, in
places where the Parliament of
England has no Jurisdiction)[1] *which*
5   *have not receiv'd*[2] *our Assent*; the
People of *England* will consider[3]
whether they also are not the King's
Subjects, and may therefore (by this
way of Reasoning) be bound by
10   Laws which the King may Assign
them without their Assent, in
relation to their Actions *Abroad*, or
Foreign Trade: [4]Or whether they
had not been Subjects to the *King of*
15   *France*, had our Kings continu'd
their Possession of that Country,
and there kept the Seat of the
Monarchy; and then, had *France*
been stronger than *England*, it
20   might seem that the Subjects of
these Kingdoms[5] might have been
bound by Laws made at *Paris*,
without their own Consent.[6] But let
this Doctrine never be mention'd
25   amongst the *Free-born* Subjects of
these Nations.[7]

Thus I have done with the *Three*
Principal Instances that are usually
brought against us, on the Stress[8]
30   that is laid on English Acts of

---

1 (in … Jurisdiction)] *not in* **H orig & H f/copy** | `(in … abroad, `in … Jurisdiction´)´ (*add. after cancellation of*
del. of passage in previous note) **PC**   2 which … receiv'd] to which we do not give **H orig** | *which* … *reciv'd* **I**
original state G7v   3 the People … consider] Let the … England consider **H orig & H f/copy** | [Let] the …
`will´ consider **PC**   4 – 6 Or whether … Consent.] *not in* **H orig**   5 *England* … Kingdoms] England (as ten
to one but it would be, under a Mild Benigne Government) the Subjects in these Realms **H f/copy** | England
[(as … Government)] `it … that´ … [Realms] `Kingdoms´ **PC**   6 Consent.] Consent. `and who knows what
may happen in Generations to Come amongst the various changes and chances of states and Kingdoms.´ **H**
f/copy | Consent. [and … changes and Revolutions of States and Kingdoms.] **PC**   7 But … Nations.] `but
this is a most (*cont. margin f.* 121v) pernicious doctrine. Let it never … Nations.´ (*returns to f.* 120r) [But] `For´
within the Land of Ireland they [all] are `all´ Positive that the [Jurisd<iction>] Authority of the Parliament of
England will not [reach them] `affect us´. They [only] (Nations. *end of interpolation begun p.* 93, *n.* 4 *above*) **H**
orig (*signum indicating intended interpolation occurs after* `affect us´) | But this Doctrine is most Pernicious on
all Hands, and let it never … (*as printed text*) … Nations. **H f/copy** | But `let´ this Doctrine [is … (*as* **H f/copy**)
… let it] never … Nations. **PC**   8 on … Stress] upon the force **H orig**

94, 23–6 *But … Nations* – Molyneux returned to this question in his discussion of Coke's arguments on Calvin's
case, *Case*, pp 116–22.

Parliament, particularly *Naming Ireland.*[1]

Members from *Ireland* in the Parliament of *England*.

There have been other Statutes or Ordinances made in *England* for 5 *Ireland*, which may reasonably be of force here, because they were made and Assented to by our own Representatives. Thus we find in the *White Book* of the Exchequer in 10 *Dublin*, in the 9th year of *Edward* the First, a Writ sent to his Chancellour of *Ireland*, wherein he mentions *Quaedam Statuta per nos de Assensu Prelatorum Comitum* 15 *Baronum & Communitatis*[2] *Regni nostri Hiberniæ, nuper apud Lincoln & quaedam alia Statuta postmodum apud Eborum facta.*[*] These we may suppose were either Statutes made 20 at the Request of the States of *Ireland*, to *Explain* to them the *Common Law of England*; or if they were introductive of *New Laws*, yet they might well be of force in *Ireland*, 25 being Enacted by the Assent of our own[3] Representatives, The Lords Spiritual and Temporal, and Commons of *Ireland*; as the Words afore-mention'd do shew: And 30 indeed, these are Instances so far

[*]Some statutes lately made by us at Lincoln, and some others afterward at York, with the consent of the Prelates, Earls, Barons, and Commons of our kingdom of Ireland]

---

1 *Naming Ireland.*] *end of passage starting p. 92 , n. 2; for which there are two versions of* **H** 2 *Communitatis*] Communitatis **H & PC** | *Communitates* **I** 3 the … own] `the … our´ own Proper **H**

95, 9 *White … Exchequer* – according to Ware, *The Works* (Dublin, 1739), i, p. 47, the White Book of the Dublin Exchequer had been burnt in 1610. **95, 9–18** *White … Eborum facta* – as in *Case*, pp 86, 88, this writ was wrongly assumed to belong to the reign of Edward I rather than Edward II. Neither Ussher's transcript from the White Book (Gutch, *Collectanea* (Oxford, 1781), i, p. 27) nor the version in the Red Book of the Exchequer (*ESI*, i, p. 296–7) included the word 'Hiberniæ', as given in Molyneux's extract. Surprisingly, Ussher cited this same writ as evidence that English statutes *were* directly binding in Ireland. **95, 13–18** *Quaedam … Eborum facta* [transl. *some … Ireland*] – the English Statutes of Lincoln (9 Edw. 2) and of York (12 Edw. 2), which both included provisions applying exclusively to Ireland, were re-enacted in the Irish statute 17 Edw. 2 (1324): *ESI*, i, pp 300–5. **95, 20–1** *States of Ireland* – the three estates of the realm: *OED*, s.v. state, 22.

from making *against* our Claim, that I think nothing can be more plainly *for* us; for it manifestly shews, that the King and
5   Parliament of *England* would[1] not Enact Laws to Bind *Ireland*, without the *Concurrence* of the Representatives of this[2] Kingdom.

Formerly, When *Ireland* was but
10   thinly Peopled, and the English Laws not[3] fully currant in all parts of the Kingdom, 'tis probable that then they could not frequently Assemble with conveniency or
15   safety to make Laws in their own Parliaments at home; and therefore during the Heats of Rebellions, or Confusion of the Times, they were forced to Enact Laws in *England*.
20   But then this was always by their proper *Representatives*: For we find that in the Reign of *Edward* the Third, (and by what foregoes, 'tis plain 'twas so in *Edward* the First's
25   Time) Knights of the Shire, Citizens, and Burgesses, were Elected in the Shires, Cities and Burroughs[4] of *Ireland*, to serve in Parliament in *England*, and have so
30   served accordingly. For amongst

---

1 would] could **H** | [could] `would´ **PC**    2 this] [that] this **H**    3 and ... not] [nor] `and´ ... `not´ **H**
4 Shires ... Burroughs] [[C]]Shires ... Burroughs ([[C]] *perhaps for* [[C<ounties>]], *cf.* Counties ... Burroughs *p. 97, l. 10*) **H**

96, 4–8 *the King ... Kingdom* – as in the discussion of the *Statutum Hiberniæ* and *Ordinatio pro Statu Hiberniæ, Case*, pp 86–9, Molyneux again turned an apparent weakness in Ireland's case into an effective rebuttal of England's claims.   **96, 17–19** *during ... England* – perhaps intended as a quasi-precedent for English legislation in favour of Irish Protestants in 1689–91. See further, *Case*, pp 106–9.   **96, 30–97, 21** *For amongst ... re-imburse him* – cf. 'Legislative power in Ireland', f. 129v. Prynne, *Brief animadversions* (London, 1669), p. 305, however, pointed out that the entry on membr. 23. distinguished between payments to Irishmen coming 'to our Council' and to English representatives coming 'to our Parliament'.

the Records of the *Tower* of *London*,
Rot. Claus. 50. *Edw.*3. *Parl.*2.
Membr.23. We find a Writ from
the King at *Westminster*, directed to

5 *James Butler*, Lord Justice of
Ireland, and to R. Archbishop of
Dublin, his Chancellour, requiring
them to issue Writs under the
Great Seal of *Ireland*, to the several

10 Counties, Cities and Burroughs, for
satisfying the Expences of the Men
of that Land, *who last came over to
serve in Parliament in England*. And
in another Roll the 50th[1] of

15 *Edw.*III. Membr.19. On Complaint
to the King *by John Draper*, who
was Chosen Burgess of *Cork* by
Writ, and served in the Parliament
of *England*, and yet was deny'd his

20 Expences by some of the Citizens,
Care was taken to re-imburse him.

If from these last mention'd
Records, it be concluded that the
Parliament of *England* may *Bind*

25 *Ireland*; it must also be Allow'd that
the People[2] of *Ireland* ought to have
their *Representatives* in the
Parliament of *England*. And this, I
believe we should be willing enough

---

1 50th] [[3]]50th **H**   2 people] [Shires and Corporations] ʼPeopleʼ **H**

97, 2–7 *50. Edw. 3 ... Dublin* – i.e. 1376–7, when James Butler, 2nd earl of Ormond, was viceroy, and Robert Wikeford, archbishop of Dublin.   **97, 22–8** *If from ... of England* – passage denounced by English commons committee (omitting the phrase 'from these ... Records'): *Commons Jnl [Eng.]*, xii, p. 325.
97, 22–98, 7 *If from ... Inconvenient* – Cary, *Vindication*, p. 106, pointed to the contradiction between the 'Happiness' that Molyneux envisaged being brought about by union and the claim in the previous paragraph that sending representatives to England had in the past proved 'Troublesome and Inconvenient'.
97, 28–98, 2 *And ... hope for* – this sentence was omitted from the 1782 edition of *The Case*, leading to its being described as the 'castrated' (T. Swift, *The utility of union* (Dublin, 1800), p. 36), or 'mutilated' edition (Gay, *Strictures* (Dublin, 1799), p. 24). Opinions have differed as to whether Molyneux's reference to union was a serious proposal, or merely a rhetorical thrust, see further intro. pp 36–7.

to embrace; but this is an Happiness we can hardly hope for.¹

This sending of Representatives
out of *Ireland* to the Parliament in
5   *England*,² on some occasions, was
found in process of time to be very
Troublesome and Inconvenient; and
this, we may presume, was the
Reason, that afterwards, when Times
10   were more settled, we fell again into
our old Track, and regular course of
Parliaments in our own Country:
and hereupon the Laws afore-
noted, pag. 64. were Enacted,
15   Establishing that *no Law made in
the Parliament of England, should be
of force in Ireland, till it was Allow'd
and Publish'd in Parliament here.*³

I have said before, pag. 85. that I
20   would only consider the *more
Antient Precedents* that are offered
to prove, That Acts of *England* particularly *Naming Ireland*, should bind
us in this Kingdom; and indeed it
25   were sufficient to stop here, for the
Reason above alledged. However, I
shall venture to come down lower,
and to enquire into the *Modern*

**Modern Acts of
the Parliament
of *England*,
naming *Ireland*.**

1 but … hope for] but *Nobis non Licet esse tam Beatis* **H** |{but} [nobis … Beatis] `but … for´ **PC**   2 to … *England*] `to … England´ **H**   3 Parliaments … *here*] Parliaments [here again] … `in the Parliament of´ … [t]here **H**

98, 3–12 *This … Country* – similar explanations in terms of a rational reconstruction of events posing as an historical narrative served to account for the Anglo-Irish refugees' accepting legislative assistance from the English parliament in 1689–90, and for the practice of appeals by writ of error to the English king's bench. Cf. *Case*, pp 106–9, 133–8. **98, 13–19** *the Laws … here* – that is from the early C.15 with the act of 10 Hen. 4, cited in the note to Bolton, *Statutes of Ireland* (Dublin, 1621), p. 67. Cary, *Vindication*, pp 70–1, countered with five instances of English Tudor statutes legislating specifically for Ireland, including 32 Hen. 8., c. 24, dissolving the Knights Hospitallers, and 8 Eliz. c. 1, prohibiting the export of sheep. **98, 27** *lower* – later in time: Johnson, *Dictionary*, s.v. low 10.

Precedents of English[1] Acts of Parliament alledged against us: But still with this Observation, That 'tis these we *Complain against* as

5 Innovations, and therefore they *ought* not to be brought in Argument against us.

I do therefore again assert, that before the Year 1641. there was

10 no Statute[2] made in *England* introductory of a *New Law* that interfered with the Right which the People of *Ireland*[3] have to make Laws for themselves, except only

15 those which we have before mentioned, and which we have discuss'd at large, and submit to the Readers Judgment.

But in the Year 1641, and

20 afterwards in *Cromwel*'s time, and since that, in King *Charles* II.[4] and again very lately in King *William*'s Reign,[5] some Laws have been made in *England* to be of *Force* in *Ireland*.

25 But how this came to pass, we shall now Enquire.

In the 17th Year of K. *Charles* I. which was in the Year 1642. there

Acts in favour of Adventurers in 1641.[6]

---

1 English] 'English' H   2 Statute] [Law] 'Statute' H   3 *Ireland*] [England] Ireland H   4 *Cromwel's ... Charles* II.] [ye Usurpers] 'Cromwels' ... 'and since Charles ye 2ds' H   5 Reign] Reigns H & PC
6 *marginal heading* **1641**] 41 PC

99, 20 *Cromwel's time* – Molyneux's decision not to refer to Cromwell as 'ye Usurper' (cf. app. crit.) was perhaps connected with the point made, *Case*, pp 101–2, as to the significance of Ireland's sending representatives to the union parliaments of the 1650s.   **99, 27–100, 31** *In the 17th Year ... Kingdom* – passage denounced by English commons committee: *Commons Jnl [Eng.]*, xii, p. 325. The four Adventurers' Acts of 1642, namely 16–17 Car. 1, c. 33 ('An act for the speedy and effectual Reducing of the Rebels in His Majesty's Kingdom of Ireland to their due Obedience to His Majesty and to the Crown of England') and three explanatory acts, cc 34, 35 and 37, were among the last legislation of the Long Parliament to escape being annulled at the Restoration. (Molyneux's initial dating of the acts to 1641 derived from the old practice of beginning the new year on 25 March, though he subsequently spoke of 1642).

were three or four Acts of Parliament made in *England* for incou-
raging *Adventurers* to raise Money
for the speedy suppression of[1] the

5   Horrid Rebellion which broke out
in *Ireland* the 23*d* of *October* 1641.
The Titles of these Acts we have in
Pulton's Collection of Statutes: But
with this Remark, *That*[2] *they are*

10 *made of no Force by the Acts of*
Setlement and Explanation passed in
King *Charles* II's. time in the Kingdom of *Ireland*. So that in these we
are so *far* from finding Precedents

15 for *England's* Parliament binding
Ireland, that they plainly shew, that
the Parliament of *Ireland* may
Repeal an Act passed in *England*, in
relation to the Affairs of *Ireland*.

20 For 'tis very well known, that
Persons who were to have Interests
and Titles in *Ireland* by virtue of
those Acts passed in *England*, are
cut off by the *Acts of Settlement and*

25 *Explanation*.[3] And indeed there is
all the[4] Reason in the World that it
should be so, and that Acts made in
a Kingdom by the Legal Representatives of the People, should take

30 place of those made in another
Kingdom. But however, it will be

---

1 suppression of] [reducing] `suppression of´ **H**   2 *That*] that, [besides their being Expired], **H**   3 For ...
Explanation.] `for ... [had] `were to have´ ... Explanation´ (*interpolation in margin*) **H**   4 the] *not in* **H & PC**

100, 7–8 *The Titles ... Statutes* – editions of collected statutes printed only the titles of expired acts, sometimes
followed (as here) by an explanatory note.   **100, 9–19** *That they ... Ireland* – the note, in Pulton, *A Collection*
(London, 1670), p. 1248, read 'See an Act for the settlement of Ireland, passed in that Kingdom, Anno ... 1662.
by which this and the following Acts concerning Ireland are besides their expiration of no force.' The discovery
that privy council scrutiny of the act of settlement had been unusually rigorous (cf. J. Kelly, *Poynings' Law*
(Dublin, 2007), pp 29–30) supports Molyneux's claim that England accepted Ireland's right to set aside the
Adventurers' Acts. In addition, Attorney General Heneage Finch told the privy council in Feb. 1671 that, while
the English parliament had the right to legislate for Ireland, the Irish parliament had an equal right to repeal
any English act relating to Ireland: Carte, *History* (Oxford, 1851), v, pp 122–4. Cary, *Vindication*, pp 72–5,
however, rejected Molyneux's interpretation as rendering the English parliament subordinate to the Irish, while
Clement, *Answer*, epist. dedic., argued that in awarding compensation from the adventurers' estates the Irish
act perforce conceded the validity of these statutes.   **100, 30** *place* – precedence: *OED*, s.v. 27c.

said, that by those Acts 'tis manifest
that *England* did presume they had
such a *Right* to pass Acts binding
Ireland, or else they had ne'er done
5   it. To which I answer, That
considering the condition *Ireland*
was in at that time, *viz.* under[2] an
horrid *Intestine Rebellion*, flaming
in every corner of the Kingdom;
10   'twas impossible to have a
Parliament of our own; yet it was
absolutely necessary that something
should be done towards suppressing
the Violences then raging amongst
15   us: And the only means could then
be practised, was for the Parliament
of *England* to interpose, and do
something for our Relief and
Safety; these were the best
20   Assurances could be had at that
juncture: But when the Storm was
over, and the Kingdom quieted, we
see new Measures were taken in a
Legal Parliament of our own.

25   As to what was done for *Ireland*   **Acts in**
in the Parliament of *England* in   **Cromwels**
Cromwel's time[3], besides the Con-   **time.**
fusion and Irregularity of all Procee-
ding[4] in those days, which hinders
30   any of them to be brought in-

---

1 by ... that] `by ... that´ **H**   **2** done ... under] [have] done ... `under´ **H**   **3** time] time[s] **H**
4 Proceeding] Proceedings **H & PC**

101, 6–11 *considering ... our own* – the reference to the disappearance of the relevant volumes of the
Commons Journal (only recovered in 1764) in Molyneux's 1693 compendium of parliamentary precedents
(MS TCD 622, f. 2) showed he was aware that sessions of the Irish parliament had continued
intermittently from the outbreak of the Irish rebellion in Oct. 1641 to 1647. *Intestine* – civil, or domestic:
OED, s.v. 1. **101, 25–102, 12** *As to ... Obligatory to us* – 'Cromwel's time' presumably designated the
Nominated Parliament of 1653, as well as the three parliaments of the Protectorate, 1655–8. Though these
irregular assemblies were rejected as precedents, attention was drawn to their belief that Irish
representatives were necessary for legislation to bind Ireland.

to Precedent in these times; We
shall find also that then there were
Representatives[1] sent out of this
Kingdom, who sate in the
5   Parliament of *England*,[2] which then
was *only* the *House of Commons*. We
cannot therefore argue from hence,
that *England* may bind us; for[3] we
see they allow'd us *Representatives*,[4]
10   without which, they rightly
concluded, they[5] could not make
Laws *Obligatory* to us.

[6]I come now to King *Charles* the
2ds time: And in it we shall find the
15   following English Statutes made, in
which the Kingdom of *Ireland* is
concerned.[7]

Cattle Act.

The first is an *Act against
Importing Cattle from* Ireland *or
20   other Parts beyond Seas*. It was only
temporary by 18 *Ch*.2. c.2. but made
perpetual 20 *Ch*.2. c.7. and 32 *Ch*.2.
c.2.[8] This Act, however prejudicial
to the Trade that was then carried
25   on between *Ireland* and *England*,
does not *properly Bind us*, more
than it does any other Country of
the World. When any thing is
Imported,   and   Landed   in

---

1 *Representatives*] Representatives [(tales Quales)] such as they were **H** | Representatives [(such ... were)] **PC** (*cf. n. 4 below*)   **2** of *England*] `of England´ **H**   **3** us; for] us; [for had they been the Most regular in their Proceedings yet we see] (new line) for **H**   **4** *Representatives*]Representatives (tales Quales) **H** | Representatives [(tales Quales)] **PC** (*cf.* OED, *s.v. tales: representatives chosen at random to make up a deficiency in the number of a jury, &c.*)   **5** they] [that] they **H**   **6** I come] *preceded by del. para.* [I now come to our Present Days under the Happy Government of his [Presen<t>] Majesty King WILLIAM (*emphatic*) ye 3d.] **H** (*cf. Case*, p. 105)   **7** following ... concerned.] `following´ ... `in´ which [Bind] the ... Ireland [their Tities are as follows.] `is concerned.´ **H**    **8** and ... c.2.] *not in* **H** | `and ... c.2.´ **PC**

102, 5–6 *which then ... Commons* – until the introduction of an upper house under the terms of the Humble Petition and Advice in January 1658. See Woolrych, 'Last Quests' in Aylmer (ed.), *The Interregnum* (London, 1972), pp 184–5.   **102, 18–26** *an Act ... Bind us* – the heavy tax imposed on Irish cattle imports in 1663 (15 Car. 2, c. 7, sect. 13) was replaced by a ban in 1666, made permanent in 1667. Resentment at the cattle acts was reawakened by the threat to Irish woollen exports in 1697–8. Cf. [Petty], *Observations* (London, 1673), and *Some thoughts on the bill ...* (London, 1698), pp 13–14. For the circumstances of the prohibition, see Edie, 'The Irish cattle bills', *Transactions of the American Philosophic Society*, n.s. 60:2 (1970).

England, it becomes immediately subject to the Laws thereof, so that[1] herein we cannot be said *properly* to be *bound*.

5   Secondly, The Acts against Planting *Tobacco* in *England* and *Ireland*, 12 *Ch*.2. c.34. and 15 *Ch*.2. c.7. and 22 and 23 *Ch*.2. c.26, &c.[2] do *positively Bind Ireland*. But there

10   has never been an Occasion of Executing it here; for I have not heard that a Rood of Tobacco was ever Planted in this Kingdom.[3] [4]But however that takes not off the

15   *Obligation* of the Law: 'Tis only want of our Consent, that I urge against that. I see[5] no more Reason for sending a Force to Trample down an Acre of *Tobacco* in *Ireland*

20   by these Statutes, than there would be for Cutting down the Woods of *Shelela*; were there an Act made in *England* against our Planting or Having *Timber*.[6]

25   Thirdly, The *Act for Encouraging Shipping and Navigation*, by express *name* Mentions and Binds *Ireland*; and by the last Clause in the Act, Obliges all Ships belonging thereto

Tobacco Act.

Navigation Act.

---

1 thereof ... that] [of] thereof ... th[[e]]at **H**   2 &c.] *not in* **H** | `&c´ **PC**    3 But ... Kingdom.] `but [I believe was n<ever>] there never has been... [never] not ... Kingdom´ **H**   4 – 6 But ... Timber.] *not in* **H** | `but ... Timber.´ (*interpolation partly in margin*) **PC**   5 I see] And I see **PC**   6 Timber.] *end of interpolation begun n. 4 above*

103, 3 *properly* – distinctively, specially: *OED*, s.v. 2.   **103, 21–2** *the Woods of Shelela* – extensive oak woods at Shillelagh in south Co. Wicklow, remnants of which still survive.   **103, 25–104, 3** *The Act for ... England* – namely the clause in the 1663 Navigation Act (15 Car. 2, c. 7), which excluded Ireland from the direct trade to the plantations that she had been permitted under the 1661 Act (12 Car. 2, c.18). Further restrictions were imposed in the 1671 Act (22 & 23 Car. 2, c. 26). The reference to 'our Foreign Plantations' was merely an inconsistency.

[104]

importing any Goods from our Foreign Plantations, to touch first at *England*.

Fourthly, the Acts Prohibiting the Exportation of Wooll from *Ireland*, to any Country except to *England*, do likewise *strongly Bind us,* and by the 12 *Car.*2. c.32. it was made highly penal on us, and by the 14th of *Car.*2. c.18. 'tis made Felony.

To these three last Acts, I must confess, I have nothing to urge, to take off their Efficacy;[2] *Name* us they do most certainly, and *Bind* us so, as we do not transgress them. But how *Rightfully* they do this, is the matter in Question[3]. This I am sure of, that before these Acts in King *Charles* the Second's Time, (the Eldest of which is not over Thirty-Seven years) *there is not one positive full Precedent to be met with in all the Statute-Book, of an English Act Binding the Kingdom of Ireland.* And on this Account we may venture to assert, That these are at least *Innovations* on us,[4] as not being warranted by any former Precedents.

Note, Exporting Wooll from *Ireland,* is made penal by the Irish Stat. 13 *Hen.*8. c.2. 28 *Hen.*8. c.17. But both these Statutes are obsolete: The like may we observe of the 11 Eliz. Ses.3. c.10 & 13 El. c.2.[1]

---

1 13 *Hen.* 8. c.2. .... 11 Eliz. Ses.3. c.10 & 13 El. c.2.] 13 *Hen.* 8. c.2. .... 11 Eliz. Ses.8. c.10 & 13 El. c.2. **ed** | 13 *Hen.* 8. c.1. .... 11 Eliz. Ses.3. c.10 & 13 El. c.4. **H, PC & I**   2 Efficacy] [Binding] Efficacy **H**   3 in Question] Complaind of, and in Question **H** | [Complained of and] in Question **PC**   4 *English* ... us,] `English´ ... [an] `at Least´ innovation´s´ on us [at least] `,´ **H**

104, 4–10 *the Acts Prohibiting ... Felony* – a new system for licensing wool exports from Ireland was introduced at the Restoration, under which export was permitted under bond to certain specified English ports: P. Kelly, 'The Irish Woollen Export Prohibition Act', *Irish Economic and Social History*, 7 (1980), p. 24.   **104, 17–29** *This I am ... Precedents* – passage denounced by English commons committee: *Commons Jnl [Eng.]*, xii, p. 325.

And shall *Proceedings only of Thirty-Seven Years standing*, be urg'd against a Nation, to Deprive them of the Rights and Liberties

5   which they Enjoy'd for Five Hundred Years before, and which were Invaded without and against their *Consent*, and from that day to this have been constantly com-

10 plain'd of ? Let any English Heart that stands so *Justly* in Vindication of his own *Rights* and *Liberties*, answer this Question, and I have done.

15 I am now[1] arriv'd at our Present Days, under the Happy Government of His Majesty King *WILLIAM*[2] the Third; and I am sorry to reflect, That since the late

20 Revolution[3] in these Kingdoms, when the Subjects of *England* have more strenuously than ever Asserted their own *Rights*, and the *Liberty* of Parliaments, it has pleased

25 them to bear harder[4] on their Poor Neighbours, than has ever yet been done in many Ages foregoing.[5] I am sure what was then done by[6] that Wise and Just Body of Sena-

English Acts Binding *Ireland* since King *William*'s Reign.

---

1 I am now] [And Now] I am `now´ **H**   2 *WILLIAM*] WILLIAM (*emphatical*) **H & PC**   3 Revolution] Revolutions **H & PC**   4 bear harder] encroach more freely **H** | [encroach ... freely] 'bear harder' **PC** 5 has ... foregoing.] `has ... done´ in [m]any ages [precedent] `foregoing´ **H**   6 what ... by] this was done by the greatest part of **H** | [this] `what´ was `then´ done by [the ... part of] **PC**

105, 1–14 *And shall ... done* – passage denounced by English commons committee: *Commons Jnl [Eng.],* xii, p. 325. Intentionally, or otherwise, Molyneux's words echoed the Jacobite act of 1689 establishing legislative independence and abolishing appeals to England; cf. Bergin & Andrew (eds), *The Acts* (Dublin, 2016), pp 54–5. Cary, *Vindication*, pp 79–81, countered Molyneux's emotive appeal by listing a number of English statutes binding Ireland prior to 1641, both medieval and Stuart.   **105,** 16–18 *Happy ... William the Third* – cf. Cary, *Vindication*, p. 82, 'more especially happy to the Protestant Interest in *Ireland*, else I fear their Lands had had other Owners before this time'.   **105,** 19–27 *since the ... foregoing* – cf. dedication, p. A2r–v above. The ensuing discussion ignores by far the most significant action of the English Convention with regard to Ireland, namely declaring William and Mary King and Queen of Ireland in Feb. 1689, as well as of England, an omission made much of by Clement, *Answer*, pp 109–10, 121.

tors, was[1] perfectly out of Good Will and Kindness to us, under[2] those Miseries which our Afflicted Country of *Ireland* then suffered:

5 But I fear some Men[3] have since that, made use of what was then done, to other Purposes than at first intended. Let us now see what that was, and consider the Circum-

10 stances under which it was done.

[4]In the Year 1689. when most of the Protestant Nobility, Gentry, and Clergy of *Ireland*, were driven out of that Kingdom by the Insolencies

15 and Barbarities of the *Irish Papists*, who were then in Arms throughout the Kingdom, and in all Places of Authority under King *James*, newly[5] Return'd to them out of

20 *France*; the only Refuge we had to fly to was in *England*, where Multitudes continued for many Months, destitute of all manner of Relief, but such as the Charity of

25 *England* afforded, which indeed was very *Munificent, and never to be forgotten.*[6]

1 was] *not in* **H** | `was´ **PC**   **2** under] [in] `under´ **H**   **3** Men] men of self Interest **H** | Men [of …
Interest] **PC**   **4** In the …] (*marginal heading for following paragraph incorrectly placed here in* **PC**)
5 Nobility … newly] `Nobility´ … `throughout … Kingdom´ … [who] newly **H**   **6** in *England* … *forgotten*]
[to] in … Multitudes [of us] … [of our Brethren] of England… afforded [us] … forgotten [by us] **H**

106, 3–4 *those Miseries … suffered* – namely, the depredations of James II's French troops and Irish
supporters, followed by the impact of the actual war, for which see Dickson, *Ireland, 1600–1800* (Dublin,
2000), p. 42.   **106, 5–8** *some Men … intended* – i.e. in arguing that in accepting the help provided by
England the Anglo-Irish had acquiesced in the loss of their legislative independence, see further *Case*,
p. 110. See app. crit. for change from 'Men of self-interest'.   **106, 11–18** *when … James* – Gillespie, 'The
Irish Protestants', *IHS*, 28 (1992), p. 129, puts the number of refugees at around 5,000. Among them were
Molyneux, his wife, child, and brother Thomas: intro. pp 5–6.   **106, 24–7** *the Charity … forgotten* – this
included extensive private charity, as well as the legislation in favour of the refugees, described in *Case*,
pp 107–9.

The Protestant[1] Clergy of *Ireland* being thus Banish'd from their Benefices, many of them Accepted such small Ecclesiastical
5 Promotions in *England*, as the Benevolence of well dispos'd Persons presented them with. But this being directly contrary to a Statute[2] in this Kingdom, in the 17
10 and 18 of *Charles* the Second, *Cap*.10. Intituled, *An Act for Disabling*[3] *of Spiritual Persons from holding Benefices or other Ecclesiastical Dignities in England or*
15 *Wales, and in Ireland at the same time*. The Protestant Irish[4] Clergy thought they could not be too secure in avoiding the Penalty of the[5] last mention'd Act, and
20 therefore Apply'd themselves to the Parliament of *England*, and obtain'd an Act in the first year of King *William* and Queen *Mary*, c.29. Intituled, *An Act for the Relief of*
25 *the Protestant Irish Clergy*. And this was the first Attempt that was made for *Binding Ireland* by an Act in *England*, since his Majesty's Happy Accession to the Throne of
30 these Kingdoms.

Act for the
Protestant Irish
Clergy.

---

1 Protestant] *not in* **H** | `Protestant´ **PC**  2 Ecclesiastical … a Statute] `Eclesiatical´ … [the] a Statute **H** 3 *Disabling*] disabili[[ty]]ing **H** 4 Protestant Irish] `Protest: Irish´ **H** | `Protestant´ Irish **PC** 5 the] this **H & PC**

107, 1 *Protestant Clergy … Ireland* – the interpolation of 'Protestant' here (and line 16 below, cf. app. crit.) denoted members of the Church of Ireland rather than Protestants in general. **107, 16–25** *The Protestant … Clergy* – for the petition from the refugee clergy, see *Commons Jnl [Eng.]*, x, pp 97–8 (22 Apr. 1689). Cary, *Vindication*, p. 84, commented: 'here you see … the Opinion of the Clergy of *Ireland* [of the authority of the English parliament] … notwithstanding any Gloss you may think fit to put on it.' *Secure* – safe from anxiety or worry: *OED*, s.v. 1.

**Act against
Commerce with
France.**

Afterwards in the same year, and same Session, Chap.34. there pass'd an Act in *England*, *Prohibiting all Trade and Commerce*
5 *with France*, both from *England* and *Ireland*. This also binds *Ireland*, but was during the Heat of the War in that Kingdom, when 'twas impossible to have a regular
10 Parliament therein, all being in the hands of the Irish Papists. Neither do we complain of it, as hindring us from corresponding with the King's Enemies, for 'tis the Duty of all
15 Good Subjects to abstain from that. But as *Scotland*, tho' the King's Subjects, Claims an Exemption from all Laws but what they Assent to in Parliament; so we think this
20 our Right also.[1]

When the Banish'd Laity of *Ireland* observ'd the Clergy thus Careful to[2] secure their Properties, and provide[3] for the worst as well as
25 they could in that Juncture, when no other means could be taken by a Regular Parliament in *Ireland*; they thought it likewise adviseable for them to do something in relation to
30 their Concerns. And[4] ac

---

1 Neither ... also.] *not in* **H** | `Neither ... `tho ... Subjects´ ... also.´ (*interpolation largely in margin*) **PC**
2 Banish'd ... Careful to] `Banishd´ ... Clergy [to] ... to **H** 3 provide] to provide **H & PC** 4 it ... And] [themselves] `it´ ... `And´ **H**

108, 9–10 *a regular Parliament* – in contrast to the 'irregular' Jacobite parliament held in Dublin, May–July 1689, which under the terms of Poynings' Law, James II was arguably no longer entitled to summon, once he ceased to reign in England. Cary, *Vindication*, p. 90, and Clement, *Answer*, pp 118–21, ironically conjectured that if Ireland were truly a separate and independent kingdom, James' authority there could not have been compromised by his abdication in England. **108, 16–19** *Scotland ... in Parliament* – cf. Scottish Claim of Right, 1689: *English historical documents* (London, 1956), viii, pp 635–6. **108, 27–109, 4** *they thought ... Ireland* – pace Cary, *Vindication*, pp 88–9, no formal petition was recorded from Irish lay refugees, unlike the clergy (see *Case*, p. 107 nn).

cordingly they obtain'd the *Act for the better Security and Relief, of their Majesties Protestant Subjects of Ireland*, 1 W. and M. *Ses*.2. c.9.

5 Wherein King *James*'s *Irish Parliament* at *Dublin*, and all *Acts* and *Attainders* done by them, are declared *void*. 'Tis likewise thereby Enacted, that no Protestant shall suffer any

10 Prejudice in his Estate or Office, by reason of his absence out of *Ireland*, since *December* 25. 1685. and that there should be a Remittal of the Kings Quit-Rent, from 25 *December*

15 1688. to the end of the War. Thus the Laity thought themselves secure[1].

And we cannot wonder that during the Heat of a Bloody War in this Kingdom, when it was

20 impossible to Secure our Estates and Properties by[2] a Regular Parliament of our own; we should have recourse to this Means, as the only which then could be had. We

25 concluded with ourselves, that when we had obtained these Acts from the Parliament in *England*, [3]we had gon a great way in securing the like Acts to be passed[4] in a regular

30 Parliament in *Ireland*,[5] whenever it

Act for Security of the Protestants of Ireland.

---

1 secure] secured **H**   2 this ... by] [that] `this´ ... [an<d>] by **H**   3 – 5 we had ... *Ireland*,] (*enclosed within square brackets by printer and marked* out *in margin* **PC**)   4 passed] past [for our security] **H**
5 *Ireland*,] (*end of passage marked for deletion by printer, cf. n. 3 above*)

109, 1–8 *Act for ... void* – the English legislation voiding the acts of 'the late pretended Parliament' was confirmed in 1695 by the Irish act 7 Will. 3, c. 3. An earlier attempt to do so had failed in the 1692 parliament. Cf. *Case*, pp 75–6.   **109, 19–24** *when ... be had* – a similar view of the propriety of the English parliament's legislating for Ireland, when it proved impossible to hold a parliament in Ireland, was advanced by Attorney General Heneage Finch in Feb.1670/1: Carte, *History* (Oxford, 1851), v, pp 122–4.
109, 24–110, 22 *We concluded ... Kingdom* – the concept of 'virtual consent' that Molyneux sought to exploit was far from convincing. Cary, *Vindication*, pp 88–9, was particularly scathing of the Irish parliament's having failed to regularise the position in 1692, 'and by your Writing I suppose you were one of them'. Cf. [Leslie], *Considerations* (London, 1698), p. 8.   **109, 26–30** *we had ... Ireland* – though marked 'out' by the printer, this clause was presumably reinstated by Molyneux, cf. app. crit.

should please God to re-establish us
in our own Country:[1] For we well
knew our own Constitution under
Poynings Law, That no Act could
5   Pass in the Parliament of *Ireland* till
approved of by the[2] King and Privy
Council of *England*. And we knew
likewise, That all the Lords and
others of his Majesties Privy
10   Council in *England* are Members of
the Lords or Commons House of
Parliament there. And that by
obtaining their Assent to Acts of
Parliament in Favour of the Irish
15   Protestants, they[3] had in a manner
pre-engaged their Assent to the like
Bills when they should hereafter
come   before   them   as   Privy
Councellors, in order to be regularly
20   Transmitted to the Parliament of
Ireland, there to be passed into
Laws of that Kingdom. But instead
of all this, to meet with another
Construction of what was done
25   herein, and to have it pleaded
against us as a Precedent of our
Submission,   and   absolute
Acquiescence in the Jurisdiction of
the Parliaments of *England* over
30   this[4] Kingdom, is what we complain
of as an Invasion (we[5] humbly con

---

1 Country] [Kin<gdom>] Country **H**   2 by the] [in the] by the **H**   3 Irish ... they] `Irish´ ... [that]
`they´ **H**   4 this] [the] this **H**   5 (we] (as we **H** | ([as] we **PC**

110, 8–22 *the Lords ... Kingdom* – that is, English peers and MPs, who were also members of the privy
council and had passed the laws benefiting Ireland in 1689–90, should be understood as having pledged
themselves in their capacity as councillors to approve such legislation for future transmission to the Irish
parliament under the terms of Poynings' Law.

ceive) of that *Legislative Right* which our Parliament of *Ireland*, claims[1] within this Kingdom.[2]

Act appointing New Oaths.

5   The next Act pass'd in the Parliament of *England*, Binding *Ireland*, is that for *Abrogating the Oath of Supremacy in Ireland, and Appointing other Oaths*, 3 and 4 *William* and *Mary*, c.2. To this the

10   Parliament convened at *Dublin*, *Anno* 1692. under Lord[3] *Sydney*, and that likewise *Anno* 1695. under Lord *Capel*, paid an intire Obedience. And by this ('tis alledged) we have

15   *given up our Right*, if any we had, and have for ever acknowledged[4] our *Subordination to the Parliament of England*. But let us a little consider the force of this Argument.

20   I readily grant, that this and the other fore-mentioned Acts in *England* since the Revolution, when they were made, were look'd upon highly in our Favour, and for our

25   Benefit; and to them as *such*, we have conform'd our Selves. But then, in all Justice and Equity, our Submission herein is to be deem'd *purely voluntary*, and not at all pro-

---

1 Parliament … claims] Parliaments … claim **H** | Parliament … claim`s´ **PC**  2 Kingdom.] Kingdom. (*new para.*) The `Brittish´ Protestants of Ireland had `then´ a strong and Malicious Enemy to deal with, No les than the Irish and French Arms in Conjunction. England was then pleasd to Help us, and themselves in us, with their Money, Force and Laws. And now the war is o[[th]]ver, the Bitt which then [they put] `wee gladly received´ into our Mouths, [and which we were glad to receive, they no<w>] `is now´ retaind `there´ against our Wills. How apposite the *Fable of the Stag and Horse* is to this, I leave the Reader to Consider. **H** | [The [Brittish] Protestants … (*as final reading of* **H**) … [now] retaind … Consider.] (*del. by cross-hatching*) **PC** 3 Lord] My Lord **H** | [my] Lord **PC** 4 acknowledged] [su] acknowledged ([su] *perhaps for* [su<bmitted>]) **H**

111, 3 *this Kingdom* – cf. app. crit. for deleted paragraph comparing English help to the Anglo-Irish to Aesop's fable of the stag and the horse. The fable was cited in Aristotle, *Rhetoric* (Cambridge, MA, 1936), II, xx, 5, as a warning against giving irrevocable power to dictators. 111, 4–9 *The next … Mary, c.2* – though English imposition of these oaths seemingly violated the Treaty of Limerick, the act did provide for dispensations under the Great Seal. The Irish attempt to re-enact the statute without this proviso in 1697 was considered by the commons committee investigating *The Case*, but not taken further: Sanford Papers, Somerset Archives, Taunton, DD/SF/13/2909. 111, 9–18 *To this … England* – cf. Cary, *Vindication*, p. 93. He also asserted that in recognizing William and Mary's right to summon a parliament in Ireland the Irish parliament had established 'a *New Original Compact*, whereby *Ireland* is become *Dependant* on the Kingdom of *England*, and your Parliament on the Parliament thereof'. 111, 20–112, 2 *I readily … Legislators* – passage denounced by English commons committee: *Commons Jnl [Eng.]*, xii, p. 325.

ceeding from the *Right* we
conclude thereby in the Legislators.
If a Man, who has *no Jurisdiction*
over me, *command* me to do a thing

5   that is *pleasing* to me, and I do it;[1] it
will not thence follow, that thereby
he obtains[2] an *Authority* over me,
and that ever hereafter I must Obey
him of *Duty*. If I *voluntarily* give

10   my Money to a Man when *I please*,
and think it *convenient* for me; this
does not Authorize him at any time
to *command* my Money from me
when *he pleases*. If it be said, this

15   allows Subjects[3] to Obey only
whilest 'tis *convenient* for them. I
pray it may be considered, whether
any Men Obey *longer*, unless they
be *forced* to it; and whether they will

20   not *free* themselves from this *Force*
as soon as they can. 'Tis impossible
to hinder Men from desiring to *free*
themselves from *Uneasiness*,[4] 'tis a
Principle of Nature, and cannot be

25   eradicated. If Submitting to an
Inconvenience be a *less* Evil than
endeavouring to Throw it off, Men
will Submit. But if the Inconvenience grow upon them, and be

30   *greater* than the hazard of getting

---

1 do it] obey him **H** | [obey him] `do it´ **PC**   2 obtains] [g] obtains ([g] *perhaps for* [g<ains>]) **H**
3 Subjects] [men] subjects **H**   4 *Uneasiness*] [any] uneasyness **H**

112, 3–14 *If a Man ... pleases* – [Leslie], *Considerations* (London, 1698), pp 2–5, was highly critical of
Molyneux's concessions in this respect, pointing out that neither the 1692 nor 1695 parliaments took place
other than in time of peace, and therefore their members could be said, in Lockian terms, to have betrayed
the interest of the Irish people. Cf. *Treatises*, ii, §141–2.   **112, 21–5** *'Tis impossible ... eradicated* – the
concept of acting so as to free oneself from *uneasiness* was a basic principle of Lockian psychology. Cf.
Locke, *An Essay* (Oxford, 1975), bk II, ch. 21, sects 28–40 (material which owed its introduction in the
1694 edn to discussion with Molyneux). *Inconvenience* – danger or injury, rather than incommodity or
discomfort: *OED*, s.v. 4, 7.   **112, 25–113, 3** *If Submitting ... they can* – passage denounced by English
commons committee: *Commons Jnl [Eng.]*, xii, p. 325.

rid of it, Men will Offer at puting it by, let the Statesman[1] or Divine say what they can.

[2]But I shall yet go a little further, and venture to Assert, That the Right of being subject *Only* to such Laws to which Men give their *own Consent*, is so inherent to all Mankind, and founded on such Immutable Laws of Nature and Reason, that 'tis not to be *Alien'd*, or *Given up*, by any Body of Men whatsoever: For the End of all Government and Laws being the Publick Good of the Common-wealth, in the Peace, Tranquility and Ease of every Member therein; whatsoever Act is contrary to this End, is in it self void, and of no effect[3]: And therefore for a Company of Men to say, *Let us Unite our selves into a Society, and let us be absolutely Govern'd by such Laws, as such a Legislator, without ever Consulting us*[4], *shall devise for us*; 'tis always to be understood, *Provided we find them for our Benefit*: For to say, We will be Govern'd by those Laws, *whether they be Good or Hurtful to us,* is absurd in itself: For to what End

1 Statesman] [Politician] `statesman´ **H** **2** – p. 115, n. 5 But … thereof.] As to a Private Act or two pasd in ye Parliament at Westminster since the Revolution, relating to the Disposal and Binding of Land in Ireland, I have nothing to say more, than that I think the Noble Person concernd was not so well advised therein as he might have been. We Know Great Men [are] `need´ not [to] be supposed so well Versed in the Laws of a Kingdom as to [know] have in their View the strict bounds of Jurisdiction, especially in a Point that seems of Late to be [doubted] disputed. But then, this canot be so wel excused in those that are about them, they ought to have known better, and advised Better; and I Doubt not the[[m]]n, but their Noble Patrons [had] `would have´ acted otherwise. **H** | [*marginal heading* Private Acts] [As … Act [or two] … (*as final reading of* **H**) … than that [I think … otherwise] [`it being the only single Instance of the Kind, I hope It will not be brought in Precedent against us.´] (*add. at foot of MS page: new page*) `it being the *only single* Precedent of the kind I hope it will not be pleaded against us. If it be, I am sure, 'tis more than the Noble Person concerned could possibly forsee.´ (*interpolation in margin*)] `But … thereof´ (*final interpolation on separate quire* ff 223–4, *manu WM*) **PC** **3** Government … no effect] 'Government and' … `with the Peace … Member there of´ … no[ne] effect **PC** **4** *Let*… us] [Come,] Let … `without … us´ **PC**

113, 4–115, 19 *But … Benefits thereof* – these four paragraphs were interpolated in place of a reference to private acts of parliament confirming an unnamed nobleman's estates, who is probably to be identified as the second duke of Ormonde (cf. app. crit.). See further, English private act 8 & 9 Will. 3, c. 5 (1696), in his favour. Cary, *Vindication*, pp 81–2, referred to a similar private act benefiting the first duke in Charles II's reign (12 Car. 2, ses. 1, c. 7). **113, 5–114, 3** *That the Right … Nature* – this account of the rationale of political society may seem to derive from Locke, *Treatises*, ii, §§95–9, 131, 134–5. However, similar ideas were found in Hooker, *Of the laws of ecclesiastical politie* (London, 1666), bk I, sect. 10, and were not uncommon in the later C.17. See further intro. pp 40–1. **113, 13–20** *the End … effect* – cf. Hobart's verdict in Savage v. Day, cited *in Case*, p. 155.

do Men joyn in Society, but to avoid
Hurt, and[1] the Inconveniencies of
the State of Nature ?

    Moreover, I desire it may be
5   considered, whether the General
Application of the Chief part of the
Irish Protestants, that were at that
time in *London*, to the Parliament at
Westminster, for obtaining these
10 Laws, may not be taken for their
Consent, and on that Account, and
no other, these Acts[2] may acquire
their *Binding Force*. I know very
well, this cannot be look'd upon as[3]
15 a Regular and Formal *Consent*, such
as might be requisite at another
more favourable Juncture: But yet it
may be taken *talis qualis*,[*] as far as   [*][such as it is]
their Circumstances at that time
20 would allow, till a more convenient
Opportunity might present itself.

    I am sure, if some such Con-
siderations as these, may not plead
for us, we are of all his Majesties
25 Subjects the most Unfortunate: The
Rights and *Liberties* of the
Parliament of *England* have received
the   greatest   Corroborations

---

1 Hurt, and] `Hurt and´ **PC**   2 to the Parliament ... Acts] [may not be taken] to ... [Acts] `Laws´ ...
taken ... `these Acts´ **PC**   3 as] `as´ **PC**

114, 4–21 *I desire ... itself* – presumably through the informal committee of leading refugees in London
under the chairmanship of the duke of Ormonde; see further *Lords MSS, 1689–90*, pp 137–92 *passim*.
[Leslie], *Considerations* (London, 1698), p. 5, attributed the refugees' action to fear of James II's parliament
in Dublin.   **114, 25–115, 8** *The Rights ... for us* – cf. dedication, pp A3v–A4r above. See further *Case*, p. 83,
on the survival of the Irish court of high commission, though 'the late Bill of Rights in *England* ... has
damned all such Courts'.

since his Majesties Accession to the Throne; and so have the *Rights* of *Scotland*; but the *Rights* of the People of *Ireland*, on the other 5 hand, have received the greatest Weakening under his Reign,[1] by our Submission (as 'tis alledg'd) to these Laws that have been made for us.[2]

This[3] certainly was not the 10 Design of his Majesty's Glorious Expedition into these Kingdoms; That, we are told by Himself, (whom we cannot possibly mistrust)[4] was to Assert the Rights 15 and Liberties of these Nations; and we do humbly presume that his Majesty will be graciously pleased to permit us to Enjoy the Benefits thereof.[5]

20 And thus I have done with the *Fourth Article* proposed. As to the *Fifth*, viz. *The Opinions of the Learned in the Laws relating to this Matter*;[7] 'tis in a great measure 25 dispatch'd by what I have offered on the Fourth Head; I shall therefore be the more brief thereon. And I think indeed the only Person of Note that remains to be considered

The Opinions of the Lawyers thereon.[6]

1 have the *Rights*... Reign] [has] `have´ ... `on ... hand´ ... [Auspicious] Reign **PC**   2 'tis ... us.] [our Adversarys alledge] 'tis alledged´) ... [Yokes] `Laws´ ... [put on us] `made for us´ [and which (they say) we shall never shake off our Necks, but the Burthen of them shall dayly be increased [upon us]]. **PC**   3 This] *no new para.* **PC**   4 (whom ... mistrust)] *parentheses add. later* **PC**   5 do humbly ... thereof.] [doubt not but we shall find this made good to us] do ... thereof. (*end of interpolation begun p. 113, n. 2 above*)   6 *marginal heading* thereon] on this Question **PC**   7 viz. ... *Matter*.] [there] `viz. ... [[]]this Matter´ (this Matter *written in very compressed fashion*) **H**

115, 9-15 *This certainly ... Nations* – namely William's declarations of 20 Sept. and 1 Oct. 1688.   115, 20-1 *thus I have ... Article* – Molyneux's second reference to having finished with the fourth of the questions introduced, *Case*, pp 4-6. Cf. ibid., p. 77.   115, 21-116, 1 *As to ... Cook* – the following section dealing with Coke's verdict in Calvin's case was perhaps prompted by what Bolton, 'Declaration', pp 10-13, had to say on the implications of Coke's dictum, 'albeit Ireland be a distinct dominion from England, yet the title thereof being by conquest, the same by judgement of law, might by express words be bound by the Parliament of England'.

by us, is the Lord Chief Justice *Cook*,
a Name of Great Veneration with[1]
the Gentlemen of the Long Robe,
and therefore to be treated with all
Respect and Deference.

[2]In his Seventh Report in
Calvin's[3] Case, he is proving that
Ireland is a Dominion Separate and
Divided from *England*; for this he
quotes many Authorities (*a*) out of
the Year-Books and Reports; and
amongst others, he has that which I
have before mention'd, pag. 91. 2
R.3.f.12. which he Transcribes in this
manner, *Hibernia habet Parlia-*
mentum, & faciunt Leges, & nostra
Statuta non ligant eos, *quia non*
mittunt Milites ad Parliamentum;[*]
and then adds, in a Parenthesis,
(*which is to be understood, unless they be*
specially named) sed *Personæ eorum*
sunt subjecti Regis sicut[5] *inhabitantes in*
Calesia, Gasconia, & Guyan.[6][**] The
first thing I shall observe hereon, is
the very *unfaithful* and *broken*
Citation of this Passage, as will
manifestly appear by comparing it
with the true Transcript I have given
thereof before, pag. 91. Were[7] this all,
'twere   in   some   measure

[*][Ireland has a parliament,
and they make laws, and our
statutes do not bind them,
because they do not send
knights to our parliament]

[**][but their persons are the
King's subjects, in the same
manner as the inhabitants of
Calais, Gascony, and Guienne]

---

1 considered … with] [Examined] `considered by us´ … [among{ts}<st>] `with´ H   2 In his] *no new para.*
H & PC   3 *Calvin*'s] CALVINS (*emphatical*) H   4 *marginal ref. Pilkington's … Plowd. Com.* 368.] *Pilkington's*
… Plowd. Com. 368. ed. (*correcting misprint of* 360 *for* 368 *in* Coke, *7th Report*, f. 22v) | Sir J. Pilkingtons …
360. H | (a) [Sir J.] Pilkingtons … 360. PC | *Pilkington's … Plowd. Com.* 360. I (F *perhaps broken letter*)|
5*eorum … sicut*] [&c us̲e̲d so as before pag. —] `[ill] eorum … sicut´ H   6 *& Guyan*] `et´ Guyan (*perhaps*
add. later) H   7 Citation … Were] [Quota<tion>] Citation … `true´ … [But] were H

116, 3 *Gentlemen … Robe* – i.e. lawyers, esp. barristers: *OED*, s.v. long robe.   **116, marginal ref. (a)** *Dyer.*
360. Plowd. Com. 368. – Dyer, *Les Reports* (London, 1672), p. 360 and Plowden, *Les Commentaries*
(London, 1613), p. 368, cited points raised in two mid-Elizabethan cases, that corroborated Ireland's status
as a distinct and separate kingdom.   **116, 15–23** *Hibernia … Guyan* [transl. *but their … Guienne*] – cf.
Coke, *7th Rep.*, f. 22v, citing the verdict in the Merchants of Waterford's case.   **116, 25–6** *the very …*
Passage – cf. Cary, *Vindication*, p. 109, 'you have been too frequently guilty of the same Fault in this Book'.

pardonable.[1] But what cannot be excused, is the Unwarrantable Position[2] in his Parenthesis, without the least colour or ground for it in

5   his Text. Herein he concludes down right Magisterially, *So it must be, this is my Definitive Sentence*; as if his *Plain Assertion*, without any *other Reason*, ought to prevail[3]; nay,

10   even point blank against the irrefragable Reason of the Book he quotes. [4]I confess in another place of *Calvin*'s Case, *viz.* fol.17.b. he gives this Assertion a Colour of

15   Reason, by saying, *That tho' Ireland be a Distinct Dominion from England, yet the Title thereof being by* Conquest, *the same by Judgment of Law might by Express Words be bound*

20   *by the Parliaments of England.*[5] How far *Conquest* gives a Title, we have Enquired before: But I would fain know what Lord *Cook* means by *Judgment of Law*: Whether he

25   means the *Law of Nature* and *Reason*, or of *Nations*; or the *Civil Laws* of our *Commonwealths*; in none of which Senses, I conceive, will he, or any Man, be ever able to

30   make out his Position.[6]

---

1 pardonable] pardonable, [tho I should give [no other nạmẹ] an Hard Name for it] (*heavily scored through*) H | `in ... measure´ pardonable **PC**   2 Unwarrantable Position] odd sort of [Logick Containd] `Position´ H | [odd ... of] `unwarrantable´ Position **PC**   3 ought to prevail] `ought ... prevail´ H   4 – 6 I confess ... Position.] `I confess ... Position´ (*interpolation in margin*) H   5 England.] England. **H & PC** | England∧ I   6 Position.] *end of interpolation begun n. 4 above*

117, 11 *irrefragable* – incontrovertible, undeniable: *OED*, s.v. 1.   **117, 14–15** *Colour of Reason* – a show of reason, a specious or plausible reason: *OED*, s.v. colour, 12a.   **117, 15–20** *That tho' ... England* – this explicit reference to the parliament of England undermines the seemingly more generous position in the extract relating to the rights of a Christian conqueror cited from *7th Rep.*, 117v, in *Case*, p. 122. It also disposes of the claim in Black, 'Constitution', *University of Pennsylvania Law Review*, 124 (1976), pp 1179–82, that Coke's overall position was by no means as unfavourable to Ireland as might at first appear.

Is the Reason of *England's*
Parliament not Binding *Ireland*,
Because we do not send thither
Representatives ? And is the
5   Efficacy of this Reason taken off, by
our being Named in an English Act?
Why should sending Representatives to Parliament, Bind those that
send them ? Meerly because
10   thereby the *Consent* of those that are
Bound, is obtain'd, as far as those
sort of Meetings can possibly
permit; which is the very *Foun-*
dation of the *Obligation* of all Laws[1].
15   And is *Ireland's being Named* in an
English Act of Parliament, the least
step towards obtaining the *Consent*
of the *People of Ireland* ? If it be not,
then certainly my Lord *Cook's*
20   Parenthesis is to no purpose. And
'tis a wonder to me, that so many
Men have run upon this vain
Imagination, meerly from the
Assertion of this Judge: For I
25   challenge any Man to shew me, that
any one *before* him, or any one *since*,
but *from him*, has vended[2] this
Doctrine: And if the *bare Assertion*
of a Judge, shall Bind a *whole*[3]
30   *Nation*,   and   Dis

---

1 which … Laws] `which … laws´ (*interpolation in margin*) **H**    2 one *before* … vended] [Man] `one´ …
[Man] `one´ … ven[[t]]ded **H**   3 a *whole*] an whole **H & PC**

118, 10–14 *the Consent … Laws* – this passage neatly encapsulated Molyneux's theory of political
obligation. See further *Case*, pp 48, 56, 150–1.   **118, 27** *vended* – put forth, or give utterance to: *OED*, s.v.
vend, 3.

solve the *Rights* and *Liberties* thereof, We shall make their Tongues
very powerful[1], and constitute[2] them
greater Lawgivers than the greatest
5   Senates. [3]I do not see why my
Denying it, should not be as
Authentick as his *Affirming* it. 'Tis
true, He was a great Lawyer and a
powerful Judge; but had no more
10   Authority to *make a Law*, than I or
any Man else. But some will say, He
was a Learned Judge, and may be
supposed to have *Reason* for his
Position. Why then does he not
15   give it us ? And then what he
Asserts would Prevail, not from the
Authority of the Person, but from
the *Force of the Reason*. The most
Learned in the Laws have no more
20   power to make or alter a Constitution, than any other Man; And
their Decisions shall no farther
prevail, than supported by Reason
and Equity.[4] I conceive my Lord.
25   Ch. Justice *Cooke* apply'd himself so
wholly to the Study of the *Common
Laws* of *England*, that he did not
enquire far into the *Laws of Nature*
and *Nations*; if he had, certainly he
30   could never have been Guilty of
such   an   Erroneous   Slip;

---

1 And ... powerful] And if [At] [the Rights and Libertys of an Whole Nation must be Dissolved by] the
... Judge [we shall make their Tongues very powerfull, [more] `even as´ powerfull [than] as any A] `shall
bind´ ... we ... powerful **H**   2 constitute] make **H** | [make] `constitute´ **PC**   3 – 4 I do ... Equity] *not
in* **H** | `I do ... Equity´ (*interpolation in margin*) **PC**   4 Equity.] *end of interpolation begun n. 3 above*

119, 7 *Authentick* – authoritative, entitled to obedience and respect: *OED*, s.v. authentic, 1.

He would have seen demonstrably, that *Consent only* gives Humane Laws their Force, and that therefore the Reason in the Case he quotes is unanswerable, *Quia non mittunt Milites ad Parliamentum.*[*] More-over, the Assertion of *Cooke* in this point is directly[1] contrary to the whole tenour of the Case which he cites: For the very Act of Parliament on which the Debate of the Judges did arise, and which they deemed not to be of Force in *Ireland*, particularly names *Ireland*. So that here again Ld. *Cooke's* Error appears most plainly.[2] For this I refer to the Report, as I have exactly delivered it before pag. 90,91. By which it appears clearly[3] to be the unani-mous Opinion of all the Judges then in the *Exchequer Chamber:* That *within the Land of Ireland*, the Parliaments of *England* have no Jurisdiction, whatever they may have over the Subjects of *Ireland* on the *open Seas:* And the reason is given, *Quia Hibernia non mittit Milites ad Parliamentum in Angliâ.*[**]

[*][Because they do not send Knights to our parliament]

[**][Because Ireland doth not send Knights to parliament in England]

---

1 Reason ... directly] [Argument] `Reason´ ... [down right] `directly´ **H**   2 For ... plainly.] *not in* **H** | `For ... plainly.´ (*interpolation in margin, manu aman.*) **PC**   3 clearly] plainly **H** | [plainly] `clearly´ **PC**

120, 7–14 *the Assertion ... names Ireland* – Clement, *Answer*, pp 92–5, sought to reconcile the apparent discrepancy in terms of an overriding imperial interest.

¹This Assertion likewise is inconsistent with himself in other parts of his Works. He tells us in his 4th. Inst. pag. 349. *That 'tis plain*

5 *that not only King* John (*as all Men allow*) *but* Henry *the Second also, the Father of King* John, *did Ordain and Command, at the Instance of the Irish, That such Laws as had been in*

10 England *should be Observ'd and of Force in* Ireland. *Hereby* Ireland *being of it self a distinct Dominion, and no part of the Kingdom of* England, *was to have Parliaments*

15 *holden there as in* England. And in pag. 12. he tells us, *That* Henry *the Second sent a Modus into* Ireland, *directing them how to hold their Parliaments.* But to what end was

20 all this, if *Ireland* nevertheless were subject to the Parliament of *England?* The King and² Parliaments of these Kingdoms are the supream Legislators;³ If *Ireland* be subject to

25 Two (its Own, and that of *England*)⁴ it has *Two Supreams*; 'tis not impossible, but they may enact *different or contrary* Sanctions; which of these shall the People

30 Obey ? He tells us in *Calvin's⁵* Case

---

1 – p. 122, n. 2 This ... Point.] `This ... Point.´ (*interpolation in margin*) **H** 2 were ... and] [could be] were ... `King and´ **H** 3 Legislators] Legislat[[ures]]ors **H** | Leigislat[[iv̲ɡ̲s̲]]ures **PC** 4 (its ... *England*)] *no parentheses in* **H** 5 of these ... *Calvin's*] `of these´ ... [ye same] Calvins **H**

121, 13–14 *Kingdom of England* – Molyneux omitted a significant parenthesis in Coke's original: '(as it directly appeareth by many authorities in Calvin's Case)'. 121, 19–21 *But ... England* – cf. Bolton, 'Declaration', p. 13: 'the Parliament of *Ireland* should be nugatory and superfluous, if by naming *Ireland* in any statute made in *England*, *Ireland* should be bound; then all these Parliaments which have been holden in *Ireland* since 12 King *John*, for the space of about 400 years, should have been needless and superfluous, which is not to be imagined.' 121, 22–30 *The King ... Obey?* – Bolton, 'Declaration', p. 13, made a similar point as to Irishmen not knowing whether to obey an act passed in England, if this contradicted an Irish statute. Such of course had been the practical problem for Irish Protestants both during the early 1640s and in 1689–91. Cf. *Case*, pp 44, 171.

fol.17.b. *That if a King hath a Christian Kingdom* by Conquest, *as* Henry *the Second had* Ireland, *after* King John *had given to*[1] *them, being under his Obedience, and Subjection, the Laws of* England *for the Government of that Country, no succeeding King could alter the same without Parliament.* Which, by the way,

5

seems directly contradictory to what he says concerning *Ireland* six lines below this last cited passage. So that we may observe my Lord *Cook* enormously stumbling at every turn

10

15 in this Point.[2]

Opinions of other Judges in Favour of Ireland.

Thus[3] I have done with this Reverend Judge; and, in him, with the only *Positive Opinion against us.* I shall now consider what our Law-Books offer in our *Favour* on this Point.

20

To this purpose we meet a Case fully apposite, reported in the Year-Book of the 20th of *Henry* the 6th,

25 fol.8. between one *John Pilkington* and one *A.*

Pilkingtons[4] Case.

Pilkington brought a *Scire Facias* against *A.* to shew Cause, why Let-

---

1 *to*] `to´ **H**   2 Point.] *end of interpolation begun p. 121, n. 1 above*   3 Thus] [An<d>] thus **H**   4 *marginal heading* Pilkingtons Case.] Pilkingtons Case. **H & PC** | Pilkintons Case, **I**

122, 1–9 *That if … Parliament* – cf. 'Legislative power in Ireland', f. 128r. The point was also made in Domville, 'Disquisition', pp 57–8, (which brought in the laws granted by Henry II) and in Bolton, 'Declaration', p. 12. The implicit argument was that even if a conquest of Ireland was conceded, John's 1210 grant (cf. *Case*, pp 44, 54) had introduced laws which could not be subsequently changed without Irish consent. Though seemingly at variance with the emphasis which Molyneux placed, *Case*, pp 40–2, 54–5, on John's title being by donation not conquest, the introduction of an argument from conquest in Ireland's favour was in keeping with his overall strategy of setting out a series of legal arguments regardless of their mutual compatibility. See further intro. p. 29.   122, 9–12 *Which … passage* – i.e. the extract '*That tho' Ireland … England.*' cited *Case*, p. 117.   122, 19–20 *our Law-Books* – that is English law books, cf. *Case*, p. 77.   122, 22–6 *a Case … one A.* – a similar account of Pilkington's case (1439–41) was given in Bolton, 'Declaration', p. 5, and a briefer one in Domville, 'Disquisition', p. 68. The detailed account in Richardson & Sayles, *Irish parliament* (London, 1952), pp 255–7, shows the issue to have been more complex than the report in Year Book [Mich.] 20, Hen. 6 suggested.   25, 27 *Scire Facias* – a writ seeking to revoke royal letters patent: *OED*, s.v.

ters Patents whereby the King had granted an Office in *Ireland*[1] to the said *A*. should not be repeal'd, since the said *Pilkington* had the same

5 Office granted to him by former Letters Patents of the same King to be occupied by himself or his Deputy. Whereupon *A*. pleaded, That the Land of *Ireland*, time out

10 of Memory, hath been a Land separated and distinct from the Land of *England*, and Ruled and Governed by the Customs of the same Land of *Ireland*. That the Lords of the same

15 Land, which are of the King's Council, have used from time to time, in the absence of the King, to Elect a *Justice*, who hath Power to Pardon and Punish all Felons, &c.

20 and to call a Parliament, and by the Advice of the Lords and Commonalty to make Statutes. He alledged further, That a Parliament was Assembled, and that it was

25 Ordain'd by the said Parliament, (*a*) That every Man who had an Office within the said Land, before[4] a certain day, shall occupy the said Office by himself, otherwise, he

30 should forfeit. He shew'd that *Pilkington* Occupied by a De

[2](*a*) This Statute we may reckon, amongst the number of those that are lost during the long Intervals of our Irish Acts, noted before page 65. to be about 119[3] Years.

---

1 in *Ireland*] `in Ireland´ H   2 *marginal note*] *in* H | (*manu aman.*) PC   3 *marginal ref.* 119] 119 H & PC | 118 I   4 Land, before‚] Land, before‚ H & PC | Land‚ before, I

123, 2–3 *an Office ... said A.* – the office was escheator of Ireland, and 'A' is to be identified as Thomas Bathe: Richardson & Sayles, *Irish parliament* (Philadelphia, 1952), pp 255–7. Molyneux omitted to mention that Pilkington's case, like that of the Merchants of Waterford's (cf. *Case*, pp 89–91), was heard in the exchequer chamber. Cf. Hemmant, *Select cases* (London, 1933), i, pp 81–4.   123, 9–10 *time ... Memory* – i.e. before the limit of legal memory, namely the coronation of Richard I, 2 Sept. 1189: Jacob, *A new law-dictionary* (London, 1729), s.v. immemorial.   123, 14–22 *the Lords ... Statutes* – this claim to the right to elect a successor on the death in office of a chief governor (later characterized as 'the Statute of Henry FitzEmpress') emerged in the early C.15 and was given statutory basis in 2 Rich. 3 (1485). It was confirmed, 33 Hen. 8, ses. 2, c. 2 (1541), though without the right to summon parliament (thereby bringing it into conformity with Poynings' Law). See further, Richardson & Sayles, *Irish parliament* (Philadelphia, 1952), appendix X. Cf. Bolton, 'Declaration', pp 5–6.   123, 24–30 *it was ... forfeit* – a no-longer-extant statute to this effect was passed in Nov. 1437 (16 Hen. 6); cf. summary of its provisions in *ESI*, iii, p. 84.

puty; and that therefore his Office
was void, and[1] that the King had
granted the said Office to him the
said *A.* Hereupon *Pilkington*

5 Demurr'd in Law; and it was
debated by the Judges, *Yelverton,*
Fortescue, Portington, Markham,
and *Ascough,* whether the said
Prescription in relation to the State

10 and Government of[2] *Ireland,* be
good or *void* in Law. *Yelverton* and
Portington held the Prescription
void. But *Fortescue, Markham,* and
Ascough held the Prescription *good;*

15 and that the Letters Patents made
to *A.* were good, and ought not to
be Repeal'd. And in this[3] it was
agreed by *Fortescue* and *Portington,*
That if a Tenth or Fifteenth be

20 granted by Parliament in *England,*
that shall not Bind *Ireland,*
although the King should send the
same Statute into *Ireland* under his
Great Seal; Except they in *Ireland*

25 will in their Parliament Approve it;
Because they have not any
Commandment by Writ to come to the
Parliament of England: And this
was not Denied by *Markham,*

30 *Yelverton,* or *Ascough.*

---

1 and] `&´ **H**   2 and … of] [of] and … of **H**   3 this] This Case **H**

124, 5 *Demurr'd in Law* – accepted the facts pleaded by the plaintiff but denied he was legally entitled to relief: *OED,* s.v. demurrer, 1.   **124, 19–25** *That if … Approve it* – based on Domville, 'Disquisition', p. 68. See further, *Case,* pp 170–1.

The *Merchants of Waterford's Case* which I have observed before, pag. 90. as Reported in the Year Book of the 2d. of[1] *Richard* the 3d. fol. 11,

5 12, is notorious on[2] our behalf, but needs not be here repeated.

The Case of the Prior of *Lanthony* in *Wales*[3], mentioned by Mr. *Pryn* against the 4th Inst. ch.

10 76. p. 313. is usually cited *against* us. But I conceive 'tis so far from proving this, that 'tis very much in our Behalf. The Case was briefly thus. [4]The Prior of *Lanthony*

15 brought an Action in the *Com. Pleas of Ireland* against the Prior of[5] *Mollingar*, for an Arrear of an Annuity, and Judgment went against the Prior of *Mollingar*;[6]

20 hereon the Prior of *Mollingar* brought a Writ of Error in the *King's Bench of Ireland*, and the Judgment was affirmed. Then the Prior of *Mollingar* Appeal'd to the

25 Parliament in *Ireland* held 5 *Hen.* 6. before *James Butler* Earl of *Ormond*,[7] and the Parliament Revers'd both Judgments. The Prior of *Lanthony* removed all[8] into the *King's Bench*

30 in *England*; but the *King's*

---

1 observed ... the 2d. of] delivered ... `the ... of´ H   2 on] in H & PC   3 Case ... *Wales*] `Case of the´ ... Llanthony{s} [Case] `in Wales´ H   4 p. 126, n. 1 The Prior ... *in the*] [The Prior] [There was a suit commenced between the Prior of *Molingar* in Ireland, and the *Prior of Lanthony*, in the Common Pleas of Ireland `where judgement went against the Pr. of Lanthony´. this was removd by writ of Error into the Kings Bench of Ireland, where the Judgement was Affirmed. From the Kings Bench the Prior of *Lanthony* Appeald to Parliament in Ireland held ye 5th of Hen. 6. before James Bottiler Earl of Ormond, where likewise the Judgement was Affirmed. From the Parliament of Ireland the Prior of *Lanthony* Appeald to the [Parliament] `Kings Bench´ of England, but the Kings Bench would not meddle therwith [after having pasd `in´ the] `as not having power or Connoisance of any [[Plea]]thing] `The ... in the´ (*interpolation in margin*) H   5 Prior of] Prior of H & PC | of Prior I   6 *Mollingar*] [Lanthony] `Mullingar´ H   7 held ... *Ormond*] `held ... Ormond´ H   8 all] all [by writ of <error>] H

125, 5 *notorious* – evident, or obvious: *OED*, s.v. 3.   **125, 7–126, 11** *The Case ... p. 313* – the account of the Prior of Llanthony's case (1427–9) was a subsequent interpolation in the holograph (cf. app. crit.). The case had come to Molyneux's attention in the search for precedents in the bishop of Derry's appeal to the Irish lords in Sept. 1697, see further intro. p. 12, n. 46.   **125, 14** *the Prior of Llanthony* – identified by Prynne, *Brief animadversions* (London, 1669), pp 313–4, as 'John Pembrugge'. See further, Richardson & Sayles, *Irish parliament* (Philadelphia, 1952), pp 254–5.   **125, 24–6** *the Parliament ... Ormond* – i.e. 1427: Richardson & Sayles, *Irish parliament* (Philadelphia, 1952), pp 254–5.

Bench refused to intermeddle, *as having no Power over what had pass'd in the[1] Parliament of Ireland.* Hereupon the Prior of *Lanthony* Appeal'd to the Parliament of *England*. And it does not appear by[2] the Parliament Roll (*a*) that any thing was done on this Appeal[4]; all that is Entred being only the Petition it self at the end of the Roll. *Vid.Pryn* against the 4th Instit. chap. 76. p. 313.[5]

Now whether this be a Precedent proving the Subordination of our Irish Parliament to that of *England*, I leave the Reader to judge. To me it seems the *clear contrary.* For first we may observe, the *King's Bench* in *England* absolutely disclaiming any Cognisance of what had passed in the Parliament of *Ireland*. And next we may observe, That nothing at all was done therein upon the Appeal to the Parliament of *England*: Certainly if the Parliament of *England* had thought themselves to have a Right to Enquire into this Matter, they had so done, one way or t'other, and not left the Matter Undetermin'd and in Suspence.

[3](*a*) *Rot.Parl. An.*
8 H.6. in ult.

---

1 *the*] *end of interpolation begun p. 125, n. 4 above*   **2** does ... by] `does not´ appear[[s]]by **H**    **3** *marginal ref.] in* **H** | (*manu aman.*) **PC**    **4** Appeal] [Petition] `Appeal´ **H**   **5** Vid. ... p. 313.] `Vid ... p. 313.´ (*perhaps add. later at end of MS line*) **H**

126, 1 *intermeddle* – here clearly used in the sense 'to concern oneself with': *OED*, s.v. 3. Cf. *Case*, p. 4. **126, 12–15** *a Precedent ... England* – cf. Mayart, 'Answer' (Dublin, 1750), pp 102–3.   **126, 16–30** *To me ... Suspence* – Bishop King had expressed satisfaction to a variety of correspondents, 8 Feb. 1697–8, at finding so compelling a precedent for the English parliament's refusal to involve itself in judicial matters already decided by the Irish parliament. Cary, *Vindication*, p. 114, however, argued the English parliament's readiness to consider the Prior's petition corroborated their right to receive appeals from the Irish parliament.

It has ever been acknowledged that the Kingdom of *Ireland* is inseparably annex'd to the Imperial Crown of *England*. The Obligation
5 that our Legislature lies under by *Poyning's Act*, 10 *H*.7. c.4. makes this Tye between the two Kingdoms indissoluble. And we must ever own it our Happiness to be thus Annex'd
10 to *England*:[1] And that the Kings and Queens of *England* are by undoubted Right, *ipso facto*[2] Kings and Queens of *Ireland*. And from hence we may reasonably conclude,
15 that if any Acts of Parliament made in *England*, should be of force in *Ireland*, before they are Received there in Parliament, they should be more especially such Acts as relate
20 to the *Succession* and *Settlement of the Crown*, and *Recognition* of the Kings Title thereto, and the *Power* and *Jurisdiction* of the King.[3] And yet we find in the Irish Statutes, 28
25 *Hen*.VIII. c.2. *An Act for the Succession of the King and Queen Ann*; and another, Chap. 5 declaring the King to be *Supream Head of the Church of Ireland*; both
30 which Acts had formerly

Argument from Acts of Succession and Recognition pass'd in *Ireland*.

---

1 The Obligation ... *England*:] *not in* H | `The ... England´ (*interpolation in margin*) PC   2 *ipso facto*] *not in* H | `*ipso facto*´ PC   3 and ... King] `and ... King´ H

127, 2–13 *the Kingdom ... Ireland* – though for Molyneux Poynings' Law provided the key to the constitutional relations between England and Ireland (cf. *Case*, p. 81 nn), he failed to appreciate the superiority which it accorded to the English parliament in determining who the ruler of Ireland should be, as happened in 1689. Cary, *Vindication*, p. 45, and Atwood, *History*, dedic., both regarded the Convention's decision as conclusive demonstration of Ireland's subordinate status. Cf. *Case*, p. 105.

pass'd in the Parliament of *England*. So likewise we find amongst the Irish Statutes *Acts of Recognition of the Kings Title to Ireland*, in the

5 Reigns of *Henry* the Eighth, Queen *Elizabeth*, King *James*, King *Charles* the Second, King *William* and Queen *Mary*. By which it appears that *Ireland*, tho' Annex'd to the

10 Crown of *England*, has always been look'd upon to be *a Kingdom Compleat within it self*, and to have all Jurisdiction to an *Absolute* Kingdom belonging, and Subor-

15 dinate to no Legislative Authority on Earth. Tho', 'tis to be Noted, these English Acts relating to the Succession, and Recognition of the Kings Title, do particularly Name

20 *Ireland*.[1]

As the *Civil* State of *Ireland* is thus *Absolute* within itself, so likewise is[2] our State *Ecclesiastical*: This is manifest by the *Canons* and

25 *Constitutions*, and even by the *Articles*[3] of the *Church of Ireland*, which differ in some things from those of the *Church of England*. [4]And in all the Charters and Grants of

30 Liberties and Immunities to

Ireland's State Ecclesiastical Independent.

---

1 Tho´ ... *Ireland*.] *not in* H | `Tho ... `English´ ... Ireland´ (*add. at foot of MS page*) PC   2 is] `is´ H   3 by the *Canons* ... *Articles*] [*from*] `by´ ... `and even ... Articles´ H   4 – p. 129, n. 1 And ... knows.] *not in* H | `And ... knows.´ (*interpolation, manu WM, on separate quire; f. 232 second leaf blank and unfoliated*) PC

128, 3–8 *Acts ... Mary* – see the index of statutes cited; the Henrician legislation was presumably the 1541 act for the kingly title. An act of recognition had also been the first statute of the Jacobite parliament of 1689: Bergin & Andrew, *The Acts* (Dublin, 2016), pp 3–6. Clement, *Answer*, p. 110, dismissed Irish acts of recognition as a mere expression of allegiance, and not a parliamentary sanction of the new sovereign's title. **128, 9–16** *that Ireland ... Earth* – passage denounced by English commons committee: *Commons Jnl [Eng]*, xii, p. 325. The phrase 'a *Kingdom Compleat ...Absolute* Kingdom belonging' echoed the 1541 act for the kingly title. The term, 'Absolute Kingdom' is equivalent to 'Imperial Crown', as used *Case*, pp 41, 55, namely a state possessing untrammelled earthly sovereignty. See further, Burgess, *Absolutism* (London, 1996), pp 3–9. **128, 17–20** *English Acts ... Ireland* – as, for example, in the Act for the Recognition of James I (1 Jac.I, c. 1), cited *Case*, p. 154, which stated 'your Maiestie is of the Realmes and Kingdoms of England, Scotland, France and Ireland, the most potent and mighty King'. **128, 21–3** *As the Civil ... Ecclesiastical* – despite the assertions of Atwood, *History*, pp 20–4, the ecclesiastical settlement imposed by Henry II at the Council of Cashel (cf. *Case*, pp 56–7) effectively set aside previous claims by Canterbury to primacy over the Irish church. For these claims, see Flanagan, *Irish society* (Oxford, 1989), pp 8–38 *passim. Absolute* – independent: *OED*, s.v. 3. **128, 24–8** *the Canons ... England* – the 104 Irish Articles, drafted by James Ussher, and adopted in 1615, were superseded (though not repealed) in 1634, when the English thirty-nine articles were approved by convocation, which at the same time passed a modified version of the English canons of 1604. The 1634 articles and canons were the basis of Church of Ireland doctrine and discipline after the Restoration: H.F. Kearney, *Strafford in Ireland* (Manchester, 1959), pp 115–16; F.R. Bolton, *The Caroline tradition* (London, 1958), p. 83.

Ireland, we still find this, That *Holy Church shall be Free*, &c. I would fain know what is meant here by the word *Free*: Certainly if our *Church*
5 be *Free* and Absolute within it self, our *State* must be so likewise; for how our *Civil* and *Ecclesiastical* Government is now interwoven, every body knows.[1] But I will not
10 enlarge on this head, it suffices only to hint it; I shall detain myself to our *Civil Government*.

Another Argument against the Parliament of *England*'s Jurisdiction
15 over *Ireland*, I take from a Record[2] in *Reyley's Placita Parliamentaria*, pag. 569. to this effect: (*a*)[3] In the 14th of *Edward* the Second, the King sent his Letters Patents to the
20 Lord Justice of *Ireland*, leting him know, That he had been moved by his *Parliament* at *Westminster*, that he would give Order that the *Irish Natives* of *Ireland*, might enjoy the
25 *Laws of England* concerning *Life* and *Member*, in[4] as large and ample manner as the *English* of *Ireland* enjoy'd the same. This therefore the King gives in Com-

Argument from a Record in *Reyley*.

(*a*) 14 *Ed.* 2. *Par.*2. *Memb.* 21 *Int.*

---

1 knows] *end of interpolation begun p. 128, n. 4 above*   2 Argument ... Record] Argument [I shall use] ... [Precedent] `Record´ H   3 *marginal ref.] in* H | (*manu aman.*) PC   4 in] `in´ H

129, 11 *detain myself to* – confine myself to, a usage not found in *OED*.   **129, 21–130, 18** *That he* ... *England* – though a telling point with regard to the English parliament's view of its rights in Ireland, this episode called into question how far the original grant of English laws in Ireland extended to the population at large as opposed to the princes, nobles and prelates; see further *Case*, p. 53. Cf. Clement, *Answer*, p. 40.

mandment, and orders accordingly,
by these his Letters Patents. From
hence, I say, we may gather, That
the Parliament of *England* did not
5   then take upon them to have any
Jurisdiction in *Ireland*, (for then
they would have made a Law for
Ireland to this Effect) but instead
thereof, they Apply to[1] the *King*,
10   that he would interpose his Commands, and give Directions that this
great Branch of the *Common Law* of
England should be put in Execution
in *Ireland* indifferently to all the
15   Kings Subjects there, *pursuant* to
the *Original Compact* made with
them on their first Submission to
the Crown of *England*.

    Let us now consider the great

**Objection
drawn from a
Writ of Error.**

20   Objection[2] drawn from a *Writ of
Error*'s lying from the *Kings Bench*
of *England*, on a Judgment given in
the *Kings Bench* in *Ireland*; which
proves (as 'tis insisted on)[3] that there
25   is a *Subordination* of *Ireland* to
England; and that if an *Inferiour*
Court of Judicature in *England*, can
thus[4] take cognizance of, and over-
rule the Proceedings in the like
30   Court of *Ireland*; it[5] will

---

1 Apply to] [Move] `Apply to´ **H**   2 Let … Objection] [I shall conclude what I have to offer on this fifth Article with the Consideration of the great Argument] `Let … Objection´ **H**   3 (as … on)] (say our Adversarys) **H** | ([say … Adversarys] `as … on´) **PC**   4 and … thus] [in] and … [the] `an Inferiour´ Court[s] … `in England´ … thus [inter meddle with and] **H**   5 Proceedings … it] Proceedings [it] … it **H**

130, 19–23 *the great … Ireland* – Molyneux now considered the question of appeals on writs of error to the king's bench in England, which he had earlier raised in connection with the Merchants of Waterford's case, *Case*, p. 91. Not surprisingly, no reference was made to the Jacobite act of 1689, which had prohibited not only appeals from the Irish king's bench to the English one, but also appeals from the Irish court of chancery. See further intro. p. 26.   **130, 26–131, 5** *if an … Ireland* – cf. Bolton, 'Declaration', p. 15.

follow, that the *Supream Court* of Parliament in *England* may do the same, in relation to the Proceedings of the Court of Parliament in

5   *Ireland*.

¹It must be confess'd that this has been the constant Practice; and it seems to be the great² thing that induced my Lord *Cook* to believe

10   that an Act of Parliament in *England*, and mentioning or Including *Ireland*, should Bind here. The Subordination of *Ireland* to *England*, he seems to infer from the

15   Subordination of the *Kings Bench of Ireland*, to the *Kings Bench* of *England*. But to this I answer:

1. That 'tis the Opinion of several Learned in the Laws of

20   *Ireland*, That this Removal of a Judgment from the *Kings Bench* of *Ireland*, by *Writ of Error*, into the *Kings Bench* of *England*, is founded on an Act of Parliament in *Ireland*,

25   which is lost amongst a great number of other Acts, which we want for the space of 130 years at one time, and of 120 at another time, as we have noted before,

---

1 It] *marginal heading* Answer'd **PC**   2 great] [chief] great **H**

131, 8–17 *it seems … England* – Mayart, 'Answer' (Dublin, 1750), pp 103–4, identified Coke's assertion that Ireland's judicial subordination to the English king's bench necessarily implied legislative subordination (cf. *Case*, p. 117) as an instance of reasoning '*a Minori ad Majus* (*quod in Minori valet, valebit in Majori* [what holds good in the lesser case, will hold good in the greater])', a form of argument for which Coke, *1st Inst.*, ff 253r, 260r, asserted the authority of Littleton.   **131, 9–12** *my Lord Cook … here* – cf. *Case*, pp 117–18.   **131, 18–25** *the Opinion … lost* – Molyneux's wording is elliptical, the procedure involved an application to the English king's bench for a writ of error redirecting the Irish king's bench. Both Bolton, 'Declaration', p. 20, and, 'Legislative power in Ireland', f. 130r, took the practice to derive from long-established custom rather than common law or statute.

pag. 65. But it[1] being only a *General Tradition*, that there was such an Act of our Parliament, we *only offer it as a Surmise*, the Statute it self
5   does not appear.[2]

2. Where a Judgment in *Ireland* is Removed, to be Revers'd in *England*, the Judges in[3] *England* ought, and always do judge,
10   according to the *Laws* and *Customs* of *Ireland*, and not according to the Laws and Customs of *England*, any otherwise than as these may be of Force in *Ireland*; but if in any thing
15   the two Laws differ, the Law of Ireland must prevail, and guide their Judgment.[4] And therefore in the Case of one *Kelly*, Removed to the *Kings Bench* in *England*, in the
20   beginning of King *Charles* the First, one Error was assigned that[5] the *Præcipe* was of *Woods* and *Underwoods*, which is a manifest Error, if brought in *England*; but the
25   Judges finding the Use to be *Otherwise* in *Ireland*, judged it *No Error*. So in *Crook, Charles,* fol. 511. *Mulcarry* vers. *Eyres*. Error was assigned for that the Declaration
30   was   of   one   hundred

---

1 it] [this] `it´ **H**     2 does ... appear] `does´ not [being] appear **H**   3 in] of **H & PC**   4 any otherwise ... Judgement] `any ... Judgement´ *(interpolation largely in margin)* **H**     5 was ... that] assigned was **H** | was assigned [was] `that´ **PC**

132, 6–12 *Where ... England* – cited verbatim from 'Legislative power in Ireland', f. 130r. Cf. Bolton, 'Declaration', pp 14–15. Clement, *Answer*, p. 114, sardonically quipped: 'an Irish Cause would immediately transubstantiate them all four [English KB judges] into the real presence of one King of *Ireland*'. **132, 17–27** *And therefore ... No Error* – cited verbatim from 'Legislative power in Ireland', f. 130r, which did not identify any earlier source. *Præcipe* – a writ ordering something to be done, or to provide a justification for not doing it: *OED*, s.v. 1. Subsequent to the Kelly case, however, an English statute was enacted, 15 Car. 2, c. 2, against spoiling 'Woods and Underwoods'; this act was recommended for re-enactment in Ireland, 18 Oct. 1692, by a committee which included Molyneux: *Common Jnl [Ire.]*, ii, pp 19–20. **132, 27–133, 4** *in Crook ... Error* – Mich. 13 Car. 1, rot. 33: Croke, *Reports* (London, 1661), pp 551–2. The writ of error issue was also raised in Darcy's *Argument* (1992), p. 274, which cited Strafford v. Strafford from James I's reign rather than the Kelly or Mulcarry v. Eyres cases. Bolton, 'Declaration', pp 15–6, cited three different cases again, involving respectively dower, disseisin, and episcopal elections. The Mulcarry case is discussed in Donaldson, *Irish law* (Durham, NC, 1967), pp 13–14.

Acres of *Bogg*, which is a word not
known in *England*; but 'twas said, It
was well enough understood in
Ireland, and[1] so adjudged *No Error.*

5 From whence, I conceive, 'tis
manifest, that the Jurisdiction of the
Kings Bench in *England*, over a
Judgment in[2] the Kings Bench of
Ireland, does not proceed from any

10 Subordination of one Kingdom to
the other; but from some other
Reason,[3] which we shall endeavour
to make out.

3. We have before observed,

15 That in the Reign of K. *Henry* the
Third, *Gerald Fitz-Maurice*, Lord
Justice of *Ireland*, sent four Knights
to know what was held for Law in
England in the Case of *Coparceners.*

20 The Occasion of which Message (as
before we have noted out of the
Kings Rescript) was, because the
Kings Justice of *Ireland* was
ignorant what the Law was. We

25 may reasonably imagine that there
were many Messages of this kind;
for in the Infancy[4] of the English
Government, it may well be sup-

---

1 and] as **H & PC**   2 a Judgment in] `a ... in´ **H**   3 Reason] [Cause] Reason **H**   4 Infancy] Infancy **H**
& PC |Instance **I**

133, 11–13 *from some ... make out* – the analysis of the growth of the appeals practice which follows, *Case*,
pp 133–8, was an instance of 'genetic history' similar to the account of Irish representatives in medieval
English parliaments (*Case*, pp 96–8), and the English legislation for Ireland during the Jacobite war (*Case*,
pp 106–9). Cf. objections to this method of arguing in Cary, *Vindication*, p. 119.   **133, 15–24** *in the Reign*
... Law was – cf. *Case*, pp 86–7.   **133, 16** *Gerald Fitz-Maurice* – recte Maurice FitzGerald, cf. *Case*, p. 187 nn.
133, 27–8 *the Infancy ... Government* – that is, in Ireland.

posed, that the Judges in *Ireland* were not so deeply versed in the Laws of *England*: This occasioned Messages to *England*, *Before*

5 Judgment given in *Ireland*, to be inform'd of the Law. And *After* Decrees made, Persons who thought themselves aggrieved by *Erroneous* Judgments, apply'd

10 themselves to the King in *England* for Redress. Thus it must be, that Writs of Error (unless they had their Sanction in Parliament) became in use. Complaints to the

15 King by those that thought themselves injur'd, increased; and at last grew into Custom, and obtain'd[1] the Force of Law.

[2]Perhaps it may be Objected,

20 That if the[3] Judges of the Kings Bench in *England* ought to Regulate their Judgment by the Customs of *Ireland*, and not of *England*, it will follow, that this Original which we

25 assign of Writs of Error to *England*, is not right.

I Answer, That this may be[4] the *Primary Original*, and yet consist well enough with what we have

---

1 obtain'd] [had] obtaind **H**   2 – p. 135, n. 2 Perhaps … suggested.] ‵Perhaps … suggested.´ (*interpolation largely in margins of* ff 138r *and*139v) **H**   3 Perhaps … the] [if it be Objected that this does not so wel ‵agree with what just foregoes, viz, that The Judges ought to go according to the Customs of Ireland a̶n̶d̶´] (a̶n̶d̶ *obscured by scoring through*)] ‵perhaps … the´ (*interpolation in margin*) **H**   4 I Answer … be] (*no new para.*) I Answer… [true] this may [well enough] be **H** | (*no new para.*) **PC**

before laid down: For tho' the
Common Law of *England* was to be
the Common Law of *Ireland*, and
Ireland at the beginning of its
5   English   Government   might
frequently send into *England* to be
inform'd about it; yet this does not
hinder, but *Ireland*, in a long Process
of Time, may have some smaller
10   Customs and Laws of its own,
gradually but insensibly crept into
Practice, that may in some measure
differ from the Customs and
Practice of *England*; and where
15   there is any such, the Judges of
England[1]   must   regulate   their
Sentence accordingly, tho' the first
Rise of Writs of Error to *England*,
may be as we have here suggested.[2]
20   [3]In like manner, where the Statute-
Law of *Ireland* differs from that of
England, the Judges of *England* will
regulate their Judgments by the
Statute-law of *Ireland*: This is the
25   constant Practice, and notoriously
known in *Westminster-Hall*: From
which it appears, that removing a
Judgment from the Kings Bench of
Ireland, to the Kings Bench of
30   *England*, is but an Appeal to the
King   in   his   Bench

---

1 of *England*] `of England´ **H**   2 suggested.] *end of interpolation begun p. 134, n. 2 above*   3 – p. 136, n. 2
In like … hereafter.] *not in* **H** | `In … hereafter.´ (*interpolation in margin*) **PC**

135, 25 *notoriously* – as a matter of common knowledge: *OED*, s.v. 1.

of *England*, for his Sense, Judgement, or[1] Exposition of the Laws of *Ireland*. But of this more hereafter.[2]

5 4. When a *Writ of Error* is Returned into the Kings Bench of *England*, Suit is made to the *King only*; The Matter lies *altogether before Him*; and the Party complaining applies to *No Part* of

10 the Political Government of *England* for Redress, but to the *King of Ireland only*, who is in *England*: That the *King only* is sued to, our Law Books make Plain. This Court

15 is call'd *Curia Domini Regis*,[*] and *Aula Regia*,[**] because the King used to sit there in Person, as *Lambard* tells us[3]; and every Cause brought there, is said to be *coram*

20 *Domino Rege*,[***] even at this very day, *Cooke* 4<th> Inst. p.72. Therefore if a Writ be returnable *coram nobis ubicunque fuerimus*,[†] 'tis to be Return'd to the *Kings Bench*.

25 But if it be Returnable *coram Justiciariis nostris apud Westm.*[‡] 'tis to be Return'd into the *Common Pleas*. This Court (as *Glanvil*[4] and other Antients tells[5] us) used to

30 Travel with the King,

[*][the Court of our Lord the King]

[**][the King's Court]

[***][before our Lord the King]

[†][before us, wherever we shall be]

[‡][before our judges at Westminster]

---

1 Judgement, or] [or] Judgement or **PC**   2 hereafter.] *end of interpolation begun p. 135, n. 3 above*   3 as ... us] `as ... us´ **H**   4 *Glanvil*] Glanvil **H & PC** | *Glavnil* **I**   5 tells] tell **H**

136, 3 *But ... hereafter* – there is no further reference to Irish law being interpreted by the English king's bench.   **136, 4–7** *When ... King only* – however, Coke, *4th Inst.*, p. 350, also asserted that in C.13 and C.14 appeals from the Irish king's bench had been made *coram rege*, and decided in accordance with Irish law not English.   **136, 13–14** *our Law-Books* – that is English law books, see *Case*, p. 77.   **136, 18** *Lambard tells us* – cf. Lambarde, *Archeion* [1635] (Cambridge, MA, 1957), p. 33.   **136, 28–9** *Glanvil ... Antients* – the earliest English legal textbook, *De legibus et consuetudinibus regni Angliæ*, written *c.*1190 (traditionally ascribed to Ranulf de Glanvill, Justiciar, 1180–9), 1965 edn, pp 9, 30, together presumably with the other early texts mentioned below such as *Fleta* and *Britton*, as cited by Coke, *4th Inst.*, pp 72–3.

[*][The King hath his own court and his own judges, before whom, and nowhere else, except before himself, &c. false judgements <of facts> and errors <of law> are to be returned and corrected]

5

10

15

20

25

30

where-ever he went. And *Fleta*, in describing this Court, says, *Habet Rex Curiam suam & Justiciarios suos, coram quibus, & non alibi nisi coram semet ipso. &c.*¹ *falsa Judicia & Errores revertuntur & Corriguntur*[*]. The King then (as *Britton* says) having Supream Jurisdiction in his Realm, to judge in all Causes whatsoever; therefore it is, that *Erroneous Judgments* were brought to him out of *Ireland*. But this does not argue that *Ireland* is therefore *Subordinate to England*; for the People of *Ireland* are the *Subjects* of the King to whom they Appeal. And 'tis not from the *Country* where the Court is² held, but from the *Presence* and *Authority* of the King (to whom the People of *Ireland* have as good a Title as the People of *England*) that the *Præeminence of the Jurisdiction* does flow, And I question not, but in former times, when these Courts were first Erected, and when the King Exerted a greater Power in Judicature than he does now, and he used to sit in his own Court, that if he had Travell'd into *Ireland*, and the Court had follow'd

1 &c.] `&c´ H   2 are the ... Court is] `are´ ... [`...´] the Court [was] `is´ H

137, 1–6 *Fleta ... Corriguntur* – from the C.13 text, *Fleta*, bk II, ch. 2 (1953 edn, p. 110), but probably cited by Molyneux from Coke, *4th Inst.*, pp 72–3.   137, 7 *as Britton says* – Molyneux was again probably citing from Coke, *4th Inst.*, pp 72–3, rather than directly from the late C.13 law tract, then attributed to John Britton. Cf. *Britton* (Oxford, 1865), i, pp 3–4, 7.   137, 24–138, 4 *in former ... Ireland* – a conjecture comparable to the assertion, *Case*, p. 42, that since John had been king of Ireland before succeeding to England, the latter might properly be said to be subordinate to Ireland rather than vice versa.

him thither; Erroneous Judgments might have been removed *from England* before him *into his Court in Ireland*; for so certainly it must be,

5 since the Court Travell'd with the King. From hence it appears, that all the Jurisdiction, that the Kings Bench in *England*, has over the Kings Bench in *Ireland*, arises *only*

10 from the *Kings Presence* in the former. And the same may be said of the *Chancery* in *England*, if it will assume any Power to Controul the *Chancery* in *Ireland*: because (as

15 *Lambard* says, p.69, 70) The Chancery did follow the *King*, as the Kings Bench did; and that, as he tells us out of the[1] Lord Chief Justice *Scroope*, the *Chancery* and the

20 *Kings Bench* were once but one Place. But[2] if this be the ground of the Jurisdiction of the Kings Bench in *England* over the Kings Bench in *Ireland*, (as I am fully perswaded it

25 is) the Parliament in *England* cannot from hence claim any Right of Jurisdiction in *Ireland*, because they claim *a Jurisdiction of their own*; and their Court is not the

30 *Kings Court*, in that *proper* and *strict* sence that the *Kings Bench* is.

---

1 the] *not in* **H**   **2** But] [And] `But´ **H**

138, 11–21 *the same … Place* – cf. Lambarde, *Archeion* [1635] (Cambridge, MA, 1957), pp 57–8. (The page numbers Molyneux cited were those of the shorter, less authoritative version, *Archion*, published by Frere earlier in 1635. See further Lambarde, *Archeion* (Cambridge, MA, 1957), appendix, esp. pp 145–7). The proposal that Irish chancery appeals should be heard by a commission appointed by the English chancery was raised in connection with the bishop of Derry's appeal to the Irish lords in 1697. See Marsh's Library, MS Z 3.2.5, item 85, 'Some Reasons why an Appeal or Writt of Error does not lie to the house of Lords in England …' *Controul* – overrule the judgement of: *OED*, s.v. control, 8.   138, 18–19 *Lord … Scroope* – Lambarde, *Archeion* (Cambridge, MA, 1957), p. 58, dated this comment of Sir Geoffrey Scrope C.J. to Mich. 1 Edw. 3 (1327).

¹But granting that the *Subordination* of the *Kings Bench* in *Ireland*, to the *Kings Bench* in *England*, be rightly concluded from
5 a *Writ of Error* out of the *latter*, lying on² a Judgment in the *former*. I see no Reason from thence to conclude, that therefore the Parliament of *Ireland* is *Subordinate*
10 to the Parliament in *England*, unless we make any *one sort* of Subordination, or in any *one part* of Jurisdiction, to be a Subordination in *all Points*, and all parts of
15 Jurisdiction. The subjects of *Ireland* may Appeal to the King in his Bench in *England*, for the *Expounding* of the *Old*³ common and Statute-Law of *Ireland*; will it
20 therefore follow that the Parliament of *England* shall make *New Laws* to bind the Subjects in *Ireland*? I see no manner of Consequence in it; unless we take *Expounding Old*
25 *Laws*, (or *Laws already made*)⁴ in the *Kings Bench*, and *making New Laws in Parliament*, to be *one* and the *same thing*. I believe the best Logician in *Europe* will hardly⁵
30 make a Chain of *Syllogisms*, that from such *Premises*,

1 – p. 140, n. 1 But … Conclusion.] `But … Conclusion.´ (*interpolation on separate sheet*, 71r–v, *bound following the dedication to the King, but keyed to* PC p. 139. *The verso bears a note, manu* WM 999 Common Paper for the Ordinary sale) H | `But … Conclusion.´ (*interpolation on separate sheet* f. 238r–v *manu aman.*) PC   2 on] [in] `on´ H     3 all parts … Old] `all´ … [Besides I take it, that] the subjects … King[s] `in his´ … `old´ H   4 (or … made)] `(or … made)´ H     5 I believe … hardly] I challenge … Europe to H | I [Challenge] `believe´ … [to] `will hardly´ PC

139, 1–140, 2 *But … Conclusion* – the interpolation of this paragraph only in the printer's copy points to its being a late addition to the text (cf. app. crit.). The verso of the interpolated leaf bore a note in Molyneux's hand '999 Common Paper for the Ordinary sale' indicating that it was a specimen of the paper on which *The Case* was to be printed, see further intro. p. 66.   139, 24–8 *unless we … thing* – a further development of the distinction between declaratory and innovative laws, introduced, *Case*, pp 70–1.

will regularly induce such a
Conclusion.[1]

To close this Point, We find that
a Judgment of the Kings Bench in
5   *Ireland,* may be Removed by a Writ
of Error to the Parliament in
Ireland[2]: But the Judgment of the
Parliament of *Ireland* was never
question'd in the Parliament of
10   *England.* This Appears from the
Prior of Lanthony's Case aforegoing.

I shall conclude this our Fifth
Article with a memorable Passage
out of our Irish Statutes, which
15   seems to strengthen what we have
delivered on the Business of a *Writ
of Error,* as well as the chief Doctrine
I drive at; and that is 28 *H.* VIII.
Chap. 19. *The Act of Faculties.* This
20   Statute is a Recital at large of the
English Act of the 25 *Hen.* VIII.
c.21. In the Preamble of which
English Act 'tis Declared, *That this
Your Graces Realm Recognizing no
25   Superiour but Your Grace, hath been
and yet is free from any Subjection to
any Mans Laws, but only such as
have been Devised with-*

**Declaration in
the Irish Act of
Faculties.**

---

1 *Conclusion.*] *end of interpolation begun p. 139, n. 1 above*   2 close ... *Ireland*] [Conclude] `close´ ...
[England] `Ireland´ **H**

140, 1 *regularly* – in accordance with the rules (of logic): *OED,* s.v. 2.   **140, 7–11** *the Judgement ...
aforegoing* – cf. *Case,* pp 125–6. Surprisingly, Molyneux did not cite the reference in 'Legislative power in
Ireland', f. 130r, to a record in the Parliament Rolls, Tower of London, 8 Hen. 6, 11 Memb. 17, relating to
the Llanthony case, stating that an Irish king's bench writ of error might be taken to the Irish parliament,
and 'the Judgement of the Parliament here [in Ireland] is not to be Questioned'.   **140, 23–141, 8** *That this
... Observance of, &c.* – cited from Domville, 'Disquisition', p. 65. Re-enacting English statutes in Ireland
gave rise to similar constitutional and jurisdictional clashes on other occasions. See intro. p. 18, for the
English commons' objections to the attempted re-enactment of the English 1696 Act for the Better
Security of his Majesty's Royal Person in 1697.

in this Realm, for the Wealth of the
same, or to such others, as by
Sufferance of Your Grace and Your
Progenitors, the People of the Realm
5 *have taken at their Free Liberties by*
their own Consent; and have bound
themselves by long Use and Custom to
the Observance of, &c.[1]

This Declaration, with the other
10 Clauses of the said English Act, is
verbatim recited[2] in the Irish *Act of*
Faculties; and in the said Irish Act it
is Enacted, *That the said English*
Act, and every thing and things
15 *therein contained, shall be Established,*
Affirmed, Taken, Obey'd and[3]
Accepted within this Land of Ireland
as a good and perfect Law, and shall be
within the said Land of the same
20 *Force, Effect, Quality, Condition,*
Strength and Vertue, to all Purposes
and Intents, as it is within the Realm
of England; (if so, then the said
Clause declares our *Right*[4] of being
25 bound only by Laws to which we
Consent, as it does the *Right of the*
People of England) *And that all*
Subjects within the said Land of
Ireland, *shall*[5] *enjoy the Profit and*
30 *Commodity thereof, in like manner*

---

1 &c.] `&c´ (*perhaps add. later at end of MS line*) **H**   2 Declaration … recited] Declaration [is Recited an<d>] … recited **H**   3 *Obey'd and*] [and] obeyd, and **H**   4 *Right*] Right[s] **H**   5 *Subjects* … the said … *shall*] subjects [and resi<d>ents] … this said … shall [observe] [keep] **H** | Subjects … this said … shall **PC**

141, 1 *Wealth* – public welfare: *OED*, s.v. 3. Domville, 'Disquisition', p. 65, read: 'Health'.   141, 11–12 *Irish Act of Faculties* – 28 Hen. 8, c. 19 (1537), part of the legislation effecting the Henrician Reformation in Ireland, which re-enacted the English act, 25 Hen. 8, c. 21.   141, 30 *Commodity* – benefit, or advantage: *OED*, s.v. 3.

as the Kings Subjects of the Realm of England.

I am now arrived at our Sixth and Last Article Proposed, *viz.*, The *Reasons and Arguments that may be farther²* Offered *on one side and t'other in this Debate.*

I have before taken notice of the Title *England* pretends³ over us from *Conquest*; I have likewise enquired into the *Precedents* on one side and t'other, from *Acts of Parliament*, from *Records*, and from *Reports* of the Learned in the Laws. There remains another Pretence or two for this *Subordination* to be Considered; and one is founded on⁴ *Purchase*.

'Tis said, That vast Quantity of Treasure, that from time to time has been spent by *England* in Reducing the Rebellions and carrying on the Wars of *Ireland*, has given them a just *Title* at least to the *Lands* and *Inheritances* of the Rebels, and to the absolute Disposal thereof in their Parliament; And as particular Examples of this,

---

1 *marginal heading* Farther] Farther **ed.** | *F*arther **I** (*italic* F)   2 *farther*] `farther´ **H**    3 pretends] pretends [to] **H**    4 Laws ... founded on] laws opinions herein ... but one `other´ Colour of Title ... that is *By* **H** | Laws [opinions herein] ... [but ... Title] 'another ... `or two´ ... Subordination´ ... [that is by] `one ... on´ **PC**

142, 22–6 *a just ... Parliament* – such a claim had been made in [Toland], *A Letter* ([London], 1697), p. 2. This passage would seem to confirm that *The Case* was in part at least a response to that work, see further intro. pp 61–2. For the question of the forfeited Jacobite estates, see intro. p. 13.

we are told of the great Sums
Advanced by *England* for sup-
pressing the Rebellion of the Irish
Papists in 41. and Opposing the late
5   Rebellion since[1] King *WILLIAM*'s
Accession to the Throne.

To this I Answer, That in a
War[2] there is all Reason imaginable
that the Estates of the Unjust
10   Opposers should go to repair the
Damage that is done. This I have
briefly hinted before. But if we
consider the Wars of *Ireland*, we
shall perceive they do[3] not resemble
15   the common Case of Wars between
two Foreign Enemies; Ours are
rather Rebellions, or[4] *Intestine
Commotions*; that is, The *Irish
Papists*[5] rising against the *King* and
20   *Protestants* of *Ireland*[6]; and then 'tis
plain, that if these Latter, by the
Assistance of their Brethren[7] of
England, and their Purse, do prove
Victorious, the People of *England*
25   ought to be fully[8] Repaid: But then
the manner of their Payment, and
in what way it shall be Levied,
ought to be left to the People of
Ireland in Parliament Assembled:
30   And   so   it   was   after

---

1 the Irish ... since] `the ... in´ ... [Ir<ish>] late ... [under] since **H**    **2** a War] [an unjust] `a War´ **H**
3 do] [are] `do´ **H**    **4** Rebellions, or] *not in* **H** | `Rebellions or´ **PC**   **5** *Irish Papists*] Irish Papists [of
Ireland] **H**   **6** *King ... Ireland*] British Protestants of Ireland **H** | [Brittish] `King and´ ... Ireland [`and
Crown of´] **PC**   **7** Brethren] Brether (*obsolete plural of* brother: *OED*, s.v.) **H & PC**   **8** fully] `fully´ **H**

143, 7–12 *in a War ... before* – cf. *Case*, pp 24–5.   **143, 17** *Intestine* – civil, or domestic: *OED*, s.v. 1.   **143,**
21–4 *these Latter ... Victorious* – Clement, *Answer*, p. 125, objected to this hyperbole, asserting, *Case*, p. 120,
that Ireland was not regained 'one day the sooner for [the Irish Protestants'] help.'

the Rebellion of 41. The *Adventurers* then were at vast *Charges*, and
there were several Acts of
Parliament in *England* made for
5 their Re-imbursing, by disposing to
them the Rebels Lands. But after
all, it was thought Reasonable that
the Parliament of *Ireland* should do
this in their own way; and therefore
10 the *Acts of Settlement* and
Explanation, made all the former
English Acts of *No Force*; or at least
did very much *Alter* them in many
Particulars[1], as we have Noted
15 before. In like manner we allow that
England ought to be repaid all their
Expences in supressing[2] this late
Rebellion: All we desire is, That, in
Preservation of our own Rights and
20 Liberties, we may do it in our own
Methods regularly in our own
Parliament: And if the Re-
imbursement[3] be all that[4] *England*
stands upon, what availeth it
25 whether it be done this way or that
way, so it be done ? We have an
Example of this in Point between
England and *Holland* in the Glorious
Revolution under His Present
30 Majesty: *Holland* in Assisting
England Expended 600000

---

1 or ... Particulars] `or ... particulars´ **H**   2 supressing] `suppressing´ **H**   3 Re-imbursement] meer
Reimbursement **H & PC**   4 that] `yt´ (*perhaps add. later in MS line*) **H**

144, 1–15 *The Adventurers ... before* – cf. *Case*, pp 99–101.   144, 26–145, 7 *an Example ... themselves* – the
States of Holland had lent William £600,000 for his expedition to England; its repayment was one of the
first charges on the Convention Parliament in 1689: Horwtiz, *Parliament* (Machester, 1977), p. 35.
Clement, *Answer*, p. 133, rejected the analogy, pointing out that the Dutch did not conquer England, as
the English had conquered Ireland.   144, 28–9 *the Glorious Revolution* – probably the earliest instance of
the term in print in Ireland, and among the earliest recorded uses anywhere. Tradition holds that the phrase
was coined by John Hampden in later 1689: Schwoerer, *The Glorious Revolution* (Cambridge, 1992), p. 3.
It was current in England by 1692, the earliest substantiated use being on an inn sign at Northampton in
1690: Rees (ed.), *Phrases* (London, 1995), p. 183.

Pounds, and the English Parliament fairly repay'd them: It would have look'd oddly for *Holland* to have insisted on disposing of[1] Lord

5 *Powis's* and other Estates, by their own Laws, to re-imburse themselves.

[2]'Tis an Ungenerous thing to villifie good Offices, I am far from

10 doing it, but with all possible Gratitude Acknowledge the Mighty Benefits *Ireland* has[3] often receiv'd from *England*, in helping to suppress the Rebellions of this

15 Country; To *England's* Charitable Assistance our Lives and Fortunes are owing: But with all humble[4] Submission, I desire it may be considered, whether *England* did

20 not at the same time propose the *Prevention of*[5] their own *Danger*, that would necessarily have attended our Ruine; if so, 'twas in some measure their *own Battels*

25 they fought, when they fought for *Ireland*; and a great part of their[6] Expence must be reckon'd in their own *Defence*.[7]

[8]Another thing alledged against

30 *Ireland* is this; If a Foreign Na

---

1 of] *not in* H | `of PC     2 – 7 'Tis ... *Defence*] 'Tis ... Defense´ (*interpolation in margin*) H     3 thing ... has] [Office] `thing´ ... [Benefits] `Good Offices´ ... [[...] has H     4 To ... humble] [Upon] `to´ ... `humble´ H     5 propose ... of] `propose the´ prevent´ion of´ H   6 their] the´ir´ H   7 *Defence*.] *end of interpolation begun n. 2 above*   8 – p. 149, n. 3 Another ... Consideration.] `[But tis objected] `Another ... this´ ... Consideration´ (*interpolation on separate quire* ff 143r–4v *manu* WM, *but with addendum ref. to* PC p. 146) H | `An other ... is this´ *followed by further interpolation* `If ... Consideration.´ (*both interpolations, manu aman., on separate quire* ff 243r–4v) PC

145, 4–5 *Lord Powis's* – William Herbert, marquess of Powis, one of James II's most prominent Catholic supporters, had fled to France in 1688 and was subsequently outlawed: *Complete peerage*, s.v. **145, 8–26** *'Tis an ... Ireland* – this claim particularly angered Clement, *Answer*, epist. dedic., and pp 135–9. **145, 29–149, 14** *Another ... Consideration* – these points relating to the commercial threat from Ireland and its alleged status as a colony were late interpolations in the text (cf. app. crit.), which responded to objections raised in pamphlets attacking Irish woollen exports in early 1698. This section provided the main target of Davenant's criticism of Molyneux in *An essay upon ... the ballance of trade* (London, 1699).

Object. *Ireland*
prejudicial to
England's Trade,
therefore to be
Bound.[1]

tion, as *France* or *Spain* for instance,
prove prejudicial to *England*, in its
Trade, or any other way; *England*, if it
be stronger, redresses it self by Force

5 of Arms, or Denouncing War; and
why may not *England*, if *Ireland* lies
cross their Interests, restrain *Ireland*,
and bind it by Laws, and maintain
these Laws by Force?

10 [2]To this I answer: First, That it
will hardly be instanced, that any
Nation ever Declared War with
another, meerly for[3] over-topping
them in some signal Advantage,

15 which otherwise, or but for their
Endeavours, they might have
reaped. *War* only is Justifiable for
Injustice done, or *Violence* offer'd, or
Rights detain'd. I cannot by the Law

20 of Nations, quarrel with a Man,
because he, going before me in the
Road, finds a Piece of Gold, which
possibly, if he had not taken it[4] up, I
might have light upon and gotten.

25 'Tis true, we often see Wars
commenced on this Account *under-*
hand, and on Emulation in Trade
and Riches; but then this is never
made   the   *Open*   *Pre-*

---

1 *marginal heading* | *not in* **H & PC**   2 To] *no new para.* **H & PC**   3 for] [from] for **H**   4 it] `it´ (*add.*
later in MS line) **H**

146, 5 *Denouncing* – declaring: *OED*, s.v. denounce, 1.   **146, 17–19** *War … detain'd* – these three
justifications for making war roughly corresponded to those cited by Pufendorf, *De jure naturæ et gentium*,
bk 8, chap. 6, sect. 3 (though the order differed).   **146, 24** *light* – obsolete past participle of light, i.e. come
upon unexpectedly or by accident: *OED*, s.v. 10d.

tence, some other *Colour* it must receive, or else it would not look *fair*; which shews plainly, that this Pretence of *being Prejudicial*, or of

5 reaping Advantages which otherwise you might partake of, is not *Justifiable* in it self. But granting that it were a good Justification of a War with a *Foreign*

10 Nation, it will make nothing in the Case between *England* and *Ireland*; for if it did, why does it not operate in the same manner between *England* and *Scotland*, and

15 consequently in like manner draw after it *England's* binding *Scotland* by their Laws at *Westminster*: We are all the *same* Kings Subjects, the Children¹ of one *Common Parent*;

20 and tho' we may have our *Distinct* Rights and Inheritances absolutely within our selves; yet we ought not, when these do chance a little to interfere to the prejudice of one or

25 t'other side, immediately to² treat one another as Enemies; fair Amicable Propositions should be proposed, and when these are not hearkened to, then 'tis time enough

30 to be at Enmity, and use Force.³

---

1 consequently … *same* … Children] Consequently, [would] … `same´ … [Family] Children **H** 2 to] `to´ (*perhaps add. later in line*) **H** 3 Propositions … Force.] Compositions … `be proposed … and´… force´.´ [and Enmity.] **H**

147, 12–17 *why … Westminster* – the reference was presumably to the conflict between England and Scotland over the activities of the Darien Company. Cf. *Case*, p. 93. **147, 17–19** *We are … Parent* – cf. dedication, *Case*, p. A3r.

'Object. *Ireland*
a *Colony.*

The last thing I shall take
Notice of, that some raise against
us, is, That *Ireland* is to be look'd
upon only as a *Colony* from
5   *England*:² And therefore as the
Roman Colonies were subject to, and
bound by, the Laws made by the
Senate at *Rome*; so ought *Ireland* by
those made by the *Great Council* at
10   *Westminster.* Of all the Objections
raised against us, I take this to be
the most Extravagant; it seems not
to have the least *Foundation* or
Colour from *Reason* or *Record*: Does
15   it not manifestly appear by the
Constitution of *Ireland*, that 'tis a
Compleat Kingdom within it self?
Do not the Kings of *England* bear
the *Stile of Ireland* amongst the rest
20   of their Kingdoms? Is this
Agreeable to the nature of a *Colony?*
Do they³ use the Title of Kings of
Virginia, New-England, or *Mary-
Land?* Was not *Ireland* given by
25   *Henry* the Second in a Parliament
at *Oxford* to his Son *John*, and
made thereby⁴ an *Absolute Kingdom*, *separate* and wholly *Independent* on *England*, till they both
30   came United again in him, after the

---

1 *marginal heading*] *not in* PC   **2** from *England*] `from England' H    **3** Do they] Does[[s]]t[[he]]hey H    **4** thereby] `thereby´ H

148, 3–5 *That Ireland ... England* – later C.17 English lawyers introduced the concept of the acquisition of territory by way of plantation, a claim extended to Ireland by the Irish Society's counsel in the bishop of Derry appeal in 1698: Shower (ed.), *Cases* (London, 1698), p. 80. Other writers, such as Cary, used the term 'colony' in the sense of a dependent territory in order to justify complete control of Irish trade. See Cary, *An Essay* (Bristol, 1695), pp 3–4; [Toland], *A Letter* ([London], 1697), p. 3; [Clement], *The Interest* (London, 1698), p. 22, and Cary, *Vindication*, dedic.   **148, 3–10** *Ireland ... Westminster* – the case for Ireland's being classified as a colony was discussed at length by Clement, *Answer*, pp 140–57. He distinguished a 'Gothick' pattern of settlement with new and independent governments hived off from the metropolis, from a 'Roman' one, which retained citizenship and the laws of the mother country, as was the case of Ireland (ibid., 149–52).   **148, 6–8** *Roman ... Rome* – cf. *Letter ... on ... regulating and advancing the woollen industry* (London, 1698), pp 6, 8–9. The claim was dismissed at greater length in *Some thoughts* (London, 1698), 6–7.   **148, 10–14** *Of all ... Record* – however, cf. Davenant, *An Essay* (London, 1699), pp 105–6: 'we take them so far to be a Colony ... (by the Interpretation both of Law and Reason) as renders them still dependant upon their Mother-Kingdom'. *Extravagant* – excessive, or fantastically absurd: *OED*, s.v. 6. *Colour* – show of reason, pretext: *OED*, s.v. 12.   **148, 15–17** *by the Constitution ... it self* – under the 1541 act for the kingly title, cf. *Case*, p. 41.   **148, 23** *New England* – presumably a general reference to the six New England colonies rather than to James II's short-lived Dominion of New England, dissolved at the revolution. Cf. Barck & Lefler, *Colonial America* (New York, 1968), pp 209–12.   **148, 24–149, 2** *Was not ... Issue* – cf. *Case*, pp 46, 53.

Death of his Brother *Richard* without Issue? Have not multitudes of
Acts of Parliament both in *England*
and *Ireland*, declared *Ireland a*
5 *Compleat Kingdom*? Is not *Ireland*
stiled in them All, the *Kingdom*, or
Realm of *Ireland* ? Do these *Name*s
agree to a *Colony*?¹ Have we not a
Parliament, and Courts of
10 Judicature? Do these *things* agree
with a *Colony* ? This on all hands
involves² so many Absurdities, that
I think it deserves nothing more of
our Consideration.³
15 These being the only remaining
Arguments that are⁴ sometimes
mention'd *Against us*, I now
proceed to offer what I humbly
conceive *Demonstrates* the Justice of
20 our Cause.⁵
And herein I must beg the
Reader's Patience, if now and then I
am forced lightly to touch upon
some Particulars foregoing. I shall
25 Endeavour all I can to avoid prolix
Repetitions; but my Subject
requires that sometimes I just
mention, or refer to,⁶ several Notes
before delivered.

---

1 Is not ... *Colony* ?] *not in* H | `Is ... *Colony* ?´ (*interpolation in margin*) PC   2 involves] [con] involves
([con] *perhaps for* [con<tains>]) H   3 Consideration.] *end of interpretation begun p. 145, n. 7 above*
4 These ... Arguments ... are] This ... Argument ... is H | Th[[is]]ese ... Argument´s´ ... [is] `are´ PC
5 the Justice ... Cause.] our Cause against our Adversarys H | `the Justice of´ ... Cause [against our
Adversarys] `.´ PC    6 or ... to] `or ... to´ H

149, 8–10 *Have ... Judicature* – the kernel of Ireland's claim to legislative independence on the basis of its
having a parliament, courts, and administration *prout in Anglia*. Cf. dedication, p. A3r above.   149, 17–20
I now ... Cause – the ten numbered points which follow, taking us to the conclusion of the book, drew
extensively on Domville, 'Disquisition', pp 58–69.   149, 28–9 *Notes ... delivered* – i.e. matters already
related: *OED*, s.v. note sb. 1, 3; deliver, s.v. 11.

First therefore, I say, *That
Ireland should be Bound by Acts of
Parliament made in* England, *is
against Reason, and the Common
Rights of all¹ Mankind.*

5

All Men are by Nature in a state
of Equality, in respect of
Jurisdiction or Dominion: This I
take to be a Principle in it self so
evident, that it stands in need of
little Proof. 'Tis not to be conceiv'd,
that Creatures of the same Species
and Rank, promiscuously born to all
the same Advantages of Nature, and
the use³ of the same Faculties,
should be Subordinate and Subject
one to another; These to this or that
of the same Kind. On this Equality
in Nature is founded that Right
which all Men claim, of being free
from all Subjection to Positive
Laws, till by their own *Consent* they
give up their Freedom, by entring
into Civil Societies for the common⁴
Benefit of all the Members thereof.
And on this *Consent*⁵ depends the
Obligation of all *Humane Laws*;
insomuch that without it, by the
Unanimous Opinion of

10

15

20

25

1 *all*] `all´ **H** 2 *marginal heading*] *not in* **PC** 3 born ... use] born [together] ... `same´ ... [same] use **H**
4 their Freedom ... common] this ... [Publick] Common **H** | this ... Common **PC** 5 *Consent*] `Consent´
(perhaps add. later at end of MS line) **H**

150, 1–5 *First ... Mankind* – passage denounced by English commons committee: *Commons Jnl [Eng.]*, xii,
p. 326. 150, 6–25 *All Men ... thereof* – based on Locke, *Treatises*, ii, §4, but omitting his references to the
deity; the phrase *that Creatures ... Faculties* was taken verbatim from lines 9–12. Cf. *Case*, pp 113–14.

all *Jurists*, no Sanctions are of any *Force*. For this let us Appeal, amongst many,[1] only to the *Judicious* Mr. *Hooker's Eccles. Polity*, Book I. sec.10.

5 *Lond*. Edit 1676. Thus He.

Howbeit, Laws do not take their Constraining force from the Quality of such as Devise them, but from that Power which doth give them the

10 *strength of Laws. That which we spake before, concerning the Power of Government, must here be applied to the Power of making Laws whereby to Govern, which Power God hath over*

15 *All; and by the Natural Law, whereunto he hath made all subject, the Lawful Power of making Laws, to command whole Politick Societies of Men, belongeth so properly unto the*

20 *same entire Societies, that for any Prince or Potentate, of*[2] *what kind soever upon Earth, to exercise the same of himself,* and not either by express Commission *immediately and*

25 *personally receiv'd from God,* or else by Authority derived at the first from their *Consent,* upon whose Persons they impose Laws, *it is no better than meer Tyranny. Laws they*

30 *are not therefore, which* Publick Ap-

---

1 no ... amongst many] [Laws and] no ... `amongst many´ (*add. later at end of MS line*) **H**   2 – p. 160, n. 3 *what kind ... suffer* it.] (*corresponding pages of* **PC** *missing, see further intro. p. 66*)

151, 6–153, 17 *Howbeit ... Agreed* – taken verbatim (bar occasional link words) from Hooker, *Of the laws* (London, 1666), pp 21–2. In citing this material Molyneux followed in the footsteps of Locke, who likewise termed its author 'the Judicious *Hooker*': *Treatises*, ii, §§5, 15, 61.   **151, 17–152, 1** *the Lawful ... made so* – cited in Locke's footnote to *Treatises*, ii, §134. Sith – since: Johnson, *Dictionary*, s.v.

probation *hath not made so*: But
Approbation not only they Give,
who Personally declare their *Assent
by Voice, Sign, or Act; but also when*

5   *others do it in their Names,* by Right
Originally, at the[1] least, derived
from them: *As in Parliaments,
Councils,* &c.

     Again, Sith Men Naturally

10   *have no full and perfect Power to
command whole Politick Multitudes
of Men; therefore utterly without our
Consent, we could in such sort be at no
Mans Commandment living. And*

15   *to be commanded we do consent, when
that Society whereof we are part, hath
at any time before consented, without
revoking the same after by the like
Universal Agreement. Wherefore as*

20   *any Mans Deed past is good, as long
as himself continueth, so the Act of a
Publick Society of Men, done five
hundred years sithence, standeth as
theirs who presently are of the same*

25   *Societies, because Corporations are
Immortal; we were then alive in our
Predecessors, and they in their
Successors do still live. Laws therefore
Humane of what kind soever, are*

30   *available by Consent,* &c.

---

1 the] `ye´ H

152, 8 &c. – both Locke and Molyneux omitted several crucial lines from Hooker at this point, that
showed his requirements for consent to have been sufficiently inexigent not only to have allowed the
English parliament to legislate for Ireland but even to accommodate the commands of 'an absolute
Monarch'. 152, 9–19 *Sith Men ... Agreement* – also cited in Locke's footnote to *Treatises*, ii, §134.
152, 22–3 *five hundred ... sithence* – the period cited by Hooker conveniently coincided with the notional
(but emotive) 'five hundred years' which Molyneux, King and others ascribed to the Irish constitution
(cf. *Case*, pp A3r, 105, 172). *Sithence* – ago: *OED*, s.v. sith, adverb 4. 152, 30 *available* – valid: *OED*, s.v. 1b.

And again, *But what matter the*
Law of Nations doth contain, I omit
to search; the strength and vertue of
that Law is such, that no particular
5 *Nation can lawfully prejudice the same*
by any their several Laws and
Ordinances, more than a Man by his
Private Resolutions the Law of the
whole Commonwealth or State wherein
10 *he liveth; for as Civil Law being the*
Act of a whole Body Politick, doth
therefore over-rule each several[1] part of
the same Body; so there is no Reason
that any one Commonwealth of it self,
15 *should to the Prejudice of another,*
annihilate that whereupon the whole
World hath Agreed.

To the same purpose may we
find the Universal Agreement of all
20 Civilians, *Grotius, Puffendorf, Lock's*
Treat<ise of> Government,[2] &c.

[3]*No one or more Men, can by*
Nature challenge any *Right, Liberty*
or *Freedom,* or any Ease in his
25 *Property[4], Estate* or *Conscience,* which
all other Men have not an *Equally*
Just Claim to. Is *England* a *Free*
People? So ought *France* to be. Is
Poland so ? *Turky* likewise, and all

---

1 *several*] several **H** | (**PC** *missing*) | *Civil* **I**   2 Agreement ... Civilians ... Treat<ise of> Government]
[Consent] `agreement´ ... the Jurists ... Treat. of Government **H** | (**PC** *missing*)   3 – p. 154, n. 2 No ...
Mankind.] `No ... Mankind.´ (*interpolation in margin*) **H**    4 by ... *Property*] `by Nature´ ... Property [and] **H**

153, 19–20 *Universal Agreement ... Puffendorf* – this claim ignored the crucial distinction that for
Pufendorf, once the state was established, there was no continuing role for popular consent in the law-
making process. Future law depended solely on the will of the prince. See Pufendorf, *De jure naturae et*
gentium, bk 1, chap. 7, sect. 13 (1712 transl., i, p. 50–1).   **153, 20–1** *Lock's ... Government* – Locke's
authorship of *Two treatises* is here asserted without even the caveat in *Case,* p. 27.   **153, 22–154, 3** *No one*
... Mankind – in this Molyneux made good his claim, *Case,* p. 3, to plead the case not merely of Ireland but
of all mankind. *Challenge* – assert one's right to, or lay claim to: *OED,* s.v. 5.

the *Eastern*[1] *Dominions, ought* to be so: And the same runs throughout the whole *Race of Mankind.*[2]

Secondly, 'Tis against the Common Laws of *England,*[3] which are of Force both in *England* and *Ireland*, by the *Original Compact* before hinted. It is Declared by both Houses of the Parliament of *England*, 1 *Jac.* cap.1. *That in the High Court of Parliament, all the whole Body of the Realm, and every particular Member thereof, either in Person, or by Representation (upon their own Free Elections) are* by the Laws of this Realm *deem'd to be Personally present.* Is this then the common Law of *England*, and the Birth-right of every Free-born English Subject? And shall we of this Kingdom be deny'd it, by having Laws imposed on us, where we are neither Personally, nor Representatively present? My Lord *Cooke* in his 4th Inst. cap.1. saith, That *all the Lords Spiritual and Temporal, and all the Commons of the whole Realm, ought* ex Debito Justiciæ[*] *to be Summon'd to Parliament, and none of them ought to be Omitted.* Hence

Against the Common Law of *England.*

5

10

15

20

25

30

[*][of right]

---

1 *Eastern*] [[Ṣul]]Eastern ([Ṣul] *perhaps for* [Ṣul<tan´s>]) **H**   2 *Mankind.*] *end of interpolation begun p. 153, n. 3 above*   3 of *England*] [both] of England [and Ireland] **H**

154, 1 *the Eastern Dominions* – presumably the Ottoman empire; the change shown in app. crit. suggests Molyneux had originally intended 'the Sultan's Dominions'.   **154, 4–157, 15** *Secondly ... Contest it* – based on Domville, 'Disquisition', pp 58–60, who, as the references show, had derived much of his material from Coke's *Institutes*. The claim that England's right to legislate for Ireland was against common law, was the first of Domville's concluding arguments.   **154, 4–8** *Secondly ... hinted* – passage denounced by English commons committee: *Commons Jnl [Eng.]*, xii, p. 326.   **154, 10–17** *1 Jac. cap. 1 ... present* – cf. 1 Jac. I, c. 1, §2.

[*][General Council]

[**][Common Council]

[***][Nothing can have the force of law, that is contrary to reason]

5

it is call'd *Generale Concilium*[*] in the Stat. of *Westminst.* I. and *Commune Concilium*,[**] because it is to comprehend all Persons and Estates in the whole Kingdom. And this is the very Reason given in the Case of the *Merchants of Waterford* foregoing, why Statutes made in *England*, should not bind them in¹ *Ireland*,

10

Quia non habent Milites hic in Parliamento; because they have no *Representatives* in the Parliament of *England*. My Lord *Hobbard* in the Case of *Savage* and *Day*, pronounced

15

it for Law, That whatever is against Natural Equity and Reason, is against Law; Nay, if an Act of Parliament were made against Natural Equity and Reason, that Act was void.

20

Whether it be not against Equity and Reason, that a Kingdom² regulated within itself, and having its own Parliament, should be Bound *without their Consent*, by the

25

Parliament of another Kingdom,³ I leave the Reader to consider. My Lord *Cooke* likewise in the first Part of his Institutes, fol.97.b. saith, *Nihil quod est contra Rationem est*

30

Licitum.[***] And in the old *Modus*⁴ *Tenendi Parliamenta* of

---

1 in] [of] `in´ H    2 Kingdom] [Nation] Kingdom H    3 *without* ... Kingdom,] `without ... Consent´ ... [Laws] `Parliament´ ... Kingdom, [be not against] H   4 old *Modus*] [Case of the Island of Ely in his 10th Report, tis resolved, that all] Old *Modus* H

155, 5–13 *the very ... England* – cf. esp. *Case*, p. 120.   155, 13–19 *My Lord Hobbard ... void* – the objection was to the mayor and aldermen of London acting as judges of the legality of their own customs in violation of the rule *nemo sui iudex* [no one should be judge in his own case]: Hobart, *Reports* (London, 1671), pp 85–6 (identified in Domville, 'Disquisition', p. 58). The view that a positive law in contradiction with reason (which is to be understood as either natural law or the principles of the common law) was accordingly void was also found in St Germain's *Doctor and student* [1511] (London, 1974), p. 15.   155, 17–19 *if an Act ... void* – cf. Hobart, *Reports* (London, 1671), p. 86: 'an Act of Parliament made against natural equity, as to make a man judge in his own case is void in itself'.   155, 20–6 *Whether ... consider* – not in Domville, 'Disquisition', p. 58. 155, 21–2 *a Kingdom ... itself* – that is, presumably, an independent or absolute, as opposed to a subordinate or dependent kingdom. See *OED*, s.v. regulate 1.   155, 26–30 *My Lord Cooke ... Licitum* – Coke expressed similar views in his report on Bonham's case (1610): *8th Rep.*, f. 118r. Modern opinion interprets this as invoking a principle of strict statutory interpretation rather than judicial review, in line with Coke's attachment to parliamentary sovereignty. Cf. Weston, 'England' in *The Cambridge history* (Cambridge, 1991), p. 389; Nenner,

England, said to be Writ about
Edward the Confessor's time, and to
have been Confirmed and Approved
by *William the Conqueror*. It is
5 expresly declared, That all the *Lords*
Spiritual and Temporal, and the
Knights, Citizens, and Burgesses ought
to be summoned to Parliament. The
very same is in the *Modus* sent into
10 *Ireland* by *Henry* the 2d. And in
King John's Great Charter dated 17.
Johannis, 'tis granted in these words,
Et ad habend. Commune Concilium
Regni de Auxiliis & Scutagiis
15 *Assidendis, Submoneri faciemus*
Archiepiscopos, Episcopos, Abbates,
Comites, & Majores Barones, Regni
Sigillatim per Literas Nostras, &
faciemus submoneri in generali per
20 *Vicecomites* omnes alios, &c.[*]
Math. Paris ad An. 17. *Johann*. All
are to be Summoned to Parliament,
the *Nobility* by special Writts; the
Commons by general Writts to the
25 Sheriffs. And is this the *Common*
Law of *England* ? Is this part of
those[1] *Liberæ Consuetudines*[**], that
were contained in the Great *Charter*
of the *Liberties* of the People of
30 *England*; and were so solemnly
granted by *Henry* II.

[*][And in order to the holding
of a Common Council of the
Kingdom for settling Aids and
knights' services, we will cause
the Archbishops, Bishops,
Abbots, Earls, and greater
Barons of the kingdom to be
individually summoned by our
writ, and we will cause all
others to be summoned by the
Sheriffs.]

[**][free customs]

---

1 part of those] [th] part of those ([th] *perhaps for* [th<ose>]) **H**

'Liberty' in *Liberty secured?* (Stanford, CA, 1992), pp 98–9; Burgess, *Absolutism* (London, 1996), pp 183–5.
155, 30–156, 4 *the old Modus … Conqueror* – Molyneux was more explicit here as to the Saxon origin of
the English Modus (cf. Coke, *2nd Inst.*, p. 7) than in *Case*, p. 30. He thought better of adding a reference
to the Men of Ely's case, cited by Domville, 'Disquisition', p. 58, from Coke's *10th Rep.*, pp 142–3. Cf. app.
crit. **156, 10–21** *in King … alios, &c.* – from clause 14 of the original Magna Carta granted by John in
1215 (cf. Domville, 'Disquisition', p. 59): Paris, *Historia maior* (London, 1641), p. 257. This key clause was
omitted from subsequent reissues of the charter till the Confirmation of the Charters of 25 Edw. 1 (1297).
See further *Case*, p. 158 and nn.

King *John*, and *Henry* the 3d, to
the *People of Ireland*, that they
shou'd Enjoy and be Govern'd by;
and unto which they were sworn to
5   be Obedient; And shall they be of
Force *only in England*, and not in
Ireland? Shall *Ireland* Receive these
Charters of Liberties, and be no
Partakers of the *Freedoms* therein
10   contained? Or do these words
signifie in *England one thing*, and in
Ireland no such thing? This is so
repugnant to all Natural Reason and
Equity, that I hope no Rational Man
15   will Contest it: I am sure if it be so,
there's an end of all Speech amongst
Men; All Compacts, Agreements,
and Societies, are to no purpose.

     3. It is against the Statute Laws
20   both of *England* and *Ireland*: this
has been[1] pretty fully discuss'd[2]
before; however I shall here again
take notice. That (*a*) in the 10.[4] of
Henry the 4th it was Enacted in
25   *Ireland*, that Statutes made in
England should not be of Force in
Ireland, unless they were Allowed
and Published by the Parliament of
Ireland. And   the   like
30   Statute   was   made   the   29th

Against the Statute Law both of *England* and *Ireland*.

[3](*a*) See before
pag. 65.

---

1 this ... been] [and several Charters of Libertys granted to the Kingdom] [`In the 10th´] `this ... been´
H   2 discuss'd] discuss'd H | disuss'd I   3 *marginal note] in* H | (**PC** *missing*)   4 10.] [20] `10´th H

157, 19–159, 27 *It is against ... Effect* – where Domville, 'Disquisition', pp 60–3, treated the violation of
statutes and charters as a single matter Molyneux separated them into his third and fourth points.
157, 19–20 *3. It is against ... Ireland* – passage denounced by English commons committee: *Commons Jnl
[Eng.]*, xii, p. 326.

of *Henry* the 6th. And in the 10th
Year of *Henry* the 7th. Chap.23
Irish Statutes, The Parliament
which was held at *Drogheda*, before

5 Sir *Christopher Preston*, Deputy to
Jaspar Duke of Bedford, Lieutenant
of *Ireland*, was declared Void, for
this Reason amongst others, *That
there was no General Summons of the*

10 *said Parliament to all the Shires, but
only to Four.* And if Acts of
Parliament made in *Ireland* shall
not Bind that People, because some
Counties were omitted: how much

15 less shall either their Persons or
Estates be Bound[1] by those Acts
made in England, whereat no one
County, or Person of that Kingdom
is present ? In the (*b*) 25th of

20 *Edward* the 1st. Cap.6. It was
Enacted by the Parliament of
England in these Words, *Moreover
from henceforth we shall*[3] *take no
manner of Aid, Taxes, or Prizes, but*

25 *by the Common Assent of the Realm.*
(*c*) And again in the *Statute of
Liberties,* by the same King, Cap.I.
De Tallag. non *Concedend.*[*] it is
Enacted in these Words. *No Tallage*

30 *or Aid shall be Taken or Levy'd by Us,
or Our Heirs, in Our Realm, without*

[*][concerning the non-granting
of Tallage]

[2](*b*) Pultons Col.
Eng. Stats. Edit.
1670. pag. 63.

[4](*c*) ibid. page 75.

---

1 either... Bound] [those Acts made in *England* bind] either ... Estates, [whereof] be Bound **H**
2 *marginal ref.*] *in* **H** | (**PC** *missing*)   3 *shall*] [have] shall **H**   4 *marginal ref.*] *in* **H** | (**PC** *missing*)

158, 1–11 *in the 10th ... Four* – this parliament held in 1493 by Robert (*not* Christopher) Preston, Lord
Gormanston, as deputy to Jasper (Tudor), duke of Bedford, was voided the following year by the final act
of Poynings' Parliament (10 Hen. 7, c. 23). Cf. Domville, 'Disquisition', p. 62. See further, Richardson &
Sayles, *Irish Parliament* (Philadelphia, 1952), p. 365.   **158, 19–159, 4** *25th of Edward ... Land* – Molyneux
has been misled by Pulton, *A Collection* (London, 1670), pp 63, 75, into thinking that the 1297
Confirmation of the Charters, 25 Edw. 1, predated *De tallagio non concedendo* (which Pulton, *A Collection*
(London, 1670), p. 75, assigned to 34 Edw. 1). In fact *De tallagio* represented a preliminary baronial draft
of the Confirmation subsequently conceded by the king. See Prestwich, *Edward I* (London, 1997), pp
427–30. *De tallagio* is no longer considered a statute. *Tallage* – a feudal levy imposed by the king: *OED*, s.v.
158, 25 *Common ... Realm* – Domville, 'Disquisition', p. 62, rendered this as the 'Common Consent of
Parliament'.

the Good Will and Assent of Archbishops, Bishops, Earls, Barons,
Knights, Burgesses, and other Freemen
of the Land. The¹ like Liberties are
5   specially Confirm'd to the Clergy, (d)   ²(d) ibid. page. 113.
the 14th of Edward the 3d. And were
these Statutes, and all other Statutes
and Acts of the Parliament of
England Ratified, Confirmed, and
10   Adjudged by several Parliaments of
Ireland to be of Force within this
Realm: And shall the People of
Ireland receive no Benefit by those
Acts ? Are those Statutes of Force in
15   England only; And can they add no
Immunity or Priviledge to the
Kingdom of Ireland, when they are
received there ? Can the King and
Parliament make Acts³ in England to
20   Bind his Subjects of Ireland without
their Consent; And can he make no
Acts in Ireland with their Consent,
whereby they may receive any
Priviledge or Immunity? This were to
25   make the Parliaments of Ireland
wholly Illusory, and of no Effect. If this
be Reasonable Doctrine, To what
end was Poyning's Law in Ireland, (e)   (e) 10 H.7. c.22.
that makes all the Statutes of England
30   before that,⁴ in Force in this King

---

1 The] [And] the **H**   **2** *marginal heading*] *in* **H** | (**PC** *missing*)   **3** and ... Acts] `and Parliament´ ... Acts [of Parliament] [`and´] **H**   **4** before that] `before that´ **H**

159, 4–6 *The like ... Edward the 3d.* – 'A Statute for the Clergy ... 1340': Pulton, *A Collection* (London, 1670), p. 113.

dom ? This might as well have been done, and again undone, when they please, by a single Act of the English Parliament. But[1] let us not

5 make thus light of Constitutions of Kingdoms, 'tis *Dangerous* to those who *do it*, 'tis *Grievous*[2] to those that *suffer it.*[3]

[4]Moreover, Had the King or his

10 Council of *England*, in the 10th year of *Hen*. VII. in the least dreamt of this Doctrine, to what end was all that strict Provision made by *Poyning's Act*, Irish Stat. cap.4.

15 That no Act of Parliament should pass in *Ireland*, before it was[5] first Certified by the Chief Governour and Privy Council here, under the Broad Seal of this Kingdom, to the

20 King and his Privy Council in *England*, and received their Approbation, and by them be remitted hither[6] under the Broad Seal of *England*, here to be pass'd

25 into a Law ? The design of this Act, seems to be the Prevention of any thing passing in the Parliament of *Ireland Surreptitiously*, to the *Prejudice* of the *King*, or the *English*

30 *Interest* of *Ireland*. But this was a

---

1 when ... But] `when ... please´ ... `But´ **H**   2 Grievous] odious **H**   3 *suffer* it.] (*end of passage missing from* **PC** *starting p. 151, n. 2 above*)   4 – p. 161, n. 4 Moreover ... Times.] `Moreover ... Times.´ (*interpolation on separate sheet f.* 149r) **H**   5 was] were **H & PC**   6 to the ... hither] `to ... England´ ... `hither´ **H**

160, 4–8 *let us ... suffer it* – cf. *Case*, p. 174; the sentiment perhaps derived from Molesworth, *An Account* (London, 1694), ch. 6. Cf. B[rewster], *An Answer* (Dublin, 1698), p. 16.   **160, 19** *Broad Seal* – recte Great Seal, cf. *Case*, p. 81.   **160, 26–30** *the Prevention ... Ireland* – a major objective of the original 1494 act had been to prevent an Irish-born governor, such as the earl of Kildare, from undermining the royal interest in Ireland. See further Bradshaw, *The Irish constitutional revolution* (Cambridge, 1979), p. 147.

needless¹ Caution, if the King, and
Parliament of *England*, had Power
at any time to revoke or annul any
such Proceedings. Upon this *Act* of
5   *Poynings*, many and various Acts
have pass'd in *Ireland*, relating to the
Explanation, Suspension, or farther
Corroboration² thereof, in divers
Parliaments, both in *Henry* the
10 Eighth's, *Phil. & Mary's*, and Q.
Eliz. Reigns; for which see the Irish
Statutes. (*a*) All which shew that
this *Doctrine* was hardly so much as
Surmised in those Days, however we
15 come to have it raised in these
Latter Times.⁴

Fourthly, 'Tis against several
Charters of Liberties Granted unto
the Kingdom of *Ireland*:⁵ This
20 likewise is clearly made out by what
foregoes. I shall only add in this
place, That in the Patent-Roll of
the 17 *Rich*.2. m.34. *de Confirma-
tione*, There is a Confirmation of
25 several *Liberties* and *Immunities*
granted unto the Kingdom and
People of *Ireland* by *Edw.*III. The
Patent is somewhat long, but so
much as concerns this Particular, I
30 shall render *verbatim*, as I have it⁶

(*a*) 28 H.8. c.4. 28
H.8. c.20. 3 & 4
Ph.&M. c.4. 11
Eliz. Ses.2. c.1. 11
Eliz. Ses.3. c.8.³

**Against several
Concessions made
to *Ireland*.**

1 *Surreptitiously* ... needless] `surreptitiously´ ... [Kings] Prejudice [or Dislike] `of the King ... Ireland´ ...
[to what end was this] `this ... needles´ **H**   2 farther Corroboration] [Interpretation] `farther
corroboration´ **H**   3 and ... Statutes. (a)] `and´ ... `for ... Statutes (a)´ (*marginal note* `(a) ... Ses. 3. c.8´
also subsequently interpolated) **H** | (*marginal note, manu aman.* **PC**)   4 Times.] *end of interpolation begun*
p. 160, n. 4 above   5 *Ireland*;] Ireland. [in par] ([par] *perhaps for* [par<ticular>]) **H**   6 as ... it] `as´ ... it
[by me] **H**

161, 17–163, 22 *Fourthly ... Junii* – closely follows Domville, 'Disquisition', pp 60–3.   **161, 17–19** *Fourthly,*
'Tis ... of Ireland – passage denounced by English commons committee: *Commons Jnl [Eng.]*, xii, p. 326.

Transcribed from the Roll by Sir *William Domvile*, Attorny General in *Ireland* during [1]the whole Reign of King *Charles* II. *Rex omnibus, &c.*

5 *Salutem: Inspeximus Literas Patentes Domini Edwardi nuper Regis Angliæ, Avi nostri fact. in haec verba: Edwardus*[2] *Dei Gra. Rex Angliæ & Franciæ, & Dominus Hiberniæ,*

10 *Archiepiscopis, Episcopis, Abbatibus, Prioribus, Ministris nostris tam Majoribus quam Minoribus, & quibuscunque aliis de Terra nostra Hiberniæ fidelibus nostris ad quos*

15 *Præsentes Literæ pervenerint, Salutem: Quia, &c. Nos hæc quæ sequuntur Ordinanda Duximus & firmiter observanda, &c. Imprimis, vizt. Volumus & Præcipimus quod Sancta*

20 *Hibernicana Ecclesia suas Libertates & Liberas Consuetudines illesas habeat, & eis Libere gaudeat & Utatur. Item volumus & præcipimus quod nostra & ipsius Terræ Negotia presertim Majora*

25 *& Ardua in Consiliis per Peritos Consiliaros nostros ac Prælatos & Magnates & quosdam de Discretioribus & Probioribus Hominibus de partibus vicinis ubi ipsa Concilia teneri*

30 *Contigerit propter hoc evocandos, in Parliamentis vero per ipsos Concilia-*

[*][The King to all, &c. greeting. We have inspected the Letters Patents of Edward our grandfather, lately King of England, in these words: "Edward by the Grace of God, King of England, and France, and Lord of Ireland, to the Archbishops, Bishops, Abbots, Priors, our Officers both of lower and higher rank, and to all our other faithful subjects of the land of Ireland to whom these presents shall come, greeting. We have thought it good that the following things be ordained and strictly observed, &c. to wit. First, we will and command, that our holy Irish Church have her own liberties and free customs unimpaired, and that she use and enjoy them without restraint. Item, We will and command that our business, and that of the land itself, especially the greatest and most difficult, be managed, explained, faithfully discussed, and also determined without the influence of fear, favour, hatred, or reward, in Councils, by our skilful Counsellors and Prelates, and Magnates, and some of the most discreet and upright men, to be convened for this purpose from the neighbourhood of the places where it shall happen that such Councils shall be held; and in Parliaments, by our said Counsellors and ...]

---

1 – p. 172, n. 1 the whole ... of *Great*] (*corresponding pages of* **PC** *missing, see further intro.p. 66*)   **2** Edwardus] EDWARDUS (*emphatical*) **H**

162, 1–4 *by Sir William ... Charles II* – added by Molyneux to Domville, 'Disquisition', p. 60.

[*][... Prelates and Nobles, and others of the aforesaid land, as use requires, acccording to justice, law, custom, and reason, &c. In Testimony whereof we have caused these our letters to be made patent, Witness ourself at Westminster, the 25th day of October, in the 31st year of our reign in England, and 18th in France." Now we accounting the aforesaid appointments, ordinances, and commands, and all and singular the things contained in the above recited letters, as being already established and right, do for ourselves and our heirs, to the utmost of our power, accept, approve, ratify and confirm the same, as the aforesaid letters do fully show. In testimony whereof, witness the King at Westminster, on the 26th of June.]

ros nostros ac Prælatos & Proceres aliosque de terra predicta prout Mos Exegit secundum Justiciam Legem Consuetudinem & Rationem tractentur deducantur & fideliter timore favore odio aut prætio post positis discutiantur ac etiam terminentur, &c. In Cujus Rei Testimonium has Literas nostras fieri fecimus Patentes <.> Teste meipso Apud Westminst. 25 die Octob. Anno Regni nostri[1] Angliæ 31, Regni vero Franciæ 18. Nos autem Ordinationes Voluntates & Præcepta Prædicta ac omnia alia & singula in Literis prædictis Contenta Rata Habentes & Grata Ea pro nobis & Hæredibus nostris quantum in nobis est Acceptamus, Approbamus, Ratificamus, & Confirmamus prout Literæ præædictæ rationabiliter testantur.[2] In Cujus, &c. Test. Reg. apud Westminst. 26 die Junii.[*]

5

10

15

20

Fifthly, It is inconsistent with the *Royalties* and *Præeminence* of a *Separate* and *Distinct Kingdom.* That we are thus a *Distinct Kingdom,* has been clearly made out before. 'Tis plain, the Nobility of *Ireland* are an Order of Peers clearly Distinct from the Peerage of *England,* the

25

30

Inconsistent with the Royalties of a Kingdom.

---

1 nostri] nostri **ed** | nostris **H, PC & I**   2 testantur] testantur **H**] testanter **I**

163, 24–165, 21 *Fifthly ... the other* – based on Domville, 'Disquisition', pp 63–4, though the order of the points has been somewhat changed.   **163, 24–6** *Fifthly ... Kingdom* – passage denounced by English commons committee: *Commons Jnl [Eng.],* xii, p. 326.   **163, 25** *Royalties* – prerogatives, rights or privileges pertaining to a sovereign: *OED,* s.v. §5a.   **163, 29–164, 7** *the Nobility ... Kingdoms* – not mentioned in Domville, 'Disquisition', p. 63, but cf. Bolton, 'Declaration', p. 21. 'Legislative power in Ireland', f. 129v, argued that if the English parliament were to legislate for Ireland, Irish peers should sit in the English lords, as well as Irish representatives in the English commons. The question of English peers' privileges in Ireland had been raised when the appeal in the chancery case of the English peer Lord Ward and Dudley v. the earl of Meath came before the Irish house of lords in 1697: *Lords Jnl [Ire],* i, p. 526.

Priviledges of the one, extend not into the other Kingdom; a Lord of *Ireland* may be Arrested by his Body in *England*, and so may a Lord

5 of *England* in *Ireland*, whilst their Persons remain Sacred in their respective Kingdoms: A *Voyage Royal* may be made into *Ireland*, as the Year-Book, 11 *Hen*.4. 17.fol.7.

10 and[1] Lord *Cook* tells us; [2]and King John in the 12th year of his Reign of *England*, made a *Voyage Royal* into *Ireland*; and all his Tenants in Chief, which did not attend him in

15 that Voyage, did pay him *Escuage*, at the Rate of Two Marks for every *Knights Fee*; which was imposed *super Prælatis & Baronibus pro Passagio Regis in Hibernia*[*], as

20 appears by the Pipe-Roll, Scutag. 12 *Johannis Regis in Scaccario Angl.*3.[**], Which shews that we are a *Compleat Kingdom* within ourselves, and not little better than[4] a *Province*, as some

25 are so Extravagant as[5] to Assert; none of the Properties of a *Roman Province* agreeing in the least with our Constitution. 'Tis Resolved in Sir *Richard*[6] *Pembrough*'s Case in

30 the 44th of *Edw*.III. That Sir *Richard* might lawfully refuse[7]

[*][upon the Prelates and Barons for the King's passage into Ireland]

[**][of King John in the Exchequer of England]

---

1 the Year-Book ... and] `the ... and´ **H**   2 – 3 and ... *Angl*.] `and ... *Angl*.´ (*interpolation in margin*) **H**   3 *Angl*.] *end of interpolation began n.2 above*.   4 little ... than] [meerly] `little ... than´ **H**   5 some ... as] some of our Adversarys [have the Assurance] `are ... as´ **H** | (**PC** *missing, but presumably* Adversarys *was deleted here as were all other instances of the word in* **PC** *cf. intro. p. 39, n. 181*)   6 *Richard*] [John] Rich **H**   7 might refuse] lawfully refused **H** | (**PC** *missing*)

164, 7–10 *A Voyage ... tells us* – a military expedition overseas, for which the king was entitled to call on the service of his vassals: *OED*, s.v. voyage, 2b. The case, as reported in the Year Book, 11 Hen. 4, f. 7r, related to the seizure of Thomas, duke of Gloucester's entourage on a voyage royal into Ireland in 1410. However, Mayart, 'Answer' (Dublin, 1750), p. 112, cited a contrary judgement from 7 Edw. 4 (1468–9) that a voyage royal could not be undertaken to Ireland.   **164, 15** *Escuage* – money payment in lieu of military service: *OED*, s.v. 2.   **164, 22–8** *we are ... Constitution* – cf. *Case*, pp 148–9. Davies, *A Discoverie* (London, 1612), pp 124–5, argued against drawing any such parallel on the grounds that the Romans gave their law to their provinces. However, Bishop King complained to Bishop Gilbert Burnet, 29 Jan. 1697/8, that Ireland was a province and suffered the fate of provinces in being badly governed, referring to Davies for corroboration.   **164, 28–165, 10** *'Tis Resolved ... England* – based on Coke, *2nd Inst.*, pp 47–8, which commented on Magna Carta, cap. 29, the chapter regarded from the late C.16 as the crucial guarantee of personal freedom under the law: Baker, *The Reinvention* (Cambridge, 2017), pp 40–2, 346–9. Ch. 29 is one of only three clauses in Magna Carta remaining in force today.

[*][for service done and to be done]

[**][He is a King who has no King <over him>, so a kingdom is that which is not subject to another kingdom]

the King, to serve him as his *Deputy in Ireland*, and that the King could not *Compel* him thereto, for that were to *Banish him into another Kingdom*, which is against *Magna Charta*, Chap.29. Nay, even tho' Sir *Richard* had great Tenures from the King, *pro servitio Impenso & Impendendo*[*], for that was said must be understood *within the Realm of England, Cooks* 2d Inst. pag. 47. And in *Pilkington's*[1] Case aforemention'd, *Fortescue* declared, That the Land of *Ireland* is and at all times hath been a *Dominion Separate and Divided from England*. How then can the Realms of *England* and *Ireland*, being *Distinct*[2] *Kingdoms* and *Separate Dominions*, be imagin'd to have any *Superiority* or *Jurisdiction* the one over the other. 'Tis absurd to fancy[3] that Kingdoms are *Separate* and *Distinct* meerly from the *Geographical distinction* of *Territories*. Kingdoms become *Distinct* by *Distinct Jurisdictions*, and *Authorities Legislative* and *Executive*;[4] and as *Rex est qui Regem non habet*, so *Regnum est quod alio non Subjicitur Regno*[**]: A Kingdom can have no *Supream*; 'tis in it self Supream with-

5

10

15

20

25

30

---

1 *Pilkington's*] Sr J. Pilkingtons **H** | (**PC** *missing*)   2 Distinct] Distinct **ed** | DIstinct **I**   3 fancy] [I] fancy ([I] *perhaps for* [I<magine>)] **H**   4 *Authorities … Executive*] `Authoritys´ Legislat[ure]ive [Authoritys] `and Executive´ **H**

165, 11–16 *in Pilkington's … England* – cf. *Case*, p. 124.   **165, 21–166, 12** *'Tis absurd … Consent* – passage denounced by English commons committee: *Commons Jnl [Eng.]*, xii, p. 326. On the irrelevance of geographical separation for political separateness, cf. 'Legislative power in Ireland', f. 127r, and Mayart, 'Answer' (Dublin, 1750), p. 127.   **165, 28** *Rex … habet* – paraphrased from Martial, *Epigrams* (Cambridge, MA, 1963), i, pp 142–3. Ussher, *A Speech* (London, 1631), p. 3, rendered it, 'there being nothing so contrary to the nature of Soveraigntie, as to have another superior power to over-rule it'. Cf. Davies, *A Discoverie* (London, 1612), p. 18; Domville, 'Disquisition', p. 63.

in it self, and must have all Jurisdictions, Authorities and Præemi-
nencies to the Royal State of a
Kingdom belonging, or else 'tis

5 none: And that *Ireland* has all these,
is declared in the Irish Stat. 33 *Hen.*
VIII. c.1. The chief of these most
certainly is, the *Power of Making
and Abrogating its own Laws*, and

10 being bound only by such to which
the *Community* have given their
Consent.

Against the Kings
Prerogative.

Sixthly, It is *against the Kings
Prerogative,*[1] that the Parliament of

15 *England* should have any Co-ordinate
Power with Him, to introduce New
Laws, or Repeal Old Laws Established in *Ireland.* By the Constitution
of *Ireland* under *Poyning's Act*, the

20 King's Prerogative in the Legislature
is advanced to a much higher Pitch
than ever was[2] Challenged by the
Kings in *England*, and the Parliament
of *Ireland* stands almost[3] on the same

25 bottom as the King does in *England*;
I say *almost* on the same Bottom, for
the Irish Parliament have not only a
Negative Vote (as the King has in
England)[4] to whatever Laws the King

---

1 *Prerogative*] [Supremacy and] Prerogative **H**   2 *Ireland* ... ever was] Ireland. [For if the King be the only
supream in each of his Dominions] ... advanced [far] ... was ever **H** | (**PC** *missing*)   3 almost] [much]
`almost´ **H**    4 I say ... *England*)] [that is to say,] `I say ... for´ ... [first] `not only´ ... `(as ... England)´ **H**

166, 6–7 *Irish ... 33 Hen. VIII. c. 1.* – i.e. the 1541 act for the kingly title.   **166, 13–18** *Sixthly ... Ireland* –
passage denounced by English commons committee: *Commons Jnl [Eng.]*, xii, p. 325.   **166, 13–18** *It is ...
Ireland* – as in Domville, 'Disquisition', p. 64, but reading 'Supremacy' for 'Prerogative'. Domville further
claimed that the nature of the royal supremacy was such that neither in England nor Ireland did the two houses
of parliament have any co-ordinate legislative power with the king: 'That must alwaise Abide sole and intire in
himselfe, and Can Admitt of no Copartners.' Cf. Hale, *Jura coronæ* (London, 1680), p. 47: 'the making of laws
is the peculiar and incommunicable Privilege of the Supreme Power, and the Office of the two Houses is only
Consultative or Representative'.   **166, 18–25** *By the Constitution ... England* – namely, the king's power to
forbid the introduction of legislation of which he disapproved into the Irish parliament. *Challenge* – assert one's
right to, or lay claim to: *OED*, s.v. 5.   **166, 23–167, 3** *the Parliament ... before them* – this assertion of the
importance of the 'Negative Vote' in Ireland must have perplexed later C.18 readers, for whom Poynings' Law
had come to represent an unjustified shackle on their constitution (cf. *Case*, p. 81). Clement, *Answer*, p. 159,
however, pointed out that in England the king assented to legislation independently of the privy council.

and his Privy Councils of both or
either Kingdom, shall lay before
them; but have also a Liberty of
Proposing to the King and his Privy
5   Council here, such Laws as the[1]
Parliament of *Ireland* think expe-
dient to be pass'd. Which Laws
being thus Proposed to the King,
and put into form, and Transmitted
10   to the Parliament here, according to
Poyning's Act, must be Pass'd or
Rejected in the *very Words*, even to
a *Tittle*, as they are laid before our
Parliament, we cannot alter the least
15   *Iota*. If therefore the *Legislature* of
Ireland stand on this Foot, in
relation to the King, and to the
Parliament of *Ireland*; and[2] the
Parliament of *England* do Remove
20   it from this Bottom, and Assume it
to themselves, where the Kings
Prerogative is much *Narrower*, and
as it were *Reversed*, (for there the
King has only a *Negative Vote*) I
25   humbly conceive 'tis an *Incroachment*
on the Kings *Prerogative*: But this I
am sure, the Parliament of *England*
will be always very Tender of, and
His Majesty will be very loth to
30   have such a Precious Jewel of his
Crown handled rufly.[3]

1 both ... the] both `or either´ Kingdom[s] ... [his] the **H**   2 and] [If] `and´ **H**   3 and His ... rufly.] *not in* **H** | (**PC** *missing*)

167, 3–15 *have also ... Iota* – for the process, whereby Irish MPs came to introduce draft legislation in the form of heads of bills, despite the restrictions of Poynings' Law, see intro. p. 9. The English commons committee examining *The Case* extended its inquiries to the heads-of-bills procedure, which it regarded as a serious abuse of Poynings' Law, though nothing finally came of the matter. See Courthorpe, 'The Minutebook' in *Camden Miscellany*, 20 (1953), pp 50–1, and further Sanford Papers, Somerset Archives, Taunton, DD/SF/13/2909. **167, 15–26** *If therefore ... Prerogative* – a similar point in relation to the English lords' usurpation of the appellate jurisdiction of the Irish house was made in the Irish lords' representation to George I on the Sherlock v. Annesley case in 1719: *Lords Jnl [Ire.]*, ii, p. 656. **167, 15** *Legislature* – the exercise of the power of making law: *OED*, s.v. 2. **167, 31** *rufly* – i.e. roughly.

The happiness of our Constitutions
depending on a Right Temperament between the *Kings*[1] and the
Peoples Rights.

5   Seventhly, It is *against the Practice*
of all former Ages. Wherein can it
appear, that any Statute[2] made in
England, was at any time since the
Reign of *Henry* the Third, allowed
10   and put in practice in the Realm of
Ireland, without the *Authority* of the
Parliament of *Ireland*. Is it not
manifest by what foregoes,[3] that from
the Twentieth of King *Henry* the
15   Third, to the Thirteenth of *Edward*
the Second, and from thence to the
Eighteenth of *Henry* the Sixth, and
from thence, to the Thirty-Second of
Henry the Sixth, and from thence, to
20   the Eighth of *Edward* the Fourth, and
from thence, to the Tenth of *Henry*
the seventh, there was special care
taken to Introduce the Statutes of
England, (such of them as were
25   necessary or[4] convenient for this
Kingdom) by degrees, and always
with *Allowance*, and *Consent* of the
Parliament and *People of Ireland*. And
since the *General Allowance*, of all

**Against the
Practice of
former Ages.**

---

1 our ... *Kings*] [their] `our´ ... kings Prerogative **H** | (**PC** *missing*)   2 Statute] [Par] Statute ([Par] *perhaps*
for [Par<liament>] **H**   3 by ... foregoes] `by ... foregoes´ **H**   4 or] [and beh] `or´ ([beh] *perhaps for*
[beh<oving>] **H**

168, 2 *Temperament* – mixture or composition; alternatively, adjustment, or compromise: *OED*, s.v. 2, 9.
168, 5–6 *Seventhly ... Ages* – passage denounced by English commons committee: *Commons Jnl [Eng.]*, xii,
p. 326.   **168, 5–169, 26** *It is against ... England* – closely based on Domville, 'Disquisition', pp 65–6. The
question of binding by comprehensive words was discussed, *Case*, p. 81.   **168, 14–22** *the Twentieth ...*
Henry the seventh – 20 Hen. 3 denoted the Statute of Merton, the earliest English statute referred to in
Bolton, *Statutes of Ireland* (Dublin, 1621), p. 67 n., as having been re-enacted in Ireland (in 13 Edw. 2;
1320). The rest are other re-enactments of English statutes up to Poynings' Parliament (1494). See the
index of statutes cited.

the English Acts and Statutes in the Tenth of *Henry* the Seventh, there have several Acts of Parliament, which were made in *England* in the

5 Reigns of all the Kings from that Time, Successively to this very Day, been particularly Receiv'd by Parliament in *Ireland*,¹ and so they become of force here, and not by

10 reason of any *General Comprehensive* words, as some Men have lately fancied. For if by *General Comprehensive Words*, the Kingdom of *Ireland* could be bound by the

15 Acts of Parliament of *England*, what needed all the² former *Receptions* in the Parliament of *Ireland*, or what *use will there be of the Parliament of Ireland at any time*? If the Religion,³

20 Lives, Liberties, Fortunes, and Estates of the Clergy, Nobility, and Gentry of *Ireland*, may be dispos'd of, without their *Privity* and *Consent*, what Benefit have they of any Laws,

25 Liberties, or Priviledges granted unto them by the Crown of *England*? I am loth to give their Condition an *hard Name*; but I have no other Notion of *Slavery, but being Bound by a Law to*

30 *which I do not Consent.*

---

1 by … *Ireland*,] `By Parliament´ in[to] Ireland, [`by´] **H**   2 the] those **H** | (**PC** *missing*)   3 Religion] `Religion´ **H**

169, 19–26 *If the Religion … England* – cf. Bolton, 'Declaration', p. 19.   **169, 28–30** *I have … Consent* – cf. Locke, *Treatises*, ii, § 22. A similar claim that the English parliament sought to reduce the Anglo–Irish to slavery was found in Bishop King's unpublished answer to [Toland], *A letter from a gentleman* ([London], 1697): P. Kelly, 'A pamphlet attributed to John Toland', *Topoi* (1985), p. 89 and in various letters King wrote in the autumn of 1698.

Against the Resolution of Judges.

Eighthly, 'Tis against several *Resolutions* of the *Learned Judges*, of former times in the very Point in Question. This is manifest from
5 what foregoes in the Case[1] of the *Merchants of Waterford*, *Pilkington*'s Case, Prior of *Lanthony*'s Case, &c. But I shall not here inlarge farther thereon.

Destroys Property.

10 Ninthly, The Obligation of all Laws having the same Foundation, if *One* Law may be Imposed *without Consent*, any *Other* Law whatever, may be Imposed on us
15 *Without our Consent*. This will naturally introduce *Taxing us without our Consent*; and this as necessarily destroys our *Property*. I have no other Notion of *Property*,
20 but a *Power of Disposing my Goods as I please*, and not as another shall Command:[2] Whatever another may *Rightfully* take from me *without my Consent*, I have certainly no
25 *Property* in. To *Tax* me without Consent, is little better, if at all, than *down-right Robbing me*. I am sure the Great Patriots of Liberty and Property, the Free Peo-

---

1 Case] Cases **H** | (**PC** *missing*)   2 Command:] Command: [This the Holy Writ seems to Justify, [*Cannot I*] `Is it not lawful for me to´ *do what I will with my Own?* (*marginal note beside line reads* Mat. 20. v.15)] **H**

170, 1–3 *Eighthly … Point* – passage denounced by English commons committee: *Commons Jnl [Eng.]*, xii, p. 326.   **170, 1–9** *'Tis against … thereon* – a more extended treatment was provided in Domville, 'Disquisition', pp 67–8.   **170, 10–15** *Ninthly, … Taxing … Consent* – passage denounced by English commons committee: *Commons Jnl [Eng.]*, xii, p. 326.   **170, 18–25** *I have … Property in* – in this Molyneux combined the traditional view of property in terms of alienability with Locke's concept in *Treatises*, ii, §138 : 'I have truly no *Property* in that, which another can by right take from me, when he pleases, against my consent.' See app. crit. for biblical quotation, which Molyneux had considered inserting at this point.   **170, 25–171, 2** *To Tax … Abhorrence* – Mayart, 'Answer' (Dublin, 1750), p. 77, asserted the English parliament's right to raise revenue in Ireland as well as to legislate for it, while Cary, *Vindication*, p. 47, cited the 1353 Staple Act (27 Edw. 3) as evidence of their authority to impose customs dues in Ireland. In contrast, Clement, *Answer*, p. 104, claimed that the English parliament had never sought to raise taxes 'upon any Members of her Empire, without the Consent of their Representatives', a view shared by Atwood, *History*, pp 207–8.

ple[1] of *England*, cannot think of such a thing, but with Abhorrence.

Lastly,[2] The People of *Ireland* are left by this Doctrine in the Greatest *Confusion* and *Uncertainty* Imaginable. We are certainly bound to Obey the *Supream Authority*[3] over us; and yet hereby we are not permitted to know *Who* or *What* the same is; whether the *Parliament of England*, or *that of Ireland*, or *Both*; And in what Cases the *One*, and in what the *Other*: Which *Uncertainty* is or may be made a Pretence at any time[4] for *Disobedience*. It is not impossible but the Different Legislatures we are subject to, may Enact Different, or Contrary Sanctions: Which of these must we obey?[5]

To conclude all, I think it highly *Inconvenient*[6] for *England* to *Assume* this *Authority* over the Kingdom[7] of *Ireland*: I believe there will need no great Arguments to convince the Wise Assembly of English Senators, how *inconvenient* it may be to *England*, to do that which may

Creates
Confusion.

Inconvenient to
England to Assume
this Power.

---

1 Peo [171][ple]] Peo [171]ple **ed** |Peo [171]Ple **I**   2 Lastly] 10. Lastly **H** | (**PC** *missing*)   3 *Authority*] [power] Authority **H**   4 at … time] `at … time´ **H**   5 It is … obey ?] *not in* **H** | (**PC** *missing*) 6 *Inconvenient*] Inconvenient and Dangerous **H** | (**PC** *missing*)   7 Kingdom] [People] Kingdom **H**

171, 3–6 *Lastly … Imaginable* – passage denounced by English commons committee: *Commons Jnl [Eng.]*, xii, p. 326.   **171, 6–20** *We are … we obey* – cf. pp 44, 66 above. Such confusion could embrace conflicting jurisdictional claims as well as conflicting legislation. In March 1699 the English lords ordered the arrest of Bishop King, together with officers of the Irish lords responsible for punishing officials in Derry who had carried out the orders of the English lords in the summer of 1698: *Derry MSS*, ii, pp 263–4, 274. Cf. *Lords Jnl [Eng.]*, xvi, p. 418 (29 Mar. 1699).   **171, 21–172, 17** *To conclude … Consider* – final passage denounced by English commons committee: *Commons Jnl [Eng.]*, xii, p. 326. Bolton, 'Declaration', pp 13–14, placed great emphasis on the doctrine of inconveniency, citing Littleton to the effect: '*Argumentum ab inconvenienti est in lege fortissimum.* – An argument drawn from any inconvenience is of the greatest force in Law.' *Inconvenience* – danger or injury, rather than incommody or discomfort: *OED*, s.v. 4, 7.

make the *Lords* and *People of Ireland*
think that they are not *Well Used,*
and may drive them into *Discontent.*
The *Laws* and *Liberties of England*
5   were granted above five hundred
years ago to the People of *Ireland,*
upon their Submissions to the
Crown of *England,* with a Design to
make them *Easie* to *England,* and to
10   keep them in the Allegiance of the
King of *England.* How Consistent it
may be with True Policy, to do that
which the People of *Ireland* may
think is an *Invasion* of their Rights
15   and Liberties, I do most humbly
submit to the Parliament of *England*
to Consider. They are Men of *Great*[1]
Wisdom, Honour, and *Justice*: and
know how to prevent all future
20   *Inconveniencies.* We have heard Great
Out-cries, and deservedly, on Breaking the *Edict of Nantes,* and other
Stipulations; How far the Breaking
our Constitution, which has been of
25   Five Hundred years standing,
exceeds that, I leave the World to
judge. [2]It may perhaps be urg'd, That
'tis *convenient* for the State of
England, that the *Supream Council*
30   thereof should make their Jurisdi-

---

1 *Great*] (*end of passage missing from* **PC** *starting p. 162, n. 1 above*)   2 It may] *new para.* **H**

172, 9 *Easie* to *England* – presumably meaning, not constituting a threat or danger to England. Cf. *OED,*
s.v. easy, 10a.   **172, 12–17** *to do ... Consider* – Clement, *Answer,* p. 161, riposted that few people in Ireland
would support Molyneux's 'Menace'.   **172, 20–3** *We have ... Stipulations* – the revocation of 1685 gave rise
to accusations from across Protestant Europe that Louis had broken faith in revoking the so-called
'perpetual edict' of Henry IV: Mandrou, *Louis XIV* (Paris, 1973), pp 289–90. Given the lords' protest on
the subject by Bishop King and others (*Lords Jnl [Ire.],* i, p. 636), the 'other [broken] Stipulations' may refer
to the Irish parliament's truncated confirmation of the Treaty of Limerick in 1697. Cf. app. crit.

ction as *Large* as they can. But with
Submission, I conceive that if this
Assumed Power be not *Just*, it
cannot be *convenient* for the State.
5 What *Cicero* says in his *Offices*, *Nihil*
est Utile, nisi idem sit Honestum[*], is
most certainly true. Nor do I think,
that 'tis any wise *necessary* to the *Good*
of *England* to *Assert* this High Juris-
10 diction over *Ireland*. For since the
Statutes of this Kingdom are made
with such *Caution*, and in such *Form*,
as is prescribed by *Poyning's Act* 10
H.7. and by the 3d and 4th of *Phil.*
15 and *Mar.* and whilest *Ireland* is in
English hands,[1] I do not see how 'tis
possible for the Parliament of *Ireland*
to do any thing that can be in the
least *prejudicial* to *England.* But on
20 the other hand, If *England assume* a
Jurisdiction over *Ireland*, whereby
they think their *Rights* and *Liberties*
are *taken away; That their Parlia-*
ments are rendred meerly nugatory, and
25 that their Lives and Fortunes
Depend on the Will of a *Legislature*[2]
wherein they are *not Parties;* there
may be ill Consequences of this.
Advancing the Power of the
30 Parliament of *England*, by

[*][Nothing is profitable which is not upright]

1 and whilest ... *hands*] `and ... hands´ **H**   2 *Legislature*] Legislative **H** | Legislat[[ive]]ure **PC**

173, 5–6 *What Cicero ... Honestum* – cf. Cicero, *De Officiis*, bk III, ch. 7, sect. 34.

breaking the *Rights* of an *other*, may in time have ill Effects.[1]

[2]The *Rights of Parliament* should be preserved *Sacred* and *Inviolable*, wherever they are found. This kind of Government, once so *Universal* all over *Europe*, is now almost *Vanished* from amongst the Nations thereof. Our Kings Dominions are the only Supporters[3] of this noble *Gothick Constitution*, save only what little remains may be found thereof in *Poland*. We should not therefore make so light of that sort of Legislature, and as it were Abolish it in One Kingdom of the Three,[4] wherein it appears;[5] but rather Cherish and Encourage it wherever we meet[6] it.

5

10

15

20

───────────

FINIS.

25

──────────────[7]

1 *Advancing* … Effects] [which Almighty God Prevent] `Advancing … Effects even on the Parliament of England´ **H** | Advancing … Effects [even … England] **PC**   2 The *Rights*] *no new para.* **H**   3 *Vanished* … Supporters] [perishd_∧ These Nations are] `vanish'd … thereof´ … [up] supporters ([up] *perhaps for* [up<holders>] **H**   4 and … Three] `and … three´ **H**   5 wherein it appears] *not in* **H** | `wherein it appears´ **PC**   6 meet] find **H** | [find] `meet´ **PC**   7 [rule] FINIS. [rule]] *not in* **H & PC**

174, 2 *ill Effects* – Molyneux thought better of continuing 'even on the Parliament of England'. Cf. app. crit.   **174, 6–19** *This … meet it* – cf. Molesworth's call for the English to cherish their 'Gothic' parliamentary freedoms in the face of spreading absolutism in Europe: Molesworth, *An Account* (London, 1694), ch. 6, esp. pp 42–3.

The Modus Tenendi Parliamenta in Hibernia

AS THE TITLE IMPLIES, THE English Modus Tenendi Parliamentum consisted of instructions for summoning parliament and organizing its sessions, and was written sometime between 1311 and the early 1370s, probably in the reign of Edward III.[1] Presenting itself as the official directions issued by William the Conqueror, the Modus – despite contradicting contemporary practice in a number of respects – long enjoyed a spurious authority arising from the lack of other accounts of how parliament functioned.[2] The Modus also served as ammunition in parliamentary conflicts from the 1380s to the mid-seventeenth century. While its dating and the purpose for which it was written have been the subject of extensive historical debate, the most recent assessment by Kerby-Fulton and Justice suggests that the author of the Modus was a senior exchequer or chancery clerk familiar with parliamentary procedures, and that its divergences from what actually happened in parliament probably represented a deliberate effort to draw attention to certain contemporary issues. Emphasizing the central role of the commons as the representatives of the community at the expense of both king and lords, the Modus was the product of a civil service culture interested in fostering social and political reforms such as were later raised in the English parliaments of Richard II.[3]

Despite Sayles' ostensibly persuasive arguments in favour of the priority of the Irish Modus, it is more likely that the English Modus was the original text.[4] The manuscript stemma show the Irish version to have been adapted (in Latin) from the French text of the English Modus preserved in the Courtenay cartulary, brought to Ireland by Philip de Courtenay, who had been sent as governor in 1383–5.[5] The Irish Modus was subsequently exploited as a weapon in parliamentary conflicts by both governors and their opponents in the later 1380s and '90s. Later interpolations in the text, such as the designation of the archbishop of Cashel as guardian of parliamentary records, adapted the document for use

---

1 Cf. Taylor, *English historical literature* (Oxford, 1987), pp 212–16; Kerby-Fulton & Justice, 'Reformist intellectual culture', *Traditio*, 53 (1998), pp 150–2, 190–6.

2 For this reason manuscripts of the Modus are often found bound with statutes and other official documents: Taylor, *English historical literature* (Oxford, 1987), pp 212–13.

3 Kerby-Fulton & Justice, 'Reformist intellectual culture', *Traditio*, 53 (1998), pp 161–2, 176.

4 Sayles, *'Modus tenendi'* in Lydon (ed.), *England and Ireland* (Dublin, 1981), pp 132–9, argued this on the basis that various practices described in the Modus were more applicable to what happened in the Irish parliament than the English. See further Prestwich, 'The *Modus tenendi*', *Parliamentary History*, 1 (1982), pp 224–5.

5 Now BL Add. MS 49359, and incidentally the earliest surviving manuscript of the Modus in any form: Kerby-Fulton & Justice, 'Reformist intellectual culture', *Traditio*, 53 (1998), pp 163–6.

in the factional struggle between the Butlers and the Talbots that began in the governorship of Sir John Talbot (later first Earl of Shrewsbury). It was in the early stages of this conflict that the interpolated version of the Irish Modus was seized from Sir Christopher Preston at Clane in 1418, as recounted in *The Case* (pp 32–4).[6] While little further was heard of the document in the second half of the fifteenth century, a (no longer complete) transcript of the Irish Modus, together with a reference relating it to a dispute over parliamentary precedence, is found in Archbishop Allen's register for 1533, though there was no subsequent mention of the Irish Modus until the early the early seventeenth century.[7]

The English Modus, as known in the fourteenth and earlier fifteenth centuries, went into eclipse until its publication by John Hooker in the 1570s, after which it enjoyed a considerable vogue among parliamentarians and antiquaries. The document's significance for the English parliamentary opposition in the early seventeenth century ensured that the emergence of an Irish version of the Modus generated considerable interest. According to Maude Clarke, its 'discovery' resulted from the arrival of a copy in London in the summer of 1613, brought by recusant opponents of Sir John Davies' election as speaker of the Irish commons as evidence for an appeal to the privy council.[8] Corroboration of this claim is seemingly provided by the presence of the medieval original of Hakewill and Cotton's version of the Irish Modus among Lord Keeper Ellesmere's papers in the Huntington Library, California.[9] This text, however, differs quite considerably from the Modus published by Molyneux's brother-in-law Anthony Dopping in 1692, which (as *Case*, p. 35, related) was based on an ancient roll found by Sir Francis Aungier in the treasury at Waterford, that later came into the possession of Sir William Domville.[10] The person responsible for making the Irish Modus known in England in 1614 was the MP and antiquary William Hakewill, who obtained a copy of the version brought to London the previous year (presumably thanks to Ellesmere), which he subsequently communicated to John Selden and to Sir Robert Cotton.[11] While both Coke and Cotton accepted the authenticity of the Irish Modus, neither Selden nor William Prynne regarded it as genuine.[12] Dopping, however, refused even to consider Prynne's arguments, claiming in his preface that not only had the Irish Modus been issued by Henry II but that Domville's roll

6   Pronay & Taylor (eds), *Parliamentary texts* (Oxford, 1980), pp 121–4. For the circumstances of the seizure, see Crooks, 'The background', *Analecta Hibernica*, 40 (2007), pp 5–6.

7   M.V. Clarke, 'The manuscripts', *English Historical Review*, 48 (1933), p. 597.

8   Leading the group who went to London in 1613 was Lord Gormanston, lineal heir of the Sir Christopher Preston from whom the Irish Modus had been seized in 1418: M.V. Clarke, 'The manuscripts', *English Historical Review*, 48 (1933), p. 582.

9   This version, together with the copy of the exemplification of its seizure in 1418, is now MS EL 1699 in the Huntington Library, San Marino, California. The fact that Molyneux's grandfather Daniel sought a copy from Sir Robert Cotton (now MS TCD 581, ff 10–15) would suggest early C.17 Irish Protestant antiquaries did not previously know of its existence.

10 For the publication and its variant titlepages, see intro. p. 6, n. 11 above. Domville's roll no longer survives, though a copy he had had made in 1676 is now BL Add. MS 33505. See further *Case*, p. 32 nn.

11 Hakewill's role in the discovery was recorded by John Selden to whom he sent a copy in 1614: Selden, *Titles of honour* (London, 1672), p. 614. Hakewill's transcript was published in Steele (ed.), *A bibliography* (Oxford, 1910), i, pp clxxxviii–cxcii.

12 An opinion shared by the future Archbishop Ussher, see *Case*, p. 32 nn.

was very probably the actual document that the king had sent to Ireland.[13] The copy of the Modus that Bishop King included among the precedents submitted to the English lords in 1698 was a fresh transcript of 'the Parchment Roll supposed to be the original Record' (i.e. Domville's roll), as certified by Joseph Hardisty before Sir Richard Pine, chief justice of common pleas, 4 February 1697/8.[14] King (a long-time associate of Anthony Dopping) must therefore have been given access to the roll immediately before the bishop's son Samuel lent it to Molyneux for use in *The Case* (cf. p. 36).[15] According to Pronay and Taylor, Molyneux was the last recorded person to have seen it.[16]

13 Molyneux, however, doubted the Domville roll's association with Henry II (*Case*, 36).

14 See *Lords MSS, 1697–9*, 34–9, and King's payments to 'Haidsty/Hardesty' (described as 'Mr Justice Coote's clerk') in *Derry MSS*, ii, pp 218–19. Pronay & Taylor (eds), *Parliamentary texts* (Oxford, 1980), app. ii, regard this as a less reliable version than Dopping's.

15 The draft response from the Irish privy council to the English lords' request of 8 Jan. 1697/8 for precedents relating to chancery appeals in Ireland referred to 'a very ancient roll produced before us certainly the s[ai]d Modus', suggesting the council regarded it as the actual document that Henry II had sent to Ireland: Marsh's Library, MS Z3.2.5, item 75.

16 Pronay & Taylor (eds), *Parliamentary texts* (Oxford, 1980), p. 119.

A comparison of the references to the Waterford exemplifications of medieval statutes confirming Ireland's legislative independence found in the *Statutes of Ireland* with those in the 'Declaration'

The significant passages are printed in **bold**.

A. Bolton, *Statutes of Ireland* (Dublin, 1621), p. 67, n.

13. E. 2. per parliament en cest Realme le statutes de W[estminster]. 1. W[estminster] 2. Merton, Marlebridge, & Gloucest[er] were confirmed in this kingdome, and other statutes which were of force in Engl. were referred to be examined in the next Parliament, & so many as were then allowed and published to stand likewise for laws in this kingdome. 10. H. 4. **it was enacted in this kingdom that ye statutes made in England should not be of force in this kingdome unlesse they were allowed and published in this kingdome by Parliament, and the like statute was made again Ann. 29. H. 6.** These Statutes are not to be found in the Rolls, nor any Parliament Rolls of that time, but I have seene the same exemplified under the great seale, and the exemplification remayneth in the Treasury of the citie of Waterford.

B. Bolton, 'Declaration' [1644], p. 4

(*viz.*) in 13th. of *Edw.* 2. in a Parliament in *Ireland*, the Statutes of *Merton* and *Marlebridge*, made in the time *Hen.* 3, and the statutes of *Westminster* 1st, and *Westminster* 2d, and the Statute of *Gloucester*, made in the time of *Edw.* I were confirmed and approved to be of force in *Ireland*, and all other statutes, which were of force in *England*, were then referred to be examined in the next Parliament, and so many of them, as should be then allowed, and published, to be accepted for laws in *Ireland*. **And afterwards, in a Parliament holden in *Ireland* in 19th. of *Edw.* 2. in which it was enacted, that the statutes made in *England* should not be of force in the kingdom of *Ireland*, unless they were allowed, and published in that kingdom by Parliament; the like statute was made again in 29th of *Hen.* 6.** But these statutes are not to be found in these parliament rolls, nor any parliament rolls of that time, but the same are exemplified under the great Seal, and the exemplifications were remaining in the Treasury of the city of *Waterford*.

Pamphlets relating to the Irish woollens controversy, published between December 1697 and early 1699

1 [John Toland], *A letter from a gentleman in the country, to a member of the house of commons; in reference to the votes of the 14th instant* [London. Dec.], 1697, 4 pages. Not in Wing (ed.), *Catalogue* (New York, 1994–8); copy in NLI: shelf mark Thorpe P12; reprinted in no. 2.

2 B[rewster], [Sir] F[rancis], *An answer to a letter from a gentleman in the country, to a member of the house of commons: on the votes of the 14th inst. relating to the trade of Ireland* (also reprints text of *Letter*). Two issues: London, for Geo. Huddleston, 1697 and 1698. Reprinted in Dublin, 1697; second Dublin issue, styling the author 'Sir F. B', rather than plain 'F. B.', 1698 – both for Patrick Campbell.

2a [Sir Francis Brewster], *Answer to a letter from a gentleman* … (does not reprint no. 1). Reprinted in Dublin, for Andrew Crook, 1698.

3 [Sir Francis Brewster], *A discourse concerning Ireland and the different interests thereof, in answer to the Exon and Barnstaple petitions* [to the house of commons]. London, for T. Nott, 1698.

4 *Reasons humbly offered … to the honourable house of commons for bringing in a bill … for preventing the exporting of wool from Great Britain and Ireland to France* [?Exeter], 1698, 3 pages. With special reference to the city of Exeter.

5 B. F. [? Brewster, Sir Francis], *A letter to a member of the house of commons, on a proposal for regulating and advancing the woollen industry.* London, 1698.

6 *A letter to a member of the house of commons, on regulating and advancing the woollen industry.* London, 1698. (Raises matters answered in no. 9, below.)

7 *Some considerations offered to the honourable house of commons against a bill depending on the export of wool* … [brs]. London, 1698.

8 Exeter. Eng. Gild of Incorporated Weavers, Fullers and Shearers. *The names of several persons trading in, and depending upon the manufactury of serges, within the city of Exon, and parts adjacent, lately removed from thence into the kingdom of Ireland.* Dated 2 March 1697/8 [? Exeter. 1698].

9   [Francis Annesley], *Some thoughts on the bill depending before the right honourable the house of lords for prohibiting the exportation of the woolen manufactures of Ireland into foreign parts.* London, 1698. Reprinted in Dublin, 1698: (1) by J. Darby for Andr. Bell; (2) for Joseph Ray; and (3) J. Ray for Eliphal Dobson. (Answered in no. 10 and no. 11.)

10   [Simon Clement], *The interest of England as its stands with relation to the trade of Ireland, considered ... With short remarques on a book entituled, Some thoughts on the bill ... to forreign parts.* London, by John Astwood, 1698. Reprinted in Dublin, 'to be sold by Mr John Foster', 1698.

11   [John Gardner], *The substance of the arguments for and against the bill for prohibiting the exportation of woollen manufacture from Ireland to forreign parts ... Together with some remarks on a printed paper, entituled, Some thoughts on the said bill.* London, for J. Astwood, 1698.

12   *The linnen and woollen manufactury discoursed, with the nature of companies and trade in general; and particularly, that of the companies for the linen manufactury of England and Ireland; with some reflections how the trade of Ireland hath formerly, and may now, affect England.* London, for Geo. Huddleston, 1698. (Reprint of London edn of 1691.)

13   [Alderman John Hovell, of Cork], *A discourse of the woollen manufactury of Ireland, and the consequences of prohibiting its exportation.* London, [?Mar.] 1698. Reprinted in Dublin, by 'J.B. & S.P. to be sold by Jacob Milner', 1698.

14   *Reasons humbly offered to the most honourable the house of lords on ... the bill relating to the woollen manufactury* [brs]. London. 1698.

15   *Reasons humbly offered for passing the bill tendered, prohibiting the exportation of woollen manufactures of Ireland to foreign parts* [brs]. London, 1698.

16   *A proposal for regulating and advancing the woollen manufacture ... by one that hath 30 years experience in that trade, and in importing of wool from Ireland.* London, 1698.

17   T[homas] T[ryon], *Some general considerations offered, relating to our present trade; and intended for its help and improvement.* London, for J. Harris, 1698. (Only brief ref. to Ireland, pp 5–6.)

18   William Molyneux, *The case of Ireland ... Stated.* Dublin, 1698. (Proposed London edition with special Churchill titlepage not issued – see further checklist of printings, p. 79)

19   John Cary, *A vindication of the parliament of England, in answer to a book written by William Molyneux, of Dublin, esquire, intituled The Case ... stated.* London, printed by Freeman Collins for Sam Crouch and Eliz. Whitlock, 1698; 2nd edn, London, 1701.

20   William Atwood, *The history, and reasons, of the dependency of Ireland upon the imperial crown of the kingdom of England. Rectifying Mr. Molineux's state of The Case of Ireland's being bound by acts of parliament in England.* London, 1698. Two London issues,

differing only in titlepage: for Dan. Brown and Ri. Smith; and for Dan. Brown and Tho. Leigh.

21 [Simon Clement], *An answer to Mr. Molyneux his Case of Ireland's being bound by acts of parliament in England, stated: and his dangerous notion of Ireland's being under no subordination to the parliamentary authority of England refuted* ... London, for Dan. Brown and Ri. Smith, 1698.

22 [John Cary], *To the freeholders and burgesses of the city of Bristol.* [? Bristol], [autumn] 1698. (Election address emphasizing damage caused to Bristol by Irish woollen exports.)

23 *Some thoughts on the bill ... for prohibiting the exportation of the woolen manufactures of Ireland* ... London reissue of (no. 6), bearing date 'Dec. 21 1698'. Not in Wing (ed.), *Catalogue* (New York, 1994–8); copy in BL, shelf-mark 712 g. 16 (22). (Presumably republished on introduction of 1698–9 Irish-woollens export prohibition bill, Dec. 1698.)

24 [Leslie, Charles], *Considerations of importance to Ireland, in a letter to a member of parliament there; upon occasion of Mr. Molyneux's late book: intituled, The case of Ireland's being bound by acts of parliament in England, stated* [probably London], 1698 (dated 26 Dec. 1698).

25 Davenant, Charles, *An essay upon the probable methods of making a people gainers in the ballance of trade.* London, for James Knopt, 1699. (Consideration of Irish woollen trade and critique of Molyneux's *Case* in 'Sect. III: Of the land of England and its product'.)

'The case of the parliament of Ireland'

Isaac Newton's autograph reflections on Molyneux's *Case of Ireland*[1]

TILL THE REIGN OF HENRY II IRELAND was divided amongst many Kings and Lords without any common Parliament. Then one of those Kings vizt. Dermot Prince of Leinster, being beaten by his neighbours obteined succours of some English Lords by the consent of King Henry II who was then busied in Aquitain, and by their assistance recovered his territories<.> And a little after vizt in November 1172 King Henry went[2] into Ireland with an Army, and the Kings Lords and Prelates of Ireland being terrified by the late successes of the English arms submitted and sware fealty and homage to the King and confirmed the Kingdome of Ireland to him[3] and his Heirs by Letters with seales pendent after the manner of Charters. And thereupon the King[4] convening the Irish at Lismore caused them to receive the Laws of England and to swear to be governed thereby, and in like manner calling a Council of the Irish Clergy at Cashal he made them promis conformity to the English Church, and in April following vizt 1173 returned into England. Molyn. p. 6, 7, 8, 9, 10, 11, 12, 28, 36, 37.

About five years after in a Parliament held at Oxford the King created his younger son John then 12 years old, Lord of Ireland and at his death left the Kingdom of England to his elder son Richard I but by the death of Richard and succession of John the lordship of Ireland became again united to the Crown of England[5] and hath ever since continued so. Mol. p. 39, 40, 43.

King John about the 12th year of his reign over England vizt Jun 28 1210 went into Ireland and the Irish Princes being affrighted did him homage and fealty and he granted and enjoyed them the English Laws and Customes by a Charter or Statute under his seale swearing them thereunto and placing Sheriffs and other Ministers who might judge the Irish according to those Laws. Whence they have to this day Courts of Chancery, Kings Bench, Common Pleas and Exchequer as in England. Afterwards Henry III the son and successor of K. John in the 12th year of his reign sent a Mandate to Richard de Burgh then Justice of Ireland to convene the Irish and cause to be read to them the Charter or Statute which his Father K. John had ordeined and caused them to swear unto concerning the Laws and Customes of England to be observed in Ireland and that he should cause the Irish firmly to receive and keep the said Laws and Customes and the same to be proclaimed and

---

1 Public Record Office, Kew, MINT 19, 3, ff 456–7 (Newton MS III, ff 456–7).
2 went] [going] 'went'.
3 the Kingdome … him] [[to]]of [[him]]Ireland to him.
4 the King] 'the King'.
5 England] England [Mol. p. 39, 40].

obeyed in every County of Ireland forbidding in the Kings name that no man presume to act contrary to this his Mandate. Mol. p. 44, 52. The words of the Mandate run thus. Rex Dilecto et Fideli suo Richardo de Burgo Justic' suo Hibern. salutem. Mandamus vobis firmiter præcipientes quatenus certo die et loco faciatis venire coram vobis Archiepiscopos Episcopos Abbates Priores Comites [f. 456v] et Barones Milites et libere Tenentes et Balivos singulorum Comitatium and coram eis publice legi faciatis Chartam Domini Joannis Regis Patris nostri cui sigillum suum appensum est quam fieri fecit et jurare a Magnatibus Hiberniæ de Legibus et Consuetudinibus Angliæ observandis in Hibernia. Et praecipiatis eis ex parte nostra quod Leges illas et Consuetudines in Charta prædicta contentas de cætero firmiter teneant et observent et hoc idem per singulos Comitatus Hiberniæ clamari faciatis et teneri prohibentes ex parte nostra et super foris facturam nostram nequis contra hoc Mandatum nostrum venire præsumat &c Teste me ipso apud Westm' 8 die Maii An. Regn. nostri 12. Mol. p. 53.

Thus did the Kings of England in these Reigns by their absolute and sole authority as Conquerors impose Laws on Ireland even without a Parliament, the Irish hitherto assembling not to make Laws but to submit and swear to the laws <imposed> on them by the King's command. And therefore the present Irish Parliament is of no further authority then what it derives from the grant of the Crown of England and by consequence of no authority against an Act of an English Parliament.

Some would derive the Parliament of Ireland from the Grant of Hen. II called Modus tenendi Parliamentum, but this is of suspected authority. King John and King Henry III seem the first who granted Charters and Privileges to Ireland. Edward I neare the beginning of his reign summoned them by Writs to the Parliament of England and these summons continued till towards the end of the reign of Edward III or longer. p. 95, 96, 97. Whence the lordship of Ireland was as much annexed and united by law[6] to the crown and Kingdom of England as[7] the Principality of Wales is at present. For Ireland is so firmly annexed to the crown of England (even by Acts of Parliament of both nations and particularly by Poynings Act) that whosoever is King of England is ipso facto Lord or King of Ireland p 43, 44, 127. Whence Acts of an English Parliament for setling the succession to the crown are of force in Ireland without the authority of an Irish Parliament and an Irish Act of Settlement[8] can be no more than declarative for publishing and putting in execution the Law of England and must derive its authority from that Law. And for the same reason an English Parliament has power to impose laws on Ireland for preventing or suppressing rebellions and conserving the possession of Ireland to[9] this Crown.

When the Irish had seen the manner of Parliaments in England the King began to summon them at home, and Edward III granted them Councils and Parliaments by his Letter Patents confirmed afterward by Rich II, p. 161, 162, 163. These Parliaments examined the English Statutes not yet imposed on the Kingdom by Royal authority and by degrees received them all till the 10th year of Henry VII p. 64, 68, 69. At which time their Parliaments by Poynings Act gaining a negative voice to the Kings broad [f. 457r] seal

6 by law] 'by law'.
7 as] as [Irela<nd>].
8 an Act of Settlement] i.e. an act of recognition of the succession to the crown.
9 Ireland to] Ireland [[. . .]]to.

(p. 160, 161, 166, 167)[10] they began to make their private statutes with less regard to ours, and in the next reign aspired[11] from the title of a Lordship to that of a kingdom.

However, in memory of their ancient subjection to our laws, their Courts of Justice remain to this day subordinate to ours. For a writ of error still lies from the Kings Bench of Ireland to the Kings Bench of England and thereby the Judges of our Kings Bench are Interpreters of all[12] the Irish Laws. For we are to judge them by their own Laws whether those Laws were received from us or made originally in their own Parliament. And since A writ of Error lies from our Kings Bench to our house of lords, this House and much more the King and both Houses together are Interpreters of all the Irish Laws p 71, 87, 88, 130, 131, 132, 133, 134, 135, 136, 139. So then it lies in the breast of an English Parliament to interpret and declare the meaning extent and force of all the Irish Laws not excepting those by which they claim any power to themselves.

10   (p. 160 ... 167)] '(p. 160 ... 167)'.
11   aspire] aspire – i.e. ascend, rise up: *OED*, s.v. 5.
12   all] 'all'.

Reasons against the order of the English house of lords declaring the Irish house of lords' verdict in favour of the bishop of Derry *coram non judice*[1]

REASONS AGAINST THE Order of the English house of lords, 24 May 1698, Declaring the Irish house of lords Verdict of 24 September 1697 in favour of the Bishop of Derry *coram non judice*.

1st. Because upon the conquest of Ireland by Henry the IId. he introduced the laws of England in that Kingdom, and sent over the *Modus Tenendi Parliamentum in Terminis*, the same with that of England, in which record it is said that such things may be examined and corrected, *in Pleno Parliamento et non alibi*.

2dly. Because in the 20th year of King Henry the Third, it was provided that all laws and customs which are enjoyed in England, shall be also in Ireland, and that the land shall be subject thereunto and governed thereby *sicut Dominus Johannes Ker* [recte *Rex*: TCD MS 1180, f. 7r.] *cum ultimo esset in Hibernia statuit et fieri mandavit et quod Brevia de communi jure quæ currunt in Anglia similiter currant in Hibernia*.

3dly. Because King Edward III in the 20th [recte 29th: TCD MS 1180, f. 7r.] year of his reign, ordained for the quiet and good government of the people in Ireland, that in all cases whatsoever, errors in judgment, in records, and proceedings in the courts of Ireland, shall be corrected and amended in parliament in Ireland.

4thly. Because it appears by other ancient records, *quod terra Hiberniæ inter se omnes et omnimodas habet curias prout in Anglia*.

---

1   Attributed to William Molyneux in *Case*, 1782 edn, pp 62–4. The paper is prefaced by the following note: 'The public may depend on the authenticity of the following small, but valuable piece of the great patriot, the Author of the foregoing Case, which the Editor obtained thro' the means of the Rev. Mr. *Thos Brooke Clarke*, from *William Johnson*, of the City, Esq; who copied it from the Original Manuscript in the hand-writing of the Author, written in the blank Leaves of one of his printed Cases, which he sent to the then Lord Bishop of Meath.' The earliest manuscript version of this paper is probably TCD MS 1180, ff 7r–9v., which is endorsed 'Reasons that may be given if any of the Lords heer shall think fitt to Enter their Protests'. TCD MS 1038, ff 104r–106r, is headed 'Reasons of the Lords Protesting against the Order made in the Appeal of the Society of Londonderry against the bishop of Derry'. Archbishop King's papers in Marsh's Library, MS Z.3.2.5, contain two further copies identifying the paper as the duke of Leeds' protest against the English lords' *coram non judice* verdict of 24 May 1698. See further intro. p. 51, n. 247 above. None of the manuscript versions make any reference to Molyneux.

5thly. Because a conqueror by the laws of England and of nations, having power to introduce what laws he will in the conquered country, and King Henry II. pursuant to that power, having introduced the laws of England, and particularly that of holding parliaments in Ireland, the house of lords in parliament in Ireland, may proceed to hear and determine judicially, such matters as shall be brought before them, in the same manner as the lords in parliament in England.

6thly. Because pursuant to the many concessions made by King Henry II. King John, King Henry III, and other Kings of England. [*sic*] The Lords in parliament in Ireland, have proceeded to correct and amend errors in judgment and decrees in the courts of Ireland, (as appears by the several precedents certified over to your Lordships,) and their judgments <were> never before this called in question, many of them being very irregular. It is therefore presumed to have been by a good and lawful jurisdiction, otherwise they would have been by our ancestors (who were zealous assertors of their rights) long before this called in question.

7thly. The order declaring the appeal was *coram non judice*, and null and void, will call all other judgments and decrees in question, under which many estates have been purchased, settled, and enjoyed, which will be of fatal consequence to many families, and create great discontent and dissatisfaction in that kingdom.

8thly. Because the declaring the said appeal to be *coram non judice*, and null and void, strikes at and tends to the jurisdiction of this House, for Ireland having *omnes et omnimodas curias prout in Anglia*, must include the high court of parliament, and if their high court of parliament, being an exact picture of the high court of parliament in England, cannot judicially hear and determine appeals, writs of error, and impeachments, it may from thence be alleged that this here cannot.

9thly. Because this resolution strikes at and tends to abridge the King's prerogative in Ireland; all appeals and writs of error in parliament, being *coram rege in parliamento*, and therefore these words *coram non judice* takes from the King the judicial power which is given to him there.

10thly. Because the Peers of Ireland have little else left to them beside their judicature, which if taken away, they will be of little esteem there, and many of the Peers of England have some of their titles of honour from that Kingdom.

11thly. Because it is the glory of the English laws, and the blessing attending Englishmen, that they have justice administered at their doors, and not to be drawn as formerly to Rome, by appeals which greatly impoverished the nation, and by this order, the people of Ireland must be drawn from Ireland hither, whensoever they receive any injustice from the Chancery there, by which means poor men must be trampled upon, not being able to come over to seek for justice.

12thly. The danger of altering, changing, or lessening a constitution, for above 500 years unshaken, or so much as called in question in any one thing, (the custom and usage of Courts being the law of Courts) may occasion the destruction of the whole, for the judicial power of the House of Peers in Ireland, in criminal causes by way of impeachment or otherwise, may by the same reason be called in question, as their judicature in civil causes, which will encourage evil disposed men, especially those in employment in that Kingdom, (who are generally very arbitrary) to act wickedly; and the better we preserve the constitution of Ireland, and of those plantations dependant on England, the better we shall preserve our own – and they will be barriers to ours, to prevent any invasion of theirs, and since the Kings of England have in all times in matters relating to their revenue, their grants by letters patent, and their Ministers not only empowered the Parliament of Ireland to hear, correct, reform and amend them, but also acquiesced in their judgment, it ought not now to be questioned.

13thly. Because this taking away the jurisdiction of the lords House in Ireland, may be a means to disquiet the lords there, and disappoint the King's affairs.

14thly. Because the judicial power of the House of Peers in Ireland is in no respect altered by an act of parliament, – the statute of the 10th of Hen. 7, c. 4. called Poynings Law, only directs a new form of passing bills into laws, but alters nothing of the judicial power, and their argument of their having the interpretation of all laws by a judicial power being allowed them, will enable them to make the laws what they please, will as well hold against the jurisdiction of this House, which ought not to be suffered.

Bibliography

MANUSCRIPT SOURCES

British Library, London

Egerton MS 917: Letters from Bishop King to Sir Robert Southwell, 1698.
Sloane MS 1008: Molyneux's correspondence with Bishop Borlase of Chester, 1680.
Add. MS 4223: Thomas Birch's life of William Molyneux.
Add. MS 35505: 1676 copy of William Domville's roll containing Modus Tenendi Parliamenta in Hibernia.
Add. MS 61653: Letters to Lord Galway from John Methuen and Lord Chancellor Somers, 1697–9.

Marsh's Library, Dublin

MS Z3.2.5: Papers relating to Archbishop King's appeals to Irish house of lords, 1697, and to the English house of lords, 1698.

National Library of Ireland

MS 2055: Archbishop King Papers.

Public Record Office, Kew

MINT 19, 3, ff 456–7 (Newton MS III, ff 456–7), Isaac Newton's notes on *The Case* (summer, 1698).

Robinson Library, Armagh

Item P001733040: 'Hibernica, or ancient pieces relating to Ireland', includes the 1664 version of Sir William Domville's 'Disquisition' and Sir Richard Bolton's 'Declaration' (1644).
Item P001937770: Molyneux estate papers.

Somerset Archives and Local Studies, Taunton

DD/SF/13/2909: Edward Clarke's papers relating to the commons committee inquiry into *The Case*, June–July 1698.

Trinity College, Dublin, Library

Molyneux Papers, TCD MSS 622, 881–90.
  MS 622: Molyneux's 1693 compendium of C.17 volumes of the Irish Commons Journal.
  MS 888/1, ff 127–30: 'That the legislative power in Ireland doth belong to the king by the advice of his parliament of Ireland, not of his parliament of England'.
  MS 890: papers relating to the composition of *The Case*.

Archbishop King Papers.

    Letterbooks, 750/1–6 (1696–1722).

    MS 2331: William King, 'The authority of parlements in Ireland over inferior courts ... ought not to be questioned' [1698].

MS 581: Copies of Modus Tenendi Parliamenta in Hibernia and Archbishop Ussher's notes on English statutes in Ireland.

MSS 647, 843, 860 and 1040: Copies of Sir Richard Bolton, 'A declaration setting forth how, and by what means, the laws and statutes of *England* ... came to be of force in *Ireland*' (1644).

MSS 1038, ff 104–6; MS 1180, ff 9–7: Reasons against the order of the English house of lords, 24 May 1698.

PRINTED WORKS AND UNPUBLISHED THESES

Abbott, T.K., *Catalogue of the manuscripts in the library of Trinity College, Dublin, to which is added a list of the Fagel collection of maps in the same Library* (Dublin, 1900).

The alarm, or the Irish spy: in a series of letters on the present state of the affairs in Ireland, to a lord high in the opposition: written by an ex-Jesuit, employed by his lordship for that purpose (Dublin, 1779).

Almon, John, (ed.), *A narrative of the proceedings and debates of the parliament of Ireland: during the fifth session of the second parliament in the reign of his present majesty: began to be held in Dublin on the tenth day of October, 1776* [recte 1775] (London, 1776).

—, *Memoirs of a late eminent bookseller* [1790] (New York, 1974).

[Annesley, Francis], *Some thoughts on the bill depending before the ... house of lords for prohibiting the exportation of the woolen manufactures of Ireland into foreign parts* (London, 1698).

Another letter to Mr Almon: in the matter of libel (Dublin, 1771).

Arber, Edwin (ed.), *The term catalogues, 1668–1709 A.D.*, 3 vols (London, 1903–6).

Aristotle, *The art of rhetoric*, ed. and transl. J.H. Freese (Cambridge, MA, 1936).

Atwood, William, *The fundamental constitution of the English government* (London, 1690).

—, *The history, and reasons, of the dependency of Ireland upon the imperial crown of the kingdom of England. Rectifying Mr. Molineux's State of the case of Ireland's being bound by acts of parliament in England* (London, 1698).

—, *The superiority and direct domination of the imperial crown of England over the crown and kingdom of Scotland* (London, 1704).

Baker, John H., *Manual of law French* (Amersham, 1979).

—, *The legal profession and the common law: essays in legal history* (London, 1986).

—, 'An English view of the Anglo-Irish constitution in 1670' in *Collected papers on English legal history*, 3 vols (Cambridge, 2013).

—, *The reinvention of Magna Carta, 1216–1616* (Cambridge, 2017).

Ball, F.E., *The judges in Ireland, 1221–1921*, 2 vols (London, 1926).

Baratariana: a collection of fugitive pieces, published during the administration of Lord Townshend in Ireland (Dublin, 1773).

Barck, Oscar T., & Hugh T. Lefler, *Colonial America* (2nd edn, London, 1968).

Barnard, T.C., 'Lawyers and the law in later seventeenth-century Ireland', *IHS*, 28 (1993–4), pp 256–82.

—, 'Protestantism, ethnicity and Irish identities, 1660–1760' in Tony Clayton & Ian McBride (eds), *Protestantism and national identity: Britain and Ireland, c.1650–c.1850* (Cambridge, 1998).

Barry, James (ed.), *The case of tenures upon commission of defective titles, argued by all the judges of Ireland, with their resolution, and the reasons of their resolution* (Dublin 1637).

Bartlett, Thomas, 'The Townshend viceroyalty, 1767–72' in Thomas Bartlett & D.W. Hayton (eds), *Penal era and golden age* (Belfast, 1979).

—, & D.W. Hayton (eds), *Penal era and golden age: essays in Irish history, 1690–1800* (Belfast, 1979).

Bartolomaeus Anglicus, *De proprietatibus rerum* [London, 1495] transl. John of Trevisa, 3 vols (Oxford, 1975, 1988).

Baxter, J.H., & Charles Johnson (eds), *A medieval Latin word list, from British and Irish sources* (Oxford, 1934).

Baxter, Stephen, *William III* (London, 1966).

Belfast Newsletter for 1776 (Belfast, 1776)

Berger, Adolf, *An encyclopedic dictionary of Roman law, Transactions of the American Philosophical Society*, n.s. 43:2 (1953).

Bergin, John, & Andrew Lyall (eds), *The acts of James II's Irish parliament, 1689* (Dublin, 2016).

[Berkeley, George,] *The querist, containing several queries proposed to the consideration of the public*, part II (Dublin, 1736).

Berry, C.H., & J.F. Morrissey (eds), *Statutes and ordinances and acts of parliament of Ireland: King John to Edward IV*, 4 vols (Dublin, 1907–39).

Black, Barbara, 'The constitution of empire: the case for the colonists', *University of Pennsylvania Law Review*, 124 (1976), pp 1157–1211.

Blom, J.C.H., & E. Lambert (eds), *A history of the Low Countries*, transl. J.C. Kennedy (Providence, RI, 1999).

Bolton, F.R., *The Caroline tradition of the Church of Ireland* (London, 1958).

Bolton, Sir Richard, 'A declaration setting forth how, and by what means, the laws and statutes of England, from time to time, came to be of force in Ireland' [1644] in Walter Harris (ed.), *Hibernica: part II, or two treatises relating to Ireland* (Dublin, 1750).

—, (ed.), *The statutes of Ireland, beginning the 3rd yeare of k. Edward II untill the … 13th yeare of k. James I* (Dublin, 1621).

Borlase, Edmund, *A history of the execrable Irish rebellion* (London, 1680).

Boyce, D.G., *Nationalism in Ireland* (2nd edn, London, 1991).

—, Eccleshall, Robert, & Vincent Geoghegan (eds), *Political discourse in seventeenth- and eighteenth-century Ireland* (Houndsmills, 2001).

Boyer, Abel, *The history of King William the Third*, 3 vols (London, 1703).

Bradshaw, Brendan, *The Irish constitutional revolution of the sixteenth century* (Cambridge, 1979).

Brady, Ciaran, 'The attainder of Shane O'Neill, Sir Henry Sidney and the problems of Tudor state-building in Ireland' in Ciaran Brady & Jane Ohlmeyer (eds), *British interventions in early modern Ireland* (Cambridge, 2005).

—, & Jane Ohlmeyer (eds), *British interventions in early modern Ireland* (Cambridge, 2005).

Brampton, John, *Chronicon Johannis Brom[p]ton, abbatis Jornalensis [Jervaux]* in Sir Roger Twysden (ed.), *Historiæ Anglicanæ scriptores X* (London, 1652).

Brand, Paul, 'Ireland and the literature of the early common law' in Brand, *The making of the common law* (London, 1992).

—, 'Magna Carta in Ireland' in Peter Crooks & Thomas Mohr (eds), *Law and the idea of liberty in Ireland: from Magna Carta to the present* (Dublin, forthcoming).

B[rewster], [Sir] F[rancis], *An answer to a letter from a gentleman in the country, to a member of the house of commons: on the votes of the 14th inst. relating to the trade of Ireland* (Dublin, 1698).

[Brewster, Sir Francis], *A discourse concerning Ireland and the different interests thereof, in answer to the Exon and Barnstaple petitions [to house of commons]* (London, 1698).

B.F. [? Brewster, Francis], *A letter to a member of the house of commons, on a proposal for regulating and advancing the woollen industry* (London, 1698).

British Library general catalogue of printed books to 1955, 27 vols (New York, 1967).

Britton: the French text carefully revised, with an English translation, introduction, and notes [1540], ed. F.M. Nichols, 2 vols (Oxford, 1865).

Brooke, Sir Robert, *La grande abridgement, collect & escrie per le iuge tres-reverend Syr Robert Brooke, chevalier nadgairs chiefe iustice del common banke*, 2 vols in one (London, 1573).

Brooks, Christopher W., *Law, politics and society in early modern England* (Cambridge, 2009).

Buccleuch MSS: HMC, *Report of the manuscripts of the duke of Buccleuch and Queensbury ... preserved at Montague House, Whitehall*, ii: *The Shrewsbury Papers*, 2 parts (London, 1903).

Burgess, Glenn, *Absolutism and the Stuart constitution* (London, 1996).

Burnet, Gilbert, *A pastoral letter writ by ... Gilbert, lord bishop of Sarum, to the clergy of his diocess, concerning the oaths of allegiance and supremacy to K. William and Q. Mary* (London, 1689).

Burns, J.H., & Mark Goldie (eds), *The Cambridge history of political thought, 1450–1700* (Cambridge, 1991).

Burridge, Ezekiel, *A short view of the present state of Ireland: with regard particularly to the difficultys a chief governor will meet with there in holding of a parliament: written in the year 1700* ([Dublin], 1708).

Calendar of State Papers, colonial series, America and West Indies, 1693–6; 1698–9 (London, 1903, 1905).

Calendar of State Papers, domestic series, William III, 1695 and addenda, 1681–95; 1698 (London, 1908, 1932).

Calendar of Treasury Books, 14, 1698–9 (London, 1934).

Camden, William (ed.), *Anglica, Normannica, Hibernica, Cambrica a veteribus scripta* (Frankfurt, 1603).

—, *Britain, or a chorographical description of the most flourishing kingdoms England, Scotland, Ireland and the islands adjoining ...*, transl. Philemon Holland (3rd edn, London, 1637).

Campion, Edmund, *Two histories of Ireland: the one written by Edmund Campion, the other by Meredith Hanmer Dr of Divinity* (Dublin, 1633).

Carte, Thomas, *The history of the life of James, first duke of Ormonde, containing an account of ... Ireland under his government, with an appendix and a collection of letters*, 6 vols (Oxford, 1851).

Carty, Anthony, *Was Ireland conquered? International law and the Irish question* (London, 1996).

Cary, John, *An essay on the state of England, in relation to its trade, its poor, and its taxes, for carrying on the present war against France* (Bristol, 1695).

[Cary, John,], *To the free holders and burgesses of the city of Bristol* ([? Bristol, 1698]).

Cary, John, *The rights of the commons in parliament assembled ...* (London, 1718).

—, *A vindication of the parliament of England, in answer to a book, written by William Molyneux, of Dublin, esq., intituled, The case of Ireland's being bound by acts of parliament in England, stated* (London, 1698; 2nd edn, with additional dedication, 1701).

Catalogue of the Pitt Collection (Southampton, 1964).

Cicero, Marcus Tullius, *De Officiis* [*On Duty*], ed. and transl. Walter Miller (Cambridge, MA, 1956).

Clarendon, Edward [Hyde], 1st earl of, *The great rebellion*, 2 vols (Oxford, 1702–4).

Clarendon, Henry [Hyde], 2nd earl of, *The correspondence of Henry Hyde, earl of Clarendon, and his brother Laurence Hyde, earl of Rochester ...*, ed. S.W. Singer, 2 vols (London, 1828).

Clarke, Aidan, 'Colonial constitutional attitudes in Ireland, 1640–60', *Proceedings of the Royal Irish Academy*, 90 C:11 (1990).

—, 'Patrick Darcy and the constitutional relationship between Ireland and Britain' in Jane Ohlmeyer (ed.), *Political thought in seventeenth-century Ireland* (Cambridge, 2000).

—, *Prelude to restoration in Ireland: the end of the commonwealth, 1659–1660* (Cambridge, 1999).

Clarke, Maude Violet, 'The manuscripts of the Irish "*Modus tenendi parliamentum*"', *English Historical Review*, 48 (1933), pp 576–600.

—, *Medieval representation and consent: a study of early parliaments in England and Ireland, with special attention to the Modus tenendi parliamentum* (New York, 1936).

[Clement, Simon], *An answer to Mr. Molyneux his Case of Ireland's being bound by acts of parliament in England, stated: and his dangerous notion of Ireland's being under no subordination to the parliamentary authority of England refuted; by reasoning from his own arguments and authorities* (London, 1698).

—, *The interest of England as it stands with relation to the trade of Ireland, considered; the arguments against the bill for prohibiting the exportation of woollen manufactures to foreign parts, fairly discusst, and the reasonableness and necessity of England's restraining her colonies in all matters of trade, that may be prejudiciall to her own commerce, clearly demonstrated. With short remarques on a book entituled, Some thoughts on the bill … for prohibiting the exportation of the woolen manufactures of Ireland to forreign parts* (London, 1698).

The Clements Archive, ed. A.P.W. Malcolmson (Dublin, 2010).

Coghill, Marmaduke, *Letters of Marmaduke Coghill, 1722–1738*, ed. D.W. Hayton (Dublin, 2005).

C[okayne], G.E., *The complete peerage of England, Scotland, Ireland, Great Britain and the United Kingdom*, rev. edn ed. V. Gibbs, et al., 14 vols (London, 1910–59).

Coke, Sir Edward, *Les reports de Edward Coke* (London, 1602).

—, *Les reports; la septième part* (London, 1608).

—, *La huictième part des reports* (London, 1611).

—, *La dixme part des reports* (London, 1629).

—, *Twelfth report* (London, 1656).

—, *The first part of the institutes of the law of England* (London, 1628).

—, *The second part of the institutes of the law of England* (London, 1642).

—, *The fourth part of the institutes of the law of England* (London, 1644).

A collection of all the statutes now in use in the Kingdom of Ireland … and a continuation to the seventh day of August 1666. (Dublin, 1698).

Colles, I[? saac], *The case of Ireland's being bound by acts of parliament restated* ([?London], 1812).

Commons, House of [England], *Journal of the house of commons [England]*, vols 9–12 (London, 1742).

Commons, House of [Ireland], *Journal of the house of commons [Ireland]*, vols 1–2 (Dublin, 1796).

Connolly, S.J., *Divided kingom: Ireland, 1630–1800* (Oxford, 2008).

Cosgrove, Art, 'Parliament and the Anglo-Irish community: the declaration of 1460' in A. Cosgrove & J.I. McGuire (eds), *Parliament and community*, Historical Studies 14 (Belfast, 1983).

Costello, Kevin, *The court of admiralty, 1575–1893* (Dublin, 2011).

Courthope, James, 'The minutebook of James Courthope', ed. O.C. Williams, *Camden Miscellany*, 20:3 (1953).

Cox, Richard, *Hibernia Anglicana, or, the history of Ireland from the conquest thereof by the English to the present time*, 2 vols (London, 1689–90).

Coxe, William (ed.), *Memoirs of the life and administration of Sir Robert Walpole*, 3 vols (London, 1798).

Croke, Sir George, Kt, *The third part of the reports of Sir George Croke Kt, late one of the justices of the court of kings-bench … during the first sixteen years of King Charles the First …* (2nd edn, London, 1661).

Crooks, Peter, 'The background to the arrest of the fifth earl of Kildare and Sir Christopher Preston in 1418; a missing membrane', *Analecta Hibernica*, 40 (2007), pp 1–15.

—, 'Exporting Magna Carta: exclusionary liberties in Ireland and the world', *History Ireland*, 23:4 (2015), pp 14–17.

Cruickshanks, Eveline, Stuart Handley & D.W. Hayton (eds), *The house of commons, 1690–1715*, 5 vols (Cambridge, 2002).

Cullen, Louis, *An economic history of Ireland since 1660* (2nd edn, London, 1987).

Darcy, Patrick, *An argument delivered by Patrick Darcy, esquire; by the express order of the house of commons in the parliament of Ireland, 9. Iunii 1641. [1643]*, ed. C.E.J. Caldicott, *Camden Miscellany*, 44 (1992).

Davenant Charles, *An essay upon the probable methods of making a people gainers in the ballance of trade* (London, 1699).

—, *A discourse upon grants and resumptions, shewing … that the forfeited estates ought to be applied to the payment of the public debts* (2nd edn, London, 1700).

Davies, Sir John, *A discoverie of the true causes why Ireland was never entirely subdued, or brought under obedience to the crowne of England, until the beginning of his maiesties happie raigne* (London, 1612).

—, *Le primer report des cases et matters en ley resolues et adjuges en les courts del roy en Ireland, collect & digest per Sr. Iohn Davys chivaler, atturney generall del rey en ceste realme* (London, 1615).

Davis, Thomas, *The patriot parliament, with its statutes, votes and proceedings*, ed. Sir Charles Gavin Duffy (2nd edn, London, 1893).

Degenaar, Marjolein, *Molyneux's problem: three centuries discussion on the perception of forms*, transl. M.J. Collins (Dordrecht, 1996).

Diceto, Ralph de, *Abbreviationes chronicarum et ymagines historiarum* in Sir Roger Twysden (ed.), *Historiæ Anglicanæ scriptores X* (London, 1652).

Dickson, David, *New foundations: Ireland, 1660–1800* (2nd edn, Dublin, 2000).

Dictionary of Irish biography, ed. James McGuire & James Quinn, 9 vols (Cambridge, 2009), continued online.

Dix, E.R. McC. (ed.), '"The case … stated" by William Molyneux of Dublin, esq., list of editions', *The Irish Book-Lover*, 5 (1914), pp 116–18.

Dodrige, Sir John, *The English lawyer: describing a method for managing the lawes of this land* (London, 1631).

Domville, Sir William, 'A disquisition touching that great question, whether an act of parliament made in England shall bind the kingdom and people of Ireland without their allowance and acceptance of such act in the kingdom of Ireland', ed. Patrick Kelly, *Analecta Hibernica*, 40 (2007), pp 17–70.

Donaldson, A.G., 'The application in Ireland of English and British legislation before 1810' (PhD, Queen's University, Belfast, 1952).

—, *Some comparative aspects of Irish law* (Durham, NC, 1967).

Dopping, Anthony (ed.), *Modus tenendi parliamenta et consilia in Hibernia, published out of the antient record by … Anthony, lord bishop of Meath, to which is added the rules and customs of the house [of commons in England] … from the time of Edward the Sixth, by H[enry] S[cobell], E[squire], C[lericus] P[arliamenti]* (Dublin, 1692).

Duigenan, Patrick, *An answer to the address of the Rt Hon. Henry Grattan … to his fellow citizens of Dublin* (Dublin, 1798).

Dyer, James, *Les reports des divers select matters & resolutions des reverend juges & sages del ley … collect et report par tres-reverend Juge Sir Jaques Dyer chivaler jades chief justice del comon banke en le temps du Roign Elizabeth* (London, 1672).

Eadmerus, *Historiae novorum, sive sui saeculi, libri VI, ex Bibl[iotheca] Cottoniana, ed. Io[hanne] Seldensus, et notas adjecit et specilegium* (London, 1623).

Edie, Carolyn A., 'The Irish cattle bills: a study in Restoration politics', *Transactions of the American Philosophical Society*, n.s. 60:2 (1970).

Elliott, Marianne, *Partners in revolution: the United Irishmen and France* (London, 1982).

Ellis, S.G., 'Yorkist and Tudor Ireland in parliament and community' in A. Cosgrove & J.I. McGuire (eds), *Parliament and community*, Historical Studies 14 (Belfast, 1983).

Englefield, Dermot (ed.), *The printed records of the parliament of Ireland: a survey and bibliographical guide* (London, 1978).

English historical documents, vol. 8 (1660–1714), ed. Andrew Browning (London, 1956).

Falkner Greirson & Co., *Catalogue five: 762 interesting books* (Dublin, 1967).

Faulkner's Dublin Journal, for *1749* (Dublin, 1749).

Finch, Heneage, *Nomotechnia; cestascavoir, un description del common leys Dangleterre, solonque les rules del art* (London, 1614).

Flaherty, Martin, S., 'The empire strikes back: Annesley v. Sherlock and the triumph of imperial parliamentary supremacy', *Columbia Law Review*, 87 (1987), pp 593–622.

Flanagan, Marie Therese, *Irish society, Anglo-Norman settlers, Angevin kingship: interactions in the late twelfth century* (Oxford, 1989).

Fleta, *Fleta*, ed. H.G. Richardson & G.O. Sayles, 3 vols (London, 1955, 1972, 1983).

Fletcher (of Saltoun), Andrew, *An account of a conversation concerning a right regulation of governments for the common good of mankind* [1703] in *Political Works*, ed. John Robertson (Cambridge, 1997).

Ford, Alan, *The Protestant Reformation in Ireland, 1590–1641* (Frankfurt-am-Main, 1987).

Franklin, Benjamin, *The papers of Benjamin Franklin*, vol. 17, ed. W.B. Willcox (London, 1973).

Fraser, A.M., 'The Molyneux family in Dublin', *Dublin Historical Record*, 16 (1960), pp 9–15.

[French, R.], *The constitution of Ireland, and Poynings' Law explained* (Dublin, 1770).

Furnivall, Frederick J., ed., *The English conquest of Ireland, AD 1166–1185, mainly from the 'Expugnatio Hibernica' of Giraldus Cambrensis ...* (London, 1896)

[Gardiner, John], *The substance of the arguments for and against the bill for prohibiting the exportation of woollen manufacture from Ireland to forreign parts ... Together with some remarks on a printed paper, entituled, Some thoughts on the said bill* (London, 1698).

Garnham, Neal, *The courts, crime and the criminal law in Ireland, 1692–1760* (Dublin, 1996).

Gaskill, Philip, *A new introduction to bibliography* (Oxford, 1974).

Gay, Nicholas, *Strictures upon the proposed union between Great Britain and Ireland, with occasional remarks* (Dublin, 1799).

Gervase of Doroborn (Canterbury), *Chronicle* in Sir Roger Twysden (ed.), *Historiæ Anglicanæ scriptores X* (London, 1652).

Geraghty, J.G., *The present state of Ireland, and the means of preserving her to the empire, considered* (London, 1799).

Gilbert, Sir John T. (ed.), *Facsimiles of the national manuscripts of Ireland*, parts 3 & 4 (Dublin, 1879–84).

Gillespie, Raymond, 'The Irish Protestants and James II, 1688–90', *IHS*, 28 (1992), pp 124–33.

Giraldus Cambrensis, *Expugnatio Hibernica* in *Anglica, Hibernica, Normannica, Cambrica a veteribus scripta*, ed. William Camden (Frankfurt, 1603).

—, *Expugnatio Hibernica: the conquest of Ireland*, ed. A.B. Scott and F.X. Martin (Dublin, 1978).

—, *Topographia Hiberniæ: the history and topography of Ireland*, ed. and transl. J.J. O'Meara (Mountrath, 1982). Earlier edn in William Camden (ed.), *Anglica, Normannica, Hibernica, Cambrica a veteribus scripta* (Frankfurt, 1603).

Glanvill, *De legibus et consuetudinibus regni Angliae: the treatise on the laws and customs of the realm of England, commonly called Glanvill*, ed. G.D.G. Hall (Oxford, 1965).

Goldie, Mark (ed.), *The reception of Locke's politics*, 6 vols (London, 1999).

Grattan, Henry, *Speeches of the late Rt Hon. Henry Grattan in the Irish parliament in 1780 and 1782*, ed. James Grattan (London, 1821).

Grey, Hon. Anchitell (ed.), *The debates of the house of commons, from the year 1667 to the year 1694*, 10 vols (London, 1769).

Grimblot, Paul (ed.), *Letters of William III, and Louis XIV, and their ministers*, 2 vols (London, 1848).

Grotius, Hugo, *De jure belli ac pacis, libri tres* [1625], transl. John Morris et al., 3 vols (London, 1715).

Gutch, John (ed.), *Collectanea curiosa, or miscellaneous tracts relating to the history and antiquities of England and Ireland ...* , 2 vols (Oxford, 1781).

Hale, Sir Matthew, *Jura coronæ: his majesties royal rights and prerogatives asserted, against papal usurpations, and all other anti-monarchical attempts and practices* (London, 1680), now attributed to John Brydall.

—, *The jurisdiction of the lords house, or parliament, considered according to the ancient record* (London, 1796).

—, *The prerogatives of the crown*, ed. D.C. Yale (London, 1976).

Harris, Walter (ed.), *Hibernica: part II, or two treatises relating to Ireland* (Dublin, 1750).

Harrison, John, & Peter Laslett (eds), *The library of John Locke* (2nd edn, Oxford, 1971).

Harrison, John (ed.), *The library of Isaac Newton* (Cambridge, 1974).

Hart, H.L., *Justice upon petition: the house of lords and the reformation of justice, 1621–1675* (London, 1991).

Hayton, David, 'The beginnings of the undertaker system' in Thomas Bartlett & D.W. Hayton (eds), *Penal era and golden age: essays in Irish history, 1690–1800* (Belfast, 1979).

—, 'Constitutional experiments and political expediency, 1689–1725' in Stephen Ellis & Sarah Barber (eds), *Conquest and union: fashioning a British state, 1485–1725* (London, 1995).

—, 'Ideas of union in Anglo-Irish political discourse, 1692–1720' in D.G. Boyce, Robert Eccleshall & Vincent Geoghegan (eds), *Political discourse in seventeenth and eighteenth-century Ireland* (Houndsmill, 2001).

—, *Ruling Ireland, 1685–1742: politics, politicians and parties* (Woodbridge, 2004).

—, 'The Stanhope/Sunderland ministry and the repudiation of Irish political independence', *English Historical Review*, 113 (1998), pp 610–36.

—, 'The Williamite revolution in Ireland' in Jonathan Israel (ed.), *The Anglo-Dutch moment: essays on the Glorious Revolution and its world impact* (Cambridge, 1991).

Hemmant, Mary (ed.), *Select cases in the exchequer chamber*, 2 vols (London, 1933).

Hibernian Chronicle for 1782 (Cork, 1782).

Hibernian Journal for 1782, 1791 and 1792 (Dublin 1782–92).

Hibernian Magazine for 1782 (Dublin, 1782).

Hill, Jacqueline R., *From patriots to unionists: Dublin civic politics and Irish Protestant patriotism, 1660–1840* (Oxford, 1997).

—, 'Ireland without union: Molyneux and his legacy' in John Robertson (ed.), *A union for empire: political thought and the British union of 1707* (Cambridge, 1995).

HMC, *Appendix to second report* (London, 1874)

Hobart, Sir Henry, *The reports of the reverend and learned judge, the Right Honorable Sr. Henry Hobart ... lord chief justice of his majesties court of common pleas ...* (3rd edn, London, 1671).

Holt, James Clarke, *Magna Carta* (2nd edn, Cambridge, 1992).

Hont, István, *Jealousy of trade: international competition and the nation-state in historical perspective* (Cambridge, MA, 2005).

Hooker, Richard, *Of the laws of ecclesiastical politie*, ed. John [Gauden], bishop of Exeter (London, 1666).

Hoppen, K. Theodore, *The common scientist in the seventeenth century: a study of the Dublin philosophical society* (London, 1970).

Horwitz, Henry, *Parliament, policy and politics in the reign of William III* (Manchester, 1977).

Hoveden, Roger, *Annalium, pars prior et posterior* in Henry Savile (ed.), *Rerum Anglicarum scriptores post Bedam præcipui … nunc primum in lucem editi* (London, 1596).

[Hovell, Alderman John,] *A discourse of the woollen manufactury of Ireland and the consequences of prohibiting its exportation* (London, 1698).

Howard, Gorges, *Some questions upon the legislative constitution of Ireland* (Dublin, 1770).

Hunter, Michael, *Editing early modern texts: an introduction to principles and practice* (Basingstoke, 2007).

Irish statutes. In this volume are contained all the statutes from the tenth yere of King Henrie the Sixt, to the xiiii yere of … Queene Elizabeth, made and established in her highness' realme of Ireland (London, 1572).

Jacob, Giles (ed.), *A new law-dictionary* (London, 1729).

James, F.G., *Ireland and the empire, 1688–1770: a history of Ireland from the Williamite Wars to the eve of the American Revolution* (Cambridge, MA, 1973).

—, *Lords of the Ascendancy: the Irish house of lords and its members, 1600–1800* (Dublin, 1995).

[Jebb, Frederick], *Guatimozin's letters on the present state of Ireland, and the right of binding by British acts of parliament, &c* (London, 1779).

Johnson, Samuel (ed.), *A dictionary of the English language*, 2 vols (2nd edn, London, 1770).

Johnston-Liik, Edith Mary (ed.), *The history of the Irish parliament, 1692–1800: commons, constituencies and statutes*, 6 vols (Belfast, 2002).

Johnston, W.J., 'The English Legislature and the Irish courts', *Law Quarterly Review*, 47 (1924), pp 91–106.

Kearney, H.F., 'The political background to English mercantilism, 1695–1700', *Economic History Review*, 2nd ser. 11 (1959), pp 484–96.

—, *Strafford in Ireland, 1633–1641* (Manchester, 1959).

Keble, Joseph (ed.), *The statutes at large … to 7 Will. III*, 2 vols (London, 1695).

Kelly, James, *Henry Flood: patriots and politics in eighteenth-century Ireland* (Dublin, 1998).

—, 'The origins of the Act of Union: an examination of unionist opinion in Britain and Ireland, 1650–1800', *IHS*, 25 (1986–7), pp 236–63.

—, *Poynings' Law and the making of law in Ireland, 1660–1800* (Dublin, 2007).

—, 'Public and political opinion in Ireland, and the idea of an Anglo-Irish union, 1650–1800' in D.G. Boyce, Robert Eccleshall & Vincent Geoghegan (eds), *Political discourse in seventeenth- and eighteenth-century Ireland* (Houndsmills, 2001).

Kelly, Patrick,'Conquest versus consent as the basis of the English title to Ireland in William Molyneux's *Case of Ireland … stated*' in Ciaran Brady & Jane Ohlmeyer (eds), *British interventions in early modern Ireland* (Cambridge, 2005).

—, 'The Irish Woollen Export Prohibition Act of 1699: Kearney revisited', *Irish Economic and Social History*, 7 (1980), pp 22–44.

—, 'Irish writers and the French Revolution' in Associazione degli Storici Europei, *La storia della storiografia europea sulla rivoluzione francese*, 3 vols (Rome, 1990).

—, '"A light to the blind'; the voice of the dispossessed elite in the generation after the defeat at Limerick", *IHS*, 24 (1984–5), pp 431–62.

—, 'Locke and Molyneux: the anatomy of a friendship', *Hermathena*, 126 (1979), pp 38–54.

—, 'Nationalism and the historians of the Jacobite War in Ireland' in Michael O'Dea & Kevin Whelan (eds), *Nations and nationalisms: France Britain and Ireland in the eighteenth-century context* (Oxford, 1995).

—, 'The one that got away, or almost: the Molyneux family library and Trinity College Dublin' in W.E. Vaughan (ed.), *The Old Library, Trinity College Dublin, 1712–2012* (Dublin, 2013).

—, 'A pamphlet attributed to John Toland, and an unpublished reply by Archbishop William King', *Topoi*, 4 (1985), pp 81–90.

—, 'Perceptions of Locke in eighteenth-century Ireland', *Proceedings of the Royal Irish Academy*, 89C:2 (1989), pp 17–35.

—, 'The politics of political economy in mid-eighteenth-century Ireland' in S.J. Connolly (ed.), *Political ideas in eighteenth-century Ireland* (Dublin, 2000).

—, 'The printer's copy of the MS of "The case of Ireland's being bound by acts of parliament in England, stated", 1698', *Long Room*, 18–19 (1979), pp 6–13.

—, 'Recasting a tradition: William Molyneux and the sources of *The case of Ireland ... stated*' in Ciaran Brady & Jane Ohlmeyer (eds), *British interventions in early modern Ireland* (Cambridge, 2005).

—, 'Sir Richard Bolton and the authorship of "A declaration setting forth how, and by what means, the laws and statutes of England, from time to time came to be of force in Ireland", 1644', *IHS*, 35 (2006), pp 1–16.

—, 'William Molyneux and the spirit of liberty in eighteenth-century Ireland', *ECI*, 3 (1988), pp 133–48.

Kerby-Fulton, Kathryn, & Steven Justice, 'Reformist intellectual culture in the English and Irish civil service: the "Modus tenendi parliamentum" and its literary relations', *Traditio*, 53 (1998), pp 149–202.

Kidd, Colin, *British identities before nationalism: ethnicity and nationhood in the Atlantic world, 1600–1800* (Cambridge, 1999).

King, C.S., *A great archbishop of Dublin, William King, 1650–1729, DD: his autobiography, family, and a selection from his correspondence* (Dublin, 1906).

[King, William,] *The state of the Protestants of Ireland under the late King James' government ...* (London, 1691).

Knighton, Henry, *Chronica de eventibus Angliæ a tempore Regis Edgari usque mortem Regis Ricardi Secundi* in Sir Roger Twysden (ed.), *Historiæ Anglicanæ scriptores X* (London, 1652).

Korman, Sharon, *The right of conquest: the acquisition of territory by force, in international law and practice* (Oxford, 1996).

Lambarde, William, *Archaionomia, sive de priscis Anglorum legibus sermone Anglico, vetustate antiquissimo, aliquot ab hinc seculis conscripti ... e tenebris in lucem vocati* (London, 1568).

—, *Archeion, or, a commentary upon the high courts of justice in England* [1635], ed. C.H. McIlwain & P.L. Ward (Cambridge, MA, 1957).

Leerssen, Joep, *Mere Irish and Fíor-Ghael: studies in the idea of Irish nationality, its development and literary expression prior to the nineteenth century* (Amsterdam, 1986).

Lemmings, David, *Gentlemen and barristers: the inns of court and the English bar, 1680–1730* (Oxford, 1990).

[Leslie, Charles], *Considerations of importance to Ireland, in a letter to a member of parliament there; upon occasion of Mr. Molyneux's late book: intuled, The case of Ireland's being bound by acts of parliament in England, stated* ([London], 1698).

Leslie, Charles, *The new association of those called moderate church-men, with the modern-Whigs and fanaticks, to undermine and blow-up the present church and government, occasion'd by a late pamphlet, entituled, The danger of priest-craft, &c* (London, 1703).

A letter from a member of the house of commons in Ireland, to a gentleman of the long-robe in England: containing an answer to some objections made against the judicatory power of the parliament of Ireland, to which is added, the late duke of Leeds' reasons for protesting against a vote made in the house of lords in England, which declared a certain tryal before the house of lords in Ireland to be coram non judice (London, 1720).

A letter to a member of the house of commons, on regulating and advancing the woollen industry (London, 1698).

Locke, John, *The correspondence of John Locke*, ed. E.S. de Beer, 8 vols (Oxford, 1976–89).

—, *An essay concerning human understanding*, ed. P.H. Nidditch (Oxford, 1975).

—, *Some familiar letters between Mr. Locke and several of his friends* (London,1708).

—, *Two treatises of government*, ed. Peter Laslett (Cambridge, 1960).

Loeber, Rolf, 'The rebuilding of Dublin Castle, 1661–90', *Studies*, 69 (1980), pp 45–68.

Lords, House of [England], *The manuscripts of the house of lords [England]*, vol. 1 (1689–90), and n.s. vol. 3 (1697–9) (London, 1889, 1905).

—, *Journal of the house of lords [England]*, vol. 16 (London, [1767]).

Lords, House of [Ireland], *Journal of the house of lords [Ireland]*, vols 1–2 (Dublin, 1779–80).

Lucas, Charles, *A tenth address to the free citizens and free-holders of the city of Dublin* (Dublin, 1748 [1749]).

Ludington, Charles C., 'From ancient constitution to British empire: William Atwood and the imperial crown of England' in Jane H. Ohlmeyer (ed.), *Political thought in seventeenth-century Ireland* (Cambridge, 2000).

Luttrell, Narcissus, *The parliamentary diary of Narcissus Luttrell, 1691–1693*, ed. Henry Horwitz (Oxford, 1972).

Lutz, Donald S., 'The relative influence of European writers on late eighteenth-century American political thought', *American Political Science Review*, 78 (1984), pp 189–97.

Lydon, J.F.M., 'Ireland and the English crown, 1171–1541', *IHS*, 29 (1995), pp 281–94.

McBride, Ian, *Eighteenth-century Ireland: the isle of slaves* (Dublin, 2009).

McCormack, W.J., 'Vision and revision in the study of eighteenth-century Irish political rhetoric', *ECI*, 2 (1987), pp 7–35.

—, *The pamphlet debates on the union between Great Britain and Ireland, 1797–1800* (Dublin, 1996).

MacGillivray, Royce, *Restoration historians and the English Civil War* (The Hague, 1974).

McGowan-Doyle, Valerie, *The book of Howth: the Elizabethan re-conquest of Ireland and the Old English* (Cork, 2011).

McGrath, Charles Ivar, *The making of the eighteenth-century Irish constitution: government, parliament and the revenue, 1692–1714* (Dublin, 2000).

McGuire, James, 'The Irish parliament of 1692' in Thomas Bartlett & D.W. Hayton (eds), *Penal era and golden age* (Belfast, 1979).

McIlwain, Charles H., *The American Revolution: a constitutional interpretation* [1923] (New York, 1973).

McLoughlin, Thomas, *Contesting Ireland: Irish voices against England in the eighteenth century* (Dublin, 1999).

Madden, Richard Robert, *The history of Irish periodical literature from the end of the 17th to the middle of the 19th century, its origin, progress and results ... during the past two centuries*, 2 vols (London, 1867).

Mandrou, Robert, *Louis XIV en son temps* (Paris, 1973).

Martial, *Epigrams*, ed. and transl. D.P. Shackleton Bailey, 2 vols (Cambridge, MA, 1963).

Mayart, Samuel, Sir, 'Answer to a declaration setting forth how, and by what means, the laws and statutes of England, from time to time, came to be of force in Ireland' in Walter Harris (ed.), *Hibernica: part II, or two treatises relating to Ireland* (Dublin, 1750).

Molesworth, Robert [1st Viscount], *An account of Denmark, as it was in the year 1692* (London, 1694).

Molyneux, Sir Capel, Bt., *An account of the family and descendants of Sir Thomas Molyneux, Kt., chancellor of the exchequer in Ireland to Queen Elizabeth* (Evesham, 1820).

Molyneux, Samuel, Jnr, *A catalogue of the library of the Honble. Samuel Molyneux, deceas'd …* *consisting of many valuable and rare books in several languages … with several curious* *manuscripts …* (London, 1730).

Molyneux, William, *Anecdotes of the life of the celebrated patriot and philosopher William* *Molyneux, author of The case of Ireland: published from a manuscript written by himself*, ed. Sir Capel Molyneux, Bt. (Dublin, 1803).

—, *The case of Ireland's being bound by acts of parliament in England, stated* (Dublin, 1698). (For subsequent editions, see checklist of printings of *The Case*).

—, *Dioptrica nova: a treatise of dioptricks, in two parts* (London, 1692).

—, *Sciothericum telescopicum, or, a new contrivance for adapting a telescope to an horizontal dial for* *observing the moment of time by day or night … with proper tables requisite thereto* (Dublin, 1686).

Monck Mason, Henry Joseph, *An essay on the antiquity and constitution of parliaments in Ireland* (Dublin, 1820).

Moody, T.W., & J.G. Simms (eds), *The bishopric of Derry and the Irish Society of London, 1602–* *1705*, 2 vols (Dublin, 1968, 1983).

Morres, Hervey-Redmond, Lord Mountmorrres, *The history of the principal transactions of the* *Irish parliament, from the year 1634 to 1666 … to which is prefaced a preliminary discourse on* *the ancient parliaments of that kingdom*, 2 vols (London, 1792).

Moxon, Joseph, *Mechanick exercises on the whole art of printing* [*1683–4*], ed. H. Davis & H. Carter (2nd edn, London, 1962).

Nenner, Howard, *By colour of law: legal culture and constitutional politics in England, 1660–1688* (Chicago, 1977).

—, 'Liberty, law, and property: the constitution in retrospect from 1689' in J.R. Jones (ed.), *Liberty secured? Britain before and after 1688* (Stanford, CA, 1992).

Nicolson, William (ed.), *The Irish historical library* (London, 1724).

O'Brien, Gerard, 'The Grattan mystique', *ECI*, 1 (1986), pp 177–207.

—, 'Illusion and reality in late eighteenth-century politics', *ECI*, 3 (1988), pp 149–55.

O'Conor, Matthew, *The history of the Irish Catholics from the settlement in 1691, with a view of the* *state of Ireland from the invasion by Henry II to the revolution* (Dublin, 1813).

Ohlmeyer, Jane H. (ed.), *Political thought in seventeenth-century Ireland: kingdom or colony* (Cambridge, 2000).

O'Flaherty, Roderick, *Ogygia, seu rerum Hibernicarum chronologica …* (London, 1685).

O'Gara, James G., 'Leibnitz and "la liberté des Anglois"', *2000: The European Journal … Rivista* *Europea*, 3:1 (2002), pp 1–3.

O'Malley, Liam, 'Patrick Darcy, Galway lawyer and politician, 1598–1688' in Diarmuid Ó Cearbhaill (ed.), *Galway, town and gown, 1484–1984* (Dublin, 1984).

O'Regan, Philip, *Archbishop William King of Dublin (1650–1729) and the constitution in church* *and state* (Dublin, 2000).

Ormonde MSS. HMC, *Papers of the marquess of Ormonde KP, at Kilkenny Castle*, vol. 8 (London, 1920).

Osborough, Nial, 'The failure to enact an Irish bill of rights', *Irish Jurist*, n.s. 33 (1998), pp 392–415.

Ó Siochrú, Micheál, *Confederate Ireland, 1642–1649: a constitutional and political analysis* (Dublin, 1999).

O'Sullivan, William, 'John Madden's manuscripts' in Vincent Kinane & Anne Walsh (eds), *Essays on the history of Trinity College Library, Dublin* (Dublin, 2000).

Otway-Ruthven, A.J. *Medieval Ireland* (2nd edn, London, 1980).

Oxford dictionary of national biography, ed. H.C. G. Matthew & Brian Harrison, 60 vols (Oxford, 2004), continued online.

Oxford English dictionary. ed. J.A. Simpson & E.S.C. Weiner, 20 vols (2nd edn, Oxford, 1989), continued online.

Paris, Matthew, *Historia maior a Gulielmo Conquestore ad ultimum annum Henrici III* (London, 1641).

The parliamentary register, or history of the proceedings and debates of the house of commons of Ireland, vol. 1 (Dublin, 1782).

Pawlisch, Hans, *Sir John Davies and the conquest of Ireland* (Cambridge, 1985).

Perceval-Maxwell, Michael, *The outbreak of the Irish rebellion of 1641* (Dublin, 1994).

[Petty, Sir William,] *Some of the observations made by W.P. upon the trade of Irish cattel*, brs. ([London], 1673).

Petyt, William, *The antient right of the commons of England asserted ...* (London, 1680).

Pitt, Moses, *The English atlas*, 4 vols (London, 1680–2).

Plowden, Edmund, *Les commentaries, ou les reportes de dyvers cases de Edmund Plowden, un apprentice de le common ley, ... en le temps de Ed[ward]. le size ... & le Royne Elizabeth* (London, 1599).

Plowden, Francis, *The history of Ireland, from its invasion under Henry II to its union with Great Britain*, 2 vols (Dublin, 1803).

Pocock, J.G.A., *The ancient constitution and the feudal law: a study of English historical thought in the seventeenth century: a reissue with a retrospect* (Cambridge, 1987).

The policy of Poynings' Law fairly explained and considered, with seasonable advice to the people of Ireland (Dublin, 1770).

Pollard, Mary, *Dublin's trade in books, 1550–1800: Lyell Lectures, 1986–1987* (Oxford, 1989).

—, (ed.), *A dictionary of the members of the Dublin book trade, 1550–1800, based on the records of the Guild of St Luke the Evangelist, Dublin* (London, 2000).

[Pollock, Joseph], *The letters of Owen Roe O'Nial* ([Dublin, 1779]). Reprinted in 1782 edn of *The Case*, see further checklist of printings, item 10, p. 84.

Portland MSS. HMC, report XIV, appendix II. *The manuscripts of his grace the duke of Portland, preserved at Welbeck Abbey*, vol. 3 (London, 1894).

Power, Thomas, 'Publishing and sectarian tension in South Munster in the 1760s', *ECI*, 19 (2004), pp 75–110.

Powicke, F.M., *Henry III and the Lord Edward*, 2 vols (Oxford, 1947).

—, & E.B. Fryde (eds), *Handbook of British chronology* (2nd edn, London, 1961).

Pressly, W.L., *The life and art of James Barry* (London, 1981).

Prestwich, Michael, 'The *Modus tenendi parliamentum*', *Parliamentary History*, 1 (1982), pp 221–6.

—, *Edward I* (London, 1997).

Prior, Thomas, *A list of the absentees of Ireland ... with observations on the present state and condition of that kingdom* (Dublin, 1729).

Pronay, Nicholas, & John Taylor (eds), *Parliamentary texts of the later Middle Ages* (Oxford, 1980).

Prynne, William, *Brief animadversions on ... the fourth part of the institutes ... compiled by Sir Edward Cooke* (London, 1669).

Pufendorf, Samuel von, *De jure naturæ et gentium, libri octo* [1672], transl. Basil Kennet, 3 vols (2nd edn, London, 1717).

Pulton, Ferdinando, ed., *A collection of sundrie statues frequent in use, with notes and references* (London, 1670).

Quinn, David B., 'Government printing and the publication of the Irish statutes in the sixteenth century', *Proceedings of the Royal Irish Academy*, 49 (1943–4), pp 45–129.

The red book of the exchequer [England], ed. Hubert Hull, 3 vols (London, 1896).

A report of the debates in the house of commons of Ireland, on the 24th... 28th of January 1799, on the subject of union (Dublin, 1799).

Rees, Nigel (ed.), *Phrases and sayings* (London, 1995).

[Reily, Hugh,] *The impartial history of Ireland ... Together with the most remarkable transactions in church and state, since the Reformation: in two parts* (London, 1742).

Richardson, H.G., 'Historical revision VII – The Preston exemplification of the *Modus tenendi parliamenta*', *IHS*, 3 (1942–3), pp 187–92.

—, & G.O. Sayles, *The Irish parliament in the Middle Ages* (Philadelphia, 1952).

—, & G.O. Sayles, *Law and legislation from Æthelbert to Magna Charta* (Edinburgh, 1966).

Robbins, Caroline, *The eighteenth-century commonwealthman* (Cambridge, MA, 1959).

Rose, Craig, *England in the 1690s: revolution, religion and war* (Oxford, 1999).

Ryley, William, *Placata parliamentaria, una cum judiciis forensibus sive sententiis diminitivis desu per latis, regnantibus Edward I & Edwardo t[ertio], Angliæ regibus ...* (London, 1661).

St Germain, Christopher, *The dialogue of the doctor and the student* [1511], ed. T.F.T. Plucknett & J.L. Barton (London, 1974).

Sachse, William, *Lord Somers: a political biography* (Manchester, 1975).

Sayles, G.O., '*Modus tenendi parliamentum*: Irish or English?' in James Lydon (ed.), *England and Ireland in the later Middle Ages: essays in honour of Jocelyn Otway-Ruthven* (Dublin, 1981).

Schelstrate, Emanuel (ed.), *Acta Constantientis Concilii ...* (Antwerp, 1683).

Schwoerer, Lois G. (ed.), *The Glorious Revolution: changing perspectives* (Cambridge, 1992).

Selden, John, *Titles of honour* (3rd edn, London, 1672).

Seward, W.W., *The rights of the people asserted, and the necessity of a more equal representation in parliament stated, and approved* (Dublin, 1783).

Sharp, Granville, *A declaration of the people's natural right to a share in the legislature. Part II, containing a declaration or defense of the same doctrine ... applied particularly to the people of Ireland: in answer to the assertions of several eminent writers...* (2nd edn, London, 1775).

Shower, Sir Bartholomew (ed.), *Cases in parliament resolved and adjudged upon petitions, and writs of error* (London, 1698).

Simms, J.G., *Jacobite Ireland, 1685–91* (London, 1969).

—, *Colonial nationalism, 1698–1776: Molyneux's The case of Ireland ... stated* (Cork, 1976).

—, *William Molyneux of Dublin, 1656–1698*, ed. P.H. Kelly (Backrock, Co. Dublin, 1982).

Smyth, James, '"Like amphibious animals": Irish patriots, ancient Britons, 1660–1707', *Historical Journal*, 36 (1993), pp 785–97.

Spelman, Henry, *Glossarium archaiologicum: continens Latino-Barbara, peregrina, obsoleta, & novatae significationis vocabula* (London, 1687).

Stanihurst, Richard, *De rebus in Hibernia gestis, libri quattuor* (Antwerp, 1584).

The statutes at large of England and Great Britain from Magna Charta to the union of the kingdoms of Great Britain and Ireland, ed. T. Tomlins et al., vols 1–3 (London, 1811–14).

The statutes at large passed in the parliaments held in Ireland: from the third year of Edward the Second, AD 1310 to the twenty-sixth year of George the Third, AD 1786, inclusive, ed. J.G. Butler, vols 1–3 (Dublin, 1786).

Steele, Robert, (ed.), *Three prose versions of the Secreta secretorum* (London, 1898).

—, (ed.), *A bibliography of royal proclamations of the Tudor and Stuart sovereigns and others published under authority, 1485–1714*, 2 vols (Oxford, 1910).

Strayer, Joseph R. (ed.), *Dictionary of the Middle Ages*, 13 vols (New York, 1982–9).

Strickland, Walter G. (ed.), *A dictionary of Irish artists*, ed. Theo J. Snoddy, 2 vols (Shannon, 1969).

Swatland, Andrew, *The house of lords in the reign of Charles II* (Cambridge, 1996).

Swift, Jonathan, *A letter to the whole people of Ireland (Fourth Drapier's letter)* [1724], and *A letter to the Right Honourable the Viscount Molesworth (Fifth Drapier's letter)* [1724] in *Prose works*, ed. Harold Davis, vol. 9 (Oxford, 1961).

—, & Thomas Sheridan, *The Intelligencer*, ed. James Woolley (Oxford, 1992).

Swift, Theophilus, *The utility of union, illustrated and set forth, in a variety of statements, extracted from the most eminent patriots and constitutional writers* ... (Dublin, 1800).

Taaffe, Dennis, *The impartial history of Ireland*, 4 vols (Dublin, 1809–10).

Taylor, John, *English historical literature in the fourteenth century* (Oxford, 1987).

Temple, Sir John, *The Irish rebellion, or a history of the beginnings and first progress of the general rebellion raised within the kingdom of Ireland, upon the three and twentieth day of October, 1641* (London, 1646).

Thompson, Faith, *Magna Carta: its role in the making of the English constitution, 1300–1629* (Minneapolis, 1948).

Toland, John, *Christianity not mysterious* (London, 1697).

[Toland, John], *A letter from a gentleman in the country, to a member of the house of commons: in reference to the votes of the 14th instant* ([London], 1697).

—, *Reasons why the bill for the better securing the dependency of Ireland, should not pass* (London, 1720).

Tuck, Richard, *The rights of war and peace: political thought and the international order from Grotius to Kant* (Oxford, 1999).

Twysden, Sir Roger (ed.), *Historiæ Anglicanæ scriptores X* (London, 1652).

Ussher, James, 'Of the first establishment of English laws and parliaments in the kingdom of Ireland: October 11th 1611' in John Gutch (ed.), *Collectanea curiosa, or miscellaneous tracts relating to the history and antiquities of England and Ireland* ... , 2 vols (Oxford, 1781).

—, *Of the religion of the antient Irish and British* (London, 1631).

[Ussher], James, *A speech delivered in the castle chamber at Dublin, the XXII of November, anno 1622, at the censuring of certaine officers, who refused to take the oath of supremacie* (London, 1631).

The usurpations of England, the chief source of the miseries of Ireland (Dublin, 1780).

Vaughan, Sir John, *The reports and arguments of the learned judge, Sir John Vaughan, Kt.* (2nd edn London, 1714).

Vernon, James, *Letters illustrative of the reign of William III, from 1696 to 1708, addressed to the duke of Shrewsbury*, ed. G.P.R. James, 3 vols (London, 1841).

Vergil, Polydore, *Historia Anglica*, 2 vols (Douai, 1603).

Victory, Isolde, 'Colonial nationalism in Ireland, 1692–1725: from common law to natural right' (PhD, Trinity College, Dublin, 1984).

—, 'The making of the Declaratory Act of 1720' in Gerard O'Brien (ed.), *Parliament, politics and people: essays in eighteenth-century Irish history* (Blackrock, Co. Dublin, 1989).

Walsingham, Thomas, *Ypodigma Neustriæ: a Thomæ Walsingham, quondam monacho monasterii S. Albani conscriptum*, ed. H.T. Riley (London, 1876). Previous edn in William Camden (ed.), *Anglica, Normannica, Hibernica, Cambrica a veteribus scripta* (Frankfurt, 1603).

Ware, Sir James, *The works of Sir James Ware concerning Ireland, revised ... by Walter Harris*, 2 vols (Dublin, 1739, 1746).

Warren, W.L., *King John* (2nd edn, London, 1981).

Weston, Corinne, 'England: ancient constitution and common law' in *The Cambridge history of political thought, 1450–1700*, ed. J.H. Burns & Mark Goldie (Cambridge, 1991).

[Wetenhall, Edward], *The case of the Irish Protestants: in relation to recognizing, or swearing allegiance to, and praying for, King William and Queen Mary, stated and resolved* (London, 1691).

Whelan, Caoimhe, 'James Yonge and the writing of history in late medieval Dublin' in Seán Duffy (ed.), *Medieval Dublin XIII* (Dublin, 2013), pp 183–95.

—, 'The transmission of the *Expugnatio Hibernica* in fifteenth-century Ireland' in *Gerald of Wales: new perspectives on a medieval writer and critic*, ed. Georgia Henley & A. Joseph McMullen (Cardiff, 2018).

[Wilde, Sir William], 'Gallery of illustrious Irishmen, no. XIII: Sir Thomas Molyneux, bart., F.R.S.', *Dublin University Magazine*, 18 (1841), pp 305–27, 470–90, 604–19, 744–64.

Williams, E.N. (ed.), *The eighteenth-century constitution* (Cambridge, 1970).

Wing, Donald (ed.), *Catalogue of books printed in England, Scotland, Ireland, Wales, and British America, and of English books printed in other countries, 1641–1700*, 4 vols (2nd edn, New York, 1994–8).

Wolfe Tone, Theobald, *The writings of Theobald Wolfe Tone*, ed. T.W. Moody, R.B. McDowell & C.J. Woods, 3 vols (Oxford, 1998–2007).

Wood, Herbert, *A guide to the records deposited in the Public Record Office of Ireland* (Dublin, 1919).

Wood, James Robert, 'William Molyneux and the Politics of Friendship', *ECI*, 30 (2015), pp 11–35.

Woolhouse, Roger, *Locke: a biography* (Cambridge, 2007).

Woolrych, Austin, 'Last quests for a settlement, 1657–60' in Gerald Aylmer (ed.), *The interregnum: the quest for settlement, 1646–1660* (London, 1972).

Year Book, 11 Hen. 4. Omnes anni Regis Henrici IV: ab anno primo usque ad ann. xv (London, 1553).

Year Book, 20 Hen. 6. Le primier part des ans del Roy Henr. VI (London, 1609).

Year Book, 2 Rich. 3; 1 Hen. 7. Anni Regium Edwardi V., Richardi III., Henrici VII. et VIII., omnes qui antea impressi fuerunt (London, 1620).

York, Neil Longley, *Neither kingdom nor nation: the Irish quest for constitutional rights, 1698–1800* (Washington, DC, 1994).

Index of statutes cited in *The Case*

The statutes (most of which are now obsolete) are listed by their calendar year, together with the regnal year as given by Molyneux, followed by the chapter number and a short title or brief description, and keyed to the page numbers of the 1698 edition.[1] English statutes re-enacted in Ireland are identified by 'Eng.', followed by the appropriate statutory ref. The phrase 'lost act' denotes an Irish medieval statute not found in Bolton, *Statutes of Ireland* (Dublin, 1621), but known of by Molyneux. A page number followed by 'n' indicates a citation found solely in a marginal reference. Occasional minor errors in Molyneux's statutory refs have been silently corrected.[2]

I. IRISH STATUTES

1320 – 13 Edw. 2	(re-enacting various Eng. statutes up to Westminster II, 13 Edw. I)[3]	64–5, 78–80, 168
1324 – 17 Edw. 2	(Eng. Lincoln, 9 Edw. 2, and York, 12 Edw. 2)[4]	95
1408–9 – 10 Hen. 4	(lost act requiring re-enactment of Eng. statutes in Ireland)[5]	64, 157
1438 – 16 Hen. 6	(lost act concerning employment of deputies in Ireland)[6]	123
1440 – 18 Hen. 6	c. 1 (all Eng. statutes concerning purveyors)	68, 168
1450–1 – 29 Hen. 6	(lost act requiring re-enactment of Eng. statutes in Ireland)[7]	64, 157–8
1454 – 32 Hen. 6	c. 1 (all Eng. statutes concerning provisors)	68, 168
1468 – 8 Edw. 4	c. 1 (Eng. 6 Rich. 2, c. 6, concerning rape)	68–9, 78–80, 168
1494 – 10 Hen. 7	c. 4 (Poynings' Law)	81, 110, 127, 159–61, 166–7, 173
	c. 22 (confirming all Eng. public acts)	64, 69–71
	c. 23 (voiding Parliament at Drogheda, 1493)	158
1499 – 14 Hen. 7	sole act (all Eng. statutes concerning customs offences)	69–70
1522 –13 Hen. 8	c. 2 (agst exporting wool)	104 n.

1 In some cases where the official short title of a statute differs from the version familiar to historians, the latter has been preferred in the interest of clarity, e.g. the Irish Act of Settlement (1662) and Act of Explanation (1665).

2 All such changes are noted in the critical apparatus.

3 Cited in Bolton, *Statutes* (Dublin, 1621), p. 67 n.

4 Wrongly attributed to 17 Edw. 1. See *Case*, p. 100 and nn.

5 Cf. Bolton, *Statutes* (Dublin, 1621), p. 67 n.

6 See *Case*, p. 123 nn.

7 Cf. Bolton, *Statutes* (Dublin, 1621), p. 67 n.

2. ENGLISH STATUTES

8 *Pace* Molyneux, this was not a simple re-enactment of the section of the English act, 2 W. & M., ses. 1, c. 1, that recognized William and Mary. See *Case*, 76 nn.

9 See further *Case*, 86 nn.

10 No longer considered a statute, see further *Case*, 158 nn.

11 See further *Case*, 88 nn.

General index

All entries, including those for the text of *The Case*, are keyed to the continuous pagination of the book. Names are listed in the common modern form, with variants employed by Molyneux appended in parenthesis where confusion may arise. A page number followed by the abbreviation 'ref.' indicates that the entry is found in a marginal reference on the page cited. A name followed by '*' indicates the person mentioned was the author of a work cited. English statutes referred to as having been re-enacted in Ireland are not included in the index, unless specifically discussed. For details of statutes cited in the pamphlet, see the index of statutes cited in *The Case*.

cases, legal
  Annesley v. Sherlock 46
  Calvin's (*post-nati*) 62, 218–19, 223–4
  Hacket, Thomas (bishop of Down) 185
  Kelly 60, 234
  Llanthony, prior of, v. prior of Mullingar
    38, 227–8, 242, 272
  Men of Ely's 257 app. crit. and n.
  Men of Waterford's 38, 41, 59, 191–6,
    227, 257, 272
  Mulcarry v. Eyres 234–5
  Pembrough, Sir Richard 266–7
  Pilkington, Sir John 38, 59, 224–6, 267, 272
  the Prince's 160
  Savage v. Day 41–2, 257
  see also appeals; coparceners
Cashel 111, 139
Castile, king of (Alfonso X) 152
Catholic Confederates' peace terms (1643)
  25, 58–9
Charles I 25, 119
Charles II 201–2
Charles VI (of France) 144
charters of liberties
  Carta de Foresta 163,
  granted to Ireland 147–50, 154, 157, 163–
    5, 258–9, 263–5
  Magna Carta of England 34, 147, 163–4,
    258, 267
  Magna Carta of Ireland 34, 147–8, 163–5,
    see also Magna Carta Hiberniæ
Chester 6
Church of Ireland, articles and canons of 231
Cicero, Marcus Tullius* 275
Clarke, Edward 18–19
Clane, Co. Kildare 134
Clarendon, assize and constitutions of *see*
  Henry II, laws of
Clarendon, Henry, earl of (lord lieutenant) 6
Clement, Simon 22, 42–4
  An answer (1698) 22
  The interest of England (1698) 16, 22
clergy, Irish
  in England (1689) 209
  submit to Henry II 112–13, 138–9
Coke (Cooke), Sir Edward*, opinions of, re:
  ancient constitution (English) 34–5
  ancient laws have force of statutes *see* the
    Prince's case

arguments from Calvin's case 218–24
authenticity of Irish Modus 131–2, 137–8
English laws established in Ireland 158, 164
English right of conquest in Ireland 31,
  39, 218–19, 223–4
Irish appeals to English king's bench 38–9,
  233–4
law and reason 257
mixed ancestry of Irish 32–3
parliament in Ireland under Henry II 31
Pembrough's case 267
right to summons to parliament 256
statutes naming Ireland 182, 219–24
voyage royal 266
commercial threat, not occasion for war 247–9
Connaught 111
conquered, rights of 29, 31–2, 123–6
conqueror
  concessions by 29, 31–2, 107, 127–9
  followers of 32, 121–2
  title of 116–17, 119
  unjust (aggressor) 31, 120, 127–9
conquest
  as title to Ireland 30, 106–7, 114–19
  definitions of 114–15
  Locke on *see under* Locke
  rights conveyed by 31–3, 106–7, 120–9,
    224
consent
  basis of legal obligation 31–2, 35, 150,
    158, 252–3
  not manifested by accepting benefit 214
  not obtained by naming Ireland 220
  right to consent to laws *see under* law
Constance, Council of (1417) 144
Constantinople 145
constitution
  ancient Irish 30–4, 42–3
  balance between king and people 270
  dangers in undermining 153–4, 262, 276
  Gothic 275–6
  Irish 153, 268–9, 273–5
coparceners (*Statutum Hiberniæ*) 27, 174,
  188–90, 235
Cork 46, 199
Cornwall, Richard, earl of 153
council
  great *see* parliament
  privy, *q.v.*; *see also* Poynings' Law

Irish Legal History Society

Established in 1988 to encourage the study and advance the knowledge of the history of Irish law, especially by the publication of original documents and of works relating to the history of Irish law, including its institutions, doctrines and personalities, and reprinting or editing of works of sufficient rarity or importance.

www.ilhs.eu